THE TAO OF CHINESE RELIGION

Milton M. Chiu

UNIVERSITY
PRESS OF
AMERICA

LANHAM • NEW YORK • LONDON

Library of Congress Cataloging in Publication Data

Chiu, Milton M., 1930-
   The tao of Chinese religion.
   Bibliography: p .
   Includes index.
   1. China—Religion.   2. Tao.   I. Title.
BL1802.C55   1984   299'.51   84-17407
ISBN 0-8191-4263-8 (alk. paper)
ISBN 0-8191-4264-6 (pbk. : alk. paper)

To All of My Chinese Ancestors
who searched for the Harmony
of Heaven, Earth, and Man.

"Heaven is my father, Earth is my mother,
                    and
     All People are my comrades,
                    and
     All things are my companions."
                    --Chang Tsai

iv

FOREWORD

There have been many books written that have examined Chinese religions; and they have all, in one
way or another, contributed to our basic understanding
of the religions and of the Chinese people's attitude
toward religion. The author would like to acknowledge
his indebtness to the many great thinkers and writers
of the past, which are impossible to list here. This
book was written in an attempt to assimilate the many
writings and to give further explanations of the many
dispositions. The author is hopeful that it will af-
ford a more coherent understanding of the essence of
Chinese religion and the ways and means through which
the Chinese people have tried to attain their goal of
religious ideals.

Chinese people define the fundamental principle
of religion as the Tao (道) or the Way and delineate
the ultimate goal of their religions as to attain the
"Harmony of Heaven, Earth and Man." Their beliefs
embodied the way of Heaven, the way of Earth, the way
of Man, and the way of Harmony.

In the course of describing them, three aspects
of Chinese religions are stressed. First, the unity
and diversity are dialectically prescribed. While in
each chapter a central theme is chosen to present
what the author considered to be the unified subject
of Chinese religions, many different views and diverse
approaches proposed by various schools of Chinese religious thinkers such as the Confucianists, Taoists,
Buddhists, Mohists, Ying-Yang philosophers, etc., are
presented evenly so that the readers can make comparative studies. At the same time, these diverse views
and ways can also be seen as multifarious approaches
which could be accommodated in the attainment of the
common goal of a higher religious ideal.

Second, in the process of delineating various
representative views and ways, many quotations are
used which have been translated from the Chinese texts
as closely as the differences in languages allow.
It was done in this manner so that the readers could
acquaint themselves with the Chinese ways of thinking,
emoting, and writing. Like the reading of the Bible
is essential for the understanding of Christianity,
some readings of Chinese religious texts are very important for better comprehension of Chinese religion.

Third, since religion is very much a cultural
phenomenon, it is not merely a theological doctrine
or a philosophical idea but it also involves the
sociopolitical lives and moral and cultural enterprises. Additionally, religion has never been static,
but always on the "rise and decline" along with the
process of historical development. Therefore, the
author attempts to describe Chinese religious development in its cultural and historical contexts, thereby
allowing the reader to comprehend the embodiment of
the Tao in Chinese culture. Although the ultimate aim
of this book as been to effect a clear and understand-
able presentation of the above three aspects, it does
not necessarily follow that this goal has been accomplished. Therefore, the author would gratefully
welcome any constructive comments applicable to this
work.

Many grateful acknowledgments are made to Professor Joseph M. Kitagawa, my mentor, for his continued
support and help in the compiling of this work; to
Professors Chester F. Galaska and N. J. Girardot, who
were generous with both their time and suggestions;
to Dorothy Owens who edited the manuscript and typed
the final copy; to Linda Frank and Lana Morse who
typed the first draft; and to the National Endowment
for the Humanities for granting two summer seminars
which allowed the writing of the manuscript. I would
like to extend special thanks to my wife, Margaret,
for her ceaseless support throughout the many years of
researching and writing involved in the completion
of this book.

Milton M. Chiu
Ithaca College
Ithaca, NY

vii

ACKNOWLEDGMENTS

Permission to use material from the following publications is gratefully acknowledged.

From The Cradle Of The East by Ping-ti Ho. Copyright 1975 by The Chinese University of Hong Kong. Used by permission.

From The Birth of China by Herrlee G. Creel. Copyright 1937 by Frederick Ungar Publishing Co. Used by permission.

From Religious Pluralism And World Community by Edward J. Jurji. Copyright 1969 by E. J. Brill. Used by permission.

From A Source Book In Chinese Philosophy by Wing-tsit Chan. Copyright 1963 by Princeton University Press. Used by permission.

From The Three Religions Of China by W. E. Soothill. Copyright 1923 by Oxford University Press. Used by permission.

From Ch'u Tz'u: The Songs Of The South by David Hawkes. Copyright 1959 by Oxford University Press. Used by permission from David Hawkes, the translator. Ch'u Tz'u: The Songs of the South first published by Oxford University Press in 1959 and shortly to be reprinted by Penguins Ltd. in a revised edition.

From BUDDHIST AND TAOIST STUDIES I Edited by Michael Saso and David W. Chappell. Copyright 1977 by The University of Hawaii Press. Used by permission.

From SCIENCE AND CIVILIZATION IN CHINA by Joseph Needham. Copyright 1956 by Cambridge University Press. Used by permission.

From THE SYNCRETIC RELIGION OF LIN CHAO-EN by Judith Berling. Copyright 1980 by Columbia University Press. Used by permission.

CHRONOLOGY OF DYNASTIES

Emperor Yao (mythical)
Emperor Shun (mythical)
Emperor Yü (mythical)
Hsia dynasty (2183-1752 B.C.?)
Shang dynasty (1751-1112 B.C.)
Chou dynasty (1111-249 B.C.)
    Spring and Autumn (722-481 B.C.)
    Warring States (403-222 B.C.)
Ch'in dynasty (221-206 B.C.)
Han dynasty (B.C. 206-200 A.D.)
    Western Han (B.C. 206-8 A.D.)
    Eastern Han (25-220 A.D.)
Wei dynasty (220-265 A.D.)
Chin dynasty (265-420 A.D.)
S. and N. dynasties (420-589 A.D.)
Sui dynasty (581-618 A.D.)
Tang dynasty (618-907 A.D.)
Five dynasties (907-960 A.D.)
Sung dynasty (960-1279 A.D.)
Yüan dynasty (1271-1368 A.D.)
Ming dynasty (1368-1644 A.D.)
Ch'ing dynasty (1644-1912 A.D.)
Republic of China (1912-present)
People's Republic of China (1949-present)

LIST OF FIGURES

x

CHAPTER 1

WHAT IS CHINESE RELIGION?

Chinese Definitions of Religion

In order to understand what Chinese religion is, we must first understand what Chinese meant by "religion." In modern usage, the Chinese use the term chung-chiao (宗教) to translate the English word "religion." Chung (宗) means "ancestral tradition" and chiao (教) means "teaching or education." Combining these two words, chung-chiao means literally "the ancestral teachings." However, in ancient usage, these two words were not combined, but used separately. Besides these two words, there were also two more words used by ancient Chinese to designate "religion":chia (家) and Tao (道). The following few pages will delineate these four words and explain their religious implication.

A. Chung (宗)

The word chung appeared in several different forms as 介,俞,令,介,介, in the oracle inscriptions of the Shang Dynasty (c. 1300 B.C.).[1] As most Chinese characters are pictographic, they often depict the original images and ideas the script-makers had perceived. For instance, the first inscription 介 seems to indicate a house or a shrine (介) in which an altar (丁) was set up to offer a sacrifice (丁 or 示). With this general interpretation, chung was primarily meant to be a shrine in which the sacrifices were offered and the ritual conducted. However, Kuo Mo-jo, former Minister of Education of the People's Republic of China, interpreted the inscription 示, to mean the statue of a god who appeared in the shrine to give instructions by extending his hands to his worshippers. Thus, he interpreted the word chung to mean a theophany (i.e., a manifestation of God) or the revelation and blessing of God. It is true that the inscript 示 is still used today as a radical to mean something divine or sacred. For examples, shen (示申) means god, she (示土) the sacred earth, tsu (示且) the divine ancestor, and li (示豊) the sacred rites.

The last inscription 介 (above) contains a cross symbol which was not related to the Christian crucifix, but an indication of four shamans practicing a

rite by holding their arms crisscrossed. Kuo's interpretation of chung seems to coincide with the meaning
of the Latin root (religare) of English word religion
which means the bond between God and human. However,
since the majority of divine beings ancient Chinese
worshipped in their shrines were their clan ancestors
and tribal patriarchs, in the end, chung came to be understood as ancestral worship and ancestral tradition.
In ancient China, the supreme God Ti (帝) did not have
a statue, and the worship of Ti was limited only to
kings, so that chung did not carry the same monotheis-
tic belief.

B. Chiao (教)

The other word chiao appeared variously in the
Shang oracle inscriptions as 敨, 敎, 效, 祥, 狳 .
These inscriptions have been interpreted as portraying
the picture of a teacher who holds a teaching staff
while giving instructions to his pupils. The last inscription 狳 has more vividly illustrated a son lying
on his chest to receive the beating of the teacher's
sticks.[2] This picture might terrify many modern pupils
and their parents, but if we remember that this kind of
discipline had been a part of traditional education,
lasting even up to a decade ago, we should not be too
critical of the Shang educational practices of almost
33 centuries ago. The imagery has definitely stressed
the authority of the teacher, the obedience of the student and the necessity of discipline. Kuo Mo-jo mentioned that many neighboring countries of the Shang
kingdom had sent their children of royal and noble
families to the royal academy of Shang at the capital
Yin to receive their training and education. From this
we can speculate that teachers of the royal academy
must have already attained a very high status and authority, and the royal academy had become the center of
great learning and cultural tradition.

In current usage, chiao is used to designate the
distinctive tradition of Chinese religions such as Confucianism (Ju Chiao), Taoism (Tao Chiao), Buddhism (Fo
Chiao), Christianity (Chi-tu Chiao), and Islam (Fei
Chiao). Chiao in this context is understood as the
teachings of Confucius, Lao Tzu, the Buddha, Christ,
and Mohammed. The common folks generally thought that
all religions contained teachings to do good; so that
in essence, all religions are the same. There is a
common saying: "San Chiao Kui I Chia" (三教歸一家)
which means that "All three religions (Confucianism,

Taoism and Buddhism) belong to the same Family." There
is even a new religious group in Taiwan proclaiming
that "All Five Religions come from the same Origin (Wu
Chiao T'ung Yen, 五教同源)."[3] Generally, the common
people do not make their religious affiliation very
specific, as do the Western Christians with their denominations; therefore, it is very difficult to have
an accurate population census of religious affiliation
in China.

C. Chia (家)

     In the traditional Chinese historical writings,
the word chia (家) was used for designating a grouping
or school of religion. For example, Ssu-ma Ch'ien, a
great historian of the second century B.C., had divided various religio-philosophical schools of his time
into Ju Chia (the Literati's Family, namely the Confucianist), Tao Chia (the Taoist's Family), Mo Chia
(the Mohists' Family), Ying Yang Chia (the Yin-yang
Cosmologists' Family), Ming Chia (the Logicians'
Family), Fa Chia (the Legalists' Family), Ping Chia
(the Military Strategists' Family), and Ch'ung-huang
Chia (the Diplomats' Family). Each family had its
founder, masters, teachings, philosophy, and disciples;
and because very often, masters and disciples lived together, worked together, and traveled together promoting their beliefs and philosophies, thus Ssu-ma
Ch'ien referred to them as Chias. It is like the word
chung; this word chia also stressed the familistic
structure and patriarchal tradition of Chinese religio-
philosophical communities. Professor Joseph Kitawaga
of the University of Chicago is right in pointing out
that "family-ism" is one of the major characteristics
of the Chinese religion.[4] Once an individual is admitted to any religious community, he or she will be
treated as a family member paying homage to the founder
and the patriarchs and observing the family code of the
group. After mastering all the teachings and maturing
in age, he or she would ascend the ladder of hierarchy
and succeed to the position of senior and master. In
modern usage, Chinese call a nation Kuo Chia, which
literally means "the nation-family" or "national
family," for Chinese conceive a nation as an extended
or enlarged family. So, in fact, "family-ism" is one
of the major components of Chinese religion.

D. Tao (道)

     There is another word the Chinese used to

designate religion in ancient times, and that was Tao
(道). The most archaic form of this word did not appear in the Shang oracle inscriptions, but in the Chou
bronze-ritual vessel inscriptions such as 衛 . It contained three radicals: a human head, 首 ; human feet, 止
; and a crossroad, 彳亍 . The inscription has been
interpreted by some paleographers to mean a tribal
chief, leading his followers, walking into a crossroad.
Combining these elements, we get the meaning of Tao--
the path or the road one has to follow.[5] By the sixth
century B.C., the inscription was simplified to appear
as 道 , which comprised two radicals: a head, 首 , and
the notion of running, 辶 . It signified a leader was
leading his followers, who were running after him. So
it still retained the original meaning of the bronze
inscription of eleventh century B.C. We can see that
the word Tao has several significant connotations: the
leader as a pathfinder or a pioneer; the path or the
way to follow; and the obedience to the leader. Thus,
when it is used to designate religion, it implies that
religion is the Way opened up by a pathfinder and to
be followed by the adherents of the Way. Tao is understood by ancient Chinese to be both a concrete path
and an abstract way; and it has its starting point, the
process or method, and a final destiny and goal. Even
in the current usage, Tao has contained many important
meanings. When it is used as a noun, it generally
means the Way, principle, norm, doctrine, theory,
method, etc. But it is also used as a verb to mean "to
speak, to read, to lead, to guide, and to expound (a
doctrine)," etc. In English translation, Tao has been
translated as the Way and has been understood mainly as
an abstract truth or universal principle. It is rather
unfortunate that the concrete and practical aspect of
Tao has been ignored. Tao is not merely an idea, but
also a path to be trodden; and the journey down this
path is to be guided by a pathfinder who does speak and
expound the Way. In Tao, theory and practice, abstract
and concrete, destiny and passage, truth and reality
are inseparable.

By the fourth century B.C., there had appeared
many such schools of philosophers who claimed that they
had found the way to rectify the chaotic situation of
the Warring States Period (403-221 B.C.). Acknowledging that each of these schools had its own Tao,
Chuang Tzu, a Taoist (300-295 B.C.), said:

> There are presently many masters in the
> schools of philosophy, and each of them

has claimed to possess the correct solution to the problems of our chaotic
society. We may ask what happened to
the philosophy of ancient Tao. I would
say that it must have been diversified
into each and every system. [Chuang Tzu
33]

Hsün Tzu, a Confucian scholar (298-238 B.C.), had analyzed such diversification of Tao as follows:

If we look upon Tao as utility, we are
only seeking profits. If we look upon
Tao as desire, we are only seeking satisfaction. If we look upon Tao as law, we
are only seeking an administrative technique. If we look upon Tao as power, we
are only seeking political manipulation.
If we look upon Tao as nature, we are
only seeking the cause and effect.
Each of these different approaches to
Tao merely represents one particular
aspect of Tao [Hsün Tzu 9]

Both Chuang Tzu and Hsün Tzu seemed to lament that the
original Tao had become divided and fragmented, so
that confusion and conflicts had occurred in the society, but they nonetheless acknowledged that while
there was the Tao, there would be many ways of ap-
proaching and realizing the Tao too.

However, among all the ancient usages, Lao Tzu
was the first one who dedicated his total life to the
study of Tao, and it was believed that he had assembled all of the Tao teachings in the now famous book
Tao Te Ching (道德經), namely, the Canon of the Way
and Virtue. Upon reading it, we soon discover that
Lao Tzu wrote his Five Thousand Words Canon (Wu Ch'ien
Tzu Ching 五千字經) in poetic and prosaic form, not in
systematic and analytic form, so that it is difficult
to grasp his concept of Tao. Perhaps Lao Tsu thought
that the poetic and prosaic forms were more adequate
forms to describe Tao than a philosophical analysis.
The first statement of Tao Te Ching is: "The Tao that
can be told of is not the Eternal Tao," and Lao Tzu
also said, "The Speaker knows not; The Knower speaks
not." He seemed to say that once you have started to
talk about Tao with human language and concepts which
have their conditions and criteria, you would condition and limit the Tao within your criteria and,

therefore, confine and distort the original Tao. So
the best way to know this Tao is to meditate and keep
silent, but Lao Tzu did not merely keep silent, he
wrote about it in five-thousand Chinese words. So a
Chinese poet, Pai Loh-t'ien, composed a poem to tease
Lao Tzu:

> The Speaker knows not;
> The Knower speaks not,
> So said Lao Tzu.
> If Lao Tzu was a knower,
> Why did he write five thousand words?[6]

Apparently, however, Lao Tzu knew that human language
would distort the Original Tao. He also knew that Tao
also meant "to speak," and language is the way humans
communicate, so Lao Tzu had to speak and write about
Tao constantly reminding himself that he was "forced
to do so." It is fortunate that he did, for his con-
ception of Tao has helped us to better understand how
the ancient Chinese conceived of religion. My analysis
of the <u>Tao Te Ching</u> reveals that Lao Tzu had conceived
of the <u>Tao</u> in the following six ways:

(1) Tao as the Ontological Reality.

In chapter 25 of <u>Tao Te Ching</u>, he said:

> There is Something undifferentiated,
> and yet complete in Itself.
> Soundless and Formless;
> Independent and Unchanging;
> Pervasive and Inclusive.
>
> It can be regarded as the Mother of the
>   Universe.
> I do not know Its name.
> I named It "Tao."
> Only I was forced to give It a name.
>
> I regard It simply "Great."
> For in greatness, It produces.
> In producing, It expands.
> In expanding, It regenerates.

Although he could not describe clearly what Tao
was, Lao Tzu was quite sure that there was a reality.
And it was not simply a reality, but the creative reality that produces and even regenerates all things in
the universe. He could have called it the Mother of

the Universe, but he decided to call it "Tao." Chapter
21 also described Tao as the Origin of All things.

> The characteristic of great virtue is
> to follow the Tao and the Tao alone.
> What then is the character of the Tao?
> It is indeed elusive and evasive.
> Evasive and elusive;
> Yet it contains within itself the Image.
> Elusive and evasive;
> Yet it contains within itself the Matter.
>
> Impenetrable and vague;
> Yet it contains within itself the Essence.
> The Essence is very real,
> In it lies the authenticity.
> Throughout the ages,
> Its name has never perished.
>
> By which we may see the Origin of all
>   things.
> How do I know the Origin of all things?
> By Such as This!

(2) Tao as the Universal Principle.

     In the same chapter 25, Lau Tzu also stated that
the Tao Itself is the law of the universe.

> The way of Man follows after the law of
>   Earth;
> The law of Earth follows after the law of
>   Heaven;
> The law of Heaven follows after the law of
>   Tao;
> And the law of Tao follows after its own
>   nature.

Chapter 34 also has some indication of it.

> The great Tao flows everywhere.
> It may turn to the right or to the left.
> All things depend on it for life.
> And it does not turn away from them.
>
> It accomplishes its tasks, but claims no
>   credit.
> It clothes and feeds all things, but does
>   not overlord.
> Always desireless,

It may be called, "the small."
All things return and belong to it,
But it does not lord over them.
It may be called, "the Great."

It is just because it does not want to be
    great,
That its greatness is fully realized.

(3) Tao as the Creative Force.

    Chapter 42 stated:

        Tao produces Oneness.
            Oneness produces Duality.
            Duality produces Trinity.
            Trinity produces Myriad things.

        All Myriad things carry the Yin and embrace
        the Yang.
        Through the blending of these vital forces,
        They achieve Harmony.

Chapter 51 has a beautiful description of how the Tao
creates life and nourishes all things.

        Tao gives them life;
            Virtue nurses them;
            Matter shapes them;
        And the environment completes them.

        Therefore all things esteem Tao and honor
            Virtue.
        Tao is so esteemed and Virtue so honored.
        Not being commanded,
        But always emerging spontaneously by
            themselves.

        It is Tao that gives them life.
        It is Virtue that nurses them, grows them,
            fosters them,
        Shelters them, comforts them, nourishes
            them and protects them.

        To give life but not to be possessive,
        To care for life but expect no reward,
        To guide them but control them not,
        This is called the Primordial Virtue.

(4) Tao as the Process of Individuation.

     Tao is not only the ultimate reality and the uni-
versal principle but also the creative force which produces and nurses all things. In the creation of all
things, Tao does not dissociate itself from its creatures; instead, it permeates all things and allows
each individual thing to be distinctive and unique.
Lao Tzu called this individuation process: Te (德).
The word Te has been oftentimes translated as a noun
to mean "virtue"; but originally, it was used as a
verb meaning "to obtain" (得). In other words, it
means what an individual has obtained from the universal Tao to become an individual. Or, from the perspective of Tao--described in his chapter 51, quoted
above--Virtue (Te) is that part of Tao's creation in
nursing, fostering, caring, and protecting an individual which also becomes the integral virtue of an individual and enables that individual to grow spontan-
eously. Thus, Lao Tzu wrote in chapter 23:

          Hence, he who cultivates Tao is one with
          Tao;
          He who practices Te is one with Te;
          And he who courts Loss shall be one with
          Loss.

(5) Tao as the Way of Manifestation and Application.

     Through the process of individuation, Tao has con-
tinuously manifested itself in the universe. Tao permeates all things, and nothing exists without Tao. As
we have read in chapter 34, Lao Tzu wrote, "The great
Tao flows everywhere." However, the manifestations of
Tao are multifarious and dialectical. Chapter 41 described it most beautifully:

          Hence, there is an established saying:
          The bright Tao appears to be dark.
          The progressive Tao appears to be
               regressive.
          The smooth Tao appears to be rugged.
          The superior Te appears to be humble.
          The great purity appears to be modest.
          The broad Te appears to be deficient.
          The established Te appears to be shabby.

Tao appears both in the Yin and Yang, heaven and earth,
great and small, East and West, life and death, and
any opposites and dichotomies. Therefore, Lao Tzu

encouraged his followers to apply the principle of Tao
in all the dimensions of their lives. In chapter 54
he postulated:

> He who is well built [in Tao] cannot be
>   pulled away.
> He who has a firm grasp [of Tao] cannot
>   be taken away.
> His descendents will carry on the sacri-
>   fices without end.
>
> When one cultivates Te in his person, it
>   becomes genuine Te.
> When one cultivates Te in his family, it
>   becomes fertile Te.
> When one cultivates Te in his county, it
>   becomes lasting Te.
> When one cultivates Te in his country, it
>   becomes abundant Te.
> When one cultivates Te in the world, it
>   becomes universal Te.
>
> Henceforth, the person shall be respected
>   as person;
> the family as the family;
> the county as the county;
> the state as the state;
> And the world as the world.
>
> How do I know the world as such?
> Through This [cultivation of Te].

(6) Tao as the Final Harmony of the Universe.

Although the Tao has multiplied and diversified
into all realms and dimensions of the universe, its
final goal is to integrate all things to unite in
harmony. Chapter 42 states very succinctly on its
final page: "All things carry the Yin and embrace
the Yang. Through the blending of these vital forces,
they achieve harmony." Chapter 2 also says:

> Indeed, being and non-being produce each
>   other;
> Difficult and easy complement each other;
> Long and short contrast with each other;
> High and low distinguish each other;
> Sound and voice harmonize with each other;
> And front and rear accompany each other.

Chapter 10 has rather provocative, but challenging,
questions:

> Can you keep your spirit and soul
> In harmony with the Oneness without di-
>   viding them?
> Can you concentrate breath and
> Attain suppleness like a new-born babe?
> Can you love people and govern a state
> Without employing [cunning] knowledge?
> Can you perform the role of the female
> In opening and closing of the Heavenly
>   gate?
> Can you comprehend all the knowledge and
>   wisdom
> And yet remain simultaneously detached
>   and non-active?

Chapter 62 has something beautiful to say about the
value of Tao.

> Tao is the hidden reservoir of all things.
> It is the treasure of the good,
> And the refuge of the bad as well.
>
> Beautiful words can buy honors,
> And fine acts can gain respect,
> Yet, even if he is bad, has Tao ever
>   rejected him?

Because Tao is such an integrating principle and harmonizing factor, I have translated the first chapter
as follows:

> Tao that can be truly Tao is not a per-
>   manently fixed Tao;
> Name that can be truly Name is not a
>   permanently fixed name.
>
> As the Origin of heaven and earth, it is
>   nameless;
> As the Mother of all things, it is namable.
>
> Without desires, one can always contemplate
>   its subtleness;
> Within desires, one can always observe
>   its manifestations.

In fact, these two are all from the same
    source;
Yet, they are differently named.
They are both called original and
The mystery of all mysteries.
Indeed this is the gate to all wonders.[7]

Tao is both nameless and namable, hidden and apparent,
diverse and unified, and one in all and all in one.
The un-initiated may find a dichotomy, but the initiated will recognize "coincidentia oppositorium" or
the mystery of all mysteries.

   Following after Lao Tzu, many religious thinkers
have used the word Tao to express their religious beliefs. For example, Chuang Tzu also described that
which is the most original, eternal, and universal as
Tao.

Tao has reality and evidence, but does not
have fixed action and forms. It may be
transmitted, but cannot be possessed.
It may be intuited, but cannot be seen.
It has its own origin and root. It existed prior to Heaven and Earth, and
indeed for all eternity. It causes the
gods to be divine, and the world to be
produced. It is above the zenith, but
it is not high. It is beneath the na-
dir, but it is not low. It is prior
to Heaven and Earth, but it is not
ancient. It is older than the most
ancient, but it is not old. [Chuang
Tzu, 6]

   Even Confucius, who was not a Taoist himself,
used the word Tao to indicate the fundamental principle of his beliefs.

There are some with whom one can associate in study, but are not yet able
to make common advance toward the Way
[Tao]; there are others with whom one
can make common advance toward the Way,
but who are not yet able to take with
you a firm stand; and there are others
with whom one can take such a firm
stand, but with whom one cannot make
emergency decisions. [Lun Yu IX, 29]

In other words, Confucius knew that there were
different levels of knowing the Tao, and he reasoned
that one who has completely lived with Tao and could
act according to the Tao, even at a time of crisis and
emergency, was at the highest level. Thus, he also
said, "In the morning, I heard [and realized] the Tao,
I could be contented to die that evening." Ssu-ma
Ch'ien mentioned that there were many sages and scholars studying the Tao and developing "the Hundred
Schools" of ancient Chinese philosophies and religion.

> Shen Tao was a native of Chao. T'ien
> P'ien and Chieh Tzu were men of Ch'i.
> Huan Yuan was a native of Ch'u. These
> all studied the arts of the Way [Tao]
> and the Power [Te], of Huang and Lao
> and put forward and arranged their
> ideas according to these. . . .
> [Shih-chi, 74:3-5]

Huai Nan Tzu of the second century B.C. made the
Tao the fundamental principle to his philosophy. Tao
is the origin of the universe, the universal principle
of all things, the creative and interpenetrating force
in everything, the moral principle of human society,
the way of spiritual and moral cultivation, and the
integrative harmony which reconciles all things. The
following quote incorporates only the first passage
of this work.

> The Tao embraces Heaven and supports
> Earth. It stretched the four quarters
> of the universe and generated the
> eight points of the firmament. There
> is no limit to its height, and Its depth
> is unfathomable. It constituted Heaven
> and Earth and endowed them with the
> primary elements, when as yet they were
> without form. . . . Hence it filled
> Heaven and Earth and stretched to the
> utmost parts of the sea. It spent it-
> self without exhaustion; there was no
> morning or evening, i.e., rise and de-
> cay, no fatigue and revival. [Huai Nan
> Tzu, 1:1-2]

By the time of Tung Chung-shu (179?-104 B.C.),
the Tao was conceived not only as a cosmological or
metaphysical principle but also as the principle of
human beings and the way of unifying Heaven, Earth,

and Man. He found a close correspondence between the
physiology of human beings and that of Heaven and
Earth. He elucidated:

> The symbols of Heaven and Earth and the
> correlations between the yin and yang
> are visible in the human body. . . . The
> body is like Heaven; it has 366 lesser
> joints correlate to the number of days
> in a year and 12 divisions of larger
> joints correlate to the number of
> months. Heaven, Earth and Man are the
> foundation of all things. Heaven pro-
> duces them, Earth nourishes them, and
> Man completes them. [<u>Ch'un-ch'iu</u> <u>Fan-lu</u>,
> 13:2-4]

Thus, the Tao is understood to be at once the principle of Heaven, the principle of Earth and the principle of Man, and the principle of their mutual correspondences. This notion of "Three in One" and "One
in Three" or the Harmony of Heaven, Earth, and Man
finally came to blossom in the religio-philosophy of
Neo-Confucianism (960-1643 A.D.). Traditionally, the
Neo-Confucianists were called, as were the Tao Hsueh
Chia (道學家), the Family which study the Tao. By
the tenth century, Buddhism had been introduced into
China and became well-established, Taoism had also
flourished, and Confucianism enriched itself by synthe-
sizing Buddhism and Taoism.

Chang Tsai (1020-1077), one of the distinguished
students of Tao, said most straightforwardly that Tao
is the Great Harmony (T'ai Ho 太和) and the Supreme
Ultimate of the Universe. In his now well-known <u>Hsi
Ming</u> (西銘) or <u>Western Inscription</u>, he expressed his
motto of life.

> Heaven is my father and Earth my
> mother. . . . I am the being that
> lies within the bounds of Heaven and
> Earth. . . . All people are my bro-
> thers, and all creatures are my
> friends. [<u>Cheng-meng</u>, 17]

Ch'eng Ming-tao (1032-1085), another great Neo-
Confucianist, stated that Tao in Its origin is undifferentiated; and when manifested, it appeared as the
way of Heaven, the way of Earth, and the way of man.
Each way is different from other ways, but all three

ways correspond to one another and harmonize all
things. In this context, the goal of the way of man
is to attain harmony with the ways of Heaven and Earth.
In order to attain such harmony, the careful investigation of all things in Heaven and Earth and human
society and the conscientious knowledge of the ways as
they are, and the spiritual and moral disciplines to
maintain sincerity and seriousness are essential. The
mind of human beings should be cultivated to maintain
its _Jen_ (仁) or impartiality in order to correspond
with the principle of Tao. This is what he believed
religion should be. Several passages from his writings
are quoted below.

> The movement of Heaven has neither
> sound nor smell. And yet its dynamic
> is transforming; its principle, the
> Tao; and its function mysterious.
> What Heaven produces in Man is called
> nature. Therefore, to follow the law
> of nature within us is called the Tao.
> To cultivate oneself according to the
> Tao is [the essence of] education.
> [_I-shu_, 1:3a-b]

His brother Ch'eng I-chuan has stated most succinctly the essence of Chinese religion:

> By identifying oneself with Heaven
> and Earth, sun and moon, the four
> seasons and the active and passive
> forces, the great man identifies one-
> self with the Tao. [_I-chuan_, 1:7-8]

The word Tao was not only used to designate the
indigenous religious tradition of China but also the
foreign religions that were introduced into China.
For example, Yuan Hung (A.D. 328-76), summarized the
teachings of Buddhism that were introduced into China
during the Han dynasty in his now famous Hou Han Chi
(The Record of the Latter Han dynasty) as follows:

> They also teach that when a man dies
> his soul does not perish, but will be
> reborn and assume another form. The
> meritous and evil deeds performed dur-
> ing this life-time will have their re-
> wards and punishments. Therefore they
> value the practice of meritous deeds
> and the cultivation of the Way [Tao],

so as to discipline the soul. By
doing so they attain to Nirvana and
become Buddha.[8]

In spite of this, there are many different teachings
in Buddhism. The Buddhists still have to "cultivate
the Way [Tao]" in order to attain to Nirvana and become Buddha. The Eightfold Path (right speech, right
action, right livelihood, right effort, right mind-
fulness, right concentration, right views, and right
intention) was translated as Pa Sheng Tao (八聖道).
The "path" and "the Way" became one.

We also witness a similar thing happening to the
incoming of Christianity. The first introduction of
Christianity into China was the Nestorian mission from
the seventh to the ninth centuries. The Nestorian
faith was called "Ching Chiao" (景教), Luminous Religion. When the Bible was to be translated into Chinese,
many important Christian doctrines were also assimilated with Chinese religious ideas. Among these various assimilations, the most important is the translation of the first verse of the Gospel according to
John. "In the beginning the Word" (ὁ λόγος) is translated into Chinese as T'ai Ch'u yu <u>Tao</u>, "In the beginning the Way." Apparently, while English speaking
people understood the Greek word ὁ λόγος to be the Word,
Chinese people found it more congenial to their idea
of the Tao which has been transmitted from generation
to generation.

<u>The Plan of this Book</u>

The main purpose of this book is to search for an
understanding of the essence and manifestation of
Chinese religion. As Chinese understood their religion
by words such as <u>chung</u>, <u>chiao</u>, <u>chia</u>, and <u>Tao</u>, we assume that Chinese have regarded religion to be ances-
tral teachings and traditions grouped by familistic
orientation in search of the realization of Tao.
First, in Chinese religious traditions, each tradition
stressed its continuity and perennial quest for the
realization of its own Tao. Second, each tradition
tends to organize its community as a family and respect the teachings of its patriarchs. Third, each
tradition has developed its own way of spiritual and
moral cultivation to realize its goal and proposed its
method of applying its own way to the world. Fourth,
while each tradition is searching its own way to reach
the ultimate goal, each also recognizes that there are

16

many other traditions also searching for the same goal,
all acknowledged to be Tao. Therefore, while sometimes
they have rivaled and debated one another to claim that
their own tradition was the best, they also learned how
to tolerate one another, and even to seek compromise
among themselves. In the end, many Chinese religious
thinkers began to realize that in the beginning, the
Tao was an undifferentiated unity, and it then diversified into many ways during the appearance of "the
Hundred Schools" of the Warring States period (403-
221 B.C.). But when the chaotic period ended and the
Han dynasty was established, Tung Chung-shu started to
build a new synthesis, incorporating all the major
teachings and traditions of his time. We find many
religious thinkers, like Tung, in Chinese history creating a new syncretism by absorbing many new and even
foreign religious teachings that came to China.
Through their syncretism, they all aimed at realizing
the harmony of Tao. Fifth, as we have already noticed,
Chinese religious thinkers have referred quite often to
the Way of Heaven, the Way of Earth, and the Way of
Man. They believed that all these three Ways are one,
or in harmony. T'ien Ti Jen Ho I (天地人合一), the
Union of Heaven, Earth, and Man, is the ultimate goal
of the long search of Chinese religion. The basic assumption is that there is a primordial unity which is
called Tao. As Tao manifested itself in three realms
of Heaven, Earth, and Man, it was conceived differently by various different schools of religion, and,
thus, Tao became diversified. But in the end, all
these diversified ways returned to, and realized, the
original unity.

Because of these characteristics of the Chinese
religion, it would appear that the one important clue
to understanding Chinese religion is to find the unity
in the diversity of traditions.

As has been illustrated thus far, most of the
Chinese religious thinkers have acknowledged that the
unity among all the traditions is the Tao, for the
Tao is the origin, the universal, the eternal, and the
ultimate. But at the same time, the Tao has appeared
in many ways, and each of these ways is produced by,
permeated with, and directly related to the Tao.
Furthermore, these ways are also by themselves organically interrelated to one another. Each way, therefore, is essential, integral, and significant to the
totality of Tao.

Thus, the plan of this book is divided into three parts: (1) to delineate the Tao of Heaven and Earth, (2) the Tao of Man, and (3) the Tao of Harmony. However, before delineating these three parts, a brief sketch of the history of Chinese religion from its beginning to present is needed for us to know its continuity and change and to discern its unity and diversity.

The first part will focus on the Chinese understandings of the Tao of Heaven and Earth by depicting four themes: (1) the Supreme God of the Shang dynasty; (2) the Heaven and Heavenly Mandate of the Chou dynasty; (3) the P'an-ku Myth of Creation; and (4) the Origin and Structure of the Universe. Chapters 3 and 4 are intended to describe the earliest phase of Chinese religion in historical time. They do not intend to account for the origin of Chinese religion, but to describe the beginning formation of Shang religion centering in the belief of the Supreme God called Ti or Shang Ti, and also to see its dynamic change when the new dynasty Chou had taken over and a new state religion formed centering in the belief of T'ien or Heaven and His Mandate. Although the P'an-Ku myth has been regarded as late and foreign in its origin, this study has determined that it represented a preliminary effort to form a cosmology at the time the Chou state religion was disintegrating and "the Hundred Schools" of philosophy and religion were about to appear. The fifth chapter is an attempt to summarize the cosmology or the world view produced by "the Hundred Schools" during the Warring States period and the Han dynasty. Although a much more refined cosmology and more sophisticated metaphysical theories appeared later--during the Sung and Ming dynasties (960-1643 A.D.), this study revealed that the basic notion and structure of cosmology and metaphysics had already been formed by the Han dynasty, which is, therefore, just cause to present its summary to represent the Way of Heaven and Earth that Chinese people understood.

The second part will be focused on the Tao of Man by elaborating the following themes: (1) the Human Position in the Universe; (2) Search for Authentic Selfhood; (3) Human Nature Good or Evil; and (4) Ideal Images of Humanity. The first theme will discuss the mode by which the Chinese conceived of the origin of human beings and the position and role of human beings in the universe. On the one hand, Chinese thinkers

seemed to distinguish the uniqueness of human beings
from other beings, but, on the other hand, tried to
stress the inseparable relationship of human beings
with other beings. The second theme will describe,
more or less historically, the search or the struggles
of ancient Chinese people to ascertain the authenticity
of human selfhood. In the process, this study has revealed certain types of selfhood delineated by different schools of religious thinkers, e.g., the Confucian
idea of responsible self, the Mohist idea of the universal self, the Taoist idea of the transcendental
self, and integrated self in the Book of Rites. The
third theme depicts one of the most hotly debated subjects in ancient China, which is "Is Human Nature Good
or Evil?" There were five different answers to that
question and had been discussed, focusing on the issues
of what is human nature, what is the criterion of good
and evil, the causes of good and evil, and their implications and applications. The last theme will describe, typologically, the ideal images of humanity
portrayed by different schools of Chinese religion.
For each school has developed its own ideal image of a
perfected man or a sage who, in spite of evilness and
deviations in the world, has accomplished his/her
spiritual and moral cultivation to attain the highest
stage of religious discipline and become the exemplary
model of his/her followers. The Confucianists called
the ideal image of humanity the Superior Man (Chün
Tzu 君子); the Taoist the True Man (Ch'en-jen 真人);
the Mohists the Great Man (Chü Tzu 鉅子); the Shamans
the Immortal Man (Shen-jen 仙人).

Part Three will cover the Tao of Harmony and will
deal with the ways in which the Chinese attempted to
harmonize the Ways of Heaven, Earth, and Man. The
common goal of Chinese religion is to attain this
final harmony, although there are various ways to do
it. Among these various ways, four themes in particular have been chosen: (1) the Way of Ritual; (2) the
Way of Self-discipline; (3) the Way of Cosmic Integration; and (4) the Way of Religious Syncretism. Inter-
estingly, it appears that Chinese people interpreted
the primary purpose of rituals as a way of realizing
the harmony within society and the universe. This
section will elaborate particularly on Hsün Tzu's interpretation of the meaning and function of Rites
(禮), for he was, perhaps, the first theoretician of
Rites in ancient China. Chinese teachers were not only
theoreticians and instructors, but also the practi-
tioners and exemplary models of their religion and

philosophy. Spiritual disciplines and moral cultivation are lifelong orientations, so that each student
of religion has to acquire and practice in order to
reach his/her utlimate goal. Following the Way of
Self-discipline will be the Way of Cosmic Integration
in which there will be a description of three popular
rituals: ancestral worship, the Monthly Ordinances, and
the Cult of Universal Salvation. Through these rituals
the Chinese attempted to integrate all the members of
society, including the living and the dead, and also
with the seasonal change and natural environment. The
last chapter will deal with the issue of religious
pluralism. As already mentioned, throughout the history of Chinese religion, there appeared a number of
religious syncretism which synthesize the past traditions and teachings to form a new religion. In fact,
there is no religion which is not syncretic, but the
important thing is to see how a syncretism is constructed and for what purpose it is constructed.
Parallel to this concept, there will also be a general
description of Chinese attitude toward other religions
and will, in particular, point out the trend of universalism in the history of Chinese religion. It is
hoped that by presenting these twelve themes, this
book will provide the reader with a comprehensive view
of Chinese religion and demonstrate its essence.

FOOTNOTES

1. Li Hsiao-ting, <u>Chia-ku Wen-tzu Chin-shih</u> (The Collective Commentaries of the Oracle-Bone Languages), vol. 7, p. 2479.

2. Ibid.

3. Officially, it is called the T'ung Shan Hui (the Society of World Religions) or Tao Yüan (The Temple of Tao).

4. See Joseph M. Kitagawa, <u>Religions of the East</u> (Philadelphia, PA: Westminster Press, 1968), pp. 74-85.

5. Wang, Jen-shou, <u>Chin Shih Ta Tsu-tien</u> (Taipei: The Dictionary of Bronze-Vessel Inscriptions, 1969), vol. 4, p. 1848.

6. R. E. Blyth, <u>Zen in English Literature and Oriental Classics</u> (New York: E. P. Dutton & Co., 1960), p. 141.

7. The translations of <u>Tao Te Ching</u> quoted in this book are those of the author, based on Wang Pi's edition of the original text. In the process of translation, the author has also consulted with the following English translations: John Wu, <u>Tao Teh Ching</u> (New York: St. John's University Press, 1961); Arthur Waley, <u>The Way and Its Power</u> (London: Allen & Unwin, 1934); Wing-tsit Chan, <u>The Way of Lao Tzu</u> (Indianapolis: Bobbs-Merrill Co., Inc., 1963).

8. D. Howard Smith, <u>Chinese Religions</u> (New York: Holt, Rinehart & Winston, 1968), p. 113.

<u>Suggested Readings</u>

Arnold Grave, "Tao: An Aged-old Concept in its Modern Perspective," <u>Philosophy East and West</u> 13 (1963):235-250.

J. Girardot, "Chinese Religion and Western Scholarship" and Laurence G. Thompson, "The Scrutable Chinese Religion" in <u>China and Christianity</u>, ed. James Whitehead (Notre Dame, Ohio: University of Notre Dame Press, 1977).

CHAPTER 2

RELIGION IN CHINESE HISTORY

There are many ways of writing a history of Chinese religion. One way would be to divide the Chinese religion into its three major traditions: Confucianism, Taoism, and Buddhism, noting the historical development, doctrine, and organization of each tradition. Another way would be to follow the political history of dynastic changes and note the major religious events which are more involved in the sociopolitical life of the nation. Both of the above mentioned approaches have their advantages, as well as disadvantages. While the first approach may present a more distinctive picture of each separate tradition, it misses a significant factor that all three traditions inherited. This is the common heritage which preceded them and by which they have interacted with one another throughout the long history of China. There is a certain unity and continuity in Chinese religion that the divisional approach cannot convey. However, even though the second approach may present a better sociopolitical understanding of Chinese religion, it does not deal with the intrinsic nature and spiritual value of Chinese religion per se. For religion is not merely the sum of social and political activities and events recorded in the chronicles of royal courts, it is an expression of people's ultimate concern with truth, value, and meaning.

This chapter is an attempt to present Chinese religion as a unified and continuous tradition representing the spiritual search for ultimate reality, the meaning of life, and the way of cosmic harmony by Chinese people. We will also be aware of religion as a dynamic historical process in which it has a distinct origin, growth, change, decline, and revival. It is impossible to consider all aspects simultaneously, so, in a sense, some dissection and division into manageable portions is necessary for analysis. For clarity, then, I shall divide religion in Chinese history into five periods: (1) the Period of Formation; (2) the Period of Diversification; (3) the Period of Importation of Foreign Religions; (4) the Period of Decline and Disintegration; and (5) the Period of Revival and Resurgence.

The Period of Formation

Although there have been great efforts among Western and Chinese archaeologists to uncover the pre-historical phase of Chinese civilization, we do not yet have a comprehensive view of religious life in pre-historical time. There are many burial remains implying belief in life after death, and some segments of bone inscription indicating certain practice of divination and the belief in the supernatural. Other than these, we still need more archaeological discoveries to be able to better account for prehistoric religion. However, by the Shang Dynasty, we have fairly extensive archaeological artifacts and oracle inscriptions to discern the original phase of Chinese religious tradition.

The Shang Religion[1]

The Shang dynasty (c. 1750-1100 B.C.) was established by King T'ang who had annexed his neighboring tribes in the northeastern China and marched to the northwestern region to take over the Hsia alliance, laying the foundation for the Shang dynasty.

With his successful agricultural settlement and pacification programs, he assimilated the hitherto existing cultures of Lung-shan, Yang-hsiao, and others to build upon them the Shang civilization. Professor Cheng Te-k'ung has pointed out ten distinctive developments of Shang civilization. In the area of material culture, he discerned that the ceramic industry, carving, bronze casting, the use of chariot, and architecture had highly advanced. In the area of social development, the feudal system and ancestral worship were already well established. In the area of intellectual and artistic activities, the calendar, writing, and the animal style had already accomplished high elaboration.[2]

In the area of religious beliefs and practices, the Shang dynasty had already established a well-articulated system. From the sources of archaeological discoveries, the oracle inscriptions, and the ancient written records, we can discern the following distinctive religious system of the Shang royal house.

<u>Belief in a Supreme God, Ti (帝), and His Pantheon</u>. Although the Shang people believed in many gods and goddesses, Ti or Shang Ti was their highest

23

God who commanded all other gods. The gods of His
pantheon were both nature deities and deified royal
ancestors, and they all worked for Ti as His agents in
charge of controlling the nature, destiny, and welfare
of the royal family and nation. Only the king himself
was entitled to worship Him through the mediatorship of
the ancestral kings (see chap. 3).

    <u>Ancestral Worship</u>. Chinese historians have been
debating among themselves whether Ti was regarded by
the Shang kings as their primordial ancestor or not,
but there is no conclusive answer. However, there is
no question that the Shang royal house had already established an elaborate ritual system of ancestral worship. The oracle inscriptions preserved a royal gene-
alogy and well-organized ritual cycle in order to worship all ancestors. Ancestors were not only believed
to be alive but also powerful in dominating the destiny and welfare of the living community. But the most
important function of an ancestor was to intercede for
descendants and to communicate with the supreme God
(see chaps. 3 and 13).

    <u>The Practice of Divination</u>. With the archaeolog-
ical discovery of more than one hundred thousand pieces
of oracle bones and tortoise shells with oracle inscriptions, there is no doubt that divination was
practiced quite extensively, especially in the latter
half of the Shang dynasty. On the matters of military
campaigns, building the royal sites, farming, hunting,
sacrifices, and health and welfare of royal family,
the kings and their diviners were in constant consul-
tation. They believed that all sociopolitical-econom-
ical affairs were determined by the divine oracles and
divination was the way to obtain immediate instructions
from gods and ancestors. We shall see that the practice of divination has been, from that time, one of
the persistent traditions in China, even though the
devices of divination have changed from time to time.

    <u>The Sacred Kingship</u>. The Shang kings were not
only rulers, commanders-in-chief, and landlords, but
also the high priests and arch-diviners who mediated
between the divine and human beings. The kings were
the heirs of the deified ancestral kings and the in-
heritors of the theocratic state, so that they had to
conduct divination and sacrifices to reinforce the
legitimacy of their sacred kingship. The position of
king was at the center of the universe and his sacred
duties were viewed as maintaining the harmony of the

universe.

<u>The Diviners and Shamans</u>. The diviners and shamans were primarily assistants to the kings for obtaining divine oracles and for performance of royal ceremonies. Because of their special charisma and their close relationship with kings, they were also involved with the political and military affairs of the nation. Many of them acted as counselors to the kings, feudal lords, and even military commanders. Moreover, they were the intellectuals who invented the writings, inscribed the oracle inscriptions, and left for us a great legacy of the Shang civilization. They seemed to have their own divided schools and traditions which later developed into various religious and philosophical schools of ancient China.

<u>A Theocratic Community</u>. The sociopolitical structure of the Shang empire is basically theocratic. With a sacred king at the top of the hierachy, the oracle of the supreme God as its guiding principle, and royal ancestral worship as the core of political legitimacy, religion and state were inseparable in Shang society. The royal ancestral temple was the center of political activities. It was the place where the appointment of feudal lords was made, the tributes of vassals received, the rank and file of government officials ordered, the weapons of war stored, military campaigns planned, and the great royal feasts held. Extensive and elaborate rituals and festivals were conducted annually in the ancestral temple. The oracle inscriptions even mentioned that, on one occasion, three hundred cattle were slaughtered as sacrifice for a celebration of annual harvest.

<u>Elaborate Burials and Concerns for Life After Death</u>. The excavation of carriages, utensils, ritual vessels, weapons, jewels, and food in numerous well-constructed royal and noble burials revealed an obsessive concern of the Shang kings and nobles for their lives after death. Especially, enormous numbers of servants, wives, and slaves together with their chariots and horses were buried alive with their deceased masters, demonstrating their belief in the continuity between their earthly life and life after death. Death was thought of as a mere transition from here to eternity, and the Shang people wanted to take all that they could from this world to the other world and to maintain their status quo.

25

What has been described above represents, for the
most part, the religious belief and practice of the
upper-class people in Shang society, since most of the
sources we can rely upon belonged to them. We do not
have much evidence to identify the religious life of
peasants and slaves, but we can assume that they were
forced to participate in the religious activities of
their kings and feudal lords. They were completely at
the mercy of their masters, so much so, they were even
forced to accompany their masters in their burial.
The modern Communist scholars have harshly criticized
the exploitation of peasants and slaves in Shang society and the hypocrisy of Shang religion in creating
such a class division and ownership of slaves. However, we shall see the change in more recent dynasties.

The Chou Religion[3]

The well-established Shang kingdom finally came to
its end by the rebellion of the Chou tribal alliance
led by Ch'ang (posthumously entitled King Wen) of the
north-western region in the middle of the eleventh century B.C. King Wu, the son of King Wen, led the Chou
army and captured the capital, Yin, and killed King
Hsin of Shang to inaugurate a new dynasty called Chou
in 1027 B.C. The Book of History (Shu Ching), the Book
of Poetry (Shih Ching), and Bronze vessels inscriptions
(Chin Wen) of the early Chou dynasty all recorded how
the Chou kings tried to legitimate the rebellion of
Chou as the Mandate of Heaven. Owing to the excessive
licentiousness of the Shang nobility and their oppression of the peasants and slaves, especially the tribe
of Chiang (羌) who were related to the Chou tribe, the
Chou alliance rose in rebellion on the call of the supreme God they now called T'ien (Heaven).

God T'ien and the Mandate of Heaven. With their
efforts to legitimate their rebellion, they gradually
developed a new religious awareness that the supreme
God must be both righteous and universal. The supreme
God could not be merely a patron deity of a ruling
tribe or class and only favor and protect his own tribe
and class. Therefore, they claimed that God T'ien was
the God of morality; He would only endow His mandate
to a righteous king to govern a given state; and He
would take away the mandate from an unworthy king. The
new consciousness of the moral nature of divinity had
enabled the Chou people to realize the universality of
God and also the moral mandate of divine kingship.
This valuable insight was preserved by Confucius and

his followers to develop a moral philosophy of government. Meantime, the new awareness that God T'ien is universal and concerned with the welfare of all human kings led the Taoists to develop a universalistic metaphysic and mysticism. Mo Tzu and his followers also tried to build a new classless fraternal community based on the "all-embrasive love of heaven."

The <u>Religious Codes</u>. The Duke of Chou, the brother of King Wu, acting as regent after the death of his brother, developed this notion of moral mandate and righteous rule further into a full-scale feudal political system supporting the central Chou authority bounded by an elaborate kinship code and hierarchical legislation. The king was titled the son of Heaven (T'ien Tzu). He had the exclusive right to worship the deceased Chou kings and God T'ien and given sovereignty over all the feudal lords and their domains. The feudal lords were to be related to the central royal family and carry out the moral mandate and righteous commands issued by the central authority. They had to pay annual tribute and homage by partaking in the annual ceremony of royal ancestral worship conducted by the son of Heaven. The whole Chou society was stratified, hierarchically, according to the lineage relationship with the royal family, by a rigidly instituted rank system for all government officials. In order to consolidate its hierarchical networks and delicate feudal relations, codes and rules were specifically written down. The <u>Book of Rites</u>, the <u>Records of Rites and Ceremonies</u>, and the <u>Temple</u> Hymns in the <u>Book of Poetry</u>, all witness to such efforts of stratification and codification. Even the hitherto random practice of divination was now well articulated and codified as the <u>Book of Changes</u>.

<u>Rise of Skepticism</u>. The hierarchical system of the Chou dynasty lasted for about three centuries. The beginning of its collapse is noted as the end of the eighth century B.C. Due to the court intrigues among the feudal lords, the constant military campaigns to resist the invasion of northern barbarians, and the subduing of rebellious tribes, the central monarchy of Chou weakened and was finally taken over by the independent and divided powers of the feudal lords in 770 B.C., when King P'ing moved his capital from the Western capital Chung-chou to the Eastern capital Cheng-chou. It signified the end of the Western Chou and the beginning of the Eastern Chou, or the Period

of Ch'un Ch'iu (春秋).

During the period of disintegration, occurring at
the end of the Western Chou period, we saw the rise of
skepticism in the traditional belief of the righteous
rule of God T'ien. In the Book of Poetry, we read the
following challenge to the supreme command of Heaven.

     Oh, universal T'ien, whom we call parent!
     I am innocent and blameless,
     Yet I suffer from such great disorders.
     Majestic Heaven, you are too stern;
        for truly I am innocent.
     Majestic Heaven, you are too cruel;
        for truly I am blameless. [Shih, 2:5, 4]

     I gaze up to August Heaven, but it does not
     favour us. For long these cruel afflictions
     which it has sent down greatly distressed us.
     The state is unsettled. Officers and people
     have suffered. [Shih, 3:3, 10]

     Now the people in their perils look up to
       Heaven,
     But they find no clear guidance. [Shih, 2: 4]

     The net which Heaven throws down is full of
       calamities.
     Good men are perishing, and my heart is grieved.
     [Shih, 3:3]

Peasant Religion. However, this skepticism did
not entirely eradicate the traditional beliefs. Instead, we see the emergence of folk religion in the
writings of some intellectuals. Of course, folk religion must have existed long before the rise of the
Shang state religion, but its beliefs and practices did
not appear in the official records until the appearance
of an anthology of folk songs in the Book of Poetry in
the eighth century B.C. Professor Marcel Granet had
elaborated on what he called "Peasant Religion" based
on the Book of Poetry. Peasant religion was basically
a communal religion of farmers conducting the spring
and autumn festivals in their holy places worshipping
the Mother Earth and Sky Father. It was a religion of
fertility, focusing on the mating of Yin and Yang
forces in nature to procreate the new life. In their
annual communal festivals, they gathered at the holy
places to rekindle their social harmony and to re-
strengthen their bond with nature. They believed that

the source of life and energy are of chthonic origin
called the Yellow Spring, and the life-substance will
go back to it after death and return again like vegetation. Human life and social process are therefore
to be in accord with the cycle of nature, and the
farmer's almanac becomes the norm and guide of agrarian
life.[4]

The Period of Diversification

With the collapse of Chou, central authority, and
the rise of warfare between the divided states, the
well-established state religion of ancient China began
to disintegrate and the diversification of various
religious schools began. The chaos created by the concurrent warfare during the Warring States period (453-
221 B.C.) caused great confusion and conflict in
Chinese society, but it also provided a great opportunity for Chinese people to develop new religious
thoughts and organizations. We see the rise of Confucianism, Taoism, Mohism, Yin-Yang Cosmology, and
Shamanism during this period. The following will describe the major tennets of these religious schools.

Confucianism (Ju Chiao 儒教).[5]

Confucianism was founded by Confucius (551-479
B.C.), who was a conservative and traditionalist of
the Chou state religion. He served as a minister of
ceremonies in the state of Lu, trying to restore the
culture and religion of Chou instituted by the Duke of
Chou. It was believed he edited the Six Classics
(Shih, Shu, Li, Yüeh, I, and Ch'un-ch'iu) and to educate his disciples with the Six arts (Poetry, History,
Rites, Music, Divination, and Political Science). He
carried on the tradition of ancestral worship
stressed filial piety as the foundation of social
ethics. He esteemed the traditional belief in the Mandate of Heaven, and he emphasized that each individual
who sensed the sacred duty of transmitting the ancient
culture would also have received the same mandate from
Heaven. He died without realizing his ideal of restoring the ancient golden age, but he left a great
legacy for Chinese people, and his disciples carried
on his unfulfilled vision.

The Confucian school developed after his death in
three directions: (1) the Mencian school which championed humanistic and idealistic causes; (2) the Hsün
Tzu school which stressed realistic and legalistic
causes; (3) the Chung-yang school which integrated with

29

Yin-Yang Cosmology to promote the way for the golden
mean and moral cultivation. After going through a
brief period of oppression under the Ch'in dictatorship
(221-206 B.C.), the Confucianists won the trust and
favor of the Han dynasty and created the so-called Confucian bureaucracy to solidify their powers which
lasted until 1911 A.D.

Since the majority of Confucianists had served as
government officials, Confucian organization was connected with the government bureaucracy, and their political and religious activities were often co-mingled.
However, the Confucian shrine instituted as early as
the beginning of the Han dynasty had become the center
of Confucian tradition. Confucius, his parents, and
all eminent Confucianists were enshrined as the objects
of Confucian veneration, and the T'ai-lao sacrifice of
three victims--an ox, a sheep, and a pig--has been offered annually on the birthday of Confucius (27 August).
It is important to note that Confucianism is not merely
a philosophy, but also a religion which has its doctrine, rituals, and shrine.

Taoism[6]

Lao Tzu was believed to be the founder of Taoism,
and Tao Te Ching has been regarded as the Bible of
Taoism. In Tao Te Ching, it was not Ti or T'ien that
was the supreme being, but Tao. Tao is the cosmic
principle which procreates the universe and permeates
it in myriad ways. Its attribute is silence, emptiness, nonactivity, simplicity, and spontaneity. The
Taoists also believed that each being has inherited a
particular nature of Tao within itself which they
called Te (virtue), and each being should fulfill its
own Te in order to unite with the primordial Tao. Because of their emphasis on metaphysics and natural mysticism, the Taoists were critical of Confucian arti-
ficality in their worldly politics and social ethics.
They proposed a political anarchy: governing without
demanding and giving the people absolute freedom.
Their slogans were: "go back to nature," "roam the
universe," "act with non-action," "be one with Tao."

The Taoists were like a group of hermits, and retired or unemployed officials, who had rather a pessimistic view of human society and sought a romantic
paradise in nature for their solace. However, their
negative politics and relativistic ethics had a positive function of checking and balancing the despotic

government and corrupted bureaucracy. From time to
time, the Taoist ideology and method of politics have
rivaled Confucianism and won the favor of some emperors.
However, the greatest contribution Taoism made in China
was in the development of metaphysics and mysticism,
and to a certain degree the advancement of sciences and
democracy.[7]

   The Taoist movement had gradually divided into
various groups during the Ch'in and Han dynasties (221
B.C.-220 A.D.): (1) the Philosophical school of Chuang
Tzu and Huai Nan Tzu who developed metaphysics and mysticism; (2) the Taoist religious groups such as the
T'ai-p'ing Tao, T'ien-shu Tao, etc., which organized
as sects and revolted against the Han regime; (3) the
Prescriptionist school (Fang Shih 方士) which developed alchemy and medicine in search of longevity. During the dynasties which followed, Three Kingdoms, Tsin
and Southern and Northern dynasties (220-590 A.D.)--all
three schools--flourished among the common populace,
as well as the intellectuals. The philosophical school
produced the so-called Neo Taoism of naturalists and
romanticists such as Wang Pi, Hsiang Hsiu, and Kuo
Hsiang. The T'ien shu Tao had become a powerful religious organization carrying many followers who had lost
their trust in the government. In the Prescriptionist
school, we see the great advancement in the sciences
of astronomy, medicine, alchemy, anatomy, and helio-
therapy, etc. In the early T'ang dynasty (618-906
A.D.), Taoism was even acknowledged to be a state religion sponsored by the T'ang royal family. By the
tenth century, the Taoists were able to collect 1464
works to compose their canon called <u>Tao Tsang</u> (道藏).

Mohism[8]

   Mo Tzu (c.a. 479-381 B.C.), the founder of Mohist
school, was an engineer, military strategist, and,
possibly, a temple keeper as well, who championed for
the cause of the oppressed people and small states.
In the collection of his teachings (referred to as
<u>Mo Tzu</u>), he criticized ritualism, fatalism, discrimina-
tory ethics, and agnosticism of Confucianism, and promoted the virtue of all-embracing love, pacifism, self-
determinism, and the reverence for God and spirits.
He organized a well-knit religious organization controlled by a Chü Tzu (鉅子, great man) and dedicated
in the worship of God (T'ien) and spirits, and the
promotion of pacifism. He trained his disciples in
the political sciences, martial arts, military

engineering, and logic of diplomacy, and he sent them
to serve in various different states to propagate the
Mohist causes.

Unfortunately, Mohism was short lived in ancient
China. After the death of Mo Tzu, the Mohist group
gradually disintegrated and disappeared into oblivion.
By the time of the Han dynasty, there remained only a
few Neo-Mohist apologists; they, however, were unable
to effectuate any significant influence, as was evidenced by their predcessor and founder, Mo Tzu.
(Nevertheless, in modern times, both Christian missionaries and Communist philosophers have shown great
interest in the studies of Mohism and in reappraising
the significance of Mohism in Chinese history.)

The Yin-Yang and Five Elements School[9]

The belief in the Yin-Yang cosmic forces and the
Five Elements and their organismic interaction had
already existed in ancient China, but it was Tsou Yen
(305-240 B.C.) who composed them into a coherent cosmology and utilized it to explain human nature, social
behavior, and political changes. Tsou Yen was invited
by many feudal lords to be their political counselor,
and he drew many followers who admired him for his
erudite knowledge. He carried over the Shang belief
in the Five Agents of Ti and sacrifice to the Lords of
the Four Corners and the Yin-Yang control of human
destiny in the Book of Changes to develop a new theory
of mutual production and mutual conquest. His interpretation of political changes, according to his
theory of mutual conquest of Five Elements, had a
great impact on Chinese philosophy of history and political sciences. Although he did not organize his own
religious society, his cosmology had influenced almost all major schools of religious thought in ancient
China. The Yin-Yang cosmology and the organism of
Five Elements have become the core of Chinese world
view and remain influential even in modern times.

Shamanism[10]

The shamans who served in the Shang royal court
as diviners, priests, dancers, scribes, healers were
in exile in the southern state of Ch'u (楚) after the
fall of the Shang dynasty, and they left for us a
beautiful legacy of shamanistic poetry which was collected as the Songs of the South (Ch'u Tz'u). Although they had already lost their political power,

their aspiration for astral traveling, communion with divine beings, transcendence from the world of miseries, and their arts of poetry, music, dance, and healing have everlasting impact on Chinese religion and culture.

Ch'u Yüan, one of the great poets in the Songs of the South, composed the song "Li Sao" (On Encountering Sorrow), lamenting the paradoxes and illusion of worldly affairs and seeking to return to roaming in heaven. He was a loyal government official serving in the court of the Ch'u State, but was put in exile by slander and court intrigues, ultimately drowning himself. Chinese people commemorate this martyr-poet, Ch'u Yüan, in the course of the May Fifth Boat Festival. The nine songs in the Songs of the South recorded the songs and dances performed, for entertainment, by shamans of their patron deities. Apparently, these shamans still preserved their religious tradition centering in their own secret shrines. However, after the destruction of the State of Ch'u by the First Emperor of Ch'in and the unification of China by the Han dynasty, shamanism had been gradually absorbed into the major current of syncretistic religious movement and lost its own identity. But although there is no longer a specific religion organization of shamanism, as such, shamans still exist today, and the influence of shamanism is still visible in the modern mythology and folk religion.

The Period of Importation

From the first century on, China had seen the incoming of many foreign religions such as Buddhism from India, Zoroastrianism, Manichaeism, Christianity, Islam, and even Judaism from the Middle East. With the opening of the silk trade route between China and Persia and India in the early Han dynasty, many traders and immigrants from the Middle East came to China carrying their religions and cultures. During the Divided dynasties period (420-590 A.D.), China also saw a great influx of the neighboring tribes, and even the establishment of their regimes in central China. As the central authority of Han Chinese was weakened, the non-Han Chinese gained more power, and many foreign religions were able to settle and flourish in China under their protection. Even when the Han Chinese restored their dynasties during the Sui and T'ang (581-906 A.D.), they had to accept a cosmopolitan policy of absorbing and assimilating these foreign religions.

The influx of foreign religions continued in the following dynasties of Sung, Yüan, Ming, and Ch'ing, and
even to modern times. The following will briefly describe the introduction of these major foreign religions.

<u>Buddhism</u> [11]

     Buddhism, founded by Siddartha Gotama in India
(563-483 B.C.), was brought into China by Buddhist
devotees through the silk route around the beginning
of the first century A.D. It was propagated among the
people in the southwestern region and gradually pene-
trated into central China and flourished. Buddhism
came in as a foreign religion, yet was able to assimilate with Chinese religion and culture to become an
integral part of Chinese tradition. Buddhism introduced many new doctrines such as the karma and trans-
migration, anatman (non-self), dharma, buddhahood,
boddhisattva, kalpa, and nirvana, and also an entirely
different religious order called samgha (monastery).
And yet Buddhists were able to adapt the Confucian
ethics and Taoist metaphysics, manifesting Buddhism as
a religion of universal salvation. They had also made
their monasteries available for social and welfare
services to many suffering poeple. They not only won
the adherence of many common people but also obtained
the favor and support of the royalty and nobility.
Thus, Buddhism had attained its golden age in the
Divided dynasties (420-590 A.D.) and its zenith in the
T'ang dynasty (618-906 A.D.).

     Many Chinese intellectuals, including the Confu-
cianists and Taoists, were drawn into the studies of
Buddhism, and they, in turn, produced the flowering of
Mahayana Buddhism. There were nine major Buddhist
schools developed in China: (1) the Disciplinary School
which emphasized the code of discipline and rigid mon-
astic training; (2) the Kosa School which followed the
Realist School of Theravada Buddhism; (3) the Sect of
the Three Stages which taught the three periods of the
Buddha's teachings; (4) the T'ine-T'ai School which
developed in the monastery on Mount T'ien T'ai and expounded the Five Periods and the Eight Teachings and
the Threefold Truth; (5) the Hua-yen School which advocated the organic and non-obstructional principle of
the universe or the dharmadhatu; (6) the Fa-Hsiang
School which developed a Buddhist psychology based on
the eight consciousnesses; (7) the Tantric School
which expounded the Tantrayana method to attain

34

enlightenment; (8) the Pure Land School which developed faith and devotion to the Buddha Amitabha of the Pure Land; and (9) the Ch'an School (or Zen in Japan) which emphasized the importance of dhyana exercises. After the great accomplishment of the Ch'an School in the T'ang dynasty, we see the gradual decline of Buddhism in China.

Zoroastrianism, Manichaeism, and Judaism.[12]

With the opening up of the silk trade route, many Western faiths were also introduced into China by traders and immigrants. Zoroastrianism came to China around the sixth century, and a Zoroastrian temple was established at Ch'ang-an in 631 A.D. There is the possibility that Manichaeism came earlier and had already left certain influences on Taoism at the end of the fourth century. Several Manichaean temples were built between 766-779 A.D. and apparently supported by large numbers of Chinese converts. Jewish immigrants came to settle in the area of Kai-feng during the Han dynasty and continued to observe their religion and customs for about eight hundred years.

Christian Missions[13]

The Nestorian mission was the first introduction of Christianity into China. With the discovery of the famous Nestorian stele near Hsiang-fu, we can be sure that the Nestorian mission was quite active and successful in building churches and monasteries, in translating the Bible, and winning Chinese converts during the T'ang dynasty. Chinese called the Nestorian Faith <u>Ching Chiao</u>--"Luminous Religion"--and the royal house and some high-ranking officials even supported it. Especially when the Mongols established the Yüan dynasty in China, the Nestorian mission had greatly flourished with the favorable support of the Mongol emperors and tribes. Meantime, the Franciscan mission also came to China in 1300 and obtained the support of the Mongol officials, winning many Chinese converts. However, when the Mongol dynasty collapsed in 1368, Christianity lost its supporters and gradually died out in China.

China had to wait until the coming of the Portuguese traders in the beginning of the sixteenth century to see again the reintroduction of Christianity. This time it was mainly the Jesuit missionaries led by Mattaeo Ricci (1552-1610) who won approval from the Chinese emperor by demonstrating superior scientific

knowledge and astronomy to open the way for Christian
propagation. The Franciscan and Dominican missions
also followed in the early seventeetn century. Jesuit
missions were more tolerant and conciliatory toward
traditional Chinese religion, but the Dominicans and
Franciscans were suspicious of the Jesuits' approach,
and finally there erupted a great controversy about
whether or not Chinese Christians should retain ancestral worship and Confucian rites. Because the papal
authority issued a decree to put a ban on Christian
participation in Chinese rites in 1704, the Chinese
emperor responded with an imperial decree expelling all
missionaries out of China in 1706. It signified a sad
end to the first attempt of Catholic missions.

     With the defeat of the Chinese in the so-called
Opium War (1840-1842), Chinese had to yield the opening of five treaty ports for the incoming of the Protestant missions led by Dr. Robert Morrison. Subsequently, the Catholic missionaries re-entered China
under the protection of the French government. Although there were rapid increases in Chinese converts
to Christianity, concurrently, there also erupted
Chinese hostility against the Christian missionaries,
as they were viewed as agents of Western imperialism
which came to destroy the Chinese way of life. During
the years 1850-1865, the T'ai P'ing rebellion led by
Hung Hsiu-ch'üan, who claimed to be the brother of Jesus
and advocated the coming of the Kingdom of God, almost
brought down the Manchu dynasty. After many upheavals
and humiliations, Chinese finally accomplished a revolution of the imperial system to build the first Republic in 1917, and finally the People's Republic in
1949. With the rise of Communist China, Christianity
was once again rejected and missionaries expelled from
China. However, Chinese Christian churches have survived not only on mainland China but have also flourished in Hong Kong and Taiwan.

Muslim Immigration

     In contrast to Christian missions, which intended
to convert Chinese, the Muslims came to China as
traders and immigrants, married Chinese wives, and
were content to be allowed to practice their religion
and customs. The Chinese government has been tolerant
of Islam, for it did not threaten supreme authority
nor attempt to convert Chinese ways. During the cosmopolitan T'ang dynasty, the influx of Muslim immigrants
accelerated, and during the following dynasty of the

Mongols who were in favor of Islam, Muslim scholars, traders, and craftsmen were encouraged to immigrate to China. In South China, many Arab sailors and traders also settled in the ports of Canton and Fu-chien. Throughout the Ming and Manchu dynasties, the Muslim population continued to increase; by 1924, the government had estimated between fifteen to twenty million Muslims in China. Mosques are to be found in many of the larger cities, and most of the Muslims follow the Sunnite tradition. After the Republic of China, Chinese Islamic Society was organized (1912), and eighteen Muslims were elected as members in the National Assembly. The People's Republic acknowledged the ethnic autonomy of the Chinese Muslim community, and Islam is still in existence even under the Communist regime.

Thus, we have seen a great multiplication of religions in China since the diversification within the traditional Chinese religious framework and the incoming of many foreign religions. Hence, religious pluralism has become an important issue in China since the beginning of the Ch'in dynasty. This issue of religious pluralism has only recently become a hot issue in the Western Christian countries, especially in America, but Chinese poeple have confronted it for a long time. How then have Chinese people coped with it? There were, of course, concurrent episodes of sectarian conflicts, mutual antagonism, and imperial oppression. The burning of Confucian classics and the burials of Confucianists by the first Ch'in emperor in 213 B.C. was famous. The imperial decree of destruction and confiscation of Buddhist monasteries by Emperor Wu of 845 A.D. and the expelling of Christian missionaries by the Ming emperor in 1706, and also by the Communist regime in 1950, were overt anti-foreign actions. The subjugation and oppression of Taoist religions, folk religions, and Buddhism by the Confucian bureaucracy were recurrent. Meanwhile, the rebellions by the Taoists, Buddhists, and Christians in opposition to central authority were frequent.

However, there were also many occasions of healthy scholarly controversies, constructive comparative studies, mutual learnings, and inter-religious cooperation throughout early Chinese history. There then appeared a very interesting religious phenomenon of newly formed syncretistic religions. Realizing that none of the single religions had the monopoly of absolute truth and that there existed a common goodness

in all religions, many new religious groups synthesized
some religious teachings and practices they believed to
be most congenial to their own faith and organized a
new religion out of various different religious traditions. There were many varieties and patterns of such
syncretism in Chinese history.

Finally, it is important to note that there was
also a trend of universalism or universalistic aspiration in the history of Chinese religion. This will be
expanded upon in chapter 14.

The Period of Decline and Disintegration

The West not only introduced Christianity to China
but also introduced Western science, humanism, secularism, and atheism. In response to the great humiliation
Chinese had suffered under the invasion of the Western
and Japanese military powers, beginning with the Opium
War (1840-1842),many Chinese intellectuals had abandoned the traditional religions and were drawn to these
new Western learnings. Many Chinese students had
studied abroad and many Western writings had been
translated into Chinese. So the Western influence of
secularization had great impact on young Chinese intellectuals. They became very critical of Confucianism, Taoism, and Buddhism, looking down upon "folk"
religion as entirely superstitious. They considered
these traditional faiths to be the major causes for
the downgrading of Chinese culture and the obstacles
to the development of sciences and industries which
they felt could have compared with those in the West.
With the rise of the Republic, there were strong efforts to subdue the traditional faiths, if not completely eradicate them. Finally, since the Communists
gained power in 1949, there has been a wholesale
government effort to eradicate all religious beliefs
and practices, including both the traditional faiths
and Christianity. As the Communist regime embraced
the atheism of Marx and Lenin, Mao Tse-tung and his
followers have all engaged in harsh attacks on the
traditional faiths as being the defenders of feudalism; Christianity was seen as the agency of imperialism and capitalism which committed the evils of exploitation of peasants and laborers and creating inequality and discrimination in society. In the Constitution of the Chinese Soviet Republic issued on
November 7, 1931, Article 13 stated:

The Soviet government of China guarantees

true religious freedom to the workers,
peasants, and the toiling population.
Adhering to the principle of the complete separation of church and state,
the Soviet state neither favors nor
grants any financial assistance to
any religion whatsoever. All Soviet
citizens shall enjoy the right to engage in anti-religious propaganda. No
religious institution of the imperialists shall be allowed to exist unless
it shall comply with Soviet law.[14]

It is clear that, while nominally it advocated religious freedom, it sponsored the right to attack the
traditional religions which do not follow Soviet law.

Under such onslaught of secularism and atheism,
Chinese religions, as of 1949, suffered enormous oppression and began to disintegrate with some experi-
encing total extermination. Confucianism had lost its
eminent traditional status as the state-ideology and
guiding principle of education and state-examination.
Its strongfold of Confucian bureaucracy began to tum-
ble. Many intellectuals, including Confucian scholars,
no longer claimed Confucianism to be a religion, and
many Confucian temples were abandoned to the ravishes
of time. Taoism was criticized as archaic and nihil-
istic, and the Taoist religion as superstitious and
backward. Many Taoist temples were confiscated, and
Taoist societies were disbanded by the government authorities. Buddhism was criticized as hypocritical
and exploitative, and the Buddhist monks as the parasites of the society. Many Buddhist monasteries were
confiscated to become schoolhouses or soldiers' garri-
sons. Christian missionaries were severely criticized
as the agents of Western imperialism and capitalism,
and finally expelled from China. Chinese Christians
were forced to cut their ties with the Western Christian world and to be entirely patriotic and national-
istic. Islam, however, has been able to resist the
oppressions because of its strong ethnic support and
comparative isolation from the main current of political and social changes. Islam was not only a religion but also a total cultural system of large popula-
tions of Chinese Moslems who immigrated from the Middle East, and both the Kuomingtang and Communist regimes could not do much to modify the Moslems' traditional lifestyle. However, under the rule of unfriendly and oppressive regimes, all religions began to

disintegrate and could no longer exert their pre-exis-
tent traditional influences on a culture they used to
enjoy.[15]

The Period of Revival and Resurgence

In spite of the onslaught of secularism and the
systematic oppostion of organized religion under Communism, Chinese religions have not disappeared, but
have revived and regenerated. It is known that traditional religious communities were greatly weakened and
their activities severely limited by the Communist authorities, but they not only survived but also renewed
themselves to become new religions which are capable
of confronting adverse situations. Of course, we
should note that many traditional faiths were preserved
by the overseas Chinese who were able to maintain their
faiths in their newly settled lands. The traditional
religions have revived and flourished in the islands
of Hong Kong and Taiwan. In the major Chinese communities of Singapore, Manila, Bangkok, San Francisco, and
New York, the oversea Chinese are still holding onto
many of their traditional customs and faiths. Although the religious atmosphere in Mainland China,
Hong Kong, Taiwan, and oversea Chinese communities are
by no means altogether similar and congruent, we can
detect certain general trends of modern Chinese religious behavior and belief as follows.[16]

Confucianism

During the end of the Manchu dynasty, there was
an attempt to institute Confucianism as a state religion and to worship Confucius as equal to God by the
Manchu government and some Confucian scholars such as
K'ang Yu-wei and Yen Fu, but they had failed. Instead, Confucianism was increasingly criticized as a
backward defender of feudalism and not suitable to the
contemporary world by some eminent Confucian scholars
who had been influenced by the humanism and pragmatism
of the West. Liang Ch'i-ch'ao, Ts'ai Yuan-p'ei,
Ch'en Tu-shiu, and Hu Shih were the major critics of
Confucianism. In the early Republic, Confucian religious practices, political and educational institutions, and the veneration of Confucius as a god, were
all abandoned. However, Confucian emphasis on the respect of parents and belief in Heaven still remained
among the common populace.

Although Sun Yat-sen was a Christian, he readvocated the value of Confucian ethics after he

became the first President of the Republic and his
successor Chiang Kai-sek used the four Confucian Cardinal Virtues: propriety, righteousness, purity, and
self-consciousness to initiate the so-called New Life
Movement. Liang Sou-ming, originally a Buddhist, converted to champion the resurgence of Confucianism. He
claimed that in the coming world civilization, Confucianism will lead in building a humanistic world.
Even former critic, Hu Shih, changed his attitude toward Confucianism by saying, "Confuciansim will fur-
nish very fertile soil on which to cultivate modern
scientific thinking," and "you find Confucianism always the philosophy of political reform."[17] Kuo Mo-jo,
the late minister of education of the People's Republic, went even further when he stated that Confucius
and his pupils were always on the side of the rebels
and sympathetic to the liberation of the people, and
that their fundamental standpoints were social progress and social welfare. In the West, Professor Creel
of the University of Chicago, has praised Confucius as
a creative, liberal, democratic social reformer.

     Following the re-evaluation of Confucianism, the
scholarly research into the significance of Confucius
and Confucianism have rapidly advanced. Both Hu Shih
and Fu Ssu-nien had re-acknowledged the religious
origin and position of Confucius. An eminent Buddhist
philosopher, Hsiung Shih-li, had revived the idealism
of Neo-Confucianism and advocated the significance of
the Confucian concept of Jen (仁) as the source of all
transformation and the foundation of all being. Fung
Yi-lan advocated Neo-Confucian rationalism to promote
what he called New Rational Philosophy (Hsin Li Hsueh).
A group of Confucian scholars in Hong Kong and Taiwan
have organized the so-called Neo-Neo-Confucianism and
reaffirmed the religious value and significane of Confucianism. In their manifesto, they stated that the
doctrine of "hsin hsin" or the "conformity of heaven
and man in virtue" is the core of Chinese culture, and
"we must not allow the misunderstanding that Chinese
culture limits itself to external relations between
people, with neither inner spiritual life nor religious
or metaphysical sentiment."[18]

Buddhism

     Modern Buddhist reforms were led by Abbot T'ai-
hsu (1889-1947). He was so incensed by the destruction of temples and great disarray among the Buddhist
monks that he launched a reform movement to regenerate

the clergy, advocating rededication for social service
and reconstruction of Buddhist doctrines. In 1929 he
declared that new Buddhism should be humanistic,
scientific, demonstrative, and worldwide. In the same
year, the Chinese Buddhist society was organized, which
by 1936 had grown into 476 branches, claiming 4,620,000
members by 1947. T'ai-hsu had also traveled extensively abroad to Japan, Southeast Asia, and Europe to
promote a world federation of Buddhism and international cooperation among Buddhists. The Buddhist
society was also very active in reprinting the
Tripitaka (Buddhist Bible) and in publishing many journals and magazines for the propagation of Buddhism.
Professor W. T. Chan has noted seven tendencies in the
new development of Buddhism: (1) in Buddhist doctrines
--from T'ien-tai and Hua-yen philosophy to Wei-shih
idealism; (2) in experience--from Pure Land formalism
to pietism; (3) in practice--from the Disciplinary and
Meditation Schools to the Mystical School; (4) in lit-
erature--from Chinese to Pali and Tibetan Tripitakas;
(5) in attitude--from ritualistic performance to religious demonstration; (6) in leadership--from the clergy
to the laymen; and (7) in objective--from the other
world to this world.[19]

Currently, Buddhists are divided politically between the Chinese Buddhist Association in the People's
Republic and the Buddhist Association of the Republic
of China (in Taiwan). Modern Buddhism, the official
journal of the Chinese Buddhist Association, stated
four major goals of its association: (1) Doing tasks
toward fulfillment of the Boddhisattva vows, (2) participation in the commune to reduce egoism, (3) realization of the Western paradise through the Communist
revolution, and (4) eradication of social evils with
Buddhist compassion. According to the China Year Book
(1969-1970), B.A.R.O.C. had 50,137 members, 1,915 organizations, 13 study centers, and 13 periodicals. It
has made special efforts in recruiting Chinese intellectuals for Buddhist studies and in comprehensive
evangelism to propagate among the common people.[20]

Taoism

Four major schools of Taoism developed in the
twelfth century: Cheng-i, Ch'üan-chen, Ta-tao, and
T'ai-i, all of which disintegrated very rapidly in
modern times. The sixty-third T'ien-shu who claimed
to be a descendant of Chang Ling, the founder of a
Taoist religion called T'ien-shu Tao in the first

42

century A.D., took refuge from the mainland China to
Taiwan. There he reorganized a Chinese Taoist Association in an effort to revive the Orthodox rites for
ordination of Taoist priests and to propagate Taoist
philosophy and spiritual disciplines.

Professor Dubs asserts:

> Religious Taoism has been dying for cen-
> turies, and modern science is speeding
> up the process. Philosophical Taoism,
> however, with its exaltation of mystic-
> ism, naturalism, and simplicity, se-
> curing solace in misfortune by culti-
> vating inward calm, laissez faire,
> skepticism of doctrinaire programs, and
> optism, cultivating bodily as well as
> spiritual health, is likely to remain
> an important part of China's heritage.[21]

The Rise of New Religious Societies[22]

While the traditional Taoist religious organization was declining, there arose many syncretistic religious societies following the Ming and Ch'ing dynasties, and they are still active today. The Tsai-li
(Principle Abiding) Society, founded in the seventeenth
century, has propagated a syncretism of Taoism and
Buddhism for moral and spiritual discipline. The White
Lotus Society, founded in 1133, has produced many
branches after its rebellions against the Manchu regime
in 1794, 1801, and 1813. The branches such as I-Kuan
Tao (The Way of Pervading Unity), the Eight Triagram
Society, the Triad Society, and the Elders Society engaged in the Boxer uprising and are still active in
the mainland China, Hong Kong, and Taiwan.

After the Republic began, many new religious societies were organized. The Society of World Religions was organized in 1915; the International Society
of Holy Religions and the Hsi-hsin (the Purification
of the Heart) Society in 1917; the Universal Ethical
Society in 1921; and the Ethical Study Society in 1924.
These societies are syncretistic and international in
nature, for they draw their moral and religious teachings from all the major religions in the world.

The Tao Yuang (Society of the Way), also known as
the Society of the Way and Its Virtue, organized in
1921, had increased its membership to thirty thousand

with thirty-eight branches by 1927. Its ideology embraces the worship of T'ai-shang Lao-chün (the Supreme
Primordial Lord) as the Godhead of Confucius, Lao Tzu,
Buddha, Christ, and Mohammed. It practices the planchette as the medium for obtaining revelations from the
gods and sages. It also emphasizes social and charitable services. Because of its extensive participation
in Red Cross works, it is also called the Universal Red
Swastika Society. It still has many followers in
Taiwan and Hong Kong. The T'ung-shan (the Common Goodness) Society started in 1918 and had more than a
thousand branches in all parts of China by 1923. It
advocates meditation, vegetarianism, and practices
charitable works and offers educational services. The
Wu-shan (the Awakening of Righteousness) Society was
founded in 1915 and practices meditation, charity,
spiritual cultivation, and planchette divination. The
I-kuan Tao (the Way of Pervading Unity) has been, perhaps, the most powerful and active of all the religious
societies. Its origin is rather obscure, but it participated in the Boxer rebellion and has endured the oppression of both the Kuomingtang and Communist regimes.
It has gone underground both on the mainland and
Taiwan, but still holds many adherents and followers,
mainly among the peasants and laborers. It believes
in the emanation of the principle of oneness in all
things and the unity of all religions for the salvation of humankind, especially at the present time of
what they call the "third catastrophe" in world history. Followers of the society practice self-cultivation, purification of the heart, reduction of desires,
and control of the mind. They worship images of world
religious sages, consult with charms and the planchette, chant Buddhist and Taoist scriptures, and ab-
stain from meat, tobacco, and alcohol.

The rise and flourishing of these religious societies indicate that modern Chinese people, still
having a strong feeling for the need of religion, are
seeking a spiritual foundation of an international
order and a world fraternity among the believers of
world religions. They try to preserve and revive ancient religious traditions and, at the same time, to
create a new syncretism which reforms the faults of
the past and meets the needs of the present. They all
strive for the liberation from the oppressions and
miseries of this world and engage in social welfare
services to promote a better society in the future.
They all emphasize the leadership of laity and sociopolitical reforms. They also highly esteem the

personal spiritual and moral cultivation and the significance of meditation and inner tranquility.

<u>The New Awakening of Islam</u>

The Chinese Moslems, numbering about fifty million
in 1950, have maintained their ethnic community and
isolation from the main currents of both Chinese religions and Arabic Islamic movement. However, in recent
years, there has been a gradual new awakening among
the Moslems, and five trends are observable.[23] First,
a tendency toward liberalism. The New Sect, organized
by Ma Fu-ch'u around 1870, has promoted modernization
of Islam. It has emphasized lay leadership and accommodation to modern science and Western civilization.
Second, a new attitude toward the Qur'an. The first
official Chinese translation of the Qur'an was made in
1932, and the interpretation of the text of the Qur'an
to harmonize with the Chinese culture and modern
science has become the major task of many Moslem intellectuals. Third, an intellectual awakening. Started
by the pilgrimage to the Arabic world, many Chinese
Moslem intellectuals have begun to realize the challenge of new Islamic studies in the world and have
started to build schools and colleges for the study
of Islam in China and send Chinese students to study
abroad. Many significant works on Islam have been
translated into Chinese, and many periodicals have been
circulating among Moslem readers. Fourth, a closer
identification with national life. With the establishment of the Republic and the new policy of "harmony and
equality of the five races" in China by Sun Yat-sen,
the Moslems were put on equal footing with other
Chinese, and Moslems are beginning to break away from
their traditional isolation. The Moslem representation
in politics has gradually advanced and participation
in the military services have accumulated great mirits
and honors. In the area of academics and arts, Moslem
scholars have also made some contributions. Fifth, a
new law-seeking movement. Since 1930, there have been
rapid increases in Moslem pilgrimage to Mecca and
study abroad in Arabic Islamic academies and many goodwill missions sponsored by the Chinese Islamic Associations. These activities bring Chinese Moslems
closer to their fellow believers in the Islamic world
and also help to establish better diplomatic relationships between China and Central and Near Eastern countries. However, the primary interest of Chinese Moslems is to seek a renewal of Islamic spirituality to
help Islam grow and bloom in China.

<u>Christianity</u>

Restoration of Christian missions after the Opium War had brought a rapid increase of membership and expansion of Christian institutions such as churches, hospitals, and colleges over all the provinces of China. By the end of the nineteenth century, there were some two thousand missionaries from all different denominations of Protestant and Catholic orders working in China. Most of the missionaries were men and women of simple piety who saw their task as the propagation of the Gospel and the conversion of the Chinese people from their supersititions and backward customs through which all human beings might attain salvation. By their zeal and sacrifices, they contributed to the betterment of Chinese cultural and social life. But they were constantly suspect of being agents of Western imperialism and capitalism. Furthermore, the family feud among the Christian denominations and between the Catholics and Protestants has created many scandals in the eyes of Chinese intellectuals. The assumed superiority of the West and its insistence on extraterritoriality confirmed the pent-up suspicions and hatred of the foreigners, causing the uprising known as the Boxer Rebellion. After the harsh suppression of the rebellion by the government under the insistence and with the support of the Western powers, the young Chinese intellectuals realized the backwardness of their culture and the necessity to learn from the West of its sciences and industries and for reform and modification of their own government. Christian leaders grasped this opportunity to aid intelligent Chinese students to study abroad in the West and to propagate among the intellectuals the ways in which the Christian Gospel could bring democracy and great wealth and political success to China. Personnel and money were advanced to accelerate evangelism, building colleges and hospitals, and in training Chinese clergy, teachers, nurses, and doctors. By the year 1920, the Protestants had already gained more than eight hundred thousand members. Meanwhile, the interdenominational cooperation was enhanced, cultivation of Chinese leadership in the indigenous churches encouraged, and, finally, the National Christian Council came into being in 1922.

However, the rise of the Republic which was largely aided by Christian enterprises did not favor further development of Christianity in China. Intellectuals of the Chinese renaissance saw Christian missions as the agent of Western imperialism and capitalism and the destroyer of traditional Chinese culture, while they championed self-determination and national sovereignty. A complex combination of such nationalism and anti-Christian agitation and religious scepticism came to a climax with the takeover of the Communist regime in 1949. Under the harsh anti-religious policy and the program to eradicate Christian connection with foreign countries, the missionaries were expelled, the mission schools and hospitals confiscated, and the native Chinese Christian activities severely curtailed. Many Chinese Christians took refugee in Hong Kong and Taiwan whereby they enjoyed a temporary freedom. About one in twelve of the Chinese population in Hong Kong is counted to be Christian, and there are four hundred thousand Christians--both Catholics and Protestants--in Taiwan.

However, even under the harsh treatment of the Communist regime, the native Chinese churches have not only endured but also engaged in a "self-reliance" movement. Originally started as the Three Self Movement (Self-governing, Self-supporting, and Self-propagating), it was finally forced by the Communist regime into a Patriotic Association to support Communist policy. Christian leaders were forced to make many compromises in Christian teachings with the Communist ideology. Thus, we have now an independent Chinese Catholic Church which has cut off her relationship with the Vatican and has self-appointed Bishops in China. Many Chinese Protestant churches still maintain their self-supportive independent organizations. But with the upheavals of the Cultural Revolution (1966), both Catholic and Protestant churches suffered severe blows and declined rapidly. Following the death of Mao Tse-tun and with the reopening of diplomacy with the West, the sign of revival and resurgence of Christianity has become more observable. However, permission for the restoration of Foreign Christian Missions is still in great doubt.[24]

<u>Is Communism a New Faith?</u>

Professor C. K. Yang, in <u>Religion in Chinese Society</u>, argues that Communism is a new faith in China today.[25] Based on Paul Tillich's definition of religion as "ultimate concern with ultimate reality," Professor Yang pointed out that Chinese Communism has demonstrated certain qualities of religion as a new ideology which has inspired the Chinese populace to

47

move toward materialistic progress and national sovereignty and has demanded that "all other concerns, economical well-being, health and life, family, aesthetic
and cognitive truth, justice and humanity, be sacrificed for the realization of the people's paradise on
the earth."[26] In a sense, Communism has replaced the
traditional theistic religions by instituting a new
form of cult. For a time Mao Tse-tung was venerated as
the "Star of Salvation," and his sayings were collected
as the Red Book (a Communist Bible); the annual visit
and parade at the T'ien An Gate became a Communist
pilgrimage, and the party slogans decreed as the new
doctrines. However, after the death of Mao and the
rise of a new pragmatism, whether the once-colorful
Maoism or Marxist-Leninist ideology can maintain its
initial thrust and command further dedication and
sacrifice of the Chinese populace has become question-
able.

     With this brief survey of religious movements
throughout the history of China, we have seen many
great changes historically; and we are still witnessing
continual changes today. Religion is a perennial quest,
and the Chinese are still searching for their ultimate
truth, abiding value, and spiritual meaning as do
other peoples. However, in tracing back the footsteps
of the past pilgrims and sages, we can discern certain
persistent courses of what Chinese called the Way that
keep running through the historical process of diver-
gent movements. The Chinese have generally understood
it as the Way of Harmony between Heaven, Earth, and
Human Beings. The Way is One, but it appeared in di-
vergent ways as the ways of Heaven, the ways of Earth,
and the ways of human beings. The subtleness of truth
lies in the understanding of the "Unity in Diversity"
and "Diversity in Unity." In the following chapters,
there will be an attempt to elaborate on the context
and content of such a Way.

Footnotes

1. For the study of the Shang religion see H. G. Creel,
The Birth of China (London: P. Owen, 1958); Kuang-chih Chang,
Shang Civilization (New Haven: Yale University Press, 1980);
Ping-ti Ho, _The Cradle of the East_ (Chicago: University of
Chicago Press, 1975); David N. Keightley, _Sources of Shang History_ (Berkeley: University of California Press, 1978); Paul
Wheatley, _The Pivot of the Four Quarters_ (Edinburgh: Edinburgh
University Press, 1971); D. Howard Smith, _Chinese Religions_
(New York: Holt, Rinehart & Winston, 1968).

2. Cheng Te-k'un, _Archaeology in China_, vol. II Shang China
(Cambridge: Heffer, 1960), pp. 243-249.

3. For the study of the Chou religion see H. G. Creel,
The Birth of China (London: P. Owen, 1958); D. Howard Smith,
Chinese Religions (New York: Holt, Rinehart & Winston, 1968);
Cheng Te-k'un, _Archaeology in China_, vol. III Chou China (Cambridge: Heffer, 1963); L. J. Bilsky, _The State Religion of
Ancient China_ (Taipei, 1975).

4. Marcel Granet, _The Religions of the Chinese People_, tr.
Maurice Freedman (New York: Harper and Row, 1975).

5. For the study of Confucius and Confucianism see H. G.
Creel, _Confucius, the Man and the Myth_ (New York: John Day,
1949); D. Howard Smith, _Confucius_ (New York: Charles Scribner's
Sons, 1973); J. K. Shryock, _The Origin and Development of the
State Cult of Confucianism_ (New York: The Century Co., 1932).

6. For the study of Lao Tzu and Taoism see Holmes Welch,
The Parting of the Way (Boston: Beacon Press, 1957); Wing-tsit
Chang, _The Way of Lao Tzu_ (Indianapolis: The Bobbs-Merrill Co.,
Inc., 1963).

7. Joseph Needham claimed that Taoism had contributed toward the early development of sciences and democracy in ancient
China. Needham, _Science and Civilization in China_ (London:
Cambridge University Press, 1956), vol. II, chap. 10.

8. For the study of Mo Tzu and Mohism see Y. P. Mei, _The
Ethical and Political Works of Motzu_ (London: Probsthain, 1929);
Burton Watson, tr., _Mo Tzu: Basic Writings_ (New York: Columbia
University Press, 1963).

9. For the study of the Yin-Yang Cosmology see Fung Yi-lan,
A History of Chinese Philosophy, tr. Derk Bodde (Princeton:
University Press, 1952), vol. I, chap. 7; Joseph Needham,
Science, vol. II, chap. 13.

10. For the study of Shamanism see David Hawkes, Ch'u Tz'u: The Songs of the South (London: Oxford University Press, 1959); Mircea Eliade, Shamanism, tr. Willard R. Trask (Princeton: Princeton University Press, 1972).

11. For the study of Chinese Buddhism see Kenneth Ch'en, Buddhism in China (Princeton: Princeton University Press, 1964); E. Zürcher, The Buddhist Conquest of China, 2 vols. (Leiden: E. J. Brill, 1959); Holmes Welch, Buddhism Under Mao (Cambridge: Harvard University Press, 1972).

12. D. Howard Smith, Chinese Religions, chap. 12.

13. For the study of Christian missions in China see K. S. Latourette, A History of Christian Missions in China (New York: Macmillan, 1929); Wing-tsit Chan, Religious Trends in Modern China (New York: Columbia University Press, 1953).

14. Donald E. MacInnis, Religious Policy and Practice in Communist China (New York: Macmillan, 1972), p. 19.

15. For the study of the religious situation during the period of decline and disintegration see Wing-tsit Chan, Religious Trends; Richard Bush, Jr., Religions in Communist China (Nashville: Abingdon Press, 1970).

16. For the study of modern trends in Chinese religions see Wing-tsit Chan, Religious Trends; Richard Bush, Religions; C. K. Yang, Religion in Chinese Society (Berkeley: University of California Press, 1961).

17. Wing-tsit Chan, Religious Trends in Modern China; Eustace Haydon, ed., Modern Trends in World Religions (New York: Books for Libraries Press, 1968).

18. A Manifesto for a Reappraisal of Sinology and Reconstruction of Chinese Culture is recorded in the Appendix of Carson Chang, Development of Neo-Confucian Thought (New York: Bookman Associates, 1962), vol. 2, p. 464.

19. Wing-tsit Chan, Religious Trends, chaps. 2, 3.

20. For information on the current Buddhist movement see Holmes Welch, Buddhism Under Mao; H. Dumoulin, Buddhism in the Modern World (New York: Macmillan, 1976).

21. Quoted in H. F. MacNair, China (Berkeley: University of California Press, 1951), p. 289.

22. For the study of Chinese religious societies see Jean Chesneaux, <u>Secret Societies in China in the Nineteenth and Twentieth Centuries</u> (Ann Arbor: University of Michigan Press, 1971); Daniel L. Overmeyer, <u>Folk Buddhist Religions</u> (Cambridge: Harvard University Press, 1976).

23. The information is largely based on Wing-tsit Chan, <u>Religious Trends</u>, chap. 5.

24. The information is largely based on D. Howard Smith, <u>Chinese Religions</u>, chaps. 12, 13; and Richard Bush, Jr., <u>Religions</u>.

25. C. K. Yang, <u>Religion in Chinese Society</u>, chap. 14.

26. Paul Tillich, <u>Dynamics of Faith</u> (New York: Harper & Row, 1958), p. 1.

Suggested Readings

W. Eberhard, <u>History of China</u> (London: Routledge & Kegan Paul, 1977).

Herrlee G. Creel, <u>Chinese Thought from Confucius to Mao Tse-tung</u> (New York: New American Library, 1960)

Laurence G. Thompson, <u>Chinese Religion: An Introduction</u> (Encino, CA: Dickension, 1969).

Wolfgang Bauer, <u>China and The Search for Happiness,</u> tr. Michael Shaw (New York: Seabury, 1976).

Marcel Granet, <u>Chinese Civilization</u> (New York: Barnes & Noble, Inc., 1930)

Henri Maspero, <u>China in Antiquity</u>, tr. Frank A. Kierman, Jr. (Amherst, MA: University of Massachusetts Press, 1978).

CHAPTER 3

THE SUPREME GOD OF SHANG RELIGION

The supreme God in the Shang Oracle Inscriptions
has been identified by almost all paleographers as Ti
(帝) and Shang Ti (上帝), which means the Lord and
the Lord on High. The existence of such belief in a
supreme God is also shown by many early Chou texts,
e.g., the Book of Odes, the Book of Documents, the
Songs of the South, and the Canon of Mountains and
Seas. In this chapter, we will focus on the religious
implications and theological significance of such belief in Ti and Shang Ti. We will discuss four aspects
of Ti: (1) An etymological analysis of the word Ti;
(2) the Authority and Power of Ti; (3) Shang Ti and
His Pantheon; and (4) Shang Ti and the Shang Tribal
God.

An Etymological Analysis of the Word Ti

The oracle inscription of Ti appeared on almost
300 pieces of oracle bones and shells, and its form is
various: 帝,帝,帝,帝.[1] Many paleographers differ
in their analysis of these inscripts and give many different etymological interpretations. We will introduce only three representatives ones here.

帝 as the Symbol of a Flower

Wu, Ta-cheng (吳大徵), Wang Kuo-wei (王國維),
and Kuo Mo-jo (郭沫若) have analyzed the oracle inscript of Ti in this form, 帝, as a pictograph of a
flower in which the form ▽ would symbolize the peduncle, the form ⊢ would symbolize the calyx, and the
form ⋏ would symbolize the stamen or pistil.[2] This
pictographic symbol as flower would contain several
meanings of Ti. First, it indicates the cross-fertil-
ization among the male and female pistils and the production of a peduncle at the stem of the flower. The
form ▽ as a peduncle is apparently a fertility symbol
for the womb of mother, and the hidden seed inside the
peduncle is definitely the symbol of the origin of
life. This interpretation does correlate well with
the predominant preoccupation of agricultural life of
the Shang people and their agricultural rites of fertility.

Second, the peduncle at the stem also indicates the
solid core and last subsist of the plant's life. After

52

sprouting, branching, budding, flowering, and weathering, only the peduncle remains. Thus, the peduncle
would imply that which is most enduring and everlasting.
Kuo Mo-jo was so impressed, not only by the fact that
a tiny seed could bear a great number of offspring, but
also by the fact that it could endure so much change
and transformation and yet be able to regenerate itself, that he said, "There is nothing more divine than
this. This must be the sign of the supreme divinity."3

Third, the total picture of a flower, including
the peduncle, the pistils, and calyxes, indicates that
it is in full bloom showing its beauty and glory.
Flowering, therefore, implies the zenith growth and
total manifestation and completion of life. This interpretation relates well with Chinese love of flowers.
Chinese people love to call their own country Chung
Hua (中華) rather than China, and Chung Hua means,
"in the middle of flowering." The oracle inscription
of Hua (華) appears as 宋, 棻 , 枀 ,and they have the same
basic structure as the oracle inscription of Ti.4

帝 as the Symbol of Burnt Offering

Yueh Yü-hsing (葉玉森), J. M. Menzies and H. G.
Creel have analyzed the form Ti 帝 as representing a
sacrificial rack for a burnt offering.5 The form 木
would indicate the picture of fire wood, the form 口
the bundle, and the form ⊢⊣ the rack. Thus, the form
Ti is similar to the word liao (尞) which means a
burnt offering. As a matter of fact, the oracle text
records many such burnt offerings to Ti and other gods
so that the sacrifice and the object of sacrifice are
easily identified as one. By extending this notion of
similarity between Ti and liao, Professor Creel identifies Ti as originally a God of Fire. He states:

> According to the theory Ti was ori-
> ginally the name of a sacrifice. This
> statement is based on the fact in Shang
> dynasty Chinese the word Ti is almost
> (sometimes quite) identical with another
> word, pronounced liao. This word liao
> is a pictograph of a bundle of wood,
> burning, ready to have an animal placed
> on it as a burnt offering; it means "to
> present a burnt offering." Since these
> words are so nearly alike in form, we
> have on the oracle bones such sentences
> as "liao (present as a burnt offering)

53

five bulls to Ti," with liao and Ti
written identically. It is thought,
then, Ti was at first merely the name
of a way of sacrificing to the ancestors
or other deities, but that gradually men
confused the sacrifice itself with the
deity sacrificed to, and came to think
of it as a separate deity.

This process whereby the human mind
takes sacrificial techniques and thinks
of them as deities can be illustrated
elsewhere than in China. The Aryans of
India first worshipped gods who lived in
the heavens. They sacrificed to these
gods, pouring clarified butter onto a
sacrificial fire known as Agni. This
sacrifice was accompanied by the reci-
tation of a sacred formula, or Braham. . . .
But later it was pointed out that after
all there was no reason to praise the
gods, for it was not they, but the
sacrificial procedure which produced the
blessings. In fact, it was the fire,
Agni, which wafted the sacrifices to the
heavens and forced the gods to give their
worshippers what they wished. And so
Agni came to be a high god.[6]

While the oracle inscription of Ti might be a
representation of a burnt offering, Professor Creel's
interpretation of identifying liao with Ti and Ti with
the burnt offering, or fire itself, seems to be
stretching the imagination too far. Because the oracle texts record also that there are many other kinds
of sacrifices and offerings made to Ti and that there
are also many other gods receiving the same sacrifices,
it is too simplistic to argue that only the burnt offering is to be identified with Ti and conclude that
Ti is the God of Fire. However, we should not cancel
out entirely the possibility and feasibility that the
solemn scene of burnt offering may inspire a great
sense of awe in the presence of a supreme God like Ti.
For the oracle texts report spectacular practices of
burnt offerings conducted by the Shang royal house in
which, at one occasion, three hundred cattle were offered as sacrificial victims. Moreover, it is important to note that grammatically when Ti is used as a
verb, it does mean "to offer sacrifice" (示帝), so we
cannot entirely ignore the fact that a close relationship existed between the sacrifice and Ti. As

Confucius said, "When you offer sacrifice to God, you think as if God exists."7

帝 as the Symbol of a Spirit Tablet

Professor Akatsuka Kiyoshi has recently proposed a different interpretation of Ti based on a different analysis of the etymology of the inscript 帝 . He postulates that Ti consists of two basic radicals: the one is shu (示) which is a pictograph of a wooden tablet used as a cultic object for worship and a sign 八 indicating the descendance and possessing of a divine spirit upon the wooden tablet; and the other is wu (巫) which is the oracle form for the word 𝕏 which means shamans. By combining these two radicals, Akatsuka suggests that 帝 is the depiction of a cult of shamanistic divination in which several shamans gather together, surrounding a spirit tablet invoking the descent of the spirit. The crisscrossed sign 米 would then indicate the descent and possession of the spirit. Akatsuka cited many oracle texts and Chou texts to support his interpretation. He also pointed out that in the successive stages of ancient literary development, both the radical shu (示) and the radical wu (巫) have since become fixed to designate the presence of divine spirit and the practice of shamanism, respectively. Therefore, the oracle inscript Ti 帝 should be understood as a symbol of a spirit tablet and a sign of divine presence and spiritual possession.8

Akatsuka's interpretation is quite straightforward and convincing, because it is true that the morphology of Ti has definitely contained the basic emblem of the shu and that the shu has become a fixed radical to indicate anything divine and sacred. From the standpoint of phenomenology of religion, there is no better explanation than this, that the name of a supreme God is derived from the emblem of the sacred itself. However, we should accept his interpretation with reticency, since we do not have a convincing archaeological proof of the existence of wooden tablets being used in shamanistic cults of the Shang period.

The more logical interpretation is the first because of its structural analysis and convincing etymological interpretation. The symbolism of the flower which combines the elements of seed, peduncle, calyx, and pistil would make more sense and appeal to the agricultural people of Shang for their understanding of the supreme God to be the origin of life, the potency

of fertility, the power of eternal regeneration, and
the majestic glory of the universe. From the standpoint of the phenomenology of religion, one can sense
immediately the richness of flower symbolism, for it
involves simultaneously the hiddenness of the seed,
crossfertilization between the male and female forces,
and the gorgeous manifestation of totality. It is a
religious symbolism par excellence. We must be impressed by the ingenuity of Shang people in selecting
the flower to be the most sacred symbol and inscript
for their supreme God.

The Authority and Power of Ti

The oracle text described Ti as the supreme authority and power over all natural forces and human
affairs, and almost all the paleographers have acknowledged that this Ti has unquestionable sovereignty.
Kuo Mo-jo asserted:

> By the time of Yin [i.e., Shang]the idea
> of a supreme God was already in existence.
> In the beginning He was called Ti, and
> later on Shang Ti. During the transi-
> tional period from Shang to Chou, He was
> then called T'ien. From the oracle text,
> we can know that the Yin people believed
> in a supreme God to be a personality god
> who could issue orders and had the sense
> of good and evil. All the matters of
> weather and climate such as the wind and
> rain, calamities and disasters, and all
> the human affairs such as the good for-
> tune and bad fortune, happiness and sor-
> row, harvest and famine, victory and de-
> feat in wars, building and destruction
> of cities, promotion and degradation of
> officials, are under the control of
> T'ien. This is perfectly similar to
> the God of ancient Israel.[9]

Shima Kunio (島邦男), Ch'en Men-chia (陳夢家) and
Hu Hou-hsüan (胡厚宣) have made an exhaustive analysis
of the function of Ti in the oracle text.[10] Inasmuch
as Hu's presentation in his article is extremely comprehensive and succint, this section will only introduce his analysis without elaboration. In his article
"The Shang Ti and Wang Ti in the Yin Oracle Inscriptions," he described the power of Ti under the following subjects: (1) Ti's control over the wind, clouds,

thunder, and rain; (2) Ti endowed the annual harvest,
as well as brought the droughts and disasters; (3) Ti
sanctified the building of the cities of Shang, as well
as punished by ruining the cities; (4) Ti sanctified or
prohibited military campaigns; (5) Ti endowed mankind
with happiness, as well as calamities; (6) Ti could
protect, as well as harm, the Yin kings; and (7) Ti
could give orders and issue edicts.[11]

<u>Ti's Control Over the Wind, Clouds,</u>
<u>Thunder, and Rain</u>

Hu articulated: "From the rich sources of the
oracle inscriptions, we can see that the belief in a
unified sovereign diety who controls the natural forces
and human destinies existed during the reign of Wu Ting
(武丁 1339-1281 B.C.) of the Shang dynasty. The Shang
people believed in a God who has personality and will
and called him Ti or Shang Ti."[12] Then he quoted four
oracle inscriptions to prove that Ti had control over
the wind as he ordered it. Other inscriptions also
mentioned that the wind was regarded as the agent of
Ti or his messenger (帝使). Likewise, clouds were
under the command of Ti and also regarded as the ministers at the right hand and left hand of Ti. The
Shang people apparently believed that the clouds in
heaven were but the manifestation of the presence of
Ti.

Hu also quoted eight oracle inscriptions to prove
that Ti had ordered thunder to occur in the first,
second, third, and thirteenth months. These were the
months of spring when the thunder used to strike and
cause the first spring rain. The Shang people looked
forward to the first spring rain and the sound of
thunder as the sign of emergence of new life and the
beginning of a new farming season. The Shang kings
made many inquiries about thunder because they had a
duty to announce the beginning of the farming season.

The largest number of oracle inscriptions occur
concerning rainfall. There are even many concurrent
and repetitious inquiries about the rain, apparently
reflecting a case of crisis because of frequent
droughts and a great sense of urgency and desperation
on the part of diviners. Of course, there are many
happy occasions in which they are recorded to say that
Ti had sent down the rains. Here is a good example.
In one of the completely unbroken tortoise shells divined by King Wu Ting (武丁), there are four groups of

inscription (see Figure 1). On the left-hand side of
the shell is inscribed, "Is Ti going to order the rain
within the fourth month?" Then on the right-hand side,
another inquiry is inscribed, "Is not Ti going to send
down the rain within the fourth month?" At the center
of the shell, then, is inscribed, "The King has discerned the oracle, it will rain on the day of Ting
(4th) and it is not necessary to wait until the day of
Hsin (8th)." At the tail of the shell, it confirmed
the oracle by inscribing, "After ten days, on the day
of Ting, it rains." This oracle inscription is a good
example of how the divination was conducted and how the
inquiries were made and how the oracle was confirmed in
the end. There is no question about the Shang people's
belief in Ti's command of rainfall. But the oracle
record also tries to demonstrate how effective the
king's divination and oracle is and his unique relationship with Ti. However, it is not necessarily true
that he was always lucky, as this oracle would show,
and there are many other inscriptions recording that
Ti did not send down the rains, which caused disasters.

Ti Endowed the Annual Harvest, as Well as Brought the Droughts

The predominant and even obsessive concern about
rainfall in oracle divination truly reflected the climatic situation and agricultural life of Shang farmers
in Northeastern China. The irregularity of rain would
certainly cause grave disasters. While no rain or
scarce rainfall in the spring would mean drought and
famine, the sudden torrential rains would cause great
flood and calamities. Therefore, the annual harvest
of Shang farmers relied on the regularity of rainfall
and on Ti whom they believed sent down the rain. So
there are many oracle records inquiring about whether
or not Ti would endow the annual harvest, which was
called Sou Nien (受年). Hu has cited several oracle
inscriptions to prove that the Shang kings took seriously the divination about sufficient rain and the annual harvest.

On the other hand, if Ti did not bless the land
with rain and harvest, it would mean the onset of
droughts and famines, which the oracle inscriptions described as Chiang Han (降堇), meaning "the descendance
of disasters." For example, in a half-size tortoise
shell divined by King Wu Ting (see Figure 2), there is
an oracle inquiry on the right side, "Is Ti going to
send down disaster within the first month?" On the

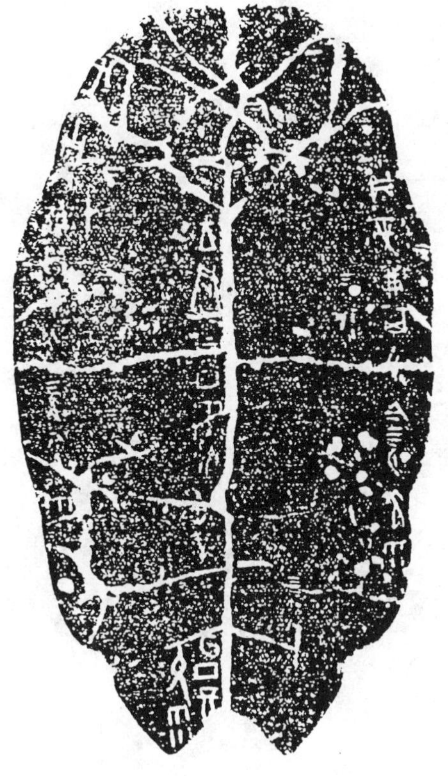

FIGURE 1
(actual length is 15 cm.)

The original text is recorded
in 乙 3090.

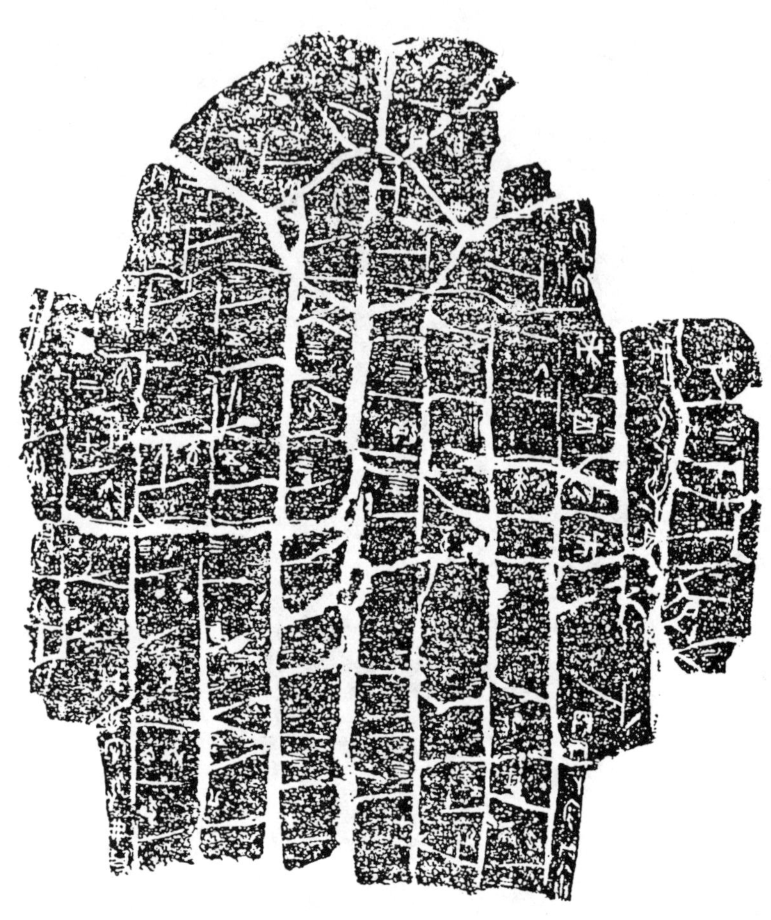

FIGURE 2
(actual length is 23 cm.)

The original texts are recorded in
乙7629, 乙7677, 乙7793, 乙7872, 7917合.

60

left side of the shell, there is another inquiry, "Is
not Ti going to send down disaster within the first
month?" We do not have the answer to these inquiries
because the lower part of the shell is missing. But
Hu was able to quote twenty-three oracle inscriptions
indicating that Ti brought down the disasters, so that
there was a real sense of urgency expressed in the
Shang king's confrontation with the emerging causalities. From the above inscriptions, we can know that
the Shang kings and people believed affirmatively in
the benevolance, as well as the malevolance, of Ti and
Ti's total command and control over all the natural
forces and human welfare.

<u>Ti Sancitified the Building of the
Cities of Shang, as Well as Punished
by Runining the Cities</u>

     Hu has quoted an inscription describing Ti coming
down into a city and another inscription describing Ti
coming into a palace, and interpreted both of these
occurrences as ominous signs by the Shang people. We
do not know exactly why the visitation of Ti would
cause such alarm, but, possibly, some previous disasters occurred which made them more alert. But there
are undoubtedly many oracle inscriptions recording the
causalities and disasters which fell upon the cities.
The words in oracle inscription for the description of
causalities are various:疾，冬，龙，不，祸，and again
we are at a loss for exact information about the de-
tails of these causalities. However, we do know that
the Shang kings were very concerned with regard to the
safety of cities. Also, there is no question about the
strong belief of Shang people that the disasters that
fell upon their cities and their final ruin was caused
by the power of Ti.

     It is interesting to note that there are two ora-
cle inscriptions inquiring about the safety of T'ang
City (唐邑), which was believed to be the formal
capital of the Hsia dynasty. It was apparently re-
built at the time of the late Shang dynasty, and yet
the Shang king was gravely concerned about its safety.
Of course, for the Shang kings, the dominant concern
would be for the safety of the Shang capital, which is
called Tzu I (蕬邑). As the Shang capital was not
only the residence of the Shang kings and their royal
families but also the headquarters of many surrounding
fiefs (封), a disaster in the capital would have meant
a great destruction, not only to the royal house but

61

also to the whole settlement. Many historical records
attest to the fact that the Shang kings had moved their
capitals many times before 1300 B.C. when the king,
Wu Ting, was able to settle down at T'ien Shang I
(天商邑). Archaeologists remind us that after settl-
ing down at T'ien Shang I, the Shang kings no longer
built other capitals. But from the oracle inscriptions, we can still see that later kings were very
concerned with the safety of the capital.

In keeping with this idea, there are also many
oracle records indicating that before building a city,
divination was practiced to secure approval of Ti for
such construction. For example, in one well-preserved
tortoise shell used for divination by King Wu Ting
(see Figure 3), on the left-hand side, an inquiry was
made: "In the eighth month, on the day of Keng-wu, a
divination was made. The diviner asked, 'if in the
Shang King Wu Ting's building of a city, will Ti approve?'" Then, on the right-hand side, another inquiry was made, "On the day of Keng-wu, a divination
was made. The diviner asked, 'The Shang King Wu Ting
is going to build a city here, is not Ti going to approve?'" Then, in the end at the bottom, one more
inquiry was made, "The Shang King Wu Ting is not
going to build the city, does Ti approve?" There are
many such inquiries about the construction of the city,
which leads to the view that the great tradition of
Chinese geomancy possibly started early in the Shang
dynasty or even earlier than Shang.

From the above records, it becomes very clear
that the Shang people believed in Ti's great command
and control over the welfare of the Shang cities and
that their construction and destruction were all ascribed to His approval and disapproval. Effects on
the ancient cities of Shang were a result of several
different causes such as the flood, earthquakes,
epidemics, and enemy attacks, but it seems that Shang
kings and people all believed them to be caused by Ti.

Ti and the Military Campaigns

In the oracle text, there are many records describing the close relationship between Ti's decree
and military campaigns. Before the Shang kings
launched their military campaigns to subdue or conquor
their neighboring countries and tribes, they had performed divinations to inquire whether or not the

FIGURE 3
(actual length is 17 cm.)

The original texts are recorded
in 乙1947, 乙6750合.

military campaigns would meet with the approval of Ti.
For example, an inscription recorded, "Now the king is
going to attack the Fang (方), does Ti endow to me his
protection?" (續 3, 3, 1). Another oracle inquired,
"To conquor the Kung-fang, would Ti bestow on me his
protection?" (龜 1, 11, 13). There are many similar
records indicating that during the reign of King Wu
Ting, several military campaigns were dispatched to the
neighboring countries such as Fang, Ma-fang, Pa-fang,
etc., which were located in the northwest of the Shangs.
Some oracle texts recorded the divinations made by a
reconnaissance patrol (启), which was apparently dispatched by the king to check the enemy. Because of
their constant exposure to the danger of the enemy's
ambush and many unpredicable dangers, they made devina-
tion for their guidance. But most important of all is
that the oracle for military campaign was also described as the decree of Ti which was inscribed as
"prescribing an edict" (尚 册   ch'eng-ts'e). For
example, there is an oracle text stating, "A divination is made to ask whether or not Ti would issue a
decree to the king to lead the campaign." (乙 1710).
It seems that by the time of King Wu Ting, a king had
to obtain a divine decree from Ti before he could summon his army and launch his military campaign. This
fact of obtaining a divine decree from Ti is important
because it implies that the war would be understood as
a holy war and the king as the agent of Ti, who has
total command of warfare. The doctrine of T'ien Ming
(the Heavenly Mandate), fully developed in the early
Chou dynasty, may have originated from this notion of
the issuance of a decree by Ti that already existed in
late Shang dynasty.

However, it was not only for the purpose of dis-
patching the military campaign that the divination
was made; there are many oracle records recording divinations inquiring about military attacks by neighboring enemies as well. A divination inquires as follows: "The diviner asked, 'if Kung-fang made attacks,
would Ti protect. . . .?'" (徵征 23). The concurrent
moving of the Shang capital and rebuilding of the
Shang cities before 1300 B.C. could attest to this
fact that there must have been concurrent warfare between the Shang and its neighboring Proto-tarcic
tribes and countries. But whether it was a military
campaign to subdue the enemy or a military attack and
invasion of the neighboring enemies, they were all regarded by the Shang kings and people as being commanded
by Ti. In the eyes of the Shang, Ti must have been an

Almighty God or the God of War par excellence similar
to the Hindu God of Warriors, Indra, and the Hebraic
Lord of Hosts, Yahweh.

Ti Could Endow Blessings as Well as Bring Disasters to Mankind

As we have seen from the above survey, the Shang
people believed that Ti had command over the annual
harvest, the safety of cities, and military activities,
and there seems to be no doubt that they also believed
in Ti's control over the happiness and sorrow in human
affairs. There are innumerable oracle records inscribed about the fortunes and misfortunes sent down
by Ti. For example, a divination asked, "Would Ti
bring good fortune?" (庫 1286, 后下 14.4) The word used
here to indicate the fortune is jo (若) which literally means "approval." But some paleographers point
out that it was originally related with the word shun
(順) which means "following, obedient, and smooth."
Metaphorically, the word shun derives from the picture
of a river running smoothly within its confining banks
or from the scene of a horse well trained and behaving
according to its master (in this case, it is written,
馬川 as 順). Therefore, jo or shun in this context
would mean that good fortune is endowed according to
the will of Ti. It could imply that the blessing will
be given to the one who follows the will of Ti. This
concept of shun becomes one of the key concepts in the
doctrine of Li (Rites or Propriety) expounded in the
Li Chi (禮記 the Book of Rites).[13]

Although the oracle text does not differentiate
clearly what are the good fortunes and what are the
bad fortunes that Ti sends down to the Shang kings and
people, we can well assume that the annual harvest,
victory in war, prosperity in cities, and health in
family would be regarded as Ti's blessings, and the
droughts, defeat in war, enemy attacks and invasions,
and sickness in the family as the misfortunes. There
are some records asking about sickness and inquiring
about whether or not it would get worse. We know well
that fortune and misfortune are the primary concerns
of individuals both in the East and West, and Chinese
are no exception; they are eager to find their fortunes by consulting the oracles in divination. We see
this preoccupation, and even an obsession, in the Shang
practice of divination, but we also see that this divination practice had developed into the fullfledged
system, during the Chou era, of sixty-four hexagrams in

I Ching (易經), and into unnumerable fortune-telling
devices for generations to come. It seems that the
West is now also taking up with this trend of divination in the vogue of reading Zodiac signs and Tarot
cards.

<u>Ti Could Protect as Well as Harm the King</u>

     A diviner asked, "Would Ti protect the king?"
(鉄 191, 4). Here a divination was made to inquire
specifically about the welfare and destiny of the king.
This could explain that either the king himself had
consulted heavily about his own fortune or his role as
the head of state should be constantly divined to inquire for his safety and success. But either way, they
show that there was a strong belief in Ti's control,
even over the destiny of kingship.

     Let us elaborate further upon the intricate rela-
tionship between a supreme God and the kingship in
Shang time. First, the word used here, "to protect"
(玉), which is the protocharacter of pao (寶), which
means "to treasure or to regard as valuable." In
modern mandarine, to treasure (pao 寶) and to protect
(pao 保) are pronounced similar (a homonym), and a
pun is frequently made to relate the meaning "to treasure" with "to protect." Thus, in fact, what the divination inquired might be interpreted as, "Would Ti
treasure the king so to protect him?" In other words,
whether or not Ti would value the king was inquired.
This inquiry is very important because it would imply
certain notions of theocracy or a theocratic state in
Shang time. We shall discuss this notion after further exploration in the relationship between Ti and the
Shang kings.

     Second, there are several oracles inquiring about
the divine assistance of Ti to the king. For example,
"On the day of 壬寅, a divination is made to ask,
"Would not Ti assist the king?" (庫 720). The word to
assist appears as 犾 which shows two hands held up.
This would imply that the divination was asking the
assistance of Ti by holding up the king. In the modern
character, "to assist" is written 左, 佐 which means
"to take the left side." The left side in Chinese custom is the honorable side where the superior and senior
take the stand.

     Third, there are many oracle texts that not only
record the inquiries about the assistance of Ti but

also about the causalities related to the kings. For
example, "A divination was made to ask whether or not
Ti would cause disaster to the king." (4525). Another example, "A divination was made to ask whether
or not Ti would allow the king's disease to worsen?"
(7913, 7304   ).   Then, there are also many oracles
asking about the fortunes and misfortunes of kings.
For example, "Would Ti bring misfortune to the king?"
(4861).   "King Wu Ting made the divination inquiring
whether or not Ti would bring calamities upon me?
(5432).   "King K'ang Ting made divination inquiring
would Ti order a god to bring harm to me?" (46.5).
These examples show us a vivid picture of not only how
the Shang kings were concerned about their welfare and
fortune, but also how superior Ti was than the Shang
kings.   Ti was believed to control and command the
personal welfare and official destiny of kings.   It
would appear that the kings were more or less the
agents or even the vassals of Ti.   The kings might be
superior to other human beings, but they are almost as
equally under the commands of Ti as everyone else.

     By viewing these three kinds of oracle texts, one
would certainly obtain a clear picture of much superiority and sovereignty.   Ti transcends beyond the level
of patron or a guardian god of Shang tribes and, particularly, the level of tribal god as the progenitor of
Shang royal families.   The kind of timidity and fear
expressed in king's oracle inquiries makes apparent the
question of the traditional interpretation that Ti was
the tribal god of Shang kings.   If Ti were to be the
patron deity or tribal god of Shang kings why, then,
would they approach Ti with such uncertainty and ner-
vousness when, after all, as a patron deity, they
should have unconditional favor and protection from
their ancestral god, but they do not show that kind of
confidence.   Later, there will be a discussion with
regard to the mediatorship between the kings and Ti
through the deceased ancestral kings and the "high ancestral" gods, which would further indicate the notion of transcendence and remoteness of Ti.

Ti Could Give Orders and Command Respect

     Since the Shang people believed that Ti could com-
mand all natural forces and human affairs, they inevitably would come to the conclusion that Ti must be
a personality who had a strong will and was capable of
issuing orders and commanding the respect of his subordinates.   There are four words used in the oracle text

to describe the nature of Ti's command; and through a
survey of these four words, we may arrive at a better
understanding of the attributes of Ti as a personal
god.

First, the word chiang (降) appeared fairly frequently in the oracle text to describe the endowment
of Ti. Chiang literary means "to bring down or to send
down." This implies that Ti is superior and high
above. For example, "Ti comes down to the cities";
"Ti comes into the palace"; "Ti brings down the
droughts"; "Ti endows his approval"; and "Ti sends
down calamities." In this survey, the word chiang has
been translated differently in English according to
its different context, but the one common notion is
unmistakably conspicious, i.e., Ti is far superior and
very commanding.

Second, another word is also used to designate
the orders of Ti, that is ling (令) which means "to
issue an order or to issue an edict." For example,
"Ti issues an order to the wind"; "Ti gives an order
to the thunder"; "Ti orders it to rain"; "Ti gives
orders to cause the calamities." Intentionally, the
diviners emphasized the notion of "ordering" between
Ti and the events to stress the fact that Ti did not
only have authority but also intelligence. Ti does not
cause the things to happen by laboring or manipulating,
but only by issuing his order. He has the total control by ordering, to bring things into existence. This
is very similar to the way Yahweh had created the universe described in the Genesis. Yahweh said, "There
should be light," and there was light. While the Bible
only states that Yahweh said, the Shang oracle text
states more precisely "Ti issues an order."

Sometimes, some oracle texts combined the ling 令
with chiang and described that Ti issues an order to
send down . . . (令降), to add more authority to Ti
and a sense of seriousness. But there is an oracle
text which gives us the most vivid picture of reaction
to the ordering of Ti. The text said, "Ti gives an
order to cause ai (伿)." The word "ai" is similar
to the Chou words 僾 and 愛, which means great wonder or sudden amazement, because the sound "ai" is
pronounced when the people saw some spectacular thing
or heard some enormous voice. The Book of Odes has a
passage using this word "ai" to indicate a shocking
amazement at seeing a gigantic whirlwind (tornado?).
Cheng Chien (鄭箋) commented that "ai" was the sound

produced by people when they were stricken by the
ceaseless hurricane.

There is no doubt that the Shang people must have
had a kind of experience, one which Rudolf Otto has described as the sense of the numinous, terrifying, and
yet fascinating.

Third, the word hu (乎) is also used to indicate
the ordering of Ti, and it means primarily "to call" or
"to provoke." This word is often connected with the
words "fa" (伐) and "ta" (它) which means "to subdue"
and "to strike," respectively. For example, "Ti calls
for subjugation" (乎戈), and "Ti calls for destruction." (乎它) (續存上 485, 1831). These oracle texts
indicate that the Shang people must have had a real
fear of Ti's provocation, for it would bring great punishment and destruction. Ti's calling is described
with such awesomeness and trembling that it would sound
like a death sentence, but one would prefer to understand it more like the lion's roar or the great summon
of a king. But the threat and danger associated with
Ti's calling is unmistakable, and we can relate it more
with what the Old Testament described as the majesty of
the Lord. Like Psalm 50 stated, "The mighty God, even
the Lord, hath spoken, and called the earth from the
rising of the sun into the going down thereof. . . .
Our God shall come, and shall not keep silent; a fire
shall devour before him, and it shall be very tempes-
tuous around about him" (Ps. 50:1, 3).

Fourth, the last word used is kuan (官), which
means "to officiate, to govern, and to command." For
example, "A divination is made to ask whether or not
Ti would officiate?" Another divination is made to ask
whether Ti would not officiate (乙 4832). Kuan is used
more in a political sense to indicate the authority of
the ruler and the power to govern. This word is used
less than the other words, but, nonetheless, it implies
a significant notion that the royal authority derives
its power from the divine sanction of Ti, who is to be
regarded as truly the King of Kings.

From the above survey of the words used for describing the great commands of Ti, we gain a clear idea
that the kings and people of Shang had definitely believed in a supreme God who had a personality, intelligence, dignity, and a great command and respect of
His people. Ti was not regarded as merely a natural

force or a cosmic principle, but He is respected as a
great commander who could issue an order and provoke
great respect.

     So far in this section, we have discussed the au-
thority and power of Ti based on the available oracle
texts, and we are able to find that in the eyes of the
Shang kings and people, Ti was definitely regarded as
the supreme God who had total control over natural
forces and human affairs. He was the one who could
cause the wind, move the clouds, and bring the rain to
effect the agricultural life of the Shang people. He
could also come down to visit the city and palace to
bring both protection and destruction. Moreover, he
was the determiner of human fortunes and misfortunes,
not only of the people in general but, particularly,
of the kings themselves. Most important of all is that
Ti is much greater than the kings, and that He seemed
to exceed beyond the level of tribal god or guardian
god. Lastly, Ti was also regarded as the "personality"
who has intelligence and great command of his authority
and dignity. It is inevitable that Shang people would
think that under such a God, there should be a pantheon
of His servant-deities, which shall be discussed in the
next section.

Ti and His Pantheon

     As we have already noticed, the wind and rain were
called the messenger of Ti (帝使) or the minister of
Ti (帝臣) in our survey about the power and authority
of Ti, so we can assume that there must exist some kind
of pantheon under His authority. As we look through
the oracle texts, we find more evidence to prove that
Ti had quite a large number of gods designated as His
agents and that sacrifices were also offered to them
for mediating between kings and Ti. In the oracle
texts, this kind of Ti's pantheon is called Ti Chung
(帝宗) which literally means the house of gods under
Ti. For example, "Sacrifices are offered to the house
of gods under Ti [Ti Chung]. Would the king thus receive protection?" (續存 2295). The formation of Ti's
pantheon must have developed early in the Shang dynasty
when the Shang royal tribe had begun to subjugate the
neighboring tribes. The Shang attempted to consolidate
them into a kingdom, incorporating these nieghboring
tribal cults into the Shang royal sacrifical system.
Thus, many tribal gods of these neighboring tribes were
either acknowledged by the Shang kings through their
pilgrimage trips to their sacred sites or assimilated

into the pantheon of Ti to be worshipped at the central
shrine of the royal temple. This kind of Ti Chung system was carried on by the Chou dynasty, and the name
was changed to T'ien Chung (天宗), the pantheon of the
Heaven.[14] Although there will be a brief description
of the major gods of Ti's pantheon, the main focus of
the following will be on the relationship between Ti
and these gods, as well as the interrelationships that
existed among these gods.

Since there are innumerable gods recorded in the
oracle texts, the task of classfying them neatly is by
no means easy because some gods are both nature deities
and tribal gods; and some are animal gods, as well as
ancestral gods. Each paleographer has a different way
of classifying these gods. However, for our purpose,
they will simply be divided into two groups: the nature deities and ancestral gods.[15]

The Nature Deities

The nature deities are the natural forces and
phenomena deified to become the objects of worship and
sacrifice. This group includes the sun, moon, cloud,
wind, rain, snow, earth, four directions, mountain,
river, etc. Following is a brief description of their
characteristics.

The Sun

The oracle text has only few inscriptions about
the sacrifies to the sun in the first and fourth periods, but they have elaborate descriptions about the
sun.

First, the sacrifices to the sun are offered in
association with the military campaigns. For example,
"On the day of Hsin I, the diviner Cheng (貞) asked,
"Shall we attack the Chi Fang (基方) with Chariots?"
On the day of Kuei-wei, the diviner Ping (丙) asked,
"Shall we let Tzu (子) attack Chi Fang (基方)?" On
the day of Mou-hsü, the diviner Ping asked, "Shall we
let the Chueh (雀) kill the cattles to offer sacrifice to the Rising Sun and the Setting Sun?" On the
day of Mou-hsü, the diviner Ping asked, "Shall we let
the Chueh kill an ox?" (合 178, I).

We do not have clear records indicating that the
sun was regarded as the "god of warriors" like the
Roman Mithra, but apparently, there was certain connection between the cult of the sun and the military

71

group and campaigns.

Second, as we can see from the oracle texts just quoted, the diviners had differentiated between the rising sun and the setting sun. Perhaps it indicated that sun worship was conducted at dawn and at dusk, the beginning and end of the day. This might imply a certain ritual cycle and the belief in the orderliness of the movement of the sun.

In connection with the notion of orderly movement of the sun, there is an oracle text describing that a human sacrifice was made to the god of earth and three cattle were offered to the sun. Professor Akatsuka thought that this connection might be an indication of a shamanistic cult trying to protect against a sun eclipse, for some Chou texts mentioned that Chou kings and feudal lords had conducted the shamanistic ritual of beating the drums at the earth shrine.[16] Another oracle text also describes a sacrifice being made to the rising and setting sun to ask for rain. Perhaps the Shang people had already a knowledge of the sun signs to read the coming weather, or had a belief that the orderly sun would bring the orderly weather.

Third, the oracle texts also referred to the sun as the Eastern Mother and the Western Mother (東母, 西母). Ch'en Meng-chia viewed the Eastern Mother as the sun and the Western Mother as the moon, but Professor Akatsuka thought that both should be identified with the sun for the notion of the rising sun and setting sun. Later on in the Chou period, much mythology developed with regard to the Eastern Mother and the Western Mother. Especially the Western Royal Mother (西王母) became very popular among the late Chou and Han peoples as the Mother of Immortality. We are not so sure whether or not the Shang people had already had a belief in immortality, but certainly the worship and sacrifice to the Eastern Mother and Western Mother could imply an awareness of an orderly cycle of birth and death and rebirth, which Mircea Eliade calls a "myth of eternal return."[17]

The Moon

There are several oracle texts describing the sacrifices that were offered to the moon, asking for rain. For example, "On the day of -wei, the diviner Cheng (爭) asked, 'Will the weather change tomorrow?' This evening, the sacrifices are offered to the Moon.

72

There is a mist, but it does not rain on the day of
Chia" (丙 59, I). Apparently, a sacrifice was offered
to ask for rain, but it did not come.

Akatsuka also tried to prove that Wang Heng (王
恒) was associated with the moon as the "god of the
moon," for the oracle inscription of Heng 𝄐 has the
picture of a crescent moon and there are some records
indicating Wang Heng was presiding over the moon. Wang
Heng was also regarded as one of the "high ancestors"
(高祖神) of the Shang tribe in the royal sacrificial
system. This is a good example of an original nature
deity transformed to become an ancestral god, or simply
an example of personification of a nature deity. We do
not have much further elaboration on the attributes
and function of the moon in the oracle texts, but there
are many mythological tales developed about the moon
in the late Chou and Han times.[18]

The Cloud

The cloud is called Ti Yün (帝雲)--the cloud that
Ti rides or the clouds of Ti--and many sacrifices were
offered to it. For example, "A burnt offering is offered to Ti Yün" (續2, 4, 11). "Five hogs and five
sheep are offered to the Six clouds" (上22,3; 22, 4).
The cloud was regarded as the manifestation of Ti, and
its various shapes and colors were interpreted as various signs of omens. Wood was burned, animal victims
offered, and the smoke rose to invoke the spirits of
the clouds to cause rains.

The Wind

"Two dogs are offered to the Wind, the Messenger
of Ti (帝使)." (卜通 398) The nature of wind as invisible, and yet powerful, could easily assimilate with
Ti as His agent either to bring down the bliss of rainfall or the calamities of hurricane and sand storms.
Thus, the wind of Ti must have been highly feared by
the Shang people and an elaborate sacrifice had to be
made to it. One text said, "Three sheep, three dogs
and three hogs are offered in order to calm down the
Wind" (續2, 15, 3). According to Er Ya (爾雅), the
sacrifice particularly prepared for calming down the
wind is called Chieh (磔) which literally means "to
crucify." Apparently, the sacrificial victims were
torn apart from the stomach and four legs were nailed
to a wooden rack to be exhibited. There should exist
certain mythological lore able to reveal the aetio-
logical reasoning for such cruel sacrifice, but we

cannot find it in the oracle text.

The Rain

As we have already seen, rain was believed to be
issued by Ti, and the request for normal rainfall was
the most frequent inquiries made in the divinations.
Rain would be inevitably looked upon as the source of
benevolence by the Shang people. Thus, many sacrifices
were offered to the rain to ensure its timeliness and
benevolence. But there are some occasions when sacrifices were made to stop the rainfall at the time of
storms or flood.

The Earth

In the Wu Ting's oracles, the earth was inscribed
as 𝌀 or 𝍁 , which were possibly depicting the earth
mound upon which the sacrifices were laid. Wang Kuo-
wei suggested that originally the characters earth
(Tu 土) and the earth cult (She 示土) were identical.[19]
The earth cult simply means the sacred ground or the
earth which is sanctified, and it has become the center
of the human community so that in modern usage, it also
means a society (She Huei). A society is formed around
the earth cult at its center. Thus, some proper names
were added to the earth to indicate certain specific
localities, e.g., Fu-tu (甫土), Hao-tu (亳土).

With regard to the earth as a nature deity,
Akatsuka found three characteristics: (1) the earth
god did not have strong positive power; (2) the earth
cult tended to be made artificially; (3) the earth cult
was used as the symbol of Shang hegemony, as well as
the sign of direction and boundary. The earth god apparently did not command the rain or the wind like
other gods did, so that the sacrifices were offered to
it mainly for the purpose of its fertility and productivity. The cult of earth could be erected at any
place men would regard as sacred ground and the tendency was for it to be distributed to four corners of
a society or a temple. The cults of earth erected at
the four corners then became the sign of direction, as
well as of boundary; and the ritual and sacrifices associated with the earth cult would become a show of
royal hegemony, as well as the demonstration of kingly
power. The earth cult was often associated with a
large banquet to which all the noble members of royal
families and local representatives were invited to
participate in order to consolidate the tie of kingship.

The Four Directions (四方 Ssu Fang)

Closely related with the earth cult were the gods of four directions. In the cult of earth, the Shang kings would face in all four directions, East, West, South, and North, to offer sacrifices and invoke the spirits to come to join in him to officiate the major sacrifices to Ti. Thus, there were the god of Eastern direction, the god of Western direction, etc.

The sacrifice is called Fang Wang (方望) which means "to gaze in a distant direction." Various animal sacrifices were offered to them and prayers were made to ask for rainfall, to appeal for the wind to be calm, and to ask for protection from enemy attacks. The four directions have such limitless horizons that very often the cult of the "four directions" was connected with the sacrifices to the gods of mountains, winds, and rivers.

According to Ch'en Meng-chia, the names of these four directions are inscribed as Hsi (析) for East, Wu (光) for South, I (彝) for West, and Yuan (元) for North. These names are somewhat correlated to the four names: Hsi (析), Yin (因), I (彝), Ao (隩) of the <u>Yao Tien</u> (堯典) and the four names: Hsi (析), Yin (因), Shih I (石彝), Wan (夗) of <u>Ta Huan-ching</u> (大荒經).[20]

Apparently, the concept of four directions and the square formation of the horizons was well established in the ritual system of Shang. It has definitely influenced the later development of an imperial ideology and orientation. But more important is the four directions plus the earth at the center to form the concept of five directions which has much greater impact on the cosmology and ecology of Chinese people. Ch'en Meng-chia continued to utilize various applications of this idea in the systematization of Chinese cosmology. Perhaps it is sufficient to give just one example here. In the T'ien Wen P'ien of <u>Huai Nan Tzu</u>, the following system was already well established.

Directions	Elements	Emperors
East	Wood	T'ai-hao
South	Fire	Yen Ti
Center	Earth	Huang Ti
West	Metal	Hsiao-hao
North	Water	Chuan-hsü

Gods	Stars	Sacred Animals
of farming	Jupiter	Blue Dragon
of Summer	Mars	Red Bird
of Earth	Saturn	Yellow Dragon
of Autumn	Venus	White Tiger
of Winter	Mercury	Black Leopard

Such understanding of an organismic universe and the interrelationships between nature and mankind which had already emerged in such early times in Chinese history is really a great surprise. The four gods of the four directions subordinated to Shang Ti at the center might not be judged to be a theology system, but clearly indicates the existence of a pantheon under Ti in Shang time.

The Mountain (山)

There are innumerable oracle texts recorded of abundant sacrifices offered to the god of the mountain, or more specifically, the gods of many mountains for rainfall and protection. Perhaps the Shang people saw the clouds hanging on the mountain tops from where the rains would come, and they imputed the mountains with divine power to bring rain. At the same time, the mountains were looked upon as mighty fortresses for defense against the invading enemies, so that the Shang people offered sacrifices to invoke the gods for their protection.

The oracle inscription of the mountain 山 has been interpreted variously as the pictograph of a volcanic mountain, a horned sheep on the tip of a hill, or a human sacrifice on the altar. The first interpretation seems to be more feasible, but it is not certain whether volcanoes existed in Shang time or not. Nevertheless, worship to the mountains was often correlated with worship to the four directions, so that we have the oracle texts mentioning "Ten Mountains" or "Five Mountains" (十山, 五山). We are not sure which mountains these ten or five mountains were, but we definitely know the notion of five mountains had influenced the cult of Feng Ch'an (封禅) in Han time. The Emperor had to make pilgrimages to the five sacred mountains to offer sacrifices on the mountains.[21]

The River (川)

The oracle texts also recorded many sacrifices

which were offered to the gods of rivers at such rivers
as Heng (洹), Wan (灅), Ngou (渴). Among these
names of rivers, we can only be certain that Heng is
the modern Heng River. Various forms of sacrifices
were conducted in the worship of river gods. First,
the Ch'u (取) ritual seems to describe a fire sacrifice of weeds and bushes cleaned up from the river
basin for the ritual site. Second, the burnt offering
(米) were animals such as the cow, dog, sheep, and
hog. Third, at some occasion Shen Pi (沈璧), to
drown a favorite concubine, was conducted. But sometimes, instead of a live sacrifice, sinking of jewels
or pearls (yü 玉) was conducted. Fourth, the sacrifice
of Mai (埋), "burying," was conducted to bury animals
on the banks of a river as offerings.

Akatsuka has found that the gods of mountains, the
gods of rivers, and the god of Wang Hai (王亥) were
three gods often worshipped together as a group cult.
For instance, "On the day of - -, the diviner Ping
asked, "Shall we offer the libation to the Gods of the
Mountain, the God of the River and the Wang Hai to ask
for the harvest?" (前 7, 5, 2). Or, "On the day of
mou-wu (戊午), a divination was made. Shall we hunt
at Shuai (率), and a burnt offering of a hog be made
to the Earth . . . to Wang Hai . . . to the River . . .
to the Mountain . . ." (粹 23). There are many interpretations about Wang Hai. Wang Kuo-wei regarded him
as one of the Shang ancestral gods who was highly venerated with abundant offerings. Ch'en Meng-chia regarded him as originally the god of bird catchers and
animal husbandry based on Chou mythology.[22] Ito
Michiharu also pointed out that Wang Hai had retained
more traces of nature deities than ancestral gods of
Shang in the Chou documents, so that he should be regarded as a personified god of natural force or simply
a wild hog who became incorporated into the cultic system of Shang ancestor worship as a tribal god.[23]

Regardless of the origin of Wang Hai, Akatsukas
illustrated a very interesting oracle text (see Figure
4) which appears to be depicting a certain kind of
pantheon, or a group of gods worshipped in the same
temple. As the figure shows, there are the gods of
the mountain, Wang Hai in the form of a sitting wild
hog, a "tiger" as the guardian god of the temple, the
"high ancestor," K'uei (夔) and the ancestral god
Fu Chia (父甲) of Chui (隹) tribe at the bottom. The
other picture also showed that the mountain god is in
the temple and the guardian god "tiger" is waiting

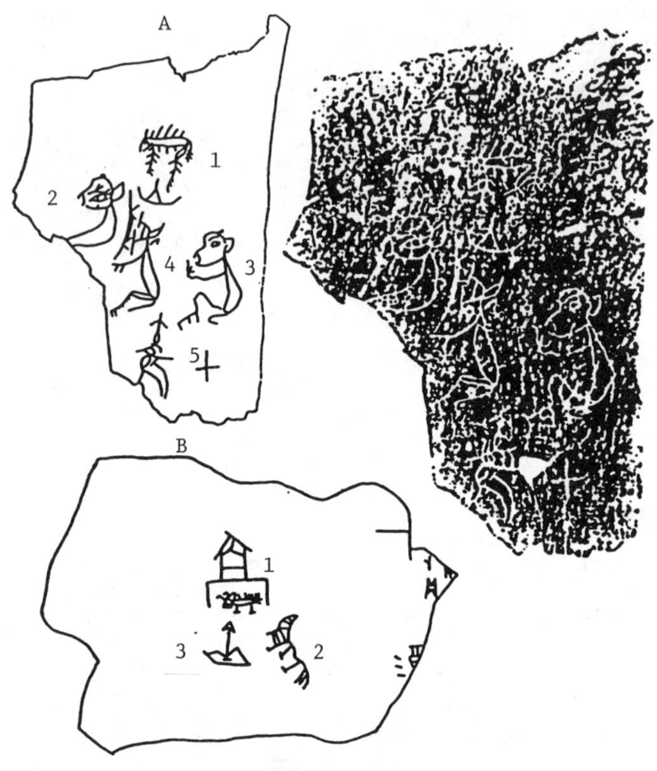

FIGURE 4

A: the plate Chia (甲) 2336
   1. the mountain god (岳)
   2. the "high ancestor" K'uei (夔)
   3. the ancestral god Wang Hai (王亥)
   4. the tiger as a guardian of temple
   5. the ancestral god Fu Chia (父甲) of Chui (雀)

B: the plate Ning (寧) 2.145
   1. the mountain god in the temple
   2. the tiger as a guardian of temple
   3. the mountain indicating the temple is on mountain

78

outside.[24] This could imply that these gods had formed
certain kind of kinship groups in that certain nature
deities became the high ancestral gods of the royal
house and both the nature deities and ancestoral gods
were worshipped together in the royal sanctuary. The
formation of a pantheon further implies that it either
reflected or was formed by the existence of certain
alliances among the royal tribes and neighboring tribes.
The cultic practices at such a pantheon temple would
serve the king in consolidating his power and authority,
as well as integrating the local tribes into a hegemony
of the Shang kingdom. Ito Michiharu made a survey of
the group formation of diviners and their origin and
suggests that these diviners might be the local tribal
chieftains who made alliances with the Shang king and
assembled in the Shang capital to partake in worship
and sacrifice at the Shang royal sanctuary to the pantheon of Ti. They brought with them the tributes to
the king, including the sacrificial animals, tortoise
shells, and local products for participating in the
royal cult. Like the assembly of these gods, there
might have been a certain kind of conference among the
king and the tribal leaders on the matter of agricultural works, mutual defense, and military mobilization,
as these were matters of primary concern in their divination.[25]

     The existence of such a pantheon and Ti's domin-
ion over this pantheon is further attested to by the
explicit oracle records regarding the "five subordinates" (Wu Ch'en 五臣) of Ti. As Ch'en Meng-chia has
pointed out, the Chou texts had many similar indications of the subordinate deities of a supreme God.
For instance, the Tso Chuan (左傳) recorded a mythical
tale about the "five pheasants" as the Wu Kung Cheng
(五工臣) which were the five agents of the supreme
God.[26] It has listed two sets of five gods to be the
subordinate gods of a supreme God: the "five birds"
(Wu Niao 五鳥) and (五鳩). Cheng Hsien (鄭玄) commented on a Chou Li (周禮) passage in Hsiao Chung Po
(小宗白) saying that there was a belief in the five
nature deities of Ti: the sun, moon, wind, rain, and
Ssu Ming (司命). Hu Hou-hsüan interpreted Ti Wu Ch'en
(帝五正) or Ti Wu Kung Ch'en (帝五工臣) to mean the
ministers or assistants of Ti like the Shang ministers
who served the king. He also thought that the five
subordinates of Ti must be the gods of four directions
and the earth god, but he would not deny that the sun,
moon, wind, and rain should be considered as a part of
the pantheon.[27]

The Ancestral Gods as Part of the Pantheon

As we have indicated above, almost all the nature deities were regarded by the Shang people as members of Ti's pantheon. Similarly, the Shang people also believed that all the ancestral gods of Shang royal lineage were an integral part of Ti's pantheon. We have already seen that Wang Hai who was originally a nature deity turned into a High Ancestral God of Shang lineage and was highly venerated by the Shang kings as a significant mediator between them and Ti, so the Shang kings must have worshipped their ancestral gods as the mediator to God. This notion of mediatorship or mediating was described in the oracle texts as Ping Yü (賓于) or Ping Yü ti (賓于帝). Hu Hou-hsüan interpreted Ping Yü to mean "to accompany." In one of the fairly well-preserved tortoise shells of the Wu Ting king's divination (see Figure 5), there were inscribed the following divinations. "Should T'ang-hsien (湯咸) accompany with Ti?" "Should Tah Chia (大甲) accompany with Ti?" "Should not Tah Chia accompany with Ti?" "Should Tsu Yi (祖乙) accompany with Ti?" Should not Tsu Yi accompany with Ti?" These three ancestral gods: T'ang Han, Tah-chia, and Tsu Yi were the most eminent patriachal kings of the Shang dynasty, and King Wu Ting made divinations asking whether they would be allowed to accompany in the cult worship and sacrifice to Ti. In other words, he asked whether or not they would be permitted to join in the pantheon of Ti. Of course, they must have been worshipped together with other nature deities in the sacrifice to Ti, but King Wu Ting wanted to obtain an approval of Ti, because only the approval of Ti would make the mediatorship between the king and Ti possible and established. As we have already noticed, there existed a genuine fear and sense of distance and transcendence in the minds of Shang kings, so that they felt they could only approach Ti through the hierarchy of their deceased ancestral kings (先王). It was not only the deceased patriarchal kings that were accompanying in the cult of Ti, but also the deceased queens who were believed to be able to accompany Ti. Akatsuka believed that these queens were worshipped, not just accompanying their husband kings, but independently with Ti, which suggests that it was due to their distinctive feminine power to procreate and to grow things that they were venerated.[28] He also mentioned that there were many other gods such as the ancestral diviners (巫先) and ancestral dukes and eminent ministers who were often incorporated into the cult of Ti.[29]

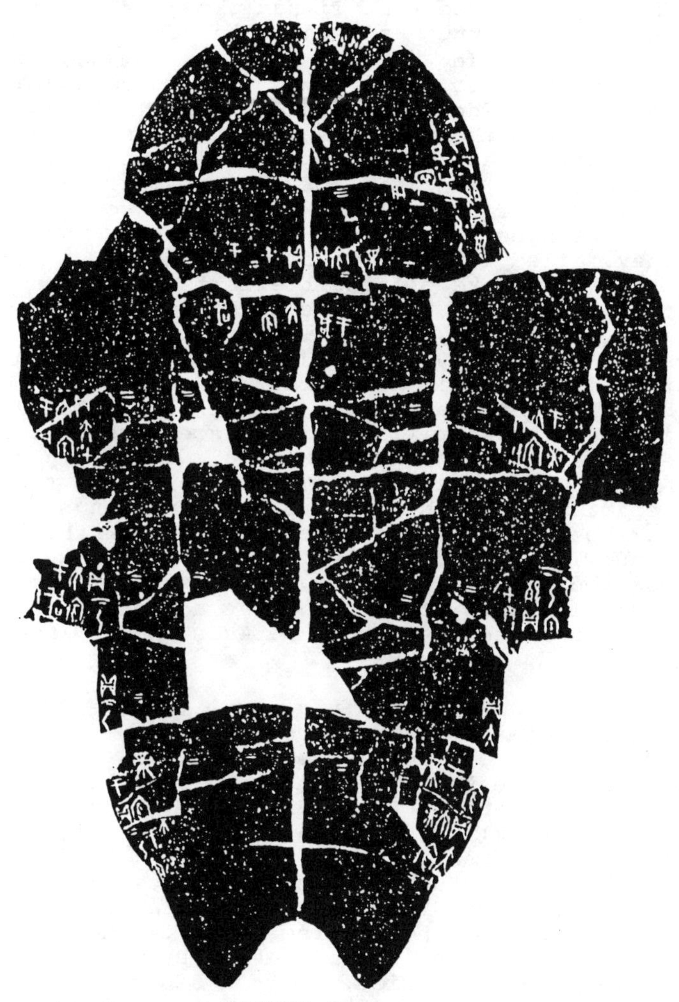

FIGURE 5
(actual length is 28 cm.)

The original texts are recorded in 乙2293, 乙2455, 乙7197, 乙7198, 乙7343, 乙7511, 乙7549, 乙8382.

Thus, we can see that Ti had a fairly large group
of gods in his pantheon and under his dominion, so
much so that a living king to approach him had to rely
on many mediators to reach him. This sense of fear and
remoteness that kings had with Ti should not be strange
to them, because that was exactly what his subjects
felt in order to approach him. As his subjects would
only approach the king's subordinates first in dealing
with political affairs, kings themselves would only
approach the subordinate gods of Ti first, and only
when they failed to answer and meet the kings' request
would the kings make all their efforts to approach Ti
directly. Of course, there is no doubt that the Shang
kings had sole right and a unique relationship with Ti
because Ti would only convey His will through the
mediatorship of royal ancestors. No one except the
king himself could enter into the inner sanctuary to
officiate at the sacrifice to his ancestors, nature
deities, and Ti. His sacred kingship certainly tied up
with his unique priesthood as the sole mediator between spiritual beings and living human beings. We
shall elaborate on the relationship between the living
kings and Ti later; but here, suffice it to say that
the deceased kings and queens, venerated posthumously
as ancestral gods, were regarded as a part of Ti's
pantheon and as the mediators between the living kings
and Ti.

Through a survey of Shang royal lineage recorded
in the oracle texts, many paleographers have immediately been able to identify certain ritual cycles
which were well established and an hierarchical order
organized according to the ordinals of T'ien Kan (天干
the Heavenly Stem). The ritual cycle consisted of five
sacrifices: Chi, Tsai, Hsieh, Yung, and I (祭,壹,會,彡,翌).
According to Shima Kunio, these five sacrifices were
further divided into two, even three groups: the first
three were a group, and the remaining two were either
a group or independent sacrifices. The duration of
total ritual cycles varied, it took 320 days in the
reign of King Tsu Chia, 380 days in the reign of King
Ti Yi, and 410 days during the reign of King Ti Chou
(帝紂). The increase of the length of ritual cycle
might be due to the increase in the number of gods
added to the pantheon. But the ritual order of these
five sacrificial acts was well organized and established
since the time of King Tsu Chia, and it did not change
much, even up to the last king of the Shang dynasty.[30]

The first ritual cycle, Chi (祭), is conducted in
82

the evening, and the wine, animal sacrifice, baked or
roasted meat, burnt oxenbeef, and millet grain were
offered accompanied by invocation music and prayers of
announcement and those seeking protection. The second
ritual cycle, Tsai (賣), is conducted also in the
evening, when raw animal sacrifice and millet grain
were offered accompanied by a prayer seeking for protection. The third ritual cycle, Hsieh (卽), was conducted in the evening and at the time of lamp lighting
and seemed to continue to the dawn, and the wine, or
millet wine, the raw animal sacrifice killed at the
moment, and the poultry sacrifice were offered accompanied by hunting and feather dancing, prayer, and
blessings. The fourth ritual cycle, Yung (彡), was
conducted from the lamp lighting, through the time of
night banquet, to the dawn, with millet wine and raw
animal sacrifice. This ceremony was accompanied by
flute music and drums and the prayers of announcement,
blessings, and seeking for protection from enemy attacks. It seems that this fourth ritual was most
elaborate of all and signified the climax of the whole
ritual cycle. The fifth ritual cycle, I (翌), was
conducted at dawn, and the millet wine and raw animal
sacrifice were offered accompanied by the prayer as a
conclusion to the whole cycle.[31]

The Shang ancestral gods both of late kings and
queens were all classified according to the rank and
order of the celestial stems ordinals: from Chia to
Kuei. With regard to the basic principle and characteristics of applying celestial stems ordinals to give
ceremonial titles (Miao Hao 廟号) to the Shang ancestors. Ho Ping-ti made the following observations.

First, the ceremonial title of a Shang king does
not indicate the date of his birth or death, but designates the specific date in sacrificial cycle on
which he was to be worshipped. Apparently, the Shang
kings did not only offer sacrifices to their direct
ancestors but also to their collateral senior ancestors.

Second, the distribution of the celestial stem
ordinals to be the ceremonial titles of deceased ancestors was not even. For example, among the thirty-
one Shang kings, only one has the chia (甲) ordinal,
and five have the i (乙) ordinal. This uneven distribution seems to indicate certain progressive

elimination of the king's collateral senior ancestors
from the network of sacrifice.

Third, the last six predynastic ancestors had
their ceremonial titles made up orderly following the
celestial system: chia, i, ping, ting, jen, and kuei.
Wang Kuo-wei thereby attested that the practice of
giving ceremonial titles to the ancestral gods was already in existence since the time of King T'ang (唐),
the founder of Shang dynasty.

Fourth, Wang Hai (王亥) was one of those predynastic ancestors who received the ceremonial title. In
contrast to the others who were believed to the deifi-
cation of natural forces, Wang Hai was portrayed as a
real historical personage who first successfully do-
mesticated sheep and cattle. He was also a leader of
predynastic Shang tribe and contributed to the welfare
of the early Shang people. This proves the endowment
of ceremonial titles was well established from the beginning of Shang dynasty.32

Such well systematized application of the ordinals
to the ceremonial names of the Shang ancestors and orderly practice and observance of the five sacrificial
cycles should positively affirm that a well-defined
system of pantheon must have been established at least
since the reign of King Tsu-chia (1258 B.C.?). This
pantheon system also reflected the accomplished soli-
dification of the Shang rule and the centralization of
its authority and power in the newly built capital
which was called T'ien Shang I (天商邑). The hierarchical order in the pantheon is also indicative of
the rank and order of mediators between the living
Shang king and the supreme God Ti.

Shang Ti and the Shang Tribal God

It has been assumed and affirmatively stated also
by some paleographers and Chinese historians that Ti
was originally a tribal god or the progenitorial pa-
triarch of the Shang tribe. Wang Kuo-wei, one of the
pioneering paleographers, first pointed out that the
character in the oracle texts could be the archaic
forms of the legendary Shang tribal god Chün (夋, 俊).
Then, he also quoted some Chou texts to prove that
Chün was both a tribal god and Shang Ti (上帝) of the
Shang tribe.33 His disciple, Wu Chi-Ch'ang (吳基昌) further suggested that the character夋,夒, seemed to

illustrate symbolically the picture of a birdhead man-
bodied demigod which might correlate with the legendary
black-bird believed to impregnate the matriarch of the
Shang tribe to produce the royal descendants of Shang.[34]
Later on, Wang also added that the same character 鳥 ,
鳥 could be identified as Ngao (夋) which was synonymous to K'u (嚳), a variant name of Chün according
to the Chou texts.

     Kuo Mo-jo (郭沫若) also quoted sixteen passages
from <u>Shan Hai Ching</u> to illustrate that Ti Chün (帝俊)
was the father of the sun and moon and some ancient
sages, so he must be Tien Ti (the Heavenly Lord). He
also pointed out that Shun (舜) who appeared in the
T'ien Wen chapter of the <u>Songs of the South</u> (楚辞)
must be identical with Ti Chün. Therefore, Ti Chün,
Ti K'u, and Shun are the same person with different
names or variant pronounciations. He then quoted the
legend of the black-bird in the <u>Book of Odes</u> (<u>Shang
Sung</u> 商頌) and T'ien-wen chapter of <u>Tzu Ch'u</u>, to say
that T'ien had orderd the black-bird to come down to
impregnate Chien Ti to give birth to Chi, the ancestor
of the Shang tribe. He even mentioned that the oracle
texts indicated that the wind was regarded as Ti's
messenger and the character Wind (Feng) was synonymous
with the character pheasant (feng 鳳), therefore
Hsien Niau (玄鳥) could also be regarded as the messenger of Ti. He further explained that the black-
bird should be translated as the "sacred bird," and the
bird and bird's egg were the symbols of fecundity.
Thus, Kuo concluded that Ti of Shang people should be
identical with Ti K'u, the tribal god of the Shangs.[35]

     Yang K'uan (楊寬), who has written about ancient
Chinese history, also agreed basically with Wang and
Kuo's hypothesis that originally Ti was the tribal god
of Shang who had several names related with bird mythology.[36]

     Ho Ping-ti was critical of Wang and Kuo's identi-
fication of Ti with the tribal god of Shang based on
the phonetic similarity between Ngao (夋) and K'u
(嚳), but agreed to their identification of the Shang
tribal god and God on High through authentic Chou
texts.[37] He emphasized that the sole reliance on the
oracle texts was insufficient and that the consulta-
tion with what Bernhard Karlgren called "free Chou
texts" could produce better evidence and support for
further understanding of Shang religion. Like Kuo Mo-
jo, he cited the <u>Book of Odes</u> and the <u>Songs of the</u>

<u>South</u> to prove that Ti and Ti Chün were to be treated as identical. This is what he stated:

> The relevant parts of the Book of Odes, "T'ien Wen," and "Li Sao" enable us to reconstruct the following. The Shang tribe's legendary male ancestor, whom the odes simply call T'ien (Heaven) and Ti (God on High), was K'u or Ti K'u (God K'u). The earliest biological ancestor of the Shang tribe was Chien Ti 簡狄, whose clan name was Sung 宋 or Yu Sung 有娀, Yu being a particle often attached to an ancient clan name. It was K'u who dispatched to Chien Ti a black bird, by which she became pregnant and gave birth to the Shang tribe. K'u was therefore at once the tribal god and God on High of the Shang.[38]

Ho furthermore supplied an illustrated reproduction of a bronze inscription of late Shang described by Yü Hsing-wu in his article, "On Totemism and Origins of Religions, with Special Reference to Hsia and Shang Totems,"showing that a late Shang aristocratic lady who married into Shang royal family, "instead of inscribing her bronze vessel with her formal name, indicated her status with an archaic compound character Hsüan-niao-fu (玄鳥婦Black-Bird-Wife)."[39]

He believed that the black-bird myth must have been very old in its origin, but how Ti K'u was evolved from the Shang tribal god to become God on High is very difficult to trace since the oracle texts were only available for the post-1300 B.C. period. But as he said:

> All we know is that God as a supreme moral ruler was so aweinspiring that the Shang dared to ask for his favor only through the medium of his ancestral spirits. Crop failures, natural calamities, and invasions of the Shang domain by alien tribesmen were all viewed as God's punishment for men's wrongdoings on earth. But close tie between God and the spirits of Shang Kings continued. It was the belief of the Shang people that when their kings died their spirits served in the heavenly court of God. Since deceased kings were also regarded as ti (gods), oracle texts occasionally refer to

them as wang ti (literally "king-gods") so
as to be distinguished from God on High.
The relationship between God on High and
king-gods was therefore just as hierarchical
as that between fathers and sons or between
the ruler and his ministers.[40]

However, Ch'en Meng-chia came to a different conclusion, as he said:

Shang Ti or Ti of the Yin people was believed to be the Lord of natural forces and
had the sun, moon, wind, and rain as His
ministers in His court. Commanding the wind
and rain, and sending down the blessings and
calamities through natural disasters were for
the manifestation of His powers. But the di-
vinationary inquiries about the regularity
of the wind and rain were related to the
basic needs of agricultural life. Therefore,
although Ti was requested to protect the
kings in warfare, He was primarily a god of
agricultural productivity. The predynastic
ancestors and the deceased ancestral kings
could accompany (Ping) Him in the celestial
court, and Ti could send down the blessings
and disasters to the living kings, but there
was no hereditary (blood) relationship which
existed between Shang Ti and human kings.[41]

Identification between Shang Ti or Ti and the Ti
Chu'n or Ti K'u or Shun, the tribal god of Shang kings
and people has been treated with reservation by this
study inasmuch as such identification would make Shang
Ti a patron deity or guardian god of the Shang tribe.
However, research for this study did not clarify that
a very intimate relationship existed between the Shang
kings and Shang Ti verifiable in the oracle texts. In
addition, what the Book of Odes stated was that T'ien
had ordered the black-bird to impregnate the mistress
Chien Ti, but it did not clearly state that T'ien was
the black-bird itself nor the black-bird an incarnation of T'ien. The black-bird was merely a messenger
of T'ien. Therefore, it would seem unjustified to
identify Shang Ti with the "black-bird" Ti K'u. According to the mythology of Ch'u Tz'u, it was not the
black-bird which came to impregnate Chien Ti, but
rather Yu Sung who went to pick up the eggs laid by
the swallows and ate them to become pregnant. According to Yang K'uang's study, Ti Chün's descendants

were variously described as not only birds, but also
as dragons, "black-teeth" monsters, "three-bodied"
monsters, the ten suns, the twelve moons, the millet,
etc.[42] Therefore, it is really too early to conclude
that "black-bird" was the totemic ancestor of the Shang
tribe, thereby jumping to a conclusion that Ti Chün was
the "black-bird" and equal to Ti or Shang Ti.

It has been also argued that since the last period
of the oracle texts, the Shang kings began to assume
the title Ti to boast of their equality with Ti like
Ti I (帝乙), Ti Hsin (帝辛), the last two kings of
the Shang dynasty, so that it was probable that Shang
Ti was, from the very beginning, believed to be the
progenitor or tribal god of the Shang people. But as
Hu Hou-hsüan has pointed out, these titles were added
posthumously to the deceased kings for their newly acquired status as the companions to Shang Ti. At the
same time, in order to differentiate these human "Ti"
from Shang Ti, the character Wang (王 king or kingly)
was added to Ti to differentiate them from Shang Ti.
Moreover, as Hu also found out, from the reign of
King Wu Ting, the character Shang (superior 上) was
added to the supreme God Ti to distinguish Him from
the human kingly "Ti". Kuo Mo-jo has explained why
Shang was added to the Heavenly God, and Wang was
added to the deceased kingly gods, because Shang (上)
and Hsia (下) were the relative terms and since there
was the Shang Ti, there should be the Hsia Ti (下帝),
i.e., the human kings to represent Shang Ti.[43] But, as
Hu Hou-hsüan said, "In the eyes of Shang people, Shang
Ti and Wang Ti were ultimately different. For example,
the Shang people thought that Shang Ti was the one who
solely controlled the volume of rainfall and abundance
of harvest. . . . To pray to Shang Ti for rainfall and
annual harvest, the kings approached to their ancestors first and never directly asked Shang Ti themselves. . . . The Shang people regarded Shang Ti as
supreme and with infinite authority. . . . This is the
most significant difference between Shang Ti and Wang
Ti."[44]

According to Akatsuka, the reason the posthumous
title Ti was added to the deceased ancestral kings was
not to boast of their power and authority, but rather
to honor them as the companions or consorts of Shang
Ti. It was rather a great necessity for kings to justify their royal authority by claiming their unique
and close relationship with Shang Ti, so they had to
add the posthumous titles of Ti or Wang to their

predecessors.[45] While the reader should not be biased
to discard the possibility that Shang Ti might be originally a tribal god of the Shang tribe who had ascended to become the supreme god when the Shang kingdom
was established, there is no clear evidence of such
evolution from a tribal god to a supreme God in our
oracle texts. It would appear to be more feasible to
conclude that from the very beginning of the oracle
text period (1300 B.C.), Shang Ti was already worshipped as the Supreme God of not only Shang kings and
people but also the non-Shang tribes. Professor Ito
has found that frequently the diviner/chieftains of
non-Shang tribes partook in the sacrifice and worship
with the Shangs and acknowledged the supreme command
of Shang Ti.[46] In this sense, Shang Ti had already
been honored as a universal God who could command authority and control over the natural forces, all four
directions, and all mankind. Shang Ti was not described merely as a tribal god or guardian deity of
Shang kings and tribe, instead, He was described as
one who could bless and punish the Shang kings and
tribe fairly, a treatment afforded to all. The only
justification the Shang kings could claim for their
kingship or divine kingship, was based on the mediatorship of their deceased ancestors and on their unique
priesthood in officiating the sacrifices to their ancestors and Shang Ti. However, the Shang kings were
much obliged to legitimatize their special divine kingship by demonstrating the efficacy of their divinations. On each crucial moment in their reigns, such
as natural calamities and invasions of the enemy, they
had to demonstrate to their people and neighboring
tribes their close contacts with Shang Ti and the ac-
curacy of their divinations. Only this could explain
why so much divination was conducted and the emphasis
on keeping perpetual divination records. Ito has suggested that the reddish and black inks which were used
to paint on some of the oracle inscriptions might be
the indication of such emphasis and demonstration of
divine sanction.

     Such common acknowledgment of the universality of
Shang Ti since 1300 B.C. can enhance better understanding and rationale for the development of Chou's doctrine of the Heavenly mandate. It would make more
sense for us to understand why and how the Book of
Odes and the Book of Documents stated it was due to
the loss of the Heavenly Mandate that the Hsia kingdom
was taken over by the Shangs, and for the same reason,
the Shang kingdom was taken over by the Chous. It is

not within the province of this study to suggest that
such belief in a universal and Supreme God already existed in Hsia time, but there is a possibility that
new archaeological discoveries may shed some light on
this since historian scholars are now becoming more
convinced of the reliability of "free" Chou texts and
the authenticated Chou texts.

At least for the Chou conquorers to be able to
condemn the corruption of Shang King Ti Hsin based on
the doctrine of Heavenly Mandate, it would be easier
for us to assume that a common belief in the existence
of a Supreme God Shang Ti and His sovereign control
over the destinies of kings had already existed long
before the rise of Chou, and that the Chou founders
were merely to invoke such doctrine and appeal to the
Shang people, as well as the non-Shang people, to
rally with them in paying homage to Shang Ti. Theolog-
ically, it is unlikely, and certainly very awkward,
for the Chou conquorers to create a new mythology to
link their ancestral lineage with the Shang ancestors
and Shang tribal god Ti K'u or Ti Chün and then to
claim a universal doctrine of Heavenly Mandate which
had never been known by the people before. As more
recent Sinologists and historians have come to acknowledge that the Chous had inherited a great deal from
the Shangs and did not radically depart from the Shang
culture and heritage, we should also assume that certain basic and primitive notions of the Heavenly Mandate must have been propagated during Shang time or
even in the Hsia era.[47]

1. Li, Hsiao-ting, ed., <u>Chia-ku Wen-tsu Chi-shih</u>
(李孝定, 甲骨文字集釋) (Taipei, 1965), vol. 1, 0025-0031.

2. Wu, Ta-cheng, <u>Shuo-wen Ku-chou-pu</u> (1898)
vol. 1 (吳大澂, 說文古籀補   ). Wang, kuo-wei, <u>Kuan-</u>
<u>t'ang Chi-lin</u> (王國維, 觀堂集林) (Chekiang, 1923),
chap. 6.

3. Kuo, Mo-jo, <u>Ch'ing-t'ung Shih-tai</u> (郭沫若, 青
銅時代) (Wen-chih, 1945), pp. 7-13.

4. Li, Hsiao-ting, <u>Chia-ku</u>, 3232. The interpretation of the character as the whole pictograph of a
flower is mine in conjunction with Wang and Kup's interpretations.

5. Yueh, Yü-hsing, <u>Chi-shih</u> (集釋) (Shanghai,
1934), L, 82; H. G. Creel, <u>The Birth of China</u> (New
York: Ungar, 1937); J. M. Menzies' interpretation is
quoted in Creel's book but without footnotes.

6. Creel, <u>The Birth of China</u>, pp. 182-84.

7. <u>Lun-yü</u>, III:12.

8. Akatsuka, Kiyos i, <u>Chugoku Kodai no Shukyo to</u>
<u>Bunka</u> (赤塚忠, 中國古代の宗教と文化) (Tokyo, 1977),
pp. 507-10.

9. Kuo, <u>Ch'ing-t'ung</u>, pp. 7-8.

10. Shima, Kunio, <u>Kokutsu Bokuji no Kenkyu</u>
(島邦男, 甲骨卜辞の研究) (Hirosaki, 1958); Ch'en Meng-
chia, <u>Yin-hsü Pu-tz'u Tsung-shu</u> (陳夢家, 殷虛卜辭綜述)
(Peking, 1956); Hu, Hou-hsüan, "Yin Pu-tz'u chung ti
Shang-ti ho Wang-ti" (The God on High and the God-kings
in Shang Oracle Inscriptions), <u>Li-shih Yen-chiu</u> (1959),
No. 9 & 10 (胡厚宣, 丁史研究, "殷卜辭中的上帝和王帝").

11. Hu, <u>Li-shih Yen-chiu</u>, No. 9.

12. Ibid., pp. 24-25.

13. Kurihara, Keisuke, <u>Reiki Shukyo Shiso no</u>
<u>Kenkyu</u> (粟原圭介, 禮記宗教思想の研究) (Tokyo, 1969).

14. Hu, <u>Li-shih Yen-chiu</u>, No. 9, pp. 47-50; Ch'en,
<u>Yin-hsü</u>, pp. 572-73.

15. <u>Chou-li</u> (Ta-chung-po) divided the gods into
three groups: (a) the celestial gods: Majestic Heaven,
Shang Ti, the sun, moon, stars, Ssu-chung, Ssu-ming,
the wind, the rain, etc.,(b) the earthly gods: She,
Ling, Wu-chi, Wu-yueh, the mountains, rivers, forest,
lake, four directions, Pai-wu, etc., (c) the spiritual
beings: Kuei, human spirits, Ta-kuei, Hsien-wang, etc.

16. Akatsuka, <u>Chugoku Kodai</u>, pp. 443-446.

17. Mircea Eliade, <u>Cosmos and History, the Myth
of Eternal Return</u>, tr. Willard Trask (New York: Harper
& Row, 1959).

18. Akatsuka, <u>Chugoku Kodai</u>, pp. 458-465.

19. Wang Kuo-wei, "Yin-li Cheng-wen" in <u>Hai-ning
wang Ching-an hsien-sheng i shu</u> (王國維, "殷礼徴文", 海寧王
清安先生遺書   ) (1936), vol. 24.

20. Ch'en, <u>Yin-hsü</u>, pp. 582-594.

21. Akatsuka, <u>Chugoku Kodai</u>, pp. 75-173.

22. Ibid., pp. 27-72.

23. Ito Michiharu, <u>Chugoku Kodai Ocho no Kei-sei</u>
(伊藤道治 ,中國古代王朝の形勢)(Tokyo, 1975), chaps. 1
and 2.

24. The Figure 4 is from Akatsuka, <u>Chugoku Kodai</u>,
pp. 30-31.

25. Ito, <u>Chugoku Kodai</u>, chaps. 2 and 3.

26. Ch'en, <u>Yin-hsü</u>, pp. 572-

27. Hu, <u>Li-shih Yen-chiu</u>, pp. 47-50.

28. Akatsuka, <u>Chugoku Kodai</u>, p. 590.

29. Ibid., pp. 305-414.

30. Shima, <u>Kokutsu</u>, pp. 40-49.

31. Ibid., pp. 140-84.

32. Ho, Ping-ti, <u>The Cradle of the East</u> (Chicago:
University of Chicago Press, 1975), pp. 242-44.

33. Wang, <u>Kuan-t'ang Chi-lin</u>, chap. 9, pp. 2a-3b.

34. Wu, Ch'i-ch'ang, "Pu-tz'u so-chien Yin-hsien-king hsien-wang sanhsü k'ao." (Third Continual Study of Shang Kings and Their Predynastic Ancestors), <u>Yen-ching hsüeh-pao</u>, XIV (December 1933), pp. 1-58.

35. Kuo, <u>Ch'ing-t'ung</u>, pp. 7-13.

36. Yang K'uan, "Chung-kuo Shang-ku-shih Tao-lun" (An Introduction to the Ancient History of China) in <u>Ku-shih Pien</u>, VII, Book I, pp. 65-421.

37. Hu, <u>Li-shih</u>, vol. 2, pp. 314-315.

38. Ho, Ping-ti, <u>The Cradle of the East</u>, p. 318.

39. Ibid., p. 318.

40. Ibid., pp. 320-321.

41. Ch'en, <u>Yin-hsü</u>, p. 580.

42. Yang Kuan, <u>Ku-shih Pien</u>, p. 245.

43. Kuo Mo-jo, <u>Ch'ing-t'ung</u>, p. 6.

44. Hu, <u>Li-shih</u>, pp. 92-93.

45. Akatsuka, <u>Chugoku Kodai</u>, chap. 2.

46. Ito, <u>Chugoku Kodai</u>, chap. 2.

47. See Kwang-chih Chang, <u>Shang Civilization</u> (New Haven: Yale University Press, 1980), chap. 7.

Suggested Readings

David N. Keightley, "The Religious Commitment: Shang Theology and the Genesis of Chinese Political Culture," <u>History of Religions</u> 17 (1978):211-225.

D. Howard Smith, <u>Chinese Religions</u> (New York: Holt, Rinehart and Winston, 1968), Chap. 1.

CHAPTER 4

THE BELIEF IN HEAVEN AND HEAVENLY MANDATE

It is interesting to note that many religions developed in widely different cultures and societies and, yet, they all address their supreme God as "Heaven" or "Heavenly God." Just as Jesus taught his disciples to pray, "Our Father Who art in Heaven, . . ." ancient Babylonians called Anu, the sky Father, the Hindus called Varuna the sky God, Japanese called Amaterasu the "Goddess Who shines forth from Heaven," and the Chinese simply addressed Heaven as T'ien (天). Apparently, the heaven or the blue sky above us, has drawn many religious people in the world to speculate upon the mysterious nature of a supreme divine being with whom they have deep religious experience.

Mircea Eliade has pointed out that the Heaven is a universal hierophany (i.e., the manifestation of the sacred) through which the divine nature of a supreme being has been manifested.[1] For the Heaven has such attributes of being high above, infinite, encompassing, overwhelming, all knowing, pervasive, universal, transcendental, etc., that it is natural for religious people to use it as a symbol to express their understanding of a supreme divine being. Instead of describing God in discursive philosophical concepts, religious people found the symbolism of Heaven easier, simpler, and more integrative to address in their worship. Western philosophers like Aristotle called God the First Cause, and theologians like Paul Tillich suggested calling God the Ground of Being, but these terms are rather awkward for religious people to use in praying to God.

Besides, these philosophical and theological titles of divine being cannot combine all the attributes of divine being into a single title. But religious symbols like Heaven can contain not only many attributes but also integrate many diverse and even conflicting attributes of divine being into one symbolism. This is the great value of natural and yet religious symbolism that many religious people had adopted in their liturgies.

The following will elaborate specifically upon the way ancient Chinese people used T'ien to express their understandings of a supreme divine being, and how their

understandings had changed from time to time according
to different leaders or interpreters and schools of
philosophy and religion.

T'ien in the Shang Oracle Inscriptions

T'ien appeared in the Shang oracle inscriptions in
these forms:天, 吞, 呆, 吞, 天, and there are several different paleographical interpretations of the etymology
of T'ien. Lo Chin-yu interpreted the character 吞 to
signify "The One Above the human being," for the Shang
people used the character ニ to mean "above or superior,"
and 大 to mean "man or men" in general.[2] Wang Kuo-wei
took the character 呆 and compared it with the Chou
bronze inscription 呆 and defined it to mean "the Head
of Mankind."[3] For Shuo Wen (說文), an authoritative
dictionary of ancient China edited by Hsu Shen (許慎),
the original meaning of T'ien was found to be "Top, or
Head." H. G. Creel also followed this interpretation
when he said,

> The original meaning of this word was simply
> "a great man," that is a man of power, pre-
> stige, and importance. As such it applied es-
> pecially to rulers and to kings. From this
> it was applied to the same men after death,
> when, as spirits, they became still greater;
> here then we have it as meaning the "Great
> Spirits," that is the spirits of the former
> kings and great personages of the past, con-
> sidered as a body. By an easy transition it
> was used also to mean "the abode of the Great
> Spirits," that is the heavens, the sky. Here
> then we have the idea of Heaven as a vague
> symbol of the vast power of the great spirits
> and the place where they dwell. Since Chinese
> does not commonly distinguish singular and
> plural, it was easy to think of this vague,
> overruling power as a single person, and thus,
> from the "Great Spirits," we get the idea of
> a single "Great Spirit," Heaven, a vast, some-
> what impersonal overruling deity.[4]

However, Ch'en Pang-fu pointed out that the character T'ien simply meant to be "the Great One" or "the
Greatest One" for Shou Wen defined T'ien as "Top or
Head, that which is nothing superior and the greatest."
In the oracle texts, T'ien was rarely used by itself to
mean a person or a god, but mostly used as an adjective
to mean "great or greatest." For instance, in the case

95

of T'ien I Shang (天邑商), it simply means "the great
City of Shang," for T'ien and Ta (大) are interchangeable.[5] Ch'en Meng-chia also agreed that the oracle texts
of Shang did not have T'ien as a heavenly god. He said
that the idea of T'ien as the supreme God had to wait
until the time of Chou King K'ang (c. 1056 C.B.).[6] So
let us see in the following how T'ien had become the
supreme God of the Chou dynasty and how the associated
ideas of T'ien Tsu (天子, the Son of Heaven) and T'ien
Ming (天命, the Mandate of Heaven) developed in the
Chou dynasty.

<u>T'ien in the Chou Bronze Inscriptions</u>

Ch'en Meng-chia has pointed out that in the earliest period of the Chou dynasty, the Chou royal court
still acknowledged the Shang supreme God Ti and His
decree (Ti Ling 帝令) and worshipped Him as superior,
to be differentiated from Heaven. The kings were still
called Wang (王), to be at the right and left sides of
Ti to serve Him, and not yet being called as T'ien Tzu
(天子, the Son of Heaven). Starting with the bronze inscription of Ta Yü Ting (大盂鼎) ritual vessel casted
in the twenty-third year of King K'ang (1056 B.C.), we
can see the idea clearly developing of T'ien as the
supreme God of the Chou dynasty. Here is the entire
translation of that bronze inscription.

> In the ninth month, King K'ang, at the
> temple of the Chou royal family, issued an
> order to his minister, Yü (盂). Thus said
> the King, "oh Yü, the most illustrious King
> Wen has received the Great Mandate possessed
> by T'ien (Heaven). And King Wu, succeeding
> King Wen, has established the national boun-
> dary, eradicated the enemies, pacified the
> four corners and rectified the conduct of the
> people. While he was conducting the rituals
> and sacrifices, he did not over-indulge in
> wine. Even when he was conducting the winter
> sacrifice of Cheng (烝), he would not dare
> to misbehave himself. Therefore, Heaven de-
> scended upon him and intimately endowed upon
> him to be the ruler of the four corners.
> As I heard, the reason why the mandate of
> Yin (殷, the last capital of the Shang dy-
> nasty) was lost, because the nobles, feuda-
> tories, and senior officers of Shang had over-
> indulged in the drinking of wine. Therefore,
> they had lost the leadership.

96

Oh! You should be reverent in attending
the important ritual of the Dawn. For this,
I have studied carefully (all the six arts)
in my elementary education. As for you, I
command you not to deviate from it. I have
since then followed the statutory and administrative principle established by the most virtuous King Wen. Now, I appoint you to be the
Assistant Minister. You should reverently
adhere to the canon of the Virtue, instruct
it dilligently day and night, and exert all
your effort to revere the Majesty of Heaven."

The King said, "I ordered you, Yü, to succeed to the position of your deceased worthy
grandfather, the Duke of Nan (南公). I appoint you as the Assistant Minister to administer the affairs of foreign tribes. Thus,
you should be attentive in managing the judi-
catory in order to assist me in pacifying all
the four corners. On my behalf, you should
take good care of the people and the land my
ancestral kings have given me.

Hereby, I bestow on you a ritual wine-
vessel, an official hat and robe, a chariot
with horses, and the hunting flag of your
grandfather, the Duke of Nan. In addition, I
appoint four supervisors from the State ranks
to assist you, and 659 slaves, another thirteen officers from my court, and another
1,050 servants as my gifts to you. You should
move swiftly to the palace and take charge."

The King said, "You should pay constant
attention to administrative affairs and never
neglect the royal dictates." Yü, in order to
record the King's great benevolence and to
honor his grandfather, the Duke of Nan, has
thus casted this valuable Ting-cauldron at the
twentieth-third anniversary of the King's
rule." [See picture of the Ta Yü and its
bronze inscription in Figure 6, p. 133][7]

This bronze inscription has been regarded as the
most convincing evidence of the first indication of
the idea of T'ien as the supreme God and T'ien Ming as
the Mandate of Heaven innovated in the Chou dynasty.
In order to understand more clearly how and why such
ideas started, we must trace its historical origin from
the beginning.

Referring to Figure 6, you will note that this

bronze ritual vessel was casted by Yü in the twenty-
third year of the reign of King K'ang to record the
event of being appointed Assistant Minister to take
charge of the affairs of foreign tribes. King K'ang
was the grandson of King Wu, the first formal king of
the Chou dynasty. But when he traced back to the beginning of Chou rule, he wanted to emphasize that it
was his great grandfather King Wen who revolted against
the Shang King Chou Hsin (紂辛) in 1122 B.C., thereby
laying the groundwork for the establishment of the Chou
dynasty. Thus, he wanted to claim that it was King Wen
who had received the Mandate from Heaven and his son
King Wu who had inherited it, and King K'ang himself
who had succeeded to it. But why was it that King Wen
and King Wu themselves did not lay claim to receiving
the Mandate of Heaven instead of waiting until the
time of King K'ang to make such claim. The main reason
was that it was not until the reign of King K'ang that
the Chou dynasty became more stabilized, for there were
many disturbances during the earliest period of Chou
rule. King Wen revolted against Shang King Chou Hsin
and controlled about two thirds of Shang territory,
however, he died before he was able to take over complete rule. His son Wu became king and carried on,
successfully defeating King Chou to establish the Chou
dynasty in 1115 B.C. But, unfortunately, King Wu died
two years later, leaving his infant son Cheng (成王) to
inherit his throne. Because of Cheng's infant age,
King Wu's brother, Duke of Chou, took charge of the re-
gency. During that time, there occurred rebellion of
three brothers of the Duke of Chou--Kuan Shu (管叔),
Tsai Shu (蔡叔), and Huo Shu (霍叔)--who allied with
the son of Shang King Chou Hsin, Lu Fu (录父). The
Duke of Chou had to dispatch a military contingent to
suppress the rebellion, and after his success, he decided to build a new capital in Lo Yang to control the
eastern territory. Thus, it was not very easy for the
new regime of Chou to pacify all the newly won terri-
tories and to solidify its monarchical authority. The
Duke of Chou had to send his trustworthy feudatories
to govern all the fiefs and constantly deal with the
rebellious foreign tribes. As we can see, even by the
time of King K'ang, he had to appoint Yü to assist him
in handling the affairs of foreign tribes. So it was
not until King Cheng was mature enough to take full
charge of kingship and was able to subdue all the rebellions and obstructions that the Chou king could
claim his total command. It was not until the twenty-
third year of King K'ang that the king felt confident
enough to proclaim his succession of the Mandate of

Heaven, and the idea of T'ien as supreme God became extant.

Two years after this bronze vessel was cast, Yü made another bronze vessel now called Hsiao Yü Ting (小盂鼎), in which he recorded the great victories he made through several military campaigns. History tells us that since that time, Chou rule had really established itself and began to enjoy peace. It was in such circumstances that King K'ang announced that T'ien (天) and <u>not</u> Ti (帝) of Shang dynasty would be the supreme God and T'ien Ming (天命, the Mandate of Heaven) the foundation of the Chou dynasty. Of course, when he began to claim such legitimacy of Chou rule based on T'ien Ming, he had to claim that T'ien Ming was given to the founder of the Chou dynasty--King Wen, his great-grandfather. In his claim of the legitimacy of Chou rule, he had to rationalize it by pointing out the immorality and evilness of the former regime, the rule of Shang King Chou Hsin. Thus, we see in the bronze inscription of Ta Yü Ting, that he pointed to the over-indulgence in drinking wine by Shang nobles and officers. Later on, the records of more evil doings of Shang rule were added to the over-indulgence in wine in other bronze inscriptions and written documents such as the <u>Book of History</u> and the <u>Records of the Grand Historian</u> (Shih Chi 史記). Of course, we can say that the winner in warfare can claim and rationalize his victory whichever way he wants, and that rationalization does not really count, but King K'ang's announcement of T'ien as the supreme God and his legitimation with the Mandate of Heaven have left enormous impact on the history of China. Since then, each founder of a new dynasty and each new king have to claim either a new or a succession of T'ine-ming. And as we shall see later, the rebel leaders also have to claim the "Revolution of the Mandate" (Kuo Ming 革命) to rationalize their rebellions. However, more important than using the Mandate of Heaven to make a political legitimation, what King K'ang started and developed further was the moralistic rationalization as the content of the Mandate of Heaven. As the bronze inscription of Ta Yü Ting showed us, what caused the loss of Shang rule was the evil doings of its rulers and officers. In other words, what it implied was that there is this new supreme God called T'ien, who is watchful of the moral behavior and conduct of the ruler, has full authority and power to terminate and rennovate His mandate to govern His people and land. We see here that King K'ang added a new perspective in the

interpretation of history which was not only determined
by political and military forces, but also by moral and
religious forces. King K'ang believed that his regime
can only be solidified by paying due reverence to T'ien
and attentively adhering to His moral commandment. It
is within this condition that the ruler can legitimize
his authority and power to govern.

By extending this idea of the Mandate of Heaven
and its succession as the legitimacy of government, a
new title "The Son of Heaven" (T'ien Tzu) was added to
the reign of King Hsüan (宣王 c. 827 B.C.). The inscription has eight sections; this study will quote
only four:

> (1) The King of Chou addressed Yin (厝 , Duke
> of Mao) saying: "Uncle Yin, because of our
> eminent Kings, Wen and Wu, who ruled with
> humanity and virtue, Majestic Heaven was
> greatly satisfied with them and endowed them
> with the rule of Chou. By receiving such
> mandate, they have conquored and pacified
> those who refused to pay tribute and there was
> no one who did not receive the benevolence of
> their enlightened rules. For this Heaven has
> broadened His mandate by appointing the ances-
> tors of senior officers to assist the kings,
> and the great mandate was successful and
> meritorious. Therefore, the Majestic Heaven,
> without any reproach, has protected the rule
> of Chou and strengthened the Mandate of our
> ancestral Kings. . . .
> (2) Now Mighty Heaven has sent down disasters
> and turmoil, and the affairs of the State are
> insecure, and I, a little child who succeeded
> in State am apprehensive of its gravity. The
> four corners has lost the order and become
> disturbed and disquiet. Oh, I, a little
> child, am fearful that my family will sink
> into turmoil and the spirits of my ancestral
> Kings will be offended."
> (3) The King said, "Uncle Yin, on the ground
> of succeeding the Mandate from our ancestral
> Kings, I command you to take charge of the ad-
> ministration of my State and family, great or
> small, in order to assist my throne. I ex-
> pect you to make good judgment of good and
> evil both in the ranks of high and low and to
> govern with steadfastness. For I am alone on
> the throne and knowledgeable of what has

happened, but lack the means of execution.
You should not be negligent in your duties,
but be dilligent in assisting me to dissolve
all differences of the State in a confidential
manner. May you remind me of the great virtues of our ancestral Kings, and so to be
luminous and effective of the Mandate of August Heaven, and to pacify the four countries
so that I would not cause grief to our ancestral Kings."
(8) Yin, Duke of Mao, in order to record the
benevolence of the Son of Heaven, has commissioned to cast this valuable Ting-cauldron.
May his sons and grandsons treasure it for-
ever.[8]

Apparently, King Hsüan was in a time of turmoil
and in great need of an able and trustworthy prime
minister to assist him to rectify the situation, so he
appointed his uncle Yin to take charge of all the political affairs. In this context, he reaffirmed his
succession of the Mandate of Heaven, but at the same
time, he seemed to want to share that mandate with his
uncle and prime minister by reminding him "to be luminous and effective of the Mandate of Heaven" as well.
However, he is the King, and he alone is responsible
to his succession of the Mandate, so he is to be distinguished from his family as the Son of Heaven. At
its initial stage, the title of the Son of Heaven might
simply indicate the hereditary succession of kingship,
but it later developed into a significant idea of Divine Kingship in ancient China. This shall be discussed more fully in a later chapter (chapter 10);
however, the present focus will continue to elaborate
on the further development of the idea of Heaven and
the Mandate of Heaven as depicted in the Book of Poetry
and Book of History.

T'ien and T'ien Ming in the Books
of Poetry and History

The Book of Poetry (Shih Ching, 詩經) was believed to be edited by Confucius for teaching and training his students for the civil service. It has altogether 305 poems consisting of ballads of the state,
festal songs, temple hymns, and eulogies. The Book of
Poetry has been commonly regarded by ancient and modern
scholars as one of the most trustworthy documents concerning the history of Western Chou (1122-770 B.C.).[9]
The Book of History (Shu Ching 書經) was another

classic edited by Confucius for teaching the subjects
of history, politics, and morality. It covers the
stories of ancient China from the reigns of mythic emperors Yao, Shun, and Yü to the time of the Marquis of
the Ch'in State (c. 628 B.C.).[10] Modern scholars have
generally discounted the stories about the mythic emperors of Yao, Shun, and Yü as historical, and have
only regarded the stories of King P'ang Keng (1401-
1374 B.C.) and after to be reliable sources, for they
can be verified with the parallel sources of the Shang
oracle inscriptions and the Chou bronze inscriptions.
In these historically reliable sources, we can find
innumerable statements about the belief in T'ien and
T'ien Ming; particular attention is given to the following characteristics: (a) T'ien and Ti are identical;
(b) the Attributes of T'ien; (c) the Rise of Scepticism.

(a) <u>T'ien and Ti are identical</u>

There are several passages putting the words T'ien
and Ti in parallel, and they can be regarded as interchangeable. Following are some of the examples.

    The drought is very severe.
    And I cannot make an excuse for myself.
    I am full of terror and in turmoil,
    Like the lightening and roar of thunder.
    Among the black-haired people of Chou remnants,
    There will be no half a man left.
    Majestic Heaven Supreme Lord [皇天上帝]
    Shall not even exempt and spare me.
    [<u>Shih</u>, Ta-ya, III 3]

    Oh/ August Heaven Supreme Lord [Huang T'ien
        Shang Ti 昊天上帝]
    Has changed his decree in favor of his eldest
        son,
    And this great dynasty of Yin,
    Our King has received that mandate.
    Unbounded is the happiness he receives;
    Unbounded is the anxiety he succeeds.
    Oh/ how can he be other than sincere and
        reverent.   [<u>Shu</u>, Chao Hau]

    Great is the Supreme Lord [Shang Ti],
    Beholding the lower world with His majesty.
    He surveyed the four quarters,
    Seeking for someone to open a settlement to
        the people.

102

The two earlier dynasties failed to obtain
  His approval;
So He sought and considered throughout all
  four states,
For one who he might confer the rule.
Hating all the great established states,
He turned His kind regard towards the west,
And there He gave the settlement to King Tse
[宅王].

[King Tse] raised up and removed the dead
  trunks and fallen trees.
He dressed and regulated the bushy clumps and
  tangled rows.
He opened up and cleared the tamrix trees and
  stave trees.
He hewed and thinned the mountain-mulberry
  trees.
Ti had thus removed thither this intelligent
  ruler,
And the barbarians of Chuan had all fled away.
T'ien had set up for itself a counterpart on
  earth;
And the decree he received was secured.
[Shih, Hwang I]

The above passages show that the people of Chou still
venerated Ti as their supreme God while gradually the
new title Majestic Heaven and August Heaven were added
to Him. Hitherto several scholars have postulated
that Ti was an ancestral king deified to become the
supreme God or the guardian god of the Shang dynasty,
and T'ien was likewise the guardian god of the Chou
tribe, and they were not identical. But the Book of
Poetry and Book of History show us not only that Ti
and T'ien are put in parallel and are interchangeable,
but, in fact, they are identical. However, when in
the parallel, Ti always preceeds T'ien. This indicates
that T'ien was put intentionally to be parallel to or
equal to Ti. Why then, did the people of Chou want to
make T'ien equal with Ti? Or how did Ti, the supreme
God of the Shang dynasty gradually change into T'ien
of the Chou dynasty? Perhaps we can say that originally T'ien was added to Ti as an adjective like Majestic Heavenly Supreme Lord" because Ti was believed to
be the Greatest One which was the original meaning of
T'ien, and gradually the adjective T'ien changed into
a noun or even a proper noun to designate T'ien as an
independent deity equal and identical with Ti. It also
can be explained that since Ti was the Greatest One or

the One above human beings, so Ti had assumed the title
of T'ien. Gradually, the people of Chou had realized
that the idea of T'ien,which implied clearer attributes
of vastness, majesty, height, infinity, and universality than that of Ti, and began to address more often
T'ien than Ti for it is more suitable for them to convey their idea of a supreme God. As I have already
shown earlier, it was definitely to the advantage of
the Chou kings to claim the legitimacy of reign upon
the decree of this newly-entitled God T'ien than Ti,
who had associated with the defunct dynasty. In addition, the Chou kings wanted to emphasize that this
supreme God must be a transcendental divinity not concerned with any particular ethnic group and must have
eternal and universal authority in commanding the whole
process of dynastic change. They wanted to claim that
it was T'ien who sent down the mythic gods and cultural heroes to earth to institute society and culture,
and He was the one who gave the Mandate for King Yu to
institute the Hsia dynasty, the King P'ang Keng to institute the Shang dynasty, and now the kings Wen and
Wu to establish the Chou dynasty. At each turn of
change in the Mandate, T'ien was seriously concerned
with the moral quality of the kings and welfare of the
people and land. Thus, they found that T'ien was more
suitable than Ti in indicating their belief. Now let
us see the attributes the <u>Book of Poetry</u> and <u>Book of
History</u> describe regarding T'ien.

<u>The Attributes of T'ien</u>

> T'ien is omnipresent and omniscient

Be reverent/ Be reverent/ T'ien has revealed
its will. Its mandate is not easy to preserve. Do not say that T'ien is far distant
above. It ascends and descends, concerning
itself with our affairs, and daily examines
all our doings. [<u>Shih</u>, 4:3; 3, 1]

Fear the anger of T'ien and do not give way
to dissipation. Fear lest T'ien changes towards you, and do not dare to rush into evil
ways. Majestic T'ien is clear-sighted, and
extends to wheresoever you go. Majestic T'ien
is all seeing as the rising sun, and reaches
you in all your licentious wanderings.
[<u>Shih</u>, 3:2; 10, 8]

104

T'ien created the people and
inspected their deeds

When T'ien gave birth to all the people, to
every constitutive faculty it annexed its law.
It was their natural disposition to love admirable virtue. [<u>Shih</u>, 3:3, 6]

T'ien inspects the people below, keeping account of their righteousness, and regulating
according to their span of life. It is not
T'ien who destroys men. They, by their evil
doing, cut short their own lives. [<u>Shu</u>: Kao
Tsung 3]

T'ien is clear-sighted and cannot be deceived

August T'ien is most clear-sighted.
[<u>Shih</u>, 3:3; 2, 11]

How bright is T'ien above, looking down with
care and concern upon the earth below.
[<u>Shih</u>, 2:6, 3]

T'ien sees and hears everything. The sage-
king takes it as his pattern. His ministers
respectfully follow his example, and the people are well-governed. [<u>Shu</u>, Shuo Ming
Chung 3]

T'ien blesses the virtuous and
punishes the wicked

May T'ien protect and settle you, making you
perfectly secure. That you may be truly virtuous what happiness does it withhold? It
causes you to receive many blessings. They
are indeed numerous. [<u>Shih</u>, 2:1; 6, 1]

How all-embracing is T'ien above, sovereign
over all the people below/ How arrayed in
terror is T'ien above/ It decrees many punishments. [<u>Shih</u>, 3:3, 1]

It is quite clear from the above passages that the people of Chou understood T'ien to be a creator God who
has great power and authority to inspect and govern
His people on earth. Especially noticeable is T'ien's
great concern about the moral conduct of His people,
and such strong moral implication can be seen in

105

relation to the political affairs and dynastic rules.

> The capital of Shang was full of crime. The
> king was not distressed that the kingdom of
> Yin was ruined. Nor did he care that the
> fragrance of virtue should rise up from the
> sacrifices to plead with T'ien. Instead the
> complaints of the people of our drunken orgies
> were felt on high. Therefore T'ien determined
> to destroy Yin. It loved Yin no more, because
> of Yin's excesses. It is not T'ien that is
> cruel. It is people who bring evil on them-
> selves. [Shu, Chiu Kao 11]

> I have heard it said, "Shang Ti leads men to
> tranquility." But the sovereign of Hsia [King
> Chieh] would not seek tranquility, and so Ti
> sent down corrections to show his will to the
> Hsia by timely warnings. He would not be
> warned by Ti. He plunged into great excesses
> and excused his conduct. Then T'ien refused
> to hear him, took away his mandate and in-
> flicted extreme punishment. [Shu, To Shih, 5]

> The T'ien charged your first ancestor, T'ang
> the Victorious, to remove Hsia, and able men
> ruled the land. You yourselves know that your
> Yin forerunners had their annals and archives
> which related how Yin took the mandate from
> Hsia. [Shu, 6, 19]

> Without pity T'ien has brought destruction on
> Yin, since Yin has lost its mandate to rule,
> which we of the house of Chou have received.
> I do not dare to affirm that what we have es-
> tablished will continue for ever in prosper-
> ity. Yet, if T'ien assists those who are
> sincere, I would not dare to affirm that it
> will end in misfortune. [Shu, Chün Shih, 2]

> The mandate of T'ien was not easy to keep.
> It is difficult to trust in T'ien's constancy.
> He who loses the mandate does so because he
> is not able to continue in the illustrious
> virtue which characterized the men of old
> [Shu, 4]

It is definitely a great advance in terms of the idea
of God from viewing Ti as a supreme God who governs
merely the welfares and fortunes of a state to

conceiving T'ien as a supreme God who is concerned
gravely with the moral conduct of rulers and people.
The mandate of T'ien is no longer understood as merely
a special favor given to a tribal chieftain or hereditary king by their tribal guardian God, but contains a
serious moral command on the moral quality of ruler and
moral conduct of his government. In this respect,
T'ien is very similar to the God Yahweh of ancient
prophets of Israel, who they claimed was a God of
Righteousness. For example, the prophet Amos spoke on
behalf of God, "I hate, I despise your feats, and I
take no delight in your solemn assemblies. Even though
you offer me your burnt offerings and cereal offerings,
I will not accept them, and the peace offering of your
fatted beasts I will not look upon. Take away from me
the noise of your songs; to the melody of your harps I
will not listen. But let justice roll down like
waters, and righteousness like an everflowing stream"
(Amos 5:21-24 RSV); one can almost hear the same kind
of message from the passages of poets and historians
of Ancient China. (It might be a coincidence that
they were all the works of the eighth century B.C.)

Rise of Scepticism

However, when such a high moral mandate of T'ien
was tied to the mundane affairs of political struggles,
it was bound to create contradictions, which is what
actually happened, both in the case of ancient Israel
and in ancient China. In much the same way that prophets Jeremiah and Habakkuk raised the issue of why the
righteous had suffered while the wicked became prosperous, the poet and historian of ancient China also
raised the question to T'ien. Towards the end of
Western Chou period, due to the concurrent invasions of
northern barbarians, exhaustion of labor and military
supplies, and rebellions of the feudatories against the
central monarchy, the well-established Chou kingdom had
gradually disintegrated into what the later historians
called the Spring and Autumn (Ch'un-Ch'iu 春秋) period
and into the Warring States period. During this period
of turmoil and transition, the poet and historian inevitably raised their voices of distress and doubt.

> Oh, vast- far-spreading T'ien, whom we call
>   parent/
> I am innocent and blameless, yet I suffer such
>   great disorders.
> Majestic T'ien, you are too stern; for truly
>   I am innocent.

Majestic T'ien, you are too cruel, for truly
   I am blameless. [Shih 2:5, 4]

The proud are rejoicing while the troubled
   are in great distress.
Oh, azure, T'ien/ Oh, azure T'ien/
Look upon those proud men and have pity upon
   the troubled.
Those slanderous men, who was it who devised
   their plans?
I would take those slanderous men and throw
   them to the wolves and tigers. If wolves
   and tigers refuse to devour them, I would
   throw them into the northlands.
If the northlands refused to receive them,
I would throw them into the hands of August
   T'ien. [Shih 2:5, 6]

I gaze up to August T'ien, but it does not
   favour us.
For long these cruel afflictions which it has
   sent down
greatly distressed us. The state is un-
   settled.
Officers and people suffer. [Shih 3:3, 10]

Now the people in their peril look to T'ien,
but find no clear guidance.
But let T'ien once decide, and there is none
   that it cannot overcome.
This August Shang Ti above, can he hate anyone? [Shih 2:4, 8]

The net which T'ien lets down is full of
   calamities.
Good men are perishing, and my heart is
   grieved. [Shih 3:3; 10, 6]

Overshadowing T'ien is angered.
T'ien is indeed sending down destruction,
   distressing us with famine.
The people are all perishing.
Settled lands and border fields are all
   lying waste. [Shih 3:3; 11, 1]

Where is the mandate of Heaven? Why does a good God
allow such evil in the world? Why is T'ien so uncon-
cerned about the suffering of the innocent people? Was
T'ien impotent or becoming blind? Where is the justice,
the law, and the principle of reward and punishment?

With the rise of scepticism during the Ch'un-Ch'iu period, we are beginning to see a diverse development in the belief in T'ien. We shall see the reaffirmation of T'ien and T'ien Ming in Confucius and the restablishment of the Cult of T'ien in Mo Tze, but we also see the de-mythologization of T'ien among the Taoists and Legalists.

<u>Reaffirmation of T'ien Ming in Confucius</u>

Confucius was born in the time of the Warring States when the central Chou monarchy had already lost its power and the kingdom was torn apart by the warring factions of seven divided states. Riots and rebellions, usurpation of thrones and killing of elders, infighting, and warfares were rampant and pervading. As a son of a defamed literati official, Confucius advocated the restoration of law and order established by the Duke of Chou, whom he admired as the lawmaker of the Chou dynasty. Failing to obtain an influential position in his native state of Lu, he turned to teaching and the training of his students for future civil service and wandering the divided states to promote his cause. While he again failed to obtain the support of state feudatories, he was successful in training his students to carry on his mission and to, ultimately, enter government service. However, his dream of establishing a Confucian bureaucracy did not come to realization until the time of the Han dynasty (second century B.C.). But Confucius left many inerradicable legacies for posterity, and one of them was his undying conviction in the Mandate of Heaven. I would like to quote several passages from the <u>Analects of Confucius</u> (Lun Yu 論語), the most trustworthy documents concerning the man and his teachings.[11]

In one of his brief autobiographical sketches, Confucius stated the goals of his life:

> At fifteen I set my mind upon learning.
> At thirty, I sought for personal independence.
> At forty, I suffered no more perplexities.
> At fifty, I knew the Mandate of Heaven.
> At sixty, I heard them with docile ear.
> At seventy, I could follow the dictates of my
>   mind; for I desired no longer to overstep
>   the boundaries of right. [<u>Analects</u> II, 4]

This is a very important passage, for it not only indicates Confucius' personal belief in T'ien and the mandate of T'ien but also his belief in that the Mandate of Heaven was given to him. Prior to Confucius, the Mandate of Heaven had been considered to be the special endowment and privilege given by T'ien to the kings only, but now Confucius claimed that he had personally received that mandate as well. But what kind of mandate did he receive from T'ien? Was it for him to become a new king? Yes, there had been such interpretation among the Confucian scholars, for they believed that Confucius was an "uncrowned king." But Confucius himself did not regard himself a king as such; instead, he understood his own mission as that of transmission and preservation of ancient culture and tradition. This was his mandate of T'ien. The <u>Analects</u> recorded an event in Confucius' life during his wanderings through the divided states. When the Master Kung came to a border town of four states--Cheng, Wei, Sung, and Lu--he was trapped by the people of K'uang. Even though he was mistreated by the people, he said, "When King Wen [the founder of Chou dynasty] perished, did that mean that culture ceased to exist? If T'ien had really intended to let such culture as his disappear, there would not be a mortal like me to carry on its tradition. And if T'ien does not intend to destroy such culture, why should I be fearful of the people of K'uang?" (IX, 5). At such time of crisis, he was courageous because he had a commission from T'ien to perserve and transmit the culture created by the founder of the Chou dynasty. At this point we acquire a new awareness of T'ien, that of being the "guardian" of culture, with the mandate of T'ien as being the transmission of culture; and Confucius, as an educator, took that as his personal mission. This new sense of cultural mission had produced great courage and meaning for Confucius and for those who followed him. On another occasion, when Confucius was threatened by Kung-po Liao, he said, "If it is the will of T'ien that the Way shall prevail, then the Way will prevail. But if it is the will of Heaven that the Way should perish, then it must perish. What can Kung-po Liao do against Heaven's will?" (XIV, 38). Feng Yu-lan commented on these and said, "For Confucius, Heaven was a purposeful Supreme Being; hence Fate or Ming was the purpose of that Supreme Being. As for himself, he believed that he had a holy mission which had been conferred on him by Heaven."[12] However, it does not necessarily mean that by receiving the mandate of T'ien, Confucius had smooth sailing in his life and work. Instead, like many ancient prophets of Israel, he suffered many setbacks and disappointments. In the <u>Analects</u> it says,

"When Yen Yüan [the favorite disciple of Confucius]
died, the Master exclaimed: 'Alas/ Heaven has bereft
me/ Heaven has bereft me/'" (XI, 8). However, his
sense of T'ien Ming never failed him, and he recon-
firmed his faith. "The Master said: 'I make no complaints against Heaven, nor blame men, for though my
studies are lowly my mind soars aloft. And that which
knows me, is it not Heaven?'" (XIV, 37). Confucius
also said, "The Superior Man holds three things in awe.
He holds the Will of Heaven in awe; he holds the great
man in awe; and he holds the precepts of the Sages in
awe" (XIV, 8).

There has been much speculation among scholars
with regard as to whether Confucius was a theist,
agnostic, or atheist humanist, for one can find evidence for all three in his sayings. Instead of placing
him in one or another category, it is more realistic to
say that he fits all of them. Clearly, he believed in
T'ien and in that he received the mandate of T'ien,
but at the same time, he had moments of agnosticism and
scepticism when he had setbacks or was in great dis-
tess, like any human being. Yet, instead of remaining
a religionist or antagonist, he preferred to be an
authentic humanist in advocating the cause of culture
and promoting the course of humanity.

<u>Restoration of the Cult of T'ien by
Mo Tzu (479-381 B.C.)</u>

Mo Tzu, the founder of the Mohist school, appeared after the death of Confucius to organize his
own school, or what might better be described as a
religious organization, which promoted several distinctive doctrines such as universal love, the equal
exaltation of the virtuous, agreement with a superior,
and the sovereignty of Heaven. He was critical of Confucius' teachings of graded love (sometimes differentiated love), fatalism in life, ritualism in office,
and legitimation of warfare. In his argument for his
doctrines, he used the method of utilitarianism to
prove that his teachings are more beneficial to the
majority of people in society. The following will
focus only on what Mo Tzu expounded relative to T'ien
and the Will of Heaven.

In contrast to Confucius, who had occasionally
mentioned T'ien and the Mandate of Heaven, Mo Tzu had
a full chapter in his work teaching about the "will"
of Heaven.[13] Besides, he not only talked about T'ien

and His will as a personal belief or a philosophical
idea but also organized a cultic society practicing the
worship of T'ien. Hitherto, the worship of, and sacrifice to, T'ien were the monopoly of the king, because
he himself was the only legitimate Son of Heaven (T'ien
Tzu) who was qualified to worship Him. But Mo Tzu regarded T'ien as the sovereign God of all humankind,
whose will commanded all people's welfare, so that all
humankind had a duty to worship Him and submit to His
will. He accused Confucius of only offering lip service to T'ien, and not promoting the universal practice of worship of T'ien. The worship of Heaven is
not a privilege of kings, but the duty of all humankind.

Mo Tzu pointed out that like a family has a
father, a state has a feudal lord, and a nation has a
king, the world must have a soverign ruler--who is
T'ien. T'ien is benevolent to all, like a father cares
for all members of his family and a king cares for his
citizens. He asserted:

> Moreover I know T'ien loves dearly all human-
> kind not without reason. For T'ien ordered
> the sun, moon and stars to shine upon them
> and guide them. T'ien also ordained spring,
> autumn, winter and summer to regulate the
> four seasons. T'ien sends down snow, frost,
> rain and dew to grow the five grains, flax
> and mulberry so that the people can use and
> enjoy them. T'ien also established the hills
> and rivers, ravines and valleys, so that He
> can arrange them to administer His rewards
> and punishments. T'ien appointed the dukes
> and lords to give rewards to the virtuous and
> punish the wicked. They can also administer
> the industries of metal and wood, and the
> husbandary of birds and beasts, and the agri-
> culture of five grains, flax and mulberry in
> order to provide food and clothing for the
> people. All these have taken place since
> antiquity to the present. But, unfortunately,
> the people did not know and did not return
> their love to T'ien. Suppose there is a man
> who is deeply concerned for his son and used
> all his energy and time for the benefits of
> his son, and yet his son grows up and returns
> no love to his father. The intelligent and
> virtuous men of the world will all call him
> ungrateful and un-filial. Now, T'ien loves

the whole world universally. Everything is
provided for the good of mankind. The work
of T'ien has extended to even the smallest
things that are enjoyed by mankind. Such
benevolence may indeed be said to be substantial, yet there is no gratitude and service
in return. And humankind do not even know
this to be unkind and infidel. This is the
reason why I say that the intelligent of the
world know only trifles and not things of importance. [<u>Mo-Tzu</u>, chap. XVII]

The universality of T'ien is not only proven by
His benevolence to humankind in providing natural resources and governmental institutions but also by his
sanction of religious and moral institutions. In an-
swering the question: How do we know that T'ien loves
all the people in the world universally, Mo Tzu predicated:

Because T'ien accepts sacrifices from all.
How do we know that T'ien accepts sacrifices
from all? Because from antiquity to the present day there is no distant or isolated country that does not offer sacrifices to T'ien.
They all feed oxen and sheep, dogs and pigs,
with grass and grains, and prepare clean cakes
and wine in order to worship T'ien and the
spirits of mountain and river. So we know
T'ien accepts sacrifices from all. In accepting sacrifices from all, one can say that
T'ien must love them all. Take the case of
Lords Ch'u and Yüeh as example. In accepting
the sacrifices from all within the four borders of the state of Ch'u, Lord Ch'u expressed his care for the people of Ch'u.
Likewise, Lord Yüeh accepts the sacrifices
from his people and cares for his people.
Now T'ien accepts offerings from all the
world, so I know that T'ien loves all the
people in the world. [XVIII]

T'ien is also concerned about the moral conduct of his
people like a king administers justice for his people.
By the fact that the good has been rewarded and the
wicked punished, one can tell that T'ien is righteous
and honorable. For this Mo Tzu quoted past events.

There are those who love the people and benefit the people in obedience to the will of

T'ien and obtain a reward from T'ien. There
are those who hate the people and oppress the
people in opposition against the will of T'ien
and incur punishment from T'ien. Who are
those that love the people and benefit the
people . . .? They are the ancient sage-kings
of the Three Dynasties, Yao, Shun, Yü, Tang,
Wen and Wu. What did they do? They engaged
themselves in universality and not partiality
in love. Loving universally, they did not
attack the small states with their large
states; they did not molest the small houses
with their large houses. The strong did not
plunder the weak, the rich did not oppress
the poor, the clever did not deceive the ignorant, and the honoured did not disdain the
humble. Such regime was agreeable to T'ien
above, to the spirits in the middle sphere,
and to the people below. Being helpful to
these three, it is helpful to all. And this
was Heavenly virtue. Therefore, the most honourable titles were given to them, and they
were called noble, righteous, beloved of mankind and beneficial to the people. They were
obedient to the will of T'ien and rewarded of
T'ien.

Now, who are those who hated the people
and oppressed them . . .? They are the ancient wicked kings of Three Dynasties: Chieh,
Chou, Yü and Li. What did they do? They were
selfish and vicious. Being selfish they attacked the small states with their large
states, they molested the small houses with
their large houses. The strong plundered the
weak, the rich oppressed the poor, the clever
deceived the ignorant, and the honoured dis-
dained the humble. Such regime was not helpful to T'ien above, to the spirits in the
middle sphere, and to the people below. Since
they were not helpful to these three, they
were not helpful to anyone. And they were
called the enemies of T'ien. The most evil
names were thus given to them. They were
called vicious, unrighteous, haters of mankind and oppressors of the people. They were
disobedient to T'ien and punished by T'ien.

Therefore, the will of T'ien is like the
compasses to the wheel-wright and the square
to the carpenter. . . . Similarly, with the
will of T'ien, Mo Tzu can measure the

jurisdiction and government of the feudal
lords in the empire on the one hand, the doctrines and teaching of the multitudes in the
empire on the other.

In the end, Mo Tzu said, "If the rulers
and the intellectuals really desire to follow
the way of virtuous kings in benefitting the
people, they have only to obey the will of
T'ien, Who is the origin of nobility and
righteousness. Obedience to the will of T'ien
is the standard of righteousness." [XXVII]

To Mo Tzu, T'ien is the origin of righteousness and the
standard of morality and the ultimate judge who endows
reward and punishment. Even though he did not develop
a full theory for the argument of the existence of God,
his teachings definitely contained some elements of
cosmological and moral arguments.

With regard to the belief in the mandate of T'ien,
as we have already observed, Mo Tzu changed it from
T'ien Ming (天命) to T'ien Chih (天志, the Will of
Heaven). Why did he want to make such a change? Because he believed that T'ien is a Personal Being who
is the source of righteousness and universal love, and
it is His will rather than His mandate that inspired
and encouraged the sage-kings to promote the good
cause of government with righteousness and universal
love. In addition, he opposed the traditional and
Confucian interpretations of T'ien Ming as "fate" or
fatalism predetermined by T'ien with no freedom of will
to change it. Mo Tzu wrote three chapters championing
his opposition against such fatalistic interpretations
of T'ien Ming. He used three points of argument to
indicate the error of fatalism: (1) it was not based
on the deeds of the ancient sage-kings; (2) it could
not be verified according to common sense of the majority of people; (3) it could not be applied to
government and produce benefits.

First, he pointed out that the sage-kings of
Three Dynasties and the Founders of Shang and Chou
dynasties did not believe in fatalism. In the codes
of laws, punishment and declarations issued by them,
one cannot find the notion of fatalism. Instead, the
belief in fatalism was issued and instructed by the
wicked kings of Hsia and Shang dynasties to evade
their moral duties and make excuses for their mis-
government. Peace, prosperity, and blessing during
the rule of sage-kings all came from the virtue of

ruler and merits of officers and moral efforts of the
people, and not by predetermined fate. It was only
those wicked kings, insolent officials, and lazy people
who would manufacture fatalism to evade their moral
responsibility and make excuses for their failures.

Second, it is quite clear according to common-
sense that the vicious deed will cause harm, and the
laziness will not produce harvest; only the virtuous
will bring blessings and the hardworking will bear
fruit. Mo Tzu quoted the example of four evil kings
of ancient times as an example:

> The ancient wicked kings of the Three Dynas-
> ties, Chieh, Chow, Yu and Li, were appointed
> as kings and possessed the whole world of
> wealth. Yet they did not control their
> sensuality of ears and eyes, but gave in to
> the reign of their passions. Going out they
> would race, hunt, and trap. Staying indoors
> they indulged themselves in wine and music.
> They did not attend to government duties, but
> did much that was of no avail. And they op-
> pressed the people and violated their rights.
> Thus they lost the domain they had inherited
> from their ancestors. But they would not con-
> fess: "I am insolent and stupid. I did not
> attend to government diligently." Instead,
> they said: "It is but my fate that I lose it."
> [XXXVII]

Third, fatalism cannot be applied to practice in
government and in society. If fatalism is applied to
kingly rule, to government, and to social life, it will
definitely create chaos, destruction, and poverty. If
a king believed that it was simply his fate and he was
predetermined to be king, he would not administer his
rule according to the "will" of T'ien, his kingdom
would definitely suffer in anarchy and dissolution.
Likewise, if the people simply believed in fatalism
and did not put their efforts in improving their lives
and work hard in their jobs, eventually they would
suffer poverty and misery.

However, on the contrary, the worship of T'ien
and inspiring "will" of T'ien and T'ien's good example
of universal love and righteousness will encourage the
rulers and ruled and give certain incentive to do their
best in promoting themselves and bringing blessing.

Now the rulers go to court early and retire late, hearing lawsuits and meeting out justices the whole day, and dare not be negligent. Why do they do so? For they think that diligence will bring about order, and negligence chaos; diligence will produce safety and negligence danger. Therefore they dare not be negligent. The ministers and secretaries exhaust the energy in their limbs and stretch the wisdom of their minds to look after the court and to collect taxes from passes, markets and products from mountain, woods, ponds, and fields to fill the treasury, and dare not be negligent. Why do they do so? For they know that diligence will procure honour and negligence dishonour; diligence will procure glory and negligence disgrace. Therefore, they dare not be negligent. The farmers set out at day break and come back at dusk, diligently sowing seeds and planting trees to produce much soybeans and millet, and dare not be negligent. Why do they do so? For they know that diligence will result in wealth, and negligence in poverty; diligence will produce plenty and negligence famine. Therefore they dare not be negligent. . . .

Therefore, Mo Tzu said: if the intelligent men of the world really want to procure benefits for the world and destroy its calamities they cannot but vigorously refute the doctrine of fatalism. For fatalism was an invention of the wicked kings and the practice of miserable men. It was not a doctrine of nobility. Therefore, those who practice nobility and righteousness must examine it and vigorously refute it. [XXXVII]

In Mo Tzu, we have seen much greater emphasis on the universal worship and sacrifice to T'ien and the moral character of T'ien. T'ien is not merely a principle, but a person whose will is to inspire all humankind to love one another and do justice to all and do their best in promoting the welfare of society and state. T'ien is the paradigm of all virtues and the most honorable in the universe. Mo Tzu said, "I have not yet heard of T'ien invoking the kings for blessing. So I know T'ien is more honourable and wise than the kings. And, this is not all. We also learn of this from the book of ancient kings which instructs us in the vast and ineffable Way of T'ien. It says,

'Brilliant and majestic T'ien on High/ Who enlightens
and watches over the earth below/'" (<u>Mo Tzu</u>, XXVII).

As a conclusion to our survey of the idea of
Heaven and Heavenly Mandate developed in ancient China
from the sources of Shang oracle texts to the works of
Mo Tzu (381 B.C.), we should say that it was diverse
and complex in appearance, but a certain trend is also
discernable. The belief in T'ien as a supreme God
might have gradually developed from the beginning of
the Chou dynasty, but it did not come to its official
fruition until the time of King K'an, the fifth king
of Chou. Although it intended to supercede the previous belief in Ti or Shang Ti of the Shang dynasty,
nevertheless, it carried over many attributes and characteristics of Ti. However, the emphasis on the universality and moral character of T'ien was quite visible. Moreover, the idea of T'ien Ming (Heavenly Mandate) had also become more dominant than T'ien himself, for the purpose of legitimation of Chou's takeover from the rule of Shang and interpretation of the
cause of dynastic change.

Through its re-emphasis of moral character, a
feature of the Heavenly Mandate in the <u>Book of Poetry</u>
and <u>Book of History</u>, we see, finally, its universali-
zation in the beliefs of Confucius. To Confucius,
the mandate of T'ien is no longer the monopoly of
kings, but is shared by any individual who experienced
a sense of sacred vocation in his life. And the belief in Heavenly Mandate provided an individual a life
goal and sense of destiny, inducing the courage to cope
with many difficulties. Even though he was critical of
some of Confucius' teachings, Mo Tzu further advanced
the moral character and universal nature of T'ien, emphasizing the universal worship and sacrifice to T'ien
as the primary condition for peace and prosperity in
human society. Mo Tzu also made an effort to emphasize
the personality of T'ien and the "will" rather than
"fate" of T'ien, so that the rulers and people alike
would not fall into the errors of fatalism. In Mo Tzu,
we can see the idea of T'ien advance to an almost identical level with that of God in the teachings of Jesus.
Both Mo Tzu and Jesus emphasized universal love and
equal justic to all humankind. Both also stressed absolute homage and total dedication to the Heavenly God.
Both have presented the Heavenly God to be a paradigm
of morality for everyone to follow in order to promote
a society of love. However, the idea of forgiveness
and grace is not particularly apparent in Mo Tzu's

teachings; in parallel, the idea of close relationship
between belief in the Heavenly God and worldly politics is not very apparent in Jesus' teachings.

As we have already noticed, there were certain
trends of skepticism in the belief of T'ien and T'ien
Ming developed in the writings of poetry and history.
We shall also see in the following chapter a new trend
of metaphysics and cosmology developing with the idea
of the Way (Tao 道) of Heaven, rather than the mandate
or "will" of T'ien in the philosophy of Lao Tzu, Chuang
Tzu, Tsou Yen, and the Book of Changes. Although in
this new trend of metaphysics and cosmology, T'ien and
T'ien Ming had not occupied a central position, we can
see that the idea of T'ien and T'ien Ming has never
died out throughout the history of China. Instead,
from time to time we see its revival. For instance,
the Taoist religious society organized by Chang Ling
T'ien-shu (d. 157-178 B.C) believed in Yuan Shih T'ien
Tsun (元始天尊, Celestial Honoured Being of the Original
Beginning). When Buddhism was introduced into China,
the Hindu God, Indra, was translated as T'ien Ti (天帝
Heavenly Lord), and the Buddha was understood to claim
for himself "In the heavens above and below, I alone
am the honoured one" (天下惟我獨尊). It is more interesting to note that the Roman Catholic Church in
China addressed God as T'ien Chu (天主 the Heavenly
Master) and entitled itself as T'ien Chu Chiao (天主教,
the Teaching or Religion of the Heavenly Master).
Among the common people of China and Taiwan, the highest God is honored as T'ien Kung (天公 Heavenly Grandfather) and the most popular goddess is entitled as
T'ien Hou (天后, the Empress of Heaven). So we can
see that the idea of Heaven is one of the central
themes in Chinese religion, and the symbolism of Heaven
is quite pervasive in Chinese tradition.

FOOTNOTES

1. Mircea Eliade, <u>Patterns in Comparative Religion</u> (New York: Meridian Books, 1958), chap. 2.

2. Lo, Chin-yu, <u>Yin-hsü Shu-ch'i k'ao-shih</u> (殷虛書契考釋), revised (1928), p. 4.

3. Wang, Kuo-wei, <u>Kuang-t'ang Chi-lin</u> (觀堂集林) (Chekiang, 1923), pp. 10-11.

4. H. G. Creel, <u>Birth of China</u> (New York: Ungar, 1937), pp. 342-43.

5. Ch'en, Pang-fu, <u>Yin Chi Shuo-tsun</u> (殷契說存) (1943), p. 2.

6. Ch'en, Meng-chia, <u>Yin-hsü P'u-tz'u Tsung-shu</u> (殷虛卜辭綜述), (1956), p. 581.

7. The dimensions of the ritual vessel are: height-101.9 cm., diameter of mouth-77.8 cm., inside depth-49.4 cm., and weight-153.5 kg. Altogether there are 12 rows of 291 characters in two columns, inscribed in the inside of cauldron. Ta Yü Ting was uncovered from the earth during the reign of Tao Kwang (1821-50 A.D.) in the Mt. Chi of Shansi Province. During the Sino-Japanese War, it was hidden under earth and unearthed after the war, and now it is preserved in the Shanghai Museum of Natural History. See <u>Shanghai Po-wu-kuan Ts'ang Ch'ing-t'ung-ch'i</u>, (1964), 2 vols.

8. The inscription is on the inside of the Mao Kung Ting, the Ting-cauldron of the Duke of Mao (毛公). Its overall dimensions are height-53.8 cm., diameter of mouth-47.9 cm., inside depth-27.8 cm., and weight-34.5 kg. The vessel assumes ox-head and ox-leg shape and possibly is related to the sacrifice of T'ai-lao (太牢) in which an ox is the main sacrificial victim. It also has a single decor of a simple dragon scale design.

9. <u>Shih Ching</u> has been translated in several different English versions; the following two are most popular. James Legge, <u>The She King</u> in <u>The Chinese Classics</u> (Hongkong: Hongkong University Press, 1960), vol. IV; Arthur Waley, <u>The Book of Songs</u> (New York: Grove Press, 1937).

120

10. <u>Shu Ching: Book of History</u> was translated by
James Legge and modernized by Clae Waltham (Chicago:
Gateway, 1971).

11. <u>Lun Yü</u> (論語) has several English translations; the most popular one is Arthur Waley, tr., <u>The
Analects of Confucius</u> (New York: Vintage Press, 1938).

12. Fung Yu-lan, <u>A History of Chinese Philosophy</u>,
(Princeton: Princeton University Press, 1952), vol. I.,
p. 58.

13. The work of Mo Tzu is translated by Yi-pao
Mei, <u>The Ethical and Political Works of Motse</u> (London:
Probsthain, 1929).

Suggested Readings

D. Howard Smith, <u>Chinese Religions</u> (New York: Holt,
Rinehart and Winston, 1968), Chap. 2.

T'ang Chun-I, "The T'ien Ming (Heavenly Ordinance) in
Pre-Ch'in China" in <u>Philosophy East and West</u> 11 (1962):
195-218; 12 (1962):29-49.

CHAPTER 5

THE P'AN-KU MYTH OF CREATION

How did the universe come into being? Is there
any purpose in cosmic movement? What is the position
of man in the universe, and what is the significance of
our being in the universe? These and similar questions
have been raised by many people--ancient, as well as
modern; Eastern, as well as Western--and there have
been many answers attempting to solve these questions.
The Bible said that the universe was created by a Creator God called Yahweh, and He has a total design and
control over the universe. Modern physics proposed
many cosmogonic theories such as the Big Bang, the
Quantum, the Black Hole, etc. Ancient Chinese also developed various theories such as the Tao, the Yin-yang,
and the Five Elements, etc. Among them, the Yin-yang
theory is rather well known to the West. However,
there is a cosmogonic myth called P'an-ku K'ai-t'ien
(the Opening of Heaven by P'an-ku), which is more popular among the Chinese folks but less known to the West
and ignored by Chinese intellectuals as a folktale in-
valid to be a metaphysical theory. However, evolving
from the research of the present study is the feeling
that the P'an-ku contains most of the basic motifs
which developed in later metaphysic of Taoism and Neo-
Confucianism. Even though it is a myth, it should be
recognized that many ancient people believed it to be
true and valuable, and they lived upon that ancient
world view and were able to find their significance of
living in the universe. Charles H. Long described succintly the function of cosmogonic myth as follows:

> The Creation myth expresses in symbolic
> manner what is most essential to human life
> and society by relating it to a primordial
> act of foundation recorded in the myth. In
> the most general sense we could say the
> creation myth is an expression of man's cos-
> mic orientation. This orientation involves
> his apprehension of time and space, his par-
> ticipation in the world of animals and plants,
> his judgment concerning other men and the
> phenomena of the sky, the interrelationship
> of these dimensions, and finally the powers
> which have established and continue to main-
> tain his being in the world.[1]

With this understanding of the value and function

of cosmogonic myth, let us read the myth of P'an-ku
K'ai-t'ien.

The P'an-ky Myth of Creation

In the San-wu Li-chi (Record of Cycles in Three
and Fives) of the third century A.D., there appears the
following myth:

> Before there were heaven and earth [the uni-
> verse] was in Chaos [hun-tun] like a chicken's
> egg. At the time of dawn, when the darkness
> was about to dawn, P'an-ku was engendered
> within it. After 18,000 years, Chaos split
> apart, what was bright and light formed the
> heaven, and what was dark and heavy formed
> the earth. P'an-ku had daily transformed
> nine times within the Chaos. He was more di-
> vine than the heaven and holier than the
> earth. Thereafter, during another 18,000
> years, the heaven daily increased ten feet
> in height, the earth daily increased ten feet
> in thickness, and P'an-ku, between the two,
> also daily increased ten feet in size. This
> is how the heaven and earth came to be separ-
> ated by their present distance of 90,000 li
> [roughly 30,000 miles].

In the Ssu-i Chi (Record of Strange Events) edited
by Jen Fan of the sixth century A.D. is recorded another
creation myth related to P'an-ku.

> Long time ago when P'an-ku died, his head
> became four mountains, his eyes the sun and
> the moon, his blood the rivers, and his hairs
> the plants and trees. In the folklore of
> Ch'in Han time [third century B.C. to third
> century A.D.], it said that P'an-ku's head
> became the eastern mountain, his belly the
> central mountain, his left arm the southern
> mountain, his right arm the northern moun-
> tain, and his legs the western mountains.
> According to the ancient scholars, P'an-ku's
> tears became the rivers, his breath the wind,
> his voice the thunder, and his eyesight the
> lightening. An ancient story also said that
> when P'an-ku was happy, the weather would be
> clear, and when he was angry, the weather
> turned cloudy and dark. . . . In the South
> Sea, there is a country called the P'an-ku

Kuo, and all the people living there have
P'an-ku as their family name. I think it is
natural since P'an-ku is the primordial ancestor of all things, and all living beings
came from P'an-ku.

It is believed that the P'an-ku myth has at least
five major motifs: (1) Primeval Chaos (Hun-tun) as the
origin of the universe, (2) the symbol of the Cosmic
Egg as the structure of the universe, (3) the Birth of
P'an-ku as the Birth of the World, (4) the Death and
Transformation of P'an-ku as the process of creation.

Primeval Chaos

First, the word chaos is composed of two Chinese
characters: Hun (混) which means "chaos, confusion,
conglomeration," and tun (沌) which means "ocean,
abyss, deep." It is very similar to what the Bible
said about the beginning of the universe before God's
creation, "The earth was without form and void, and
darkness was upon the face of the deep . . ." (RSV,
Genesis 1:2). The Hebrew canon used two words, "bohu"
(darkness) and "tohu" (abyss) to describe this primeval
chaos prior to creation.

This notion of primeval chaos appeared in China as
early as the fifth century B.C. Lao Tzu (C 470-490
B.C.) wrote in <u>Tao-te Ching</u> about the origin of the universe:

> There is Something undifferentiated and yet
>   complete in itself.
> It existed before the birth of heaven and
>   earth.
> Soundless and Formless,
> Independent and Unchanging,
> Pervasive and Invincible.
> It can be regarded as the Mother of the Uni-
>   verse.
> I do not know Its name.
> I name It "Tao,"
> Only when I was forced to give It a name.
> I regard It simply "Great";
> For in greatness, It produces.
> In producing, It expands;
> In expanding, It regenerates . . .
> [Chap. 25]

Although Lao Tzu did not name that "Something

undifferentiated" as Hun-tun, what he described of that
"Something" was poetically beautiful and expressive of
the nature of Hun-tun as well.

Lü Pu-wei, a Taoist of the third century B.C.,
followed Lao Tzu by saying: "From the Great Monad proceed the two modes, which again give rise to the Yin
and Yang. The one ascends and the other descends.
First in the state of chaos they separate, but reunite
later. Their reunion and separation change continually,
which refers to the production of the organic world"
(Lu-shih Ch'un-ch'iu, V. 4). Lieh Tzu, another Taoist
of the fifth century B.C. also described Hun-tun more
specifically: "When force, form and substance, though
existing they were still undifferentiated; this state
is called chaos (hun-lun). Chaos designates the conglomeration and inseparability of things" (Lieh Tzu,
I). Huai-nan Tzu, a Taoist philosopher of the second
century B.C. stated more systematically the process of
creation:

> Tao begins in the Great Void, which engenders
> the universe, producing the fluid. In this
> a separation takes place. The purer and
> brighter particles are thinner and finer and
> form heaven. The coarse and more turbid ac-
> cumulate and become earth. The blending of
> the purer and finer parts is easy, the con-
> densation of the heavier and turbid parts
> more troublesome and difficult, therefore
> heaven is created before earth. The combined
> essence of heaven and earth is Yin and Yang,
> the activity of Yin and Yang produces the
> four seasons, and the dispersion of the es-
> sence of the four seasons produces ten thou-
> sand things. From the hot Yang fluid comes
> fire, and the essence of fire becomes the sun.
> From the cold Yin fluid comes water, and the
> essence of water forms the moon. The inter-
> course between the sun and the moon gives the
> stars. Heaven has thus harboured the sun,
> the moon and stars; earth has comprised water,
> the rivers, the soil and dust. [Huai-nan
> Tzu, III, 1]

From the above quotations, we can see that even
though the P'an-ku myth was recorded in the work of
the third century A.D., it's Hun-tun motif could be
traced back to the Taoist tradition of the fifth

century B.C. We can see here that Taoists perceived
that the universe came from Chaos, which was expressed
variously as Hun-tun, Hun-lun, Great Void, Great Monad,
Tao, etc., and its characteristics are formless, emptiness, fluid, undifferentiated, undivided, and nothingness. Perhaps Lao Tzu stated the characteristics of
Chaos most succinctly:

> What, then, is the character of the Tao?
> It is indeed elusive and evasive.
> Evasive and elusive;
> Yet it contains within itself, Image.
> Elusive and evasive;
> Yet it contains within itself, Matter.
> Impenetrable and vague;
> Yet it contains within itself, Essence.
> Essence is very real,
> In it lies unfailing certainty.
> [Chap. 21]

Chuang Tzu, a great Taoist of the fourth century B.C.,
stated most emphatically that Chaos is Nothingness.

> At the Great Beginning (t'ai ch'u 太初) there
>   was nothingness (wu 無).
> It had neither being nor name and was that
>   from which came the One.
> When the One came into existence, there
>   was the One, but still no form. . . .
> [Chuang Tzu, XII]

After reading these passages, perhaps one would
wonder why the P'an-ku myth and Taoist sages emphasized, to such a great extent, the negative notion of
Chaos in origin and did not sufficiently stress the
positive force of God's creation such as Light, Life,
Order, Love, etc. It is quite clear that they did not
conceive of a Creator God who stood beyond the universe
to create the cosmos. Yet, we should not forget that
even Christian doctrine teaches and emphasizes that
God created the universe out of nothing (creatio ex
nihilo). In other words, in all aspects of positive
creation, one cannot negate entirely the negative side
of creation. The idea of creation from nothingness is
also found in Greek philosophy in that while "cosmos"
(the orderly universe) is emphasized, it is always
thought to have been evolved from "chaos" (the non-
orderly universe). Again Lao Tzu stated it most

clearly, "Heaven and Earth and the myriad things are
produced from Being; Being is the product of Non-being"
(chap. 42). What, then, is the significance of preserving the notion of Hun-tun or Chaos?

In order to answer this question completely, we
would need to explain the whole scope of Taoist philosophy, which is beyond the bounds of our specific task
here, but a few basic points are in order. First, the
ultimate origin of all things should be beyond and pre-
cede all things, because if it is a thing (i.e.,
exists), one seeks its origin. Therefore, the ultimate
origin might indeed be no-thingness, which cannot be
defined by categories we use for defining the things
and phenomena in this world. Since it is beyond the
categories of phenomena, it is better to be expressed
by negation (via negativa) rather than by preposition.
With negative expression, Taoists tried to point out,
on the one hand, the limitations of human knowledge,
and on the other hand, the unconditionality, infinite-
ness, and great mystery of the universe. One should
always give credence to the idea that there is "Something" beyond our knowledge, beyond our control, and
beyond our power. This is what Lao Tzu meant when he
said:

> Tao that can be truly Tao when It is not
>   permanently fixed;
> Name that can be truly Name when it is not
>   permanently fixed.
>
> As the origin of heaven and earth, It is
>   nameless;
> As the Mother of all things, It is namable.
>
> Without desires, one can always contemplate
>   Its subtleness;
> Within desires, one can always observe Its
>   manifestations.
>
> In fact, these two are from the same source;
> Yet they are differently named.
>
> They are both called original and mysterious.
> The Mystery of All mysteries,
> Indeed is the Gate to All Wonders.
> [Chap. 1]

Second, the Taoists wanted to preserve the spirit
of flexibility, freedom, simplicity, spontaneity, naturalness, and emptiness, which are the major characteristics of Chaos. Although Hun-tun appeared to be

chaotic and confusing, it is fluid and flexible, and it
can move to any direction and it can become anything it
wants. It is straightforward and simple without hesitation and artificiality. It is spontaneous and natural just like the sun shines forth, the wind blows,
the river flows, the rain falls, and the season changes.
While nature gives all benefits such as light, life,
water, soil, vegetation, food, energy, nature has never
demanded us to pay taxes nor dominated our lives. Lao
Tzu called this the nonaction (wu-wei 無為) of Tao, and
he persuaded the government of his time to follow the
virtue of naturalness and avoid artificiality and dictatorship. Chuang Tzu has a very interesting story to
tell about how artificiality had killed Hun-tun.

> The ruler of the South Sea was called Shu
> [Change], the ruler of the North Sea was
> called Hu [Uncertainty], and the ruler of the
> Central region was called Hun-tun [Chaos].
> Shu and Hu from time to time came together
> for a meeting in the region of Hun-tun, and
> Hun-tun treated them very generously. Shu
> and Hu then discussed how they could repay
> his kindness. "All men," they said, "have
> seven holes so they can see, hear, eat and
> breathe. But Hun-tun alone does not have
> any of these. Let's try to bore some for
> him." Every day thereafter, they bored one
> hole, and on the seventh day Hun-tun died."
> [Chap. 7]

Chuang Tzu urged that we should not always use our
human value of judgment and self interests in destroying the naturalness of Chaos. He also said humorously:

> The duck's legs are short, but if we try to
> lengthen them, the duck will feel pain. The
> crane's legs are long, but if we try to cut
> off a portion of them, the crane will feel
> grief. Therefore we are not to amputate
> what is by nature long, nor to lengthen what
> is by nature short. [Chap. 8]

Third, the Taoists discovered the power of regeneration in Chaos because it still contained the unex-
haustible potency to re-create, while the created
cosmos has already become fixed and stagnant. The Taoists did not feel quite satisfied with what they saw
in the society within which they lived because the society was dominated by military monarchy and legalistic

bureaucracy, and the spirit of simplicity, spontaneity, freedom, and creativity had already been lost. But how to transform it? The Taoists found this by returning back to Chaos and being regenerated by Chaos, so that a new ideal universe could be re-created. In other words, this old and decaying social system, contaminated by superficiality and artificiality, should go through total regeneration, so that a new society full of freedom, simplicity, and creativity could be created. Lao Tzu advised:

> Reversion is the movement of Tao.
> Gentleness is the function of Tao.
> All things in the world come from Being,
> And Being comes from Non-Being. [Chap. 40]
>
> In greatness, It [Tao] produces;
> In producing, It expands;
> In expanding, It regenerates. [Chap. 25]
>
> While all things are stirred together,
> I only contemplate the Return. [Chap. 16]

In order to regenerate the world, the only way is to return to the primordial Chaos, because this world has already exhausted its energy of regeneration, and only inexhaustible Chaos can resupply that energy for re-creation. We see the same teaching in Jesus when he said to Nicodemus, a ruler of the Jews, "Truly, truly, I say to you, unless one is born anew, he cannot see the kingdom of God" (RSV John 3:3). In order to symbolize this regeneration, Christianity has instituted the rite of baptism, so that the repented can immerse in water and emerge from it to symbolize dying with Christ with one's old mode of life and rising with Christ to be reborn into a New Being. (This is Paul's interpretation of baptism, see Romans, chap. 6.)

It is interesting to note that baptism has used water to symbolize the process of regeneration, and that Hun-tun means exactly this: abyss,deep or ocean. In fact, Chaos and the water are almost identical in many ancient myths. Mircea Eliade has summarized most succinctly the significance of the water symbolism:

> Principle of what is formless and potential,
> basis of every cosmic manifestation, con-
> tainer of all seeds, water symbolizes the
> primal substance from which all forms come
> and to which they will return either by their
> own regression or in a cataclysm. It existed

at the beginning and returns at the end of
every cosmic or historic cycle; it will always exist, though never alone, for water is
always germinative, containing the potentiality of all forms in their unbroken unity. In
cosmogony, in myth, in ritual and icono-
graphy, water fills the same function in
whatever type of cultural pattern we find it;
it precedes all forms and upholds all creation. Immersion in water symbolizes a return to the pre-formal, a total regeneration,
a new birth, for immersion means a dissolution of forms, a reintegration into the form-
lessness of preexistence; and emerging from
the water is repetition of the act of creation in which form was first expressed. . ."2

With this understanding of the value in water symbolism, it might be interesting for us to inquire if
such water symbolism appears in our daily life, in fine
arts, in literature, in architecture, in religious
life, etc., and reevaluate the significance and meaning
of water symbolism. It is so pervasive as a reality
and as a symbolic feature of our culture, it is no wonder that the Taoists referred to water as the mysterious given of preexistence. If those early Taoist philosophers had had the privilege of traveling for hours
by ship or plane over the vast oceans, they would have
been even more convinced that before the universe existed, there was but the chaotic deep.

The Symbolism of the Cosmic Egg

The P'an-ku myth describes Hun-tun as a chicken's
egg, and it may not appear to be so significant to pay
attention to such a casual remark; however, since the
symbolism of cosmic egg has appeared in so many cosmogonic myths over the world, we should not ignore its
significance in this study. It is interesting to note
that the Bible also used the metaphor of cosmic egg
when "the Spirit of God was moving over the face of
the waters" (Genesis 1:2), and the Hebrew verb
"rachaph" translated as "moving over" was originally
meant to be like a mother-hen brooding over or hatch-
ing an egg. Alfred Forke, formerly a professor of
Chinese at the University of Hamburg, pointed out that
there were six astronomical systems developed in ancient China, and the second system called Hun-t'ien
described the cosmos like an egg. He noted:

"Wang Fan [third century A.D.], . . . states that
according to the views of former scholars the universe
was shaped like the egg of a bird. Heaven encloses
the earth from without as the shell does the yolk of
the egg, its curve being without beginning or end,
having a perfectly round shape, not that of a hemi-
sphere. . . . Hence the name Hun-t'ien [Chaotic Heaven]
. . . [Sung shu 23, 1 r]."

     Ko Hung (葛 洪 253-333?) maintains that "heaven
is like a hen's egg and earth like the yellow in the
egg, suspended lonely in the midst of heaven. Heaven
is great, earth is small, heaven is outside and water
inside. Both heaven and earth rest on the air and
move, carried by the water. . . . One celestial hemi-
sphere covers the earth, the other spreads around it
underneath. Consequently only half of the twenty-eight
solar mansions are visible, the other half are invisible. Heaven turns around like the nave of a wheel"
(Chin-shu, XI. 2 v.).

     It is surprising to note that even long before the
West discovered that the earth is round, Chinese had
already thought the earth as round as an egg-yolk hanging in the universe. But, it is more important to find
the meaning behind the symbol of the egg.

     The egg is, of course, immediately conceived of as
the source of life like a seed, because it contains all
the potentiality for creation of a new being. It symbolizes at once creativity, fertility, fecundity, and
productivity. Because of it, we do egg hunting in the
Easter festival; hanging eggs or egg-shells for Chris-
mas decorations; the Persians present colored eggs as
New Year gifts; and the German farmers bury blessed
eggs in their fields; and Chinese people place eggs to
accompany their dead in a coffin hoping for their rebirth.

     Moreover, since the egg contains within itself
egg white, yellow yolk, two spiral bands called
chalazas, a cicatricle from which the embryo develops,
and the thin skin-like membrane attached to the shells,
the egg is also understood to symbolize the mystery of
multiplicity in unity or the unity in multiplicity.
In one egg, all the diverse forms and variety of modes
are already present, and they are ready to evolve and
burst out. Charles Long did a comprehensive survey on
the motif of cosmic egg in mythology and concluded,
"In the cosmic-egg symbolism the beginning of things is

131

spoken of as a totality which includes the opposite
modes of sexuality in relation. This is a <u>coinci-
dentia oppositorium</u>. . . . In the cosmic egg the concrete forms of the two sexual principles are united.
This unity is a symbol of perfection."[3] (See Figure 7)

P'an Ku, The Cosmic Giant Man

     The P'an-ku myth relates that from the Hun-tun or
Cosmic Egg, P'an-ku was born. P'an in Chinese character 盤 means a vase or container, and Chinese also use
the word T'ai-p'an 胎盤 to mean the embryo, womb and
foetus. Ku (古) means ancient, old, and long time.
Thus, P'an-ku could mean an "everlasting womb" or
"eternal foetus." We can see here another important
symbolism: mother's womb, which always appears to be
associated with the cosmogony, theogony, and anthropo-
gony in mythology. The symbolism is, on the one hand,
literal, physical, and materialistic; but on the other,
symbolic, spiritual, and metaphysical. This is one of
the great functions of symbol which is capable of
transforming a metrail thing into a spiritual force,
and changing the secular into the sacred, and at the
same time, is capable of maintaining each entity and
mode in its own integrity.

     Continuing with the P'an-ku myth, we learn that
P'an-ku gradually grew from a small womb into a vast
firmament which has the heaven above and earth below.
This is again very similar to the creation story in the
Bible. On the second day, God "separated the waters
into above and below in order to create a firmament in
between" (Genesis 1:6-8). However, the basic difference is while the Bible emphasized the existence of a
creator God standing outside of the creation, the
P'an-ku myth did not have a creator God but a cosmic
giant man grew from within the universe. Therefore,
while Christianity tries to differentiate sharply between the creator and the created, the P'an-ku myth
tries to emphasize the organic growth from within and
the essential unity between the producer and that which
is produced. The original Tao permeates all things,
and all things share the same substance of Tao. There
is an interesting story telling us about such a radical view. Chuang Tzu had such a strong belief in the
universality of Tao that one day his friend Tung Kuo
Tzu asked him:

     Where is the so-called Tao? Chuang Tzu said:
     "There is nowhere where it is not." Tung

FIGURE 6

The Bronze Vessel Ta Yü Ting and Its Inscription
(see pp. 96-97)

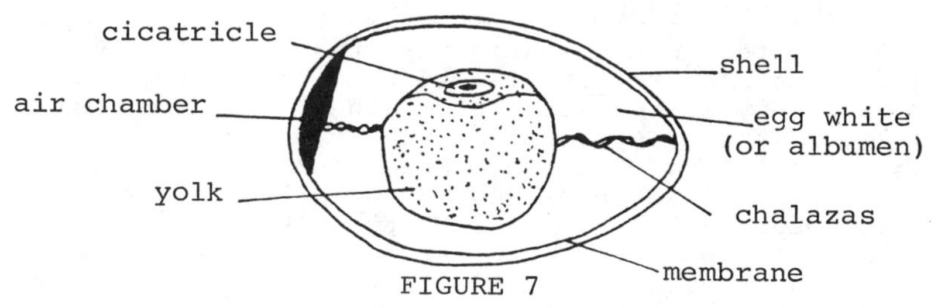

FIGURE 7

A Structure of Egg

133

Kuo Tzu said: "Specify an instance of it."
Chuang Tzu said: "It is in the ant." "How
can it be so low?" "It is in the panic
grass." "How can it be still lower?" "It
is in the earthenware tile." "How can it be
even lower:" "It is in excrement." To this
Tung Kuo Tzu made no more questions. . . .
Then,Chuang Tzu said, "There is not a single
thing without Tao. There are three terms:
Completeness, All-embracingness and the whole.
These three names differ but denote the same
reality; all refer to one thing."[4]

This basic belief in the organic unity of the universe and the interrelatedness of chaos and cosmos is
what the P'an-ku myth tried to exemplify. P'an-ku as
embryo is a <u>microcosm</u>, and P'an-ku as cosmic giant is
a <u>macrocosm</u>, and they are mutually interrelated. The
purpose of using this cosmic giant man P'an-ku is to
symbolize the totality of the cosmos and to illustrate
the organic untiy within the universe. The universe is
like a human body; his breath is the wind and cloud,
his eyes the sun and moon, his four limbs the four corners of the earth, his five fingers the five great
mountains known to Chinese, his blood the rivers of
the world, his muscles and veins the strata of the
earth, his flesh the soil, etc. Each thing in the universe has its position, its role, its value, and its
function, and yet each is related to one another and
to the totality like all the parts of the body are organically integrated. It is interesting to note that
St. Paul also used the metaphor of body to symbolize
the relationship between Christ and his church and
among all the members of the church (see Romans 12).
The Hindu myth of Purusha also used the same metaphor
to illustrate the cosmic unity between nature and man
and among the four castes.

Creation by Self Transformation

One of the most dramatic aspects in the P'an-ku
myth is that P'an-ku <u>died</u> in order to create the whole
universe. Why is the motif of death at the beginning
of cosmic birth? Is it not contradictory to talk about
death in the story of birth? Yes, it may appear to be
contradictory if we think death and birth are dichotomous, and especially when we love to talk of birth and
life and hate and fear death. But to the Taoist sages,
they regarded death and life as interrelated. As soon
as we are born, we are in the process of dying, as well

as in the process of living. In order to live and
grow, we have to die and transform. Although we are
not conscious of it, biologists tell us that thousands
and thousands of cells in our body "die" daily; while,
at the same time, thousands and thousands of them are
"born" anew. In order to become an adult, we have to
leave behind our infancy, just as the snake sheds its
skin.

Death is a necessary process for rebirth, both
physically and spiritually. Therefore, death is not
to be resisted but to be integrated within the process
of re-creation. Jesus had complete understanding of
this truth when he said, "Truly, truly, I say unto you,
unless a grain of wheat falls into the earth and dies,
it remains alone; but if it dies, it bears much
fruit" (John 12:24). He also said, "For whoever would
save his life will lose it; and whoever loses his life
for my sake and the gospel's will save it" (Mark 8:35).
As we all know, self-sacrifice is one of the central
motifs in Christianity, and yet it is astonishing to
see that the same motif has already appeared in the
P'an-ku myth. P'an-ku had sacrificed himself in order
to recreate the universe. He is at once both the
progenitor and the redeemer of the world.

1. Charles Long, <u>Alpha: The Myths of Creation</u> (N.Y.: Macmillan, 1963), pp. 18-19.

2. Mircea Eliade, <u>Patterns in Comparative Religion</u> (N.Y.: Meridian Books, 1958), p. 188.

3. Long, <u>Alpha</u>, pp. 116-117.

4. Feng Yi-lan, <u>A History of Chinese Philosophy</u> (Princeton: Princeton University Press, 1952), vol. I, p. 223.

<u>Suggested Readings</u>

Derk Bodde, "Myths of Ancient China" in <u>Mythologies of the Ancient World</u>, ed. Samuel N. Kramer (New York: Doubleday, 1961), pp. 357-408

N. J. Girardot, "The Problem of Creation Mythology in the Study of Chinese Religion," <u>History of Religions</u> 15 (1976):289-318.

David C. Yu, "The Creation Myth and Its Symbolism in Classical Taoism," <u>Philosophy East and West</u> 31 (1981): 479-500.

N. J. Girardot, <u>Myth and Meaning in Early Taoism</u> (Berkeley, CA.: University of California Press, 1983).

John Ferguson, "Chinese Mythology," <u>The Mythology of All Races</u>, ed. John A. MacCulloch (Boston, 1928), pp. 1-203.

Edward T. C. Werner, <u>Dictionary of Chinese Mythology</u> (Shanghai, 1932).

CHAPTER 6

ORIGIN AND STRUCTURE OF THE UNIVERSE

In the previous chapter, we dealt with the P'an-ku myth of creation, which was one way of describing how the universe came into being. In this chapter we will survey the various essential world views developed in ancient China. One can almost detect a distinct world view from each writing or each school of ancient Chinese philosophy and discover that each is unique as well as overlapping in some characteristics. The process leading toward formation of a metaphysical theory was long and complicated, and we do not have enough space to go into exhaustive detail. What we will do here is to present some representative theories of cosmology which can best summarize the general characistics of the Chinese world view.

Lao Tzu (老子), the founder of Taoism, was the first one attempting to present a monistic view. He believed that the universe must come from one origin which he named Tao, or "the Way." Then we see Tsou Yen (騶衍), the founder of the Yin-Yang school, proposing a popular theory of the dualism of Yin and Yang. Later on, another theory of the Five Elements was added to the Yin-Yang cosmology, and we have the beginning of the cosmology of pluralism. Finally, we see a great synthesis of Chinese world views in the sixty-four hexagrams elaborated in the Book of Changes (I Ching 易經). In the following, these four theories will be presented based on the primary sources of their writings and their implications and interrelationship will be discussed.

The Metaphysic of Tao in Lao Tzu

According to Ssu-ma Ch'ien, a great historian of the Han dynasty, Lao Tzu was an official of the archives in the capital Chou of the State of Ch'u. As he began to practice the Way and its virtue, his learning was aimed at self-effacement, and seeking no fame, he resigned from his job and retired into the mountains. When he was traveling through a pass, Yin-shi, the passkeeper requested him to write a book for posterity. Thus, Lao Tzu wrote Tao Te Ching (道德經, the Canon of Way and Virtue) in two parts, expounding the ideas of the Way and its virtue, and then left. No one knew where he went afterwards. There are some other legends about Lao Tzu, but historians are not

sure of their reliability, or even who Lao Tzu really
was. But we now still have the work attributed to him,
<u>Tao Te Ching</u>, which has over time become one of the
holy books in the world. The following is taken from
<u>Tao Te Ching</u> to elaborate on Lao Tzu's idea of Tao.[1]

Lao Tzu believed that there must be one origin of
all things, but he had difficulty defining what it was.
He said:

> There is Something undifferentiated and yet
>   complete in Itself.
> It existed before the birth of heaven and
>   earth.
> Soundless and formless,
> Independent and unchanging;
> Pervasive and invincible.
> It can be regarded as the Mother of the Uni-
>   verse.
> I do not know Its name.
> I name It "Tao," only when I was forced to
>   give It a name.
> I regard It simply "Great,"
> For in greatness, It produces.
> In producing, It expands;
> In expanding, It regenerates.
>
> Hence, Tao is great;
> Heaven is great; Earth is great;
> And the king is also great.
> In the universe, there are four great things,
> And the king is one of them.
>
> The way of man follows after the law of Earth.
> The law of Earth follows after the law of
>   Heaven.
> The law of Heaven follows after the law of
>   Tao.
> The law of Tao follows after Its own natural-
>   ness. [Chap. 25]

As we can see in this passage, Lao Tzu felt that there
is "Something undifferentiated and yet complete in Itself" to be the ultimate origin of the universe, but
he could not designate clearly what "it" was, so he
called "it" variously the Mother of the universe,
Great or the Greatest One (太乙), and Tao. He said he
named "it" Tao "only when he was forced to give It a
name." This is an important point to make, for in all
honesty, no one can define what is the ultimate origin

of the universe because none of us were present at the
time of creation and our knowledge of early beginnings
is fragmentary and speculative. Therefore, whatever we
do in defining the origin of the universe, should be
done with humility and with deference to universal
truth like Lao Tzu.

     This modesty or humility in acknowledging the
limits of human knowledge and to preserve the transcendental nature of that "Something undifferentiated
and yet complete in Itself" has a great virtue in religion. Rudolf Otto, a German theologian and historian of religions, in his book <u>The Idea of the Holy</u>
pointed out that one of the essential elements of the
numinous or the Holy is the sense of "Wholly Other"
which transcends our conceptualization and categorization.[2]

     Within this context of humility, let us elaborate
what Lao Tzu meant by Tao, since he used this word
more often than others in naming the ultimate origin
of the universe. However, Lao Tzu did not invent this
word himself. The word Tao had already appeared a long
time ago in the Chou bronze texts as 復 , and it has
been considered by paleographers to consist of three
radicals: representing a human head (𝌟), a human foot
(𝋡), and a crossroad (彳亍). It has been interpreted
to portray a chief and his followers walking into a
crossroad. By the sixth century B.C., the word Tao was
simplified, but still retained its original meaning.
It appeared as 道 , composed of two radicals: a head
(首) and the notion of running (辶). It signified that
a leader was leading, while his follwers were running
after him. By combining all these notions, one grasps
the idea that Tao is a passage which is opened up by a
leader, who is being followed by running devotees. In
the current usage, Tao, as a noun, means in a concrete
sense,a path, road, and avenue; and in an abstract
sense, the way, truth, and principle. When it is used
in association with a proper noun, it means a school
of philosophy or religion. For example, T'ai-p'ing Tao
(太平道) means the Religion of Great Peace, and Tao
implied its doctrine, practice, and fellowship. Tao is
also used as a verb to mean "to speak, to expound, to
read and to guide." In English translation, it has
often been translated as the Way, and understood as an
abstract idea or principle. It is unfortunate that
the concrete and practical aspect of Tao has been ignored. Tao is not merely an idea, but also a path to
be trodden, a passage to run through, and the way to be

acted upon.

Before Lao Tzu, in the writings of Tso Chuan and
Kuo Yi (左傳,國語), there frequently appeared the notion of the Way of T'ien (天道), the Way of Human
beings (人道), and the Way of Earth (地道). The Way
of Heaven is to indicate the way the Supreme God T'ien
governs the universe, in general, and the mandate of
kings, in particular. The former points to the laws of
nature, e.g., the phases of the moon, the changes of
seasons, and growth and weathering of vegetation. The
latter points to the rule of rewards and punishments
T'ien laid upon the rulers and ruled, and the laws of
social ethics, and the course of cultural and historical changes.[3] Carrying over these notions, Lao Tzu
wanted to synthesize them into a coherent principle
which governs all things related to the dimensions of
Heaven, Earth, and Humankind. Thus, he concluded by
saying:

> The way of man follows after the law of Earth.
> The law of Earth follows after the law of
>   Heaven.
> The law of Heaven follows after the law of
>   Tao.
> The law of Tao follows after Its own natural-
>   ness.   [Chap. 25]

Tao is, therefore, the ultimate, universal, and absolute principle of the universe. Here we can see that
Lao Tzu's understanding of Tao is not the result of
revelation from a creator God, but a result of reflection from the observation and categorization of what
happened in natural phenomena and human affairs. This
is one of the characteristics of a Chinese world view
in which the knowledge of the origin of the universe
is traced within from what has been created, rather
than claiming that it has received from a creator outside of creation.

Moreover, Lao Tzu contemplated further about the
nature and attributes of Tao from his keen observation
within nature itself. As he propounded, the "law of
Tao follows after Its own naturalness." This word
"naturalness" is a key word for understanding Lao Tzu's
Tao. "Naturalness" in Chinese characters Tzu-Jen (自
然), has two words representing the Self (自) and
Thusness (然). Its original meaning implied a profound metaphysical understanding of "Being as Such" or
"autonomous Selfhood." However, because of its modern

usage, the word Tsu-Jen is now used to mean "nature,"
or "natural," in terms of natural phenomena or natural
science, and it has lost its archaic and metaphysical
meanings. This study evaluates Tzu-Jen of Tao as having equal depth in its meaning with the Buddhist idea
of "tathata" and the Biblical notion of Yahweh (or I
am that I am), and the Existentialist understanding of
"Being as Such" or the Ground of Being. In order to
understand better what Lao Tzu meant by Tao, let us
look more into his work Tao Te Ching for what he said
about Tao. In the first chapter of Tao Te Ching, Lao
Tzu wrote:

> Tao that can be truly Tao is not a permanently
>   fixed Tao;
> Name that can be truly Name is not a perman-
>   ently fixed name.
> As the Origin of heaven and earth, It is name-
>   less;
> As the Mother of all things, It is namable.
>
> Without desire, one can always contemplate Its
>   subtleness;
> Within desires, one can always observe Its
>   manifestations.
> In fact, these two are from the same source;
> Yet they are differently named.
>
> They are both called original and mysterious.
> The Mystery of All Mysteries,
> Indeed it is the Gate to All Wonders.
> [Chap. 1]

Many have translated the first stanza as "Tao that can
be told is not a permanent Tao; Name that can be named
is not a permanent Name," but this study has translated it differently. Because, while it may emphasize
the undefinable and un-namable character of Tao, it
will make a rather unbalanced statement with the following stanzas which also emphasized the namable and
phenomenal character of Tao. Therefore, after a careful study of Chapter 1 and the whole context of Lao
Tzu's philosophy, in this study it will be emphasized
that Tao should not be permanently fixed,for Tao has
both noumenal and phenomenal, un-namable and namable,
subtle and apparent aspects, and only those who know
the unity of these diverse aspects can be initiated
into the Mystery of All Mysteries. It is obvious that
Lao Tzu considered that Tao was the Origin of heaven
and earth and the Mother of all things, but the problem

was how to integrate the Unity of Tao with the diversity of myriad things. Here Lao Tzu resorted to a
religious intuition of mysticism: <u>union mystica</u>, unifying the stage of "with desires" with the stage of
"without desire." Lao Tzu described more of this mystical aspect of Tao and "its" adepts in Chapter 15:

> In ancient Time,
> The adepts of Tao were subtle and mysterious,
>   profound and comprehensive.
> Their minds were too deep to be fathomed.
> Because they were unfathomable,
> We can only vaguely describe their appear-
>   ances.
> They are:
> Hesitant, like one wading a stream in winter;
> Timid, like one afraid of dangers on all sides;
> Reserved, like a waiting guest;
> Supple, like an ice that is about to melt;
> Genuine, like a piece of uncarved block;
> Hollow, like a valley;
> Chaotic, like a muddy pond.
> And yet who else could emerge from muddiness
>   to clarify with such calmness?
> Who else could evolve from inertness to
>   vitality with such steadiness?
>
> He who embraced this Tao does not want to
>   reach the extreme.
> Precisely because he does not reach the ex-
>   treme,
> He can remain hidden like a seed and be re-
>   born in spring.

In this poem, Lao Tzu tried to describe the primeval
state of Tao to be unfathomable and chaotic, similar
to the muddy pond and hollow valley where no distinctions and differentiation are made. This poetic imagery of Tao coincides with the imager of Chaos (Hun-
tun 混沌) which appeared in the P'an-ku myth of crea-
tion.4 However, "like a seed hidden underneath the
muddy pond, Tao will be reborn in spring," so the cosmos came out of chaos, returns to it, and will be reborn again. Such a mysterious nature of Tao is also
expressed beautifully in Chapter 14:

> Looking at it you cannot see it/
> Its name is invisible.
> Listening to it you cannot hear it/
> Its name is the Inaudible.

Grasping it you cannot possess it/
Its name is the Incorporeal.
These three attributes are unfathomable.

For indeed, in merging, they all become One.
Its upper side is not bright,
    Nor its under side dark.
Infinite and boundless,
    It cannot be called by any name;
    It returns again to nothingness.
This may be called:
    The Form of Formless;
    The Image of Nothingness.

Indeed, It is Elusive and Ecstatic.
Confront It and you do not see Its back/
And yet equipped with this timeless Tao,
You can harness all present realities.
To know the primeval origin
Is to be initiated into Tao.

In this Chapter, we see the same description of Tao as
unfathomable and elusive as we see in Chapter 15, but
Lao Tzu, in conclusion, stated here that Tao is
nothingness (Wu 無), for It is invisible, inaudible,
incorporeal, and formless. He explains the attribute
of nothingness more succintly in Chapter 40:

Reversion is the movement of Tao.
Gentleness is the function of Tao.
All things in the world come from Being,
And Being comes from Non-Being.

It is easier for us to understand that "all things come
from Being" because we often think that the origin of
the universe should be something more absolute, ultimate, substantial, and real than the ordinary things,
but it is surprising to hear Lao Tzu say that Tao is
nothingness and Non-Being. Perhaps we can easily say
that Lao Tzu wanted simply to explain the no-thing attribute of Tao because Tao is not a thing. Fung Yu-lan
interpreted it to mean that, logically speaking, if
the origin of all things is a thing or a being, it
must have another origin of its own, and ad infinitum;
therefore, the ultimate origin of all things should be
something or "somebeing" which is no longer a thing or
a being; therefore, it should be only nothingness and
Non-Being.[5] However, Wing-tsit Chan tried to emphasize

that what Lao Tzu meant by nothingness or Non-Being is
to point to the hidden potentiality which is more potential and inexhaustible than that which has been
realized or appeared.[6] Chapter 11 illustrates this aspect more clearly:

> Thirty spokes are converged upon the hub
>   to make a wheel,
> Yet, it is the emptiness within
>   that makes the wheel useful.
>
> A lump of clay is molded
>   to make a vessel,
> Yet, it is the emptiness within
>   that makes the vessel useful.
>
> Door and windows are cut out
>   to make a room,
> Yet, it is the emptiness within
>   that makes the room useful.
>
> Thus, while the being has advantage,
> It is the non-being that makes it useful.

Here, Tao is described metaphorically as the emptiness
within a hub, the emptiness within a vessel, and the
emptiness within a room. And even though we have con-
ventionally defined a wheel as consisting of spokes
and hubs, it is really the emptiness-nothingness within that gives it form. In other words, nothingness or
emptiness is as real as substance, and moreover, more
important and potential than a ready-made thing. Because we do not often pay attention to the nothingness
and emptiness, Lao Tzu tried to stress its significance.
Nothingness or emptiness also indicates the inexhaustible nature of Tao. The universe not only consists
of myriad planets of solid matter but also of enormous
vacuity which support all these planets. Chapter 4
noted:

> Tao is empty.
> Though it is used, It never exhausts.
> Fathomless,
> Yet It appears to be the progenitor of all
>   things.
>
> It blunts Its sharpness,
> It solves Its tangles,
> It harmonizes all brilliant lights,
> And It unites the dusty world into one.

> Deeply hidden,
> Yet It seems to exist forever.
> I do not know whose child It is,
> Yet It seems to have existed even prior to
>   the Lord God.

Chapters 5 and 6 also described the inexhaustible nature of Tao very well:

> When heaven and earth are not gracious,
> They treat all things like straw-dogs.
> When the sages are not gracious,
> They treat their people like straw-dogs.
>
> The space between heaven and earth is like a
>   bellows.
> It is empty, but never fails to give supply.
> When it is in motion, it never stops producing.
> Even many words cannot fathom it;
> But keep it in its center.   [Chap. 5]
>
> The Spirit of the Valley dies not.
> It is called the Mysterious Feminine.
> The gate of Mysterious Feminine
> Is called the Root of heaven and earth.
> Hidden and covered, it has faint existence,
> And yet in using it, it is inexhaustible.
> [Chap. 6]

Now, how does this Tao of nothingness and Non-Being create or produce the whole universe? Lao Tzu used a very simple and yet a succint statement to describe it in Chapter 42:

> Tao produces the One,
> The One produces the Two,
> The Two produces the Three,
> And the Three produces myriad things.
> And myriad things carry the Yin and embraces
>   the Yang.
> Through the blending of these vital forces,
> They achieve harmony. . . .

It is almost like an athletic coach calling "one, two, three," and all athletes start to run, or like a magician saying "one, two, three," and a rabbit jumps out. But "One, Two, Three" also has profound implications in terms of metaphysics and cosmology. It could mean the cosmological theories of monism, dualism, and pluralism, and <u>universism</u> of Tao.[7] It could also mean

the process of creation from production, division, and
multiplication. It could also connote a mystery of
Trinity: creation, destruction, and regeneration. However, whichever interpretation we want to take, to Lao
Tzu, Tao is the ultimate origin of all things, and Tao
is the unifying principle permeating all things, which
is what he wanted to emphasize in Tao Te Ching. He
left it up to later generations to elaborate upon the
process of creation which developed into the dualism
of Yin and Yang.

The Yin Ynag Dualism of Tsou Yen

According to Ssu-Ma Ch'ien's Grand Record of History, three famous scholars appeared in the State of
Ch'i, and one of them was Tsou Yen (305-240 B.C.). He
saw that the rulers of his day were incapable of applying moral principles in their government and instruction, he began to investigate the evolution of the Yin
and Yang forces in natural phenomena and the cycles of
the great ancient sage-rulers and wrote essays about
their mutual correlations. He tried to connect the
great events in history and the rise and fall of dynasties to various omens which appeared in heaven and
earth. He also surveyed and classified notable mountains, rivers, valleys, and their birds and beasts
and the products of their soils. He was the first one
to point out that China was not the only continent,
but only one part of eighty-one in the whole world. He
named China the Sacred Continent of the Red Region
(赤縣神洲) within which are nine provinces laid out
by Yü, the legendary emperor who controlled the flood.
Around each of these continents, there is a small en-
circling ocean; and around the outer edge of these
nine continents, there is a vast ocean encompassing
them at the point where heaven and earth meet. From
this he extended his survey to what is beyond the sea
and to the beginning of the separation of heaven and
earth and made notation of the evolution and transmutation of the Five Elements (i.e., earth, wood,
metal, fire, and water), arranging them in sequence
and allocating each force its correlation in history.

He then tried to correlate these Five Elements
with the Virtues of human-relatedness (jen 仁), righteousness (i 義), discipline, frugality, and the cor-
dial relationships between the ruler and subject, superior and inferior, and among the six other human relationships. Thus, kings, dukes, and great officials
were fascinated when they learned his theory, and he

was invited with high honor by King Hui of Liang, Prince
of Chou, and King Chao of Yen to give lectures on his
cosmic theory and the principle of government. Tsou
Yen composed the <u>Chu Yün</u> (主運, i.e., Major Evolution),
but it was lost. We know of his theory only through
secondary sources.[8]

In this account, Tsou Yen was credited with the
invention of both the theory of Yin-Yang and the theory
of Five Elements, perhaps due to the fact that by the
time of Ssu-Ma Ch'ien (145-90 B.C.), these two theories
were synthesized. But according to many studies of modern scholars, the theory of Five Elements was highly
developed long before Tsou Yen and only much later were
synthesized by the Yin-Yang philosophers with Tsou
Yen's theory of Yin-Yang.[9] For the purpose of clarifi-
cation, this section will only elaborate on the theory
of Yin-Yang; the theory of Five Elements will be the
focus of the next section.

The Chinese character of Yin (陰) and Yang (陽)
signify the shadowy and sunny sides of the same mountain, which indicates the idea of two sides of the
same existence very similar to the Western proverb:
"two sides of the same coin." With this observation,
Tsou Yen's insight that all things must have two sides,
two aspects, two genders, or two forces. The universe
has heaven and earth, day and night, the sun and moon,
land and ocean, mountain and valley, life and death,
male and female, senior and junior, etc. Polarity is
part of all existence, and it divides and differentiates, even creating tension between two poles,but it
does not necessarily conflict and tear apart the two
poles. It works like a swinging pendulum or an elec-
tric charge between the plus and minus poles to create
balance and dynamism. In religious terms, realization
of "diversity in unity" and "unity in diversity" becomes the clue for producing creativity as well as
harmony. We see such extended application of Yin-Yang
theory into the practices of human relationships and
government administration in the later writings of
<u>Kuan Tzu</u> (third century B.C.) and <u>Lü-shih Ch'un-ch'iu</u>
(200-235 B.C.).

Chapter 40 of <u>Kuan Tzu</u> informs:

Therefore the Yin and the Yang are the
great principles of Heaven and Earth. The
four seasons are the great path of Yin and
Yang. Likewise, punishment and reward in

government are to be in harmony with the four
seasons. When punishment and reward are in
harmony with the seasons, happiness will be
produced; when they disregard them, they will
produce calamity. So what shall the ruler do
in spring, summer, autumn and winter? For example; the direction of spring is east, and
its sign the stars, and its force the wind.
Its characteristics are joyfulness, plenty
and growth. The duties of spring are to clean
the place of spirits, to make Yang supreme,
to repair the dykes, to cultivate and plant
the fields, to adjust bridges and dams properly, to repair canals, rooms and gutters, to
compromise with resentments, to pardon those
who have sinned, and to open communication between the four quarters. Thereupon the soft
wind and sweet rains will come; the common
people will live to a great age; and the various animals will flourish. . . .

Likewise, each season has its direction,
sign, force and characteristics and certain
specific duties that the people and government have to observe in order to maintain harmony between natural phenomena and human affairs, and to ensure happiness.

Therefore withering in spring, flourishing in autumn, thunder in winter and frost in
summer, are all perversions of these forces.
When punishments and rewards become confused
and lose their orderliness, perversions of
the forces come ever more frequently. And
when this happens, the country will suffer
many calamities. Therefore, a Sage-King establishes government in accordance with the
seasons, accompanies education with the art
of war, and performs sacrifices to display
virtue. It is through these three that the
Sage-King can put himself into union with the
movements of Heaven and Earth."[10]

In the thirteenth book of <u>Lu-shih Ch'un-ch'iu</u>, it says:

Heaven, Earth and all things are like the
body of one man, and this is what is called
the Great Unity (ta t'ung 大同). The multiplicity of ears, eyes, noses and mouths and
the multiplicity of the five grains and cold
and heat: this is what is called the Multiplicity of Differences (chung i 衆異). Thus

all things are made complete. Heaven makes
all things flourish. The Sage observes them,
so as thereby to examine his own kind. He
finds the explanation of how Heaven and Earth
became concrete form, how thunder and light-
ning are produced, and how the Yin and Yang
form the essence of things, and how people,
birds, and beasts are in a state of peace.[11]

It is interesting to note that the idea of looking
at the whole universe as one body appearing here in
Lu-shih Ch'un-ch'iu is very similar to the idea of
looking at the whole world as the body of a giant creation figure P'an-ku in the P'an-ku myth.[12] We shall
see later on that this idea of Ta T'ung (大同) has developed into a cosmopolitan-universalistic One-World
philosophy of K'ang Yu-wei (1958-1927) in modern
times.[13] The Yin-Yang theory of Tsou Yen has left a
permanent influence on the Chinese way of thought.
Basically, what the theory of Yin-Yang tried to emphasize was the ideal of "unity in duality" and "duality in unity" and avoidance of the extreme of undifferentiated monism and dichotomous dualism. Perhaps the idea of "coincidentia oppositorium" or the
identification of macrocosm and microcosm in Western
philosophy comes closest to the idea of Yin-Yang.[14]

The Theory of Five Elements

As we have already seen in the previous section,
theory of Five Elements was synthesized with the
theory of Yin-Yang by the first century B.C., but its
origin can be traced back separately long before, from
Tsou Yen. Several scholars have pointed out that the
notion of Five Elements had already appeared in relation to the discovery of the five directions of the
world: east, west, south, north, and the center of
the earth and the winds blew from all these directions,
according to the Shang oracle texts (c. thirteenth
century B.C.). The Shang oracle diviners were quite
apprehensive about the direction from which the wind
came, for irregular blowing of the wind at inopportune
times will cause great calamity to farming, hunting,
and military campaigns. The oracle texts witnessed
that the Shang kings and officials had offered extensive sacrifices to the gods of the winds and they even
identified their specifi names. The winds of four
directions were called Hsi (析) for east, Wu (光)
for south, I (彝) for west, and Yuan (元) for north,
and the sacrifice conducted was called Fang Wang

(方望 , i.e., to gaze in a distant direction), in which
dogs and cattle were crucified and burnt. The wind was
also believed to be the Messenger of God (Ti Ssu 帝使)
and the oracle texts had indicated that there were Five
Ministers of Assistants to Ti (Ti Wu Ch'en 帝五臣 or Ti
Wu Kung Ch'en 帝五工臣), which presumably signified the
beginning of the idea of Five Elements.[15]

The "Grand Norm" in the Book of History, one of
the Confucian classics, had already a clear notation
about the idea of Five Elements.

> I have heard that in ancient time Kun had
> dammed up the flood waters and disturbed the
> order of Five Elements. Thus Ti [the Lord]
> was angered and did not endow him with the
> Grand Norm of Nine Categories. Because of
> this, the social relationships were ruined
> and Kun was condemned to die. Then, Yü [Kun's
> son] had followed him and succeeded in stop-
> ping the flood. Thereupon Heaven gave Yü the
> Grand Norm of Nine Categories to set forth
> proper social relationships. The first cate-
> gory is the Five Elements. . . . The first
> element is water, the second fire, the third
> wood, the fourth metal, and the fifth earth.
> The nature of water is to moisten and descend;
> of fire, to burn and ascend; of wood, to be
> crooked and straight; of metal, to yield and
> to be modified; of earth, to provide for
> sowing and reaping.

Here the water, fire, wood, metal, and earth are
identified as the basic elements of the world, and
their individual nature, characteristic, and correlation with human senses and behavior are demonstrated.
How and why did ancient Chinese pick up these five to
be the elements of the world? And how do they correlate with human senses and behavior? Joseph Needham,
a British scientist who has mastered the science of
ancient China, has attempted the following explanation.

> The association of saltiness with water,
> while natural indeed to a costal people, sug-
> gests primitive experiments and observations
> on solution and crystallization. The associa-
> tion of bitterness with fire, while perhaps
> the least obvious of the five, may imply the
> use of heat in preparing decoctions of

medicinal plants, which would be the bitter-
est substances likely to be known. The association of sourness and wood can readily
be explained, since wood, as vegetal, would
be connected with all kinds of plant substances which becomes sour on decomposition.
The association of acridity with metal points
directly to smelting operations, many of
which would give off highly acrid fumes,
e.g., sulpher dioxide. Lastly, the association of sweetness with earth would be due to
the finding of honey in bees' nests in the
earth, and to the general sweet taste of
cereals.[16]

Such correlation between the Five Elements and
natural phenomena, and the Five Elements and human
senses and affairs were further extended and elaborated in the writings of the Han dynasty. Such symbolic
correlations can be summarized in tables 1, 2, and 3.

One can see how extensively the theory of Five
Elements was applied in ancient China and that almost
everything in the universe can be reduced into these
five elements. However, we should also notice that
what ancient Chinese were interested is not merely to
identify with exact elements but to discover the cyclical process of change from one element to another and
the mutual correlations among the five elements.
Therefore, some scholars have pointed out that English
translation of Chinese words Wu Hsing (五行) into Five
Elements may not be quite adequate, for Hsing (行)
here is meant to be "active or action" rather than a
substance or element. Therefore, they have preferred
to translate it as "Agent" or "Force," but again it
goes to another extreme of emphasizing too much of a
dynamic aspect and ignoring the aspect of substance.[17]
In fact, Wu Hsing has connotations of both element and
force, agent and interaction, so that while we do not
have a better translation, we just have to use either
of them and be reminded that it also has other implied
meanings as well. Since Chinese are more interested
in the correlations among the five elements, they have
detected three different orders of cyclical changes
among these five elements in ancient writings.

The Cosmogonic Order (Sheng Hsu 生序)

In the Grand Norm chapter of the Book of History,
quoted above, is indicated this order of cosmogonic

151

TABLE I

Elements	Yin-Yang	Planets	Weather	Seasons	Cardinal Points
Wood	Lesser Yang	Jupiter	Wind	Spring	East
Fire	Greater Yang	Mars	Heat	Summer	South
Earth	Equal Balance	Saturn	Thunder	6th month	Center
Metal	Lesser Yin	Venus	Cold	Autumn	West
Water	Greater Yin	Mercury	Rain	Winter	North

TABLE II

Elements	Sense Organs	Tastes	Viscera	Moods	Psycho-Physical Functions
Wood	Eye	Sour	Spleen	Anger	Demeanour
Fire	Tongue	Bitter	Lungs	Joy	Vision
Earth	Mouth	Sweet	Heart	Desire	Thought
Metal	Nose	Acrid	Kidney	Sorrow	Speech
Water	Ear	Salt	Liver	Fear	Hearing

TABLE III

Elements	Rulers	Ministries	Sacrifices	Styles of Government
Wood	Hsia	Agriculture	Inner-door	Relaxed
Fire	Chou	War	Hearth	Enlightened
Earth	Pre-dynasty	The Capital	Inner Court	Careful
Metal	Shang	Justice	Outer Door	Energetic
Water	Ch'in	Labors	Well	Quiet

152

evolution from the element of water to other elements:
Fire, Wood, Metal, and Earth. This order emphasized
that water is the origin of all things. In the P'an-
ku myth of creation, and many other cosmogonic myths
of the world, we can also easily detect that water has
been universally regarded as the source of life and
cause for regeneration.[18] In chapter 39 of the <u>Book
of Kuan Tzu</u>, we see a fairly elaborate explanation
about the water as the origin of life.

> Now water is the blood and breath of the
> earth, flowing in through its sinews and
> veins. Thus we say that water is the raw ma-
> terial of all things. How do we know this?
> Because although water is yielding, weak and
> clean, it likes to wash away the evils of
> humankind--this is the benevolence of water.
> Although it looks sometimes black, sometimes
> white, that signifies the flexibility of
> water. When you measure it, you cannot force
> it to level off at the top, for when the ves-
> sel is full it does so by itself--this is the
> rectitude of water. There is no space into
> which it will not penetrate, and it occupies
> the spaces of all vessels to its level--this
> is the impartiality of water. People all
> like to go up higher, but water runs to the
> lowest possible place,--this virtue of humil-
> ity is the principle of Tao and the instru-
> ment of true rulers.
> The water-level instrument (chun 准) is
> the ancestor of the five measurements. The
> white color [of water] is the base of the
> five colors. The insipidness [of water] is
> the center of the five tastes. Thus water
> is the standard level of all things and the
> common factor of all life. It is the medium
> (chih 質) in which all gains and losses
> take place. Therefore there is nothing which
> water cannot fill and dwell in. It is ac-
> cumulated in Heaven and on Earth, and stored
> up in all things. It is produced amidst meat
> and rocks, and collected in all living things.
> It is thus mysterious and spiritual (shen
> 示申). Being collected in plants and trees,
> their roots grow in orderly progress, their
> flowers in due profusion blossom, and their
> fruits ripen proportionally. Being collected
> in birds and animals, they get their form and
> flesh, their feathers and furs, their obvious

153

stripes and markings. Thus there is nothing
which cannot achieve its germination. The
reason why creatures can realize their potentialities and grow orderly and normally
is because the inner regulation of their
water is in accord. . . .
     Human beings are made of water. When
the producing elements of male and female
unite, and water flows, forming a new body.
. . . The water congeals to form human beings,
and nine orifices and five viscera appear.
These are but part of its essence. Such essence, being thick and viscous, can continue
to live and never die. The turtle and dragon are two things which are able to live for
ever although they may appear to be not living. Though the turtle lives in the water,
when its shell is put on fire, it can still
perform divination. The dragon lives in the
water and acquires the five colours of water,
so it becomes a spirit. Thus it can make itself as small as a caterpillar, and alternatively, it can make itself as large as if it
can cover the whole world. . . . People all
drink water, but I alone make it my model.
People all have water, but I alone know how
to make use of it. Why do we call water the
preparative element? Because all things receive their life from it. People ask what
water is. It is the origin of all things
and the ancestral temple of Life.
     Water produces the beautiful and the
ugly, the virtuous and the wicked, the foolish and the clever. How do we know this?
For the waters of the state of Ch'i are rapid
and turning backwards [in rocky gorges]; thus
its people are rough, brave and covetous.
The waters of Ch'u are soft, weak and pure;
thus its people are light minded and sure of
themselves. The waters of Yüeh are turbid,
heavy and soaking through the land; thus its
people are stupid, jealous and dirty. The
waters of Ch'in are muddy, stagnant and
clogged with dust; thus its people are greedy,
deceptive and quarrelsom. . . . Hence the
sage's strategy for transformation of the
world lies in solving the problem of water.
When the water is uncontaminated, the human
heart will be upright. When the water is
pure, the people's heart will be at ease.

154

When the human heart is upright, their desires will not become dissolute. When the
people's heart is at ease, their conduct will
be without evil. Hence the Sage when he
rules the world, does not teach the people
one by one or family by family, but takes
water as his clue.

Although Kuan Tzu's saying about water may appear
to be like a soothsayer's prognostication, it contains
certain careful observations of natural phenomena and
profound contemplation on the characteristics of water.
It also has certain validity in terms of ecological
concerns and some intuitive wisdom beneficial for us
modern men to follow. While this cosmogonic order of
Five Elements emphasized so much the element of water
and its significance as the primal source of life, it
does not give us much detailed explanation of the
evolutionary process that took place from water to the
other elements: fire, wood, metal, and earth. In the
following two orders, we shall see that intercorrela-
tion and interaction among the five elements are more
fully elaborated.

<u>The Mutual Production Order</u>
<u>(Hsiang Sheng 相生)</u>

In the same writing of Kuan Tzu, we discover that
there is another description of the order of Five Elements in which the cyclical process of mutual production among the Five Elements was developed. For each
season, beginning with spring, the element Wood begins
to rise, and then the element Fire was produced for
the summer season, and the element Earth for the mid-
year, and the element Metal for the autumn, and finally
the element Water for the winter, and the annual cycle
goes on.

In the chapter "On the Five Elements," Tung Chung-
shu also write about the mutual productive process of
Five Elements.

Heaven has five elements: Wood, Fire, Earth,
Metal and Water. Wood comes first in the
cycle, water comes last, earth being in the
middle: this is the order by which Heaven has
made the universe. Wood produces fire, fire
produces earth [i.e., as ashes], earth produces metal [i.e., as ores], metal produces
water [like rocks issue water], and water

155

produces wood. This is a sort of causal,
father and son relationship. Wood dwells on
the left, metal on the right, fire in front,
and water behind, with earth in the center;
each receiving from the other in its turn.
Wood receives from water, fire from wood,
and so on. As transmitters they are fathers,
and receivers they are sons. There is an un-
varying dependence of the sons on the fathers,
and an orderly direction from the fathers to
the sons. Such is the Tao of Heaven.[19]

In the writing of Huai Nan Tzu, the order of mutual production is more carefully elaborated. The Five
Elements would have each, in turn, taken the process
of helping (hsiang 相), flourishing (wang 旺), retiring
(hsiu 休), imprisoning (ch'iu 囚), and dying (ssu 死).
Later on, in order to correspond with the twelve months
of the year, the twelve phases of annual cycle among
the Five Elements was elaborated as follows. Each of
the Five Elements occurs in turn: (1) to receive breath
(shou ch'i 收氣); (2) to be in the womb (t'ai 胎);
(3) to be nourished (yang 養); (4) to be born (sheng
生); (5) bathed (mu yü 沐浴); (6) to be initiated
(kuan tai 冠帶); (7) to become an official (lin kuan
臨官); (8) to flourish (wang 旺); (9) to become weak
(shuai 衰); (10) to become ill (ping 病); (11) to die
(ssu 死); (12) to be buried (tsang 葬).[20] These twelve
phases correspond with the destiny of human beings, as
well as the cyclical process of each element. With
this understanding of the cycle of rise and decline;
flourishing and decay, birth and death, a new order
among the Five Elements is discovered. It is called
the Mutual Conquest Order.

The Mutual Conquest Order (hsiang sheng 相勝)

Since each element has its time to rise and its
time of decline, finally to be taken over by others,
the Five Element theorist had quickly discovered that
the reality of mutual conquest existed in nature and
in human history as well. In the writing of Lü Shih
Ch'un Ch'iu, Tsou Yen was believed to expound the mutual conquest theory as follows:

The Five Elements dominate alternatively.
. . . Each of the Five Elements will be followed by the one it cannot conquer. The dynasty of Shun ruled under the influence of
Earth, the Hsia dynasty ruled under the

156

influence of Wood, the Shang dynasty ruled
under the influence of Metal, and the Chou
dynasty ruled under the influence of Fire.
Whenever a new dynasty is about to rise,
Heaven manifests auspicious signs to the
people. During the rise of the Yellow Emperor [Huang Ti] large earth-worms and large
ants appeared. He said, "This indicates
that the elements of Earth is in ascendancy,
therefore, yellow should be our color and
the earth should be the pattern of our
affairs." During the rise of Yü the Great,
Heaven produced the plants and trees which
would not wither in autumn and winter. He
said, "This indicates that the element Wood
is in ascendancy, therefore, green should be
our color and wood should be the pattern of
our affairs." During the rise of King T'ang,
the Victorious, a metal sword had appeared
out of the water. He said, "This indicates
that the element Metal is in ascendancy,
therefore, white should be our color and
metal should be the pattern of our affairs."
During the rise of King Wen of Chou, Heaven
manifested fire, and many fire birds holding
documents written in red flocked together at
the altar of the royal house. He said, "This
indicates that the fire element is in ascendancy, therefore, red should be our color
and fire should be the pattern of our affairs." Following Fire, inevitably the element Water will come. Heaven will manifest
the sign for the coming dominance of the
Water element. Then the color of a new dynasty should be black and water should be
the pattern of its affairs. And eventually
that dispensation will in turn come to its
end, and at the appointed time, all will return once again to Earth. But we do not
know when that time will be.[21]   [Chap. 63]

   Herein we see that the mutual conquest theory of
five elements was applied directly to interpret the
cause of dynastic changes in political history and
even to predict the future change. It also implies
that the cyclical mutation of Nature would continue
its course, and no matter how many precautions or what
opposition the rulers would take, an eternal dynasty
could not be established. This might have been a way
of "check and balance" that Tsou Yen wanted to put into

practice in order to stop dictatorship and hegemony.
It was especially during the time of the Warring States
period that his theory of mutual conquest had a certain
impact on the power struggles among the states. Such
application of the Five Element theory upon the philosophy of history and the political science of dynastic changes developed by Tsou Yen had great influence
and impact on the later development of Chinese thought.

From the theories of mutual production and mutual
conquest in the Five Elements, we can discover two
principles: the principle of Mutual Control and the
principle of Mutual Transformation. The principle of
Mutual Control is drawn from the order of Mutual Conquest, for in it the element that conquers the other
element is in turn being controlled by another element
that will conquer it. For example:

> Wood conquers Earth, but Metal controls the
> process.
>
> Metal conquers Wood, but Fire controls the
> process.
>
> Fire conquers Metal, but Water controls the
> process.
>
> Water conquers Fire, but Earth controls the
> process.
>
> Earth conquers Water, but Wood controls the
> process.

Joseph Needham commented on this principle by saying
that it is applicable to the ecological principle of
modern science.

> . . . The Chinese were following perfectly
> logical paths of thought which in our own
> time have been found applicable in numerous
> fields of experimental science, for in-
> stance, the kinetics of enzyme action, or
> the ecological balance of animal species.
> Thus the digestion of an oxidase by a pro-
> tease and the consequent inhibition of re-
> action which it would otherwise have
> catalysed would be an excellent example of
> the "principle of control" worked out by men
> such as Hsiao Chi in the sixth century. Or
> again, the "food chains" in natural

ecological communities must obviously depend on the relative abundance of the various species which prey on one another in a sequence based on their sizes and habits. A factor which increases the abundance of a certain bird will indirectly benefit a population of aphids because of the thinning effect which it will have on the coccinellid beetles [ladybirds] which eat the aphids but are themselves eaten by the birds. Modern economic entomology is full of such examples.[22]

The principle of Mutual Transformation depends upon both the order of mutual production and the order of mutual conquest. It refers to the transformation of a process of change by other processes, which produces it faster than it can be destroyed by the primary process. For example:

> While Wood conquers Earth, Fire transforms the process.
>
> While Fire conquers Metal, Earth transforms the process.
>
> While Earth conquers Water, Metal transforms the process.
>
> While Metal conquers Wood, Water transforms the process.
>
> While Water conquers Fire, Wood transforms the process.

In order to prevent the over-forestation of the earth, certain forest fires would stop the excessiveness of forestation. On the other hand, in order to prevent metal from destroying wood by cutting it up, water will transform the process by producing wood faster than metal can cut it up. Of course, these principles may not happen all the time and many of the processes depend very much upon more complex circumstances and conditions, but such an understanding of ecological balance has definite validity. When it was applied to the power politics of the Warring States period (and perhaps to our modern international politics), certain checks and balance mechanisms or arbitration of mutual control could be effected. As a matter of fact, the Five Element theory was not primarily intended to be a cosmological theory, but to be a political mechanism to control the chaos created by the Warring States.

The relationship of the Five Elements can be diagrammed by the following symbols: the black arrows indicate the Mutual Conquest Order and the dotted arrows indicate the Mutual Production Order (see figure 8).

<u>The Sixty-Four Hexagrams of</u>
<u>I Ching (易經)</u>

The <u>Book of Changes</u> is an accumulation of long tradition of divination practiced in ancient China.[23] The Shang divination applied heat to tortoise shells to create cracks and lines for the purpose of prognostication. Since those crackling and lines were rather irregular and easily exposed to abuse and misinterpretation, the unbroken line (—) and broken line (— —) and their combinations were formed to produce the triagrams and hexagrams for more specific prognostication. The unbroken line is to symbolize the Yang force and the broken line the Yin force matching the philosophy of Yin-yang dualism. Since ancient diviners believed that there must be certain mutual correlations between Heaven, Earth, and Human beings, the combination of three lines should compose the basic structure of all things in the universe; thus, eight triagrams were composed. The Appendix V of the <u>I Ching</u> explained:

> The Ch'ien triagram ☰ symbolizes Heaven; hence should be called Father. K'un ☷ symbolizes Earth; hence should be called Mother. Chen ☳ has its first [i.e., lowest] line as yang or male, signifying it to be the first son. Sun ☴ has its first line as yin or female, signifying it to be the first daughter. K'an ☵ has its second line as yang or male; signifying it to be the second son. Li ☲ has its second line as yin or female, signifying it to be the second daughter. Ken ☶ has its third line [i.e., upper] as yang; signifying it to be the third son. Tui ☱ has its third line as yin, signifying it to be the third daughter.

Here we see that human family life is taken to reflect the process of cosmogony. Like a human being is produced by the union of man and woman, so the

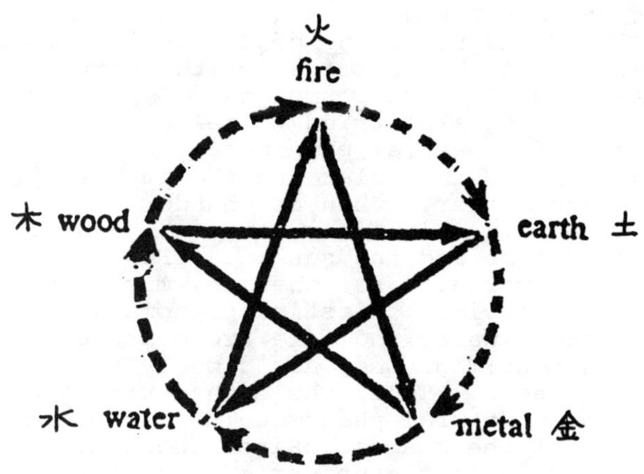

FIGURE 8

The Interrelationship of the Five Elements

The black arrows indicate the direction in which the Five Elements "conquor" one another; the dotted arrows indicate the directions in which they "produce" one another.

161

universe has Ch'ien-Heaven and K'un-Earth to produce
all things. This understanding of family life as a
microcosm related to the macrocosm of the universe is
the basic belief of Chinese cosmology. By extension,
Appendix V of I Ching also tried to relate each family
member with specific natural phenomena. "Ch'ien is
Heaven, round, and is the ruler and the father . . .
K'un is Earth and mother. Chen is thunder . . . Sun
is wood and rain . . . K'an is water . . . and is
moon . . . Li is fire and the sun . . . Ken is mountain . . . Tui is marsh." For the sun, moon, thunder,
and wind are most obvious celestial phenomena; the
mountains, marshes, water and fire are most obvious
terrestial phenomena; and they are closely related to
the basic human needs. Thus, the eight triagrams
representing these natural phenomena are to become the
basic symbolism of the cosmos. Since there are myriad
things and phenomena in the universe, the thinkers of
the I Ching tried then to multiply these eight triagrams to compose sixty-four hexagrams (8 x 8 = 64).
The Book of Changes was composed to give exposition to
each of these sixty-four hexagrams. It gives each
hexagram a title to indicate its basic nature, then
the general explanation of the whole hexagram and
finally the exposition and prognostication of each
line. For exposition of sixty-four hexagrams and 384
lines, the Book of Changes had accumulated many
archaic divinatory prognostications which contained a
profusion of peasant-omens, mythic imageries, and almanacs, many of which are no longer intelligible to
us modern men. However, ten chapter of Appendices
added to the original text were possibly by the Yin-
Yang philosophers in the third century B.C. to give a
comprehensive and philosophical interpretation to the
total structure and meaning of the sixty-four hexagrams.

    First of all, the title of the book, I (易),
could be interpreted as "easy or simple" as well as
"change." Easy or simple indicates the purpose of
the book which is to simplify the complex phenomena
in the universe into a structured composition of
lines, triagrams and hexagrams, and make it easier to
see the interrelationship and interactions in all the
existence in the universe. The symbolism of sixty-
four hexagrams is definitely much more spontaneous and
efficient in conveying the totality of the universe
than the discursive and analytical preposition of any
metaphysical theories.

_I_ as "Change" expresses the basic philosophy of the _I Ching_ that the universe is in constant flux or change. The universe is not static but dynamic, not stagnant but in process, and not an end-result but a continuous transformation. Like the sun rises and sets, the seasons change, the moon phases, and a dynasty rises and declines, there is a constant change. But at the same time, underlying all the changes there is an unchangeable principle of change. The _Book of Changes_ is to demonstrate simultaneously the phenomenal aspect of changes and the numenal aspect of the unchangeable principle. The ignorant one may just look at one side and ignore the other, but the wise one tries to see both sides at once and to be at home with both. In other words, he can go along with all changes while he dwells on the eternal, and he can also enjoy eternity while he lives in the world of innumerable changes. Incidentally, the word "I" (易) was believed to be originally a pictograph of a lizard or chameleon, 蜴 , for the chameleon changes quickly the color of its skin according to different circumstances to protect itself from iminent dangers; thus, the idea of changes of the unchangeable was born. The Appendix defined "I" as "Change, that is unchangeable."

Second, the _Book of Changes_ tries to illustrate that all things and all phenomena are but the changes between the Yin and the Yang forces. All the lines are divided into either a broken line or unbroken line. Thus, it seems to acknowledge the polarity or dualism of two opposing forces existent in the universe, but its emphasis is rather on the correlation and interaction between the two and the balancing and harmony they idealize. Appendix III notes:

> One Yin and one Yang constitute the movement
> of Tao. Those which are perpetuated by it
> are good. . . . It is manifested in the ac-
> tivities of benevolence, and is realized in
> the things useful. . . . The abundance of
> its power is complete and its achievement
> great.

Tao is the unity of all things, and Yin-Yang is but its side appearing in all things. The mystery is to find out the "unity in diversity" and "diversity in unity."

Third, all things are patterned and structured according to the order symbolized by the hexagrams.

Each existence, each phenomenon, and each movement is
given a certain position in the universe and guided by
a certain direction. Everyone is related to one another and interacting with one another. None is isolated and alienated. Each one is essential, for it
is an integral part of the total. Each is a microcosm representing the macrocosm of the universe. The
purpose of the sixty-four hexagrams is to show an individual his/her position and significance in the
universe.

> Heaven produced the spiritual things and
> the sages followed their patterns. Heaven
> and Earth have transformed all things and
> the sages imitated their changes. Heaven
> illuminated the good and bad fortunes and
> the sages symbolized their omens. The lines
> of the hexagrams are served to indicate all
> the movements taking place under the sky.
> [I Ching, Appendix III]

The sixty-four hexagrams composed after the movement of the universe observed by the Sage is thus believed to be able to give an individual at certain
given time his/her "timely position" and "proper movement," so that he/she can have good fortune by following the prognostication prescribed in the Book of
Changes.

As we can see, the Book of Changes is a synthesis
of the monism of Tao, the dualism of Yin-Yang, and the
pluralism of the Five Elements (only Five Elements are
replaced by the Eight Triagrams), and it symbolizes
it in a cosmogram of sixty-four hexagrams which could
be diagrammed (see figure 9).

As a summary to our survey of Chinese cosmology,
we can detect the following characteristics:

(a) It is fundamentally a monistic view even
though it contains the Yin-Yang dualism and Five Elements pluralism, for Yin-Yang and Five Elements are
but the extension of Tao. Tao is the permeating
principle, as well as the ultimate reality of the universe. Tao is the origin, the process, and the con-
sequence of all cosmic movements. The mystery of
"Tao in the universe" and "the universe in Tao" is the
clue for understanding truth and reality. Therefore,
in Chinese cosmology, there is no Creator God who

FIGURE 9

The Cosmogram: The Yin-Yang, the
Eight Trigrams, and the
Sixty-Four Hexagrams

distinguished himself from the creation and creatures.
In the Chinese way of thinking, there is no separation
or conflict between the sacred and profane, spiritual
and material, and divine and human. It is not necessarily a pantheistic but, rather, a pan-Taoistic or
cosmo-ontological view of the universe. It is what
J. J. M. De Groot called "universism."

(b) Chinese cosmology is organically structured
and ecologically oriented. In the midst of the monism
of Tao, diversity and plurality are acknowledged, but
they are patterned according to the order of Tao. We
have discerned the principle of mutual control and
transformation in the order of mutual production and
conquest. We have also seen a panoramic and intricate
structure of correlations in the sixty-four hexagrams
of the Book of Changes. The notion of macrocosm-
microcosmic relationship is abundant in the explica-
tion and exposition of Chinese cosmology. The harmony
between human beings and Heaven and Earth is the recurrent theme and the final ideal in Chinese religion.

(c) Chinese cosmology is also pragmatic and
utilitarian. Chinese believed that metaphysical speculation should be applicable for daily use in all human
affairs including social, religious, political, economical, etc., and should be beneficial or profitable.
Therefore, when Lao Tzu expounded the principle of Tao,
he had also to explicate that Tao is, and should be,
applicable to the practices of government. Tsou Yen
did likewise to apply his Yin-Yang and Five Elements
theories in his interpretation of dynastic change and
political science. The Book of Changes did not only
accumulate considerable ancient wisdom and almanacs,
but also intended to make itself into a book of
prognostication for telling good and bad fortunes. As
a matter of fact, Chinese people are generally more
interested in the practicability and profitability of
prognostication than in the metaphysical theory of the
sixty-four hexagrams. However, it is true that very
often it is carried so far that it becomes arbitrary
and mere superstitious practices prevail. However,
Chinese preference of practicability and utility of
the Book of Changes has never stopped.

It is interesting to note that even Carl Jung
practiced for himself a prognostication based on the
Book of Changes.[24]

FOOTNOTES

1. Ssu-ma Ch'ien, <u>Shih Chi</u> (Historical Records), Chapter 63. There have been many different theories about the person Lao Tzu and the authorship of Tao Te Ching. See Wing-tsit Chan, <u>The Way of Lao Tzu</u> (Indianapolis: Bobbs Merrill, 1963), chaps. 2 and 3. Since it was not the intention of this study to go into detail about the person nor the books, only the traditional view of Lao Tzu and <u>Tao Te Ching</u> have been mentioned.

2. Rudolf Otto, <u>The Idea of the Holy</u>, tr. John Harvey (London: Oxford University Press, 1925).

3. <u>Tso Chuan</u> and <u>Kuo Yi</u> are the writings of the third century B.C. <u>Tso Chuan</u> is a commentary on the <u>Ch'un Ch'iu</u> which covered the chronicle-history of the State of Lu extending from 722 to 381 B.C. James Legge, tr., <u>The Chinese Classics</u> (Oxford: Claredon Press, 1895). <u>Kuo Yi</u> is a writing contemporary of <u>Tso Chuan</u> collecting the historical conversations which took place among the States during the same period as that of <u>Tso Chuan</u>. This has no full English translation.

4. See chapter 3 of this book.

5. Fung Yi-Lan, <u>History of Chinese Philosophy</u>, tr. Derk Bodde (Princeton: Princeton University Press, 1952), Vol. 1, p. 179.

6. Wing-tsit Chan, <u>The Way of Lao Tzu</u>, chap. 1, pp. 6-10.

7. The term "universism" was coined by J. J. M. De Groot to define the characteristics of Chinese religion. See his <u>Religion in China</u> (London: Putnum, 1912); also see Joseph Kitagawa, <u>Religions of the East</u> (Philadelphia: Westminster, 1960), pp. 48-51.

8. See Ssu-ma Ch'ien, <u>Shih Chi</u>, Chapter 74.

9. See Chü Wang-li, <u>Hsien Chin Liang Han chih Yin-Yang Wu-hsing Hsieh-shou</u> (The Yin-Yang and Five Element Theories of Pre-Chin and Han dynasties).

10. <u>Kuan Tzu</u> is the writing attributed to Kuan Chung (管仲, +645 B.C.), but modern literal-critics argued that it must be a work of the third century B.C.

167

It contains the writings about many schools of thought
including Legalists, Tsoists, the Five Elements
theorists, etc.

11.Lu Shih Ch'un Ch'iu (呂氏春秋) is a compilation
of various schools of thought edited under the direction of Lü Pu-wei (呂不韋 +235 B.C.).

12. See chapter 3 of this book.

13. See chapter 14 of this book.

14. "Coincidentia Oppositorium," i.e., coincidence
of the oppositories, was the idea developed by Medieval
philosophers like the pseudo-Dionysius, Meister Eck-
hardt, and Nicholas of Cusa. See Mircea Eliade, Patterns in Comparative Religion, New York: Meridian,
1958), pp. 419-420.

15. Ch'en Meng-chia, Yin Shǔ P'u-ts'u Tsung Shu
(A Comprehensive Description of the Oracle Texts of
Yin Ruins), Science Press, Peking, 1956, pp. 582-594.
Akatsuka Kiyoshi, "Chiu ko-ku Ko-dai ni okeru Kaze no
Shinko to Gogyo-setsu" (The Belief in the Winds and
the Five Elements Theory in Ancient China) in Chiu-
Koku Kankei Ron-setsu Shiryo, Shukyo to Tetsugaku,
Vol. 19, pp. 418-441.

16. Joseph Needham, Science and Civilization in
China (London: Cambridge, University Press, 1956),
Vol. 2, p. 244. Needham's treatise on the "Funda-
mental Ideas of Chinese Science" in Chapter 13 is a
valuable reading for the understanding of Yin-Yang and
Five Element Theories and the Book of Changes.

17. Needham, Science and Civilization, p. 244.

18. See Eliade, Chapter 5, The Waters and Water
Symbolism.

19. Tung Chung-shu (179-104 B.C.) was a Confucian
philosopher of the Han dynasty. He synthesized the
Confucian ethics with the Five Elements Theory in his
work, Ch'un-ch'iu Fan-lu (春秋繁露) in 82 chapters.

20. Needham, Science and Civilization, p. 250.

21. It is interesting to notice that both the
first Ch'in emperor and first Han emperor tried to
claim themselves as the legitimate inheritor of the

Water Element predicted by Tso Yen.

22. Needham, <u>Science and Civilization</u>, p. 258.

23. The <u>I Ching</u>, or the <u>Book of Changes</u>, also known as <u>Chou I</u> (周易) or the <u>Chou Book of Changes</u>, contains an original tradition of divination practiced probably from the beginning of the Chou dynasty and Ten Appendices believed to be added by the Yin-Yang philosophers. Traditionally, its Eight Triagrams were believed to be made by either Fu Hsi, a mythic cultural hero, or King Wen, the founder of the Chou dynasty, its 64 hexagrams were believed to be made by either King Wen or Duke of Chou, his brother, and the Ten Appendices (Shih I 十翼) were ascribed to Confucius. However, modern literary critics generally regard the <u>Book of Changes</u> to be compiled around the third century B.C. although it may contain some archaic sources. The translation by James Legge and edited by Ch'u Chai, <u>I Ching</u> (Chicago: Bantam Books, 1964) is a good one.

24. See the foreword written by C. G. Jung in the translation of the <u>I Ching</u> by Richard Wilhelm (Princeton: Princeton University Press, 1950), pp. xxi-xxxix.

<u>Suggested Readings</u>

C. Y. Chang, <u>Creativity and Taoism</u> (New York: Julian Press, 1963).

Wing-tsit Chan, "Synthesis in Chinese Metaphysics," <u>The Chinese Mind</u>, ed. Charles A. Moore (Honolulu: University of Hawaii Press, 1967), pp. 132-148.

Thomé Fang, "The World and the Individual in Chinese Metaphysics," <u>The Chinese Mind</u>, ed. Charles A. Moore (Honolulu: University of Hawaii Press, 1967), pp. 238-263.

Hellmut Wilhelm, <u>Change, Eight Lectures on the I Ching</u>, tr. Cary F. Baynes (New York: Pantheon Books, 1960).

Alfred Forke, <u>The World-Conception of the Chinese</u> (London: Probsthain, 1925).

CHAPTER 7

HUMAN POSITION IN THE UNIVERSE

What is the origin of human life? Evolutionists
claimed that we evolved from earlier forms of life and
related to species such as apes and chimpanzees. But
others turned in another direction for guidance on the
origin of life, taking their cues from their religious
tradition which stressed the omnipotence of a creator
God. Long before the systematic observation of physical evidence and the birth of material science, man
sought to account for our spiritual origins, so that
the unseen world and supernatural evidence was considered valid as well. In the Book of Genesis, there
are two different mythic accounts about the origin of
human life (anthropogonic myth). One described man and
woman as being created by God according to His image
(Genesis 1:26), and the other is an account of God
making a human figure out of the soil and breathing
His breath into his nostrils to make a living person
(Genesis 2:7). In spite of their differences and the
existence of various different interpretations of the
meaning of the Image of God and the Breath of God, both
anthropogonic accounts emphasized that God is the ultimate origin of human life.

Now, let us examine the Chinese concept of the
origin of human life. Chinese seem not to be divided
by the evolutionist view and the Biblical view, but
take a cosmological or naturalistic viewpoint. In
simple terms, they believed that man was born from
the union of Heaven and Earth, and man is an integral
part of the universe. Therefore, they were more concerned about finding their proper position in the universe and seeking harmony with all beings in the universe rather than with origins. The following will
first introduce two accounts of anthropogonic myths
and then elaborate on the theme of human positions in
the universe expounded by various ancient Chinese religious thinkers.

The Origin of Human Life

We have two accounts of the myth of the origin of
human life in ancient China, one is preserved in the
P'an-ku myth and the other in the Myth of Nü Kua (女
媧). We have already seen the P'an-ku myth in chapter
5. It was after the creation of heaven, earth, the
sun and moon, the ocean and mountains, the plants and

climates through the transformation of the body of
P'an-ku that "the parasites on his body, impregnated
by the wind, became human beings."[1] From the point of
view of Christians who believed that human beings were
made according to the Image of God, and that of Evolutionists who believe that the great apes are our very
distant relatives, it is quite an insult to speak of
human ancestors who were the parasites. Clearly, it
implies very low esteem to the position of human beings
in the universe. However, to the Chinese, it seems to
indicate modesty and humility when they think about
the real significance of human beings in the universe.
Instead of arrogantly inflating human beings to be the
Glory of Creation and the Masters of the World, ancient Chinese were more moderate in acknowledging that
we human beings are but parasites which do not contribute a great deal to the universe, but adhere to the
universe and suck its resources, if not spoiling it
altogether. We are not much as producers nor creator
like the Heaven and Earth, but more of the dependents
and consumers like parasites. We see this modest acknowledgment of the smallness of human beings in the
universe that appeared in Chinese writings and land-
scape paintings.

However, even though the Chinese acknowledge the
insignificant position of human beings in the universe,
they still believe that human beings came ultimately
from the same One origin which is symbolized as the
body of P'an-ku. It is also important to note that
the whole universe is portrayed as a cosmic giant man
P'an-ku, and all things are but a part of his body.
Therefore, after all, Chinese were by no means looking
down upon the value of human beings. Instead, the
P'an-ku myth tried to demonstrate that the universe
and human beings are co-substantial and totally integrated. The universe is a "giant man" and human beings
are not necessarily the masters of the world, but significant representatives of the universe. Human beings
are different from other beings, but not isolated; they
are distinctive, but not separated. There is an integral and organic relationship that existed between
human beings and the universe. This is what the P'an-
ku myth symbolized.

The second anthropogonic myth is preserved in the
myth of Nü Kua, which is recorded in two writings:
Huai-nan Tzu and Feng-su T'ung-yi.

In ancient times, the four pillars [of

heaven] were destroyed, the nine continents
were torn apart, heaven could not cover the
whole earth, and the earth could not completely support heaven. Fires flamed up and
were not able to be extinguished. Waters
flooded over and were not able to be stopped.
Fierce beasts ate up the people and birds of
prey seized the old and the weak in their
claws.

Thereupon Nü Kua had fused together stones
of five colors to patch the azure heaven,
and cut off the feet of giant turtles to set
up four pillars. She had slaughtered the
Black Dragon in order to save the province of
Chi and collected the ashes of reeds to check
the wild waters. Thus the azure heaven was
repaired, the four corners rectified, the
wild waters checked, the province of Chi
pacified, the wild beasts killed, and the
good people lived.[2]

According to a folk legend, after the creation of heaven and earth, and before the existence of human beings, Nü Kua had patted
the yellow clay together to make human beings.
Because the work tasked her strength and left
her no leisure hours, so that she had then
dragged a string through mud and heaped it
up so as to mass produce human beings. This
was the reason why the rich and the noble are
those men made of yellow earth and those who
are poor and lowly were made from the cord-
dragging.[3]

   Here, the creation of human beings was made by Nü
Kua, a cultural heroine who repaired the damage of the
four pillars. Wang Ch'ung (A.D. 27-100) pointed out
that there was a cosmic warfare between Kung Kung and
Chuan-hsü, and Kung Kung blundered against Mount Pu-
chou causing the pillar of Heaven and the cord of Earth
to break off, for he was not able to take the throne
away from Chuan-hsü. This made Chinese astronomists
ponder upon the reason astral bodies of heaven tend
to move in a westerly direction and the rivers (of
China) tend to flow easterly toward the ocean. This
is called the theory of K'ai T'ien (蓋天說), and the
Nü Kua myth seemed to correspond with it. It is interesting to note that the Nü Kua myth is also similar to
the second Biblical account (the J creation story) in

which human beings were made from clay and the creator
was portrayed as a mason or potter, although Nü Kua
was female, while the creator God was male. Another
coincidence was that Nü Kua was also believed to be the
Goddess of marriage, because she was the first one to
institute this rite, like the creator God in the Bible
who was described as a match-maker bringing Eve to
Adam. Although the Nü Kua myth did not clearly state
it, the purpose for her creation of human beings must
have had something to do with her heavy work of re-
pairing the damaged universe, because she needed many
assistants and a great amount of manual labor. This
aspect of the myth is reflected historically in the
great demands of civil engineering in building the dams
and canals of the Yellow River and the Great Walls to
defend against the invasion of the northern barbarians
(symbolized by Kung Kung) in ancient China. In other
words, the Nü Kua myth tried to convey the message that
human beings are responsible and commissioned to partake with the soteriological work of Nü Kua for re-
pairing the damage caused by hostile forces. It was
rather unfortunate that this primary motif of indicating that labor is holy and soteriological was twisted
to explain the beginning of a two-class system: the
rich and poor, the noble and the common. However, the
image of man as worker in the Nü Kua myth is definitely
a step up from that of parasite in the P'an-ku myth.
Is it possible these two myths were asking us which
image of man we want to choose, parasite or worker?

The Nature of Man

After discussing the origin of human beings, let
us now see what ancient Chinese thought about the con-
stituency of humanness. The Book of Rites, perhaps,
stated it most succinctly, "Humanness is consistent of
benevolent virtue of Heaven and Earth, the co-operative
union of Yin and Yang, the joint assembly of ghost and
spirit, and the finest breath contained in the Five
Elements."[4] Since we have already discussed the cosmology of Yin-Yang and the Five Elements, we can understand that Chinese thought of human beings as the
finest co-operative production of the universe, and
that human beings contained the basic substance and
elements of the universe. However, in this statement,
it mentions something new, the joint assembly of ghosts
and spirits, Kuei Shen chih Hui (鬼神之會). What
are ghosts (Kuei) and spirits (Shen)? It is interesting to note that the Book of Rites mentioned that Tsai
Ngo, possibly a student of Confucius, asked his master,

"Sir, I have heard about 'Kuei and Shen,' but I do not
understand what they mean." Confucius answered him
saying:

> The Ch'i (氣 Breath) is the full manifesta-
> tion of the spirits [Shen], and the P'o
> [白鬼 ,Soul] is the full manifestation of the
> ghost [Kuei]. The harmony between Kuei and
> Shen is the highest tennet of my teachings.
> For all living beings are sure to die and
> return back to the soil after death. This
> "returning back" is what is meant by Kuei.
> While the bones and flesh buried under the
> ground shall mould mysteriously with the
> Earth, the Breath [Chi'i] shall issue forth
> and ascend above to become a Shinning Light
> [Chao Ming 昭明).[5]

We are not sure whether this was really the saying of
Confucius, but it definitely represented a Confucian
thought and a general understanding in ancient China.
What does this answer mean? It means that man has two
soul elements: Shen and Kuei. While Shen comes from
Heaven and appears in the form of Breath (Ch'i) and
contains the Yang force, Kuei comes from Earth and
appears in the form of bones and flesh and contains
the Yin force. At the time of birth, these two soul
elements became integrated, and at the time of death,
they dissolve. Then, after death, Shen goes back to
Heaven, which is also called Hun (云鬼). The character Hun has two radicals: 云 means "the cloud," and 鬼
means "returning," which implies that Hun is the state
in which Shen returns back to take the abode like the
cloud in Heaven. Kuei, after death, goes back to the
Earth and becomes P'o (白鬼). The character P'o has
two radicals: 白 means "white" and 鬼 means "returning,"
which implies that Kuei has returned to its intrinsic
and pristine state of Earth.

The Book of Rites continued to explain that two
sacrifices were also instituted in association with
these two soul-elements.

> After it was established that there are two
> constituent elements of the soul, two cere-
> monies were also instituted in order to show
> gratitude to them. The morning service
> which contained a burnt offering with the
> fragrance of the meat-dishes and the lighten-
> ing of aromatic wood was to show gratitude

to the Ch'i (Breath of Heaven). By this
ritual, the multitudes were taught to turn
their minds back to their primal origin.
And in order to express gratitude to the
P'o, the offerings of millet barley, together with dainties, livers, lungs, heads,
and hearts, libationed by two earthen jars
of aromatized spirits. This sacrifice is to
teach the people to love one another. Such
proper expression of affection and polite-
ness to the souls above and below are the
most important of rites.[6]

We shall elaborate more on the meaning and function of
Chinese ritual in later chapters, but we shall focus
here more on the further elaboration of the notion of
two soul-elements. Liu An, Prince of Huai-nan, who
lived three to four centuries after Confucius, did not
only carry over the Confucian notion of two soul-elements but also added their correlations with the Five
Elements.

Anciently, before the existence of Heaven
and Earth, there were only images but without physical shapes. They were deep, vague,
vast, immobile, impalpable and tranquil.
There was a hazy, infinite, unfathomable,
abysmal and vast deep to which no one knew
its door. Then two divinities appeared and
mingled with each other, regulating Heaven
and controlling Earth. Profound indeed! No
one can know where they ended. Vast indeed!
No one can know where they ceased. Thereupon they divided into the Yin and the Yang,
and permeated into the eight extremes of the
compass. While the hard and soft are mutually completing each other, the myriad
things have gradually acquired their forms.
The murky fluids took the forms of reptiles,
and the finer essence took the forms of
human beings. Hence what is spiritual belongs to Heaven, and what is physical belongs
to Earth. If the spiritual returns to its
door, and the physical returns to its root,
how can I continue to exist?. . .
     The spiritual is what is received from
Heaven, while the physical is what is endowed by Earth. Hence the saying: "Unity
produced Duality. Duality evolved into
Trinity, and Trinity evolved into the myriad

things. The things carry the Yin and embrace the Yang. It is on the blending of
the [Yin and Yang] breaths that their harmony depends." Therefore it is said: "In
the first month, there is a fertilizing
plaster; in the second month it has form;
in the third month, it has embryo; in the
fourth month, it has skin; in the fifth
month, it has muscle; in the sixth month, it
has bones; in the seventh month, it has completed the body; in the eighth month, it
started to move; in the ninth month, it stirs
and becomes restless; and in the tenth month,
it is born." Thus the bodily form being completed, the five viscera are also formed.
Hence the lungs regulate the eyes; the kidneys the nose; the gall the mouth; the liver
the ears. The senses are the outward regu-
lators while the vicera the inward regula-
tors. Their opening and closing, expansion
and contraction, each has its fixed rule.
Hence the roundness of the head imitates
Heaven, and the squareness of the foot imitates Earth. Like Heaven has four seasons,
Five Elements, nine divisions and 360 days,
human beings also have four limbs, five
viscera, nine orifices and 360 joints. Like
Heaven has wind, rain, cold and heat, human
beings also have the qualities of accepting,
giving, joy and anger. Therefore gall corresponds to clouds, the lung to vapor, the
spleen to wind, the kidneys to rain, and the
liver to thunder. Thus human beings form a
trinity with Heaven and Earth, and the human
mind is the master. Therefore the ears and
eyes are the sun and moon, and the humors of
the blood as wind and rain.
     The Way of Heaven and Earth is great
and vast; nevertheless they conserve their
brilliant light and preserve their spiritual
intelligence. How then can human ears and
eyes work long without taking rest? How can
human spirit ever speed on without exhausting
itself?[7]

In another passage he also said:

If we look back to antiquity, to the very
Beginning, human beings were born out of
Non-being and assumed form from Being.

Having form, human beings are conditioned by
things. But he who is able to revert to that
state out of which he was born, so as to be
as if he had never had physical form, is to
be called the True Man (chen jen 真人). The
True Man is he who is as if he had not yet
separated from the Great Unity (T'ai I 太乙).[8]

The <u>Pai Hu T'ung</u>, the collection of conversations
on the classics held by scholars in the White Tiger
Hall in A.D. 79, has a fiarly detailed description of
the correlations between the Five Elements and five
viscera and virtues of human beings.

What are the five viscera? They are the
liver, heart, lungs, kidneys, and spleen.
. . . Of these five viscera, the liver corresponds to love, the lungs to righteousness,
the heart to propriety, the kidneys to wisdom, and the spleen to good faith.
    How does the liver correspond to love?
For the liver is the essence of the element
of wood, and love also likes to be productive. The east is the quarter of wood and
the rising Yang, and the place where all
things are first born. Therefore the liver
resembles wood, being green in color having
branches and leaves. . . .
    How do the lungs correspond to righteous-
ness? For the lungs are the essence of the
element of metal, and righteousness is de-
terminative like the metal. The west is the
quarter of the metal and the place where all
things reached maturity and die. Therefore
the lungs resemble metal, being white in
color. . . .
    How does the heart correspond to pro-
priety? For the heart is the essence of the
element of fire. The quarter of fire is the
south, where the exaulted Yang holds a
higher position and the lowly Yin holds a
lower position. Propriety maintains social
differences between the exaulted and the
lowly. Therefore the heart resembles fire,
being red in color and pointed. . . .
    How do the kidneys correspond to wisdom?
For the kidneys are the essence of the element of water, and wisdom proceeds unceas-
ingly without any doubt or uncertainty.
Water likewise moves forward without

177

uncertainty. The north is the quarter of water and has black as its corresponding color. Therefore the kidneys are black in color. Water is Yin, and therefore the kidneys are two in number like Yin. . . .
How does the spleen correspond to good faith? For the spleen is the essence of the element of earth. The highest function of earth is to nourish all creatures so as to give them form. It produces creatures without partiality, which is the acme of good faith. Therefore the spleen resembles earth being yellow in color. . . .[9]

It is quite obvious that Chinese conceived that human organs, senses, and even moral character, are all endowed by the interaction between the Yin and Yang forces together with the combinations of the Five Elements. No doubt, human beings are the microcosm reflecting the macrocosm of the universe.

It is important to note that the Chinese view of human beings is neither materialistic nor spiritualistic, but rather a synthesis of both. Between the two spiritual forces of Yin and Yang and the Five material Elements, human beings were born to incorporate them into becoming organic beings. Thus, human beings are the union of body, soul(s), and spirit; and each one is essential to be human, and any lack of one of them will make human beings incomplete. The knowledge of this inner organism within human beings and its correlation with the large organism of the universe becomes the central theme in Chinese anthropology, and the technique of balancing the inner organism with the external organism becomes the main subject of Chinese education and religious disciplines. However, we may ask since Chinese think that all beings are but microcosm in correlation with macrocosm of the universe, and human beings are but a part of total cosmos, then what are the differences between human beings and other beings such as natural objects and animals and plants? In other words, is there any uniqueness or distinctiveness in human beings? Or exactly what is the position of human beings in the universe? The Chinese did believe that there was some distinctiveness in human beings and that there is a unique position that human beings occupy in the universe.

<u>Distinctiveness of Human Beings</u>
Lao Tzu, in his <u>Tao Te Ching</u>, mentioned that

178

there is a certain kind of virtue human beings received from the universal principle, Tao, that makes
human beings distinctive. He named it "Te" (德),
which is generally translated as "virtue." But the
ancient Chinese lexicon <u>Shou Wen</u> said that "te" was
originally written as 得 which means "to obtain."
Therefore, "te" could mean more specifically the special quality one has obtained from the universal principle. Thus he stated:

> Cultivate virtue in your own personality,
> Its virtue shall become authentic.
> Cultivate virtue in your family,
> Its virtue shall become overflowing.
> Cultivate virtue in your community,
> Its virtue shall become everlasting.
> Cultivate virtue in your country,
> Its virtue shall become abundant.
> Cultivate virtue in the whole world,
> Its virtue shall become universal.
>
> Therefore, contemplate your personality
>   through yourself.
> Contemplate your family through the family.
> Contemplate your community through the com-
>   munity.
> Contemplate your country through the country.
> And contemplate the whole world through the
>   world.
> How do I know this is to be the state of the
>   world?
> By such as it is.[10]

Lao Tzu believed that each individual person has
received a certain special personality from Tao, therefore, he encouraged each individual to cultivate his/
her virtue to be an authentic person. Likewise, he
believed that each family, each community and each
country has also received certain distinctive character from Tao, and each in its own way has to cultivate
that virtue. Virtue is the life principle given to
each being, appropriate for each being to be unique
and distinctive, therefore, each being has only to look
into its own being to discover its true self and complete its own personality. One cannot find one's own
selfhood in other beings or groups of beings. Chuang
Tzu also agreed with Lao Tzu and stated more clearly
that this distinctive individuational quality of human
beings is obtained from Tao.

179

> When things obtained that by which they came
> into existence, it was called their Te. . .
> Form without Tao cannot have existence. Ex-
> istence without Te cannot have manifesta-
> tion. . . .
> Tao is what all things (including man) fol-
> low. Te is what things individually ob-
> tain from it.[11]

However, both Lao Tzu and Chuang Tzu did not
specify what are the distinctive qualities of human
virtue that human beings have obtained from Tao. Instead, they tried to stress that human virtue is to
return back to Tao and conform with the universal
principle. They regarded the Confucian specification
on the distinctive virtue of human beings as already
an indication of departure or even disintegration from
the original Tao. Lao Tzu expounded:

> Superior virtue is not concerned with its
> virtue,
> Therefore it has true virtue.
> Inferior virtue never stops valuing its
> virtue,
> Therefore it has no true virtue.
> Hence only when Tao is lost,
> Then does the teaching of virtue arise.
> Only when virtue is lost,
> Then does the teaching of love arise.
> Only when love is lost,
> Then does the teaching of righteousness
> arise.
> Only when righteousness is lost,
> Then does the teaching of propriety arise.
> Now, propriety is a superficial expression
> of faithfulness
> And the beginning of disorder. . . .
>
> For this reason,
> The great man dwells upon the substantial
> rather than the superficial.
> He dwells upon reality rather than the il-
> lusionary.
> Indeed, he takes what is within and leaves
> what is without.[12]

This statement represents the Taoists' criticism
of Confucian ethics, indicating its inferiority and
its deviation from the original principles of Tao.
Confucian virtues such as love, righteousness,

propriety, wisdom, and faithfulness were regarded by
Taoists to be secondary and superficial, for they were
artificially created by a group of elite as a social
code imposed upon the people. Instead, true virtue is
to conform with Nature and to be simple, spontaneous,
pure, natural, and harmonious. Huai-nan Tzu said that
the True Man is "he who is able to revert to that state
out of which he was born: and is "he who is as if he
had not yet separated from the Great Unity."

However, Confucianists regarded this "revert to
that state out of which he was born" and "yet separated
from the Great Unity" to be a return to that nondiffer-
entiated and nondistinctive state which is Chaos. In
Chaos, human beings and other beings are comingled,
and the distinctiveness of human beings is undiscerible.
Since human beings are already born and separated from
the Great Unity, and human beings had obtained from
Tao their individuational principle, Confucianists made
their endeavor to discover what were the distinctive
virtues or qualities that made human beings unique and
then to discover the special position of human beings
in this vast universe.

Confucius was the first one to state that what
makes human beings human is Jen (仁), translated variously as human-heartedness, human-relatedness, love,
charity, humanity, morality, etc. The word Jen in
Chinese 仁 is composed of two radicals: 亻 which means
"human being," and 二 which means "two." Thus, it con-
notes all the moral qualities which govern the relationships between two human beings. Etymologically,
it is to be translated simply as human-relatedness,
but philosophically, that human-relatedness should be
defined specifically as morality or love as the cardinal principle of human relationships. The <u>Lun Yü</u>
recorded a conversation between Confucius and his disciple, "Once when Fan Chih asked the meaning of Jen,
the Master replied: 'It is to love your fellow men.'"[13]
Tseng Tzu, a disciple of Confucius understood Jen to
be conscientiousness (<u>chung</u> 忠) and altruism (<u>shu</u> 恕).
The <u>Lun Yü</u> continued:

> The Master said: "Shen! My teaching contains
> one all pervading principle." "Yes, Sir"
> replied Tseng Tzu. After the Master had left
> the room the other disciples asked: "What did
> he mean?" Tseng Tzu replied: "Our Master's
> teaching is conscientiousness (chung) and
> altruism (shu), and nothing else."[14]

In other words, Tseng Tzu understood that Jen, as the
prevading principle of Confucius' teachings, is conscientiousness and altruism. The Chinese word for
conscientiousness is chung (忠) which means literally
both "honest to oneself" and "faithful to others."
Thus, Confucius advised that "Desiring to maintain
oneself, one should sustain others; desiring to develop
oneself, one should develop others." The Chinese word
for altruism is shu (恕) which literally means "having
a heart like others would have." Thus, Confucius
taught "Do not do to others what you do not like your-
self." Both chung and shu are to express the mutuality
and reciprocity in human relationships and two modes
of practices of Jen. Confucius sometimes used Jen to
include all the human virtues and morality.

> Once, Tsu Chang asked Confucius the meaning
> of Jen, whereupon Confucius replied: "To be
> able to carry five things into practice wher-
> ever one goes constitutes Jen." On begging
> to know what the five things were, he was
> told: "They are respect, tolerance, faithful-
> ness, earnestness and gracefulness. With re-
> spect you will avoid insult; with tolerance
> you will win over everyone; with faithfulness
> men will trust you; with earnestness you will
> have achievement; and with gracefulness you
> will be fitted to command others."[15]

Thus, Jen included many different virtues and summarized them into one single moral principle to indicate
the distinctive quality of human beings.

Mencius (372-289 B.C.), the most distinguished
Confucian philosopher next to Confucius, further elaborated on the distinctive quality of human beings. He
tried to explain why the virtues of love, righteousness, propriety, and wisdom should be fundamental qualities of human beings because he said:

> All human beings have a mind which cannot
> bear to see the sufferings of others. . . .
> If today some suddenly sees a child about to
> fall into a well, he/she will without ex-
> ception experience a feeling of urgency and
> anxiety. This feeling is not caused because
> he/she wants to gain the favor of the child's
> parents, nor to obtain high praise from neigh-
> bors and friends, nor to be afraid of a bad
> reputation if he/she did not rescue the

child.

From this case we can perceive that he/
she who lacks the feeling of commisseration
(ts'e yin 惻隱) is not a human being; that
he/she who lacks a feeling of shame (hsiu wu
羞惡) is not a human being; that he/she who
lacks a feeling of modesty (tz'u jang 辭讓)
is not a human geing; and he/she who lacks
a sense of right and wrong (shih fei 是非)
is not a human being.

The feeling of commisseration is the
beginning of human-relatedness (jen). The
feeling of shame is the beginning of righteousness (i). The feeling of modesty is the
beginning of propriety (li 禮). The sense
of right and wrong is the beginning of wisdom (chih 智).[16]

In another passage, he also said:

The feeling of commisseration belongs to all
human beings; so does that of shame; that of
reverence and respect; and that of right and
wrong. . . . These are not fused into us
from without. We originally are possessed
of them.[17]

That whereby human beings differ from
the birds and beasts is but slight. The
mass of people cast it away, whereas the
Superior Man preserves it.[18]

What makes human beings different from animals is
morality which has the virtues of love or commiseration,
righteousness, propriety, and wisdom. This moral quality is the essence of humanity, and it is, according
to Mencius, innate and intrinsic to human nature. Human beings are capable of doing good because such moral
possibility or potentiality has been inherent in human
nature. Without it, there would be no difference between human beings and animals. Besides moral qualities, Mencius also regarded the human mind, which can
distinguish good from evil and right from wrong, as
the distinctive nature of human beings. Like Aristotle mentioned in his Ethics, reason humans possess
is the fact which differentiates human beings from
animals. Mencius also stated that the human mind
capable of reasoning is the special prerogative of
human beings.

The senses of hearing and seeing do not
think, but are obscured by external things.
When a thing comes into contact with one of
the senses, it simply responds impulsively.
But the faculty of the mind is thinking. By
thinking, it holds the corrective view of
things, whereas without thinking, it fails
to do so. This mind is what Heaven has given
to us. Therefore, let a human being first
establish firmly this noble part of his constitution, so that the inferior part will
not be able to lead him. It is simply this
mind that constitutes the great human being.[19]

Like men's mouths agree in having the
same relishes; their ears agree in enjoying
the same sounds; their eyes agree in recog-
nizing the same beauty, so their minds shall
agree to the same principle. What is it,
then, that they approve similarly? I say it
is the principle of reason (li 理) and of
righteousness (i 義).[20]

Mencius says again:

Human-heartedness (Jen) is the mind of human
beings; righteousness is the path of human
conducts.[21]

Mencius believed that all human beings have inherited this innate good nature of moral quality and
rational mind from the beginnings of their birth and,
therefore, all human beings are equally capable of becoming sages like the ancient sages Yao and Shun.
However, he also acknowledged that for some human
beings, this innate quality is underdeveloped and de-
teriorated due to various causes; while for some human
beings, it is highly developed and improved. The
causes of such difference in subsequent development
will be discussed more fully in the chapter on the
problem of Good and Evil; but in this chapter, it is
important to note that Mencius had emphasized that this
distinctive human quality is given by Heaven. He believed in the close relationship between Heaven and the
goodness of human nature. While Heaven is the metaphysical source and basis of the moral quality of human
beings, epistemologically, human beings know Heaven
through the morality and rationality in human nature.

He who has exercised his mind to the utmost,

knows his nature. Knowing his nature, he
knows Heaven. To keep one's mind preserved
and nourished one's nature is the way to
serve Heaven. To be without doubleness of
mind, whether one is to have an untimely
death or long life; and having cultivated
one's personal character, to wait with this
for whatever there may be: this is to stand
in accord with the Mandate (ming 命).[22]

It is not depending on the revelation of God that
one knows the distinctive nature of human beings and
ultimate origin of all things, but by introspection
within one's own nature, for such thought and mind are
given by Heaven. In other words, there is an essential
unity between human nature and the universe so that
knowing one of them will lead to knowing the other.

All things are complete within us. There is
no greater delight than to find sincerity
when one examines oneself. If one acts with
a vigorous effort of altruism in one's seeking for human-heartedness, nothing will be
closer to one.[23]

We can detect certain mystical elements in Mencius'
statement, for he said that "all things are complete
within us," which implies that we are essentially one
with the universe. Here, we see that both Taoism and
Confucianism had embraced certain mysticisms in their
understanding of the close relationship between the
universe and human beings. While Lao Tzu and Chuang
Tzu were describing it as the union between Tao and
Te, Confucius and Mencius were describing it as the
union between Heaven and Human Nature. Fung Yi-lan
pointed out this common mystical element more succintly
in the following statement.

In China, the school of Mencius in Confucianism, and the school of Chuang Tzu in Taoism,
have both mysticism as the supreme state,
and mystical experience as the highest aim
of individual self-cultivation. The methods
used by these two schools to attain this
supreme state and aim have differed, however.
Through a life of "pure experience" to forget the self: this has been the Taoist method.
Through "the work of Love" [a term used by
Schopenhauer] to get rid of selfishness:
this has been that of the Confucians. Being

without self and without selfishness, the
individual can become one with the universe.[24]

Mencius called this mystical force which unites
human nature with the universe Vitality of Cosmis Air
(huo jan chih ch'i 浩然之氣).

> Such is the Cosmic Air (ch'i 氣): it is
> most great and most strong. Being nourished
> by uprightness, and sustaining no injury, it
> fills up all between Heaven and Earth. . . .
> Such is the Cosmic Air: it is the cor-
> relate of righteousness and the universal
> principle [Tao]. Without it, humanness is
> in a state of starvation. It is produced by
> the accumulation of righteous deeds, and not
> to be obtained by incidental acts of right-
> eousness. If one's mind does not feel sat-
> isfaction in one's conduct, there results
> this state of starvation.[25]

We shall come back to the mysticism of Mencius
later on, but it is sufficient to note here that what
Confucius had distinguished to be the distinctive quality of human beings, namely Jen, was further developed
by Mencius to become not only the uniqueness of humanness but also the ultimate link between the universe
and human beings. In other words, the distinctiveness
of humanness lies in knowing the moral quality and
rational mind within human nature. A human being becomes genuinely human when an individual realizes one's
distinctive nature and cultivates one's moral quality
in aspiration for the final unity between humanness
and the universe.

<u>Human Position in the Universe</u>

As we have already made a survey of Chinese understanding of the origin and nature of humanness and
the distinctiveness of human nature, let us also see
how ancient Chinese understood the human position in
the universe and discover the special role human beings
have to play. We can find this theme well stated in
the writings of Tung Chung-shu (179-104 B.C.), a great
Confucianist who synthesized the ideas of the schools
of Yin-Yang, Five Elements, and Taoism with Confucian
ethics.

He carried over the cosmology of Yin-Yang and
stated that human beings were not only one of the
creations from the union of Yin and Yang but were also

186

the noblest and finest parts of all creation.

> Nothing is more refined than the cosmic airs
> of Yin and Yang, for they are richer than
> Earth and more spiritual than Heaven. Of the
> creatures born from the refined essence
> (ching 精) of Heaven and Earth, one is more
> noble than human beings.
> Human beings receive the decree [ming]
> of Heaven, and therefore are loftier than
> other creatures. Other creatures have suf-
> fered troubles and distress and are incapable
> of unifying themselves with Heaven and Earth;
> only human beings are capable of so doing.[26]

Tung Chung-shu not only believed that human beings
had uniquely inherited a refined essence from Yin-Yang
and Heaven-Earth but also that the physical form and
structure of the human body have great resemblances
with Heaven and Earth.

> Man has 360 joints, which matches the
> number of Heaven (the days of the year). The
> Human body, with its bones and flesh, matches
> the thickness of Earth. Man has ears and
> eyes above, with their capacity for hearing
> and seeing, which corresponds to the forms of
> the sun and moon. The Human body has its
> orifices and veins, which correspond to the
> forms of rivers and valleys. The Human heart
> has its sadness and pleasure, joy and anger,
> which are in parallel with the spirit-like
> feelings of Heaven. When we observe the
> Human body, how much loftier it is than that
> of any other creature. . . .
> Other creatures derive their life from
> Heaven's Yin and Yang in a recumbent posi-
> tion, whereas Man bears brilliantly its mark-
> ings. Thus it is that among all other crea-
> tures, there are none that do not move about
> in recumbent position; only Man faces Heaven
> directly, with head erect and upright pos-
> ture. In this way, those who receive less
> from Heaven and Earth face them in a recum-
> bent position, whereas one who receives more
> faces them directly. Herein may be seen hu-
> man distinction from other creatures and how
> Man is to be equated with Heaven and Earth.
> In the physical form of Man, for this
> reason, the human head is large and round,

like Heaven's countenance. Human hair is
like the stars and constellations. Human
ears and eyes, with their brilliance, are
like the sun and moon. Human nostrils and
mouth, with their breathing, are like the
wind. The penetrating understanding that
lies within the human breast is like the
spiritual intelligence of Heaven. The human abdomen and womb, now full and then
empty, are like the hundred creatures. . . .
     The symbols of Heaven and Earth, and
the correspondences between the Yin and Yang,
are also established in the human body. The
body is like Heaven, and its numerical categories correspond with those of the latter,
so that its life is linked with the latter.
With the number of days that fills a year,
Heaven gives form to the human body. Thus
the 366 lesser joints of the body correspond
to the number of days in a year, and twelve
divisions of the larger joints correspond to
the number of months. Within the body there
are five visceras, which correspond in number to the Five Elements. Externally there
are four limbs, which correspond in number
to the four seasons. The alternating opening and closing of the eyes correspond to
day and night. The alternation of hardness
and softness corresponds to winter and summer. The alternation of sadness and pleasure corresponds to the Yin and Yang. The
mind possesses the power of thinking, which
corresponds to Heaven's power of deliberation and calculation. Human conduct follows
the principle of proper relationships, which
corresponds to the relationship between
Heaven and Earth. . . .
     In what may be numbered, there is a
correspondence in number. In what may not
be numbered, there is a correspondence of
Man with Heaven.[27]

     If, as the Bible claims, man was created by God
according to the image and likeness of God (Imago Dei),
then perhaps we can say that Tung Chung-shu was saying
that man was created by the universe according to the
image and likeness of the universe. While the Bible
did not elaborate on what the image and likeness meant,
Tung identified man as physically similar to, and
structurally corresponding to, the universe. The

emphasis is that man is the zenith of creation and the
representative of the universe. Moreover, it was not
only the physical similarity and structural correspondence but also the moral quality and rationality
that the human being has received from Heaven that
makes man distinctive and unique among all the creatures. As explained by Tung:

> Man cannot create Man, for the creator of
> Man is Heaven. The fact is that human beings
> can become human only by the power of Hea-
> ven. Heaven is indeed the supreme ancestor
> of Man. This is why Men are to be classified
> with Heaven above. The human body is formed
> through the transforming influence of the
> numerical categories of Heaven. Human vigor
> is directed to love (Jen) through the trans-
> forming influence of Heaven's will (chih 志).
> Human moral conduct is expressed in right-
> eousness through the transforming influence
> of Heaven's rational principle (li 理).
> Human likes and dislikes are influenced by
> Heaven's warmth and purity. Human joy and
> anger are influenced by Heaven's cold and
> heat. . . . The duplicate of Heaven lies in
> Man, and human feelings and nature derive
> from Heaven.[28]

In this passage, Tung Chung-shu clearly states his
strong belief in the religious foundation of human
morality and rationality. Even being human itself or
humanity itself is regarded as Heavenly given and not
made by human beings. Human capacity to love is not
simply innate but must be strengthened by the will of
Heaven. Human courage to act morally is not only implanted but is also reinforced by the Heavenly principle of reason. At times in this passage, Heaven may
be depicted as a creator or ancestor; while at other
times, it may be depicted as a natural phenomenon,
such as cold and heat, but to Tung Chung-shu, Heaven is
"one" who created man according to the image of his
physical form and cosmic structure and also endowed
them with his personal traits and moral quality. There
is no dichotomy within Heaven himself, his natural
forces and moral vitalities, cosmological structure and
rational principle are all totally integrated. The
following statement of Tung Chung-shu is not much different from the saying of Jesus: "God is Love, therefore you shall love one another."

The beautiful expression of love (Jen 仁)
lies in Heaven, for Heaven is love. Heaven
generates and produces all creatures, pro-
tects and shelters them, and nourishes and
forms them. Its works are continuous and
endless; when it reaches to the end [of its
cycle], it returns again to its beginning.
And everything that it produces it hands over
to human beings for their cares. If we want
to examine the purpose of Heaven, we shall
see that it is boundless and infinitely loving. Human beings, receiving their lives
from Heaven, receive likewise from it love
and are thereby themselves loving. Therefore
human beings . . . possess the family relationships of father and son, elder brother
and younger brother, and their hearts are one
of loyality, good, faith, kindliness, incor-
ruptibility, and blameless, and they make
decisions as to what is right or wrong, proper or improper. Their cultured principles
are obvious and abundant, and their knowledges
broad and extensive.[29]

Man is created by this Heaven of Love, and received
from Him a special nature and quality, so that Man
should govern his actions according to the Way of Heaven. Tung said it more emphatically:

Human beings have received life from Heaven
in a manner markedly different from that of
the great mass of living creatures. Within
the home, they have the family relationships
of father and son, elder and younger brothers.
Outside, they have the social relationships
of ruler and subject, superior and inferior.
In their social contacts there are for them
ways of manifesting the distinction between
the aged and the young. They possess clearly
marked patterns for their social intercourse
and joyful displays of affection in their
love toward others.
    Therefore Confucius has said: "Of all
creatures with their different natures produced by Heaven and Earth, human beings are
the noblest." Understanding their heavenly
nature, they know themselves to be nobler
than other creatures. By knowing themselves
to be nobler than other creatures, they come
to know love and righteousness. This is what

190

Confucius meant when he said: "He who does
not understand the Decree of Heaven cannot
become a superior man."[30]

Superior Man(Chün tzu君子) is the ideal image of man in
Confucianism, which we will discuss further in chapter
10; in this chapter, however, our purpose is to note
the importance of Tung's understanding of an ideal man
as the one who knows one's distinctive nature and position in the universe and conducts one's life in accordance with the decree of Heaven. Briefly, Tung mentioned that man is set within the context of human-
social relationships and relationships with vegetation
and animals, and that human beings should maintain an
orderly relationship with their environment, as well
as with other human beings. Each human being has his/
her distinctive position in family and society according to different situations and circumstances, and he/
she should know it distinctively and behave accordingly.
For example, while at home, you are a son to your parents, a brother to your brothers and siters; but in
society, you are a friend to your friends, and a young
citizen of the nation, and a junion member of a company, etc. And in each different position you are in,
you have a special duty, as well as privilege associated with that position to perform accordingly. In
addition, human relationships are mutual and recipro-
cal; while you have received something, you are supposed to give something in return. Likewise, while
man is fed and nourished by the environment, he also
has the duty to take good care of the environment as
well. Thus, the understanding of human-relatedness
(Jen) and the principle of faithfulness and altruism
becomes essential to be human in Tung Chung-shu's
teachings. Like many other Chinese thinkers who loved
to apply their metaphysics and ethics to political
science, Tung also extended his understanding of the
distinctiveness of the human position in the universe
to his political ideals. In other words, he thought
that the king, as the head of state, should also be an
exemplary model of a human being who knows one's unique
position and role in the universe.

> Heaven has endowed humankind with a nature
> containing the "basic stuff" of goodness, but
> human beings are unable to do good by them-
> selves. Therefore a monarchy [or kingship]
> was established to promote such good conducts.
> This is one of Heaven's purposes. . . .
> The kings, being entrusted by Heaven

with the task of ruling the people, hold a
lofty position and heavy responsibility.
. . . The ancient sages invented the writing
of the word "Wang" (王) by drawing three
horizontal lines which were connected
through the center by a vertical stroke to
mean a king. These three horizontal lines
signify the realms of Heaven, Earth and Man,
and the central vertical line signifies the
interrelationship of three realms. . . .
Therefore the kings should model themselves
on Heaven. . . . They should model on the
will of Heaven and commit themselves to
love (Jen 仁).[31]

Etymologically, Tung's interpretation of the word
"King" (Wang 王) might be false, for in the Shang oracle texts, it appeared as 大, which depicts a man
wearing a crown standing erect on the ground with out-
stretched arms and legs to demonstrate his greatness
(the word 大 indicates greatness). But, since by the
time of Tung, the word king was written as 王, Tung was
right in interpreting that king is the one who stands
at the center of the universe which is represented by
three horizontal lines of Heaven, Man, and Earth, and
the king's role is to unite all three realms in harmony
at the center, which is represented by the vertical
line. There is no better script to illustrate most
realistically and vividly the unique position a king
should assume and the most ideal position any human
being could occupy. It is the most simply symbol of
axis mundi, the center of the universe. It contains
the symbolism of the cross, which is the sacred symbol
of Christianity, illustrating the centering of divine-
human encounters. But the Chinese symbol of Wang
demonstrates the correspondence and union among the
three realms of the total cosmos: Heaven, Man, and Earth.
The king is understood to be the mediator between Heaven
and Earth and human beings, and his primary role is to
maintain the harmony of the universe. Tung also emphasized that the government was instituted to enhance
this goal, and the primary duties of government officials were to assist the king in advancing such harmony. This is the reason why the king was called the
son of Heaven and he was to be both a high priest and
a political leader. In ancient China, religion and
politics are inseparable, very often the identification
of them is regarded as ideal in government. The king
is regarded not only as a privileged individual but is
also the paradigm of human beings in the universe, and

the word 王 represents its ideal image.

1. The description of human beings as parasites could be an interpolation added to the P'an-ku myth. However, it is quite common among the ancient anthropogonies to describe the birth of human beings in such lowly positions and humble origin. For example, the Summerian myth described the first human beings created by gods as rather abnormal, sick, weak, and feeble in body and spirit, and lifeless creatures. See Samuel N. Krammer, "Mythology of Sumer and Akkad," in Mythologies of the Ancient World, ed. Samuel N. Krammer (New York: Doubleday, 1961), pp. 103-105.

2. Huai-nan Tzu, Lan-mi Hsün (淮南子, 覽冥訓).

3. Feng-su T'ung-yi (Comprehensive Interpretation of Customs) in T'ai-p'ing Yü-lan, 78). (風俗通義, 太平御覽).

4. The Book of Rites, Li Yün III (禮記)

5. The Book of Rites, Chi-Yi, II.

6. The Book of Rites, Chi-Yi, II.

7. Huai-nan Tzu, Hung-lieh, VII.

8. Huai-nan Tzu, XIV.

9. Pai Hu T'ung (白虎通).

10. Tao Te Ching, Chap. 54.

11. Chuang Tzu, Chap. 12.

12. Tao Te Ching, Chap. 38.

13. Lun Yü, XII, 22.

14. Lun Yü, IV, 15.

15. Lun Yü, XVII, 6.

16. Mencius, IIa, 6.

17. Mencius, VIIa, 6.

18. Mencius, IVb, 19.

19. *Mencius*, VIa, 15.

20. *Mencius*, VIa, 7.

21. *Mencius*, VIa, 11.

22. *Mencius*, VIIa, 1.

23. *Mencius*, VIIa, 4.

24. Fung Yi-lan, *A History of Chinese Philosophy* (Princeton: Princeton University Press, 1952), vol. I, p. 130.

25. *Mencius*, IIa, 2.

26. *Ch'un-ch'iu Fan-lu*, Chap. 56.

27. *Ch'un-ch'iu Fan-lu*, 13.2-4.

28. *Ch'un-ch'iu Fan-lu*, 11.1.

29. *Ch'un-ch'iu Fan-lu*, ii.9-10.

30. *Ch'ien Han Shu*, 56.16 (前漢書).

31. *Ch'un-ch'iu Fan-lu*, 11.9.

Suggested Readings

Thomé Fang, *The Chinese View of Life: The Philosophy of Comprehensive Harmony* (Hong Kong: The Union Press, 1957).

Donald J. Munro, *The Concept of Man in Early China* (Stanford, CA: Stanford University Press, 1968).

Wing-tsit Chan, "The Concept of Man in Chinese Thought," *The Concept of Man: A Study in Comparative Philosophy*, ed. P. T. Raju (London: Allen and Unwin, 1960), pp. 158-205.

CHAPTER 8

THE SEARCH FOR AUTHENTIC SELFHOOD

What is the position of an individual in society and the world? Is selfhood of any significance in the universe? How much right does an individual have in society? How does an individual relate to his/her society and the world? These are very important questions raised in Chinese religious tradition. Chinese society has been viewed as a collective society where little individuality is acknowledged. In a large family system, an individual is regarded simply as a member of a family and counted according to rank as the first son, first daughter, second son, second daughter, and so forth. It is the family name that is most often used and not the personal name. Chinese children were taught to remember that they are a member of the family and whatever they do, either good or bad, shall affect their family. Personal handwritten signatures were not officially acknowledged, instead the chop-seal was authorized. For so long, Chinese people were governed by an autocratic monarchy supported by a literate bureaucracy so that the ideal of self-independence and creativity of the individual was discouraged.

It is true that Chinese people are comparatively more family oriented and collectively conscious, but it does not mean that they negate the existence of individuality and the significance of selfhood. Instead, we shall see that Chinese have struggled from ancient times searching for the integrity of selfhood and harmonious relationships among individuals, society, and the world. The main focus of this chapter will be to define the ways in which Chinese people searched for the identity of the individual and their understanding of the significance of selfhood. In doing so, we will confine our descriptions to the period of the earliest history, namely, the time of the Shang dynasty through the Han dynasty.

The Status of the Individual in the Shang and Early Chou Dynasties

From the great archaeological discoveries of the ancient ruins of the Shang capital Yin (殷), we are now more well informed about the imperial structure and social formation of the Shang dynasty than ancient Chinese historians who had to depend on oral tradition for their information. The central administration of

the Shang dynasty is, of course, governed by the Shang
kings. The Shang kings had established their authority
by military conquests of their neighboring tribes and
consolidation by royal marriage with families of tribal chiefs. Many tribal chiefs thus became the subordinates of the king or the vassals who paid regular
tributes to the king, and maintained military alliance with the central authority. The Shang kings were
also regarded as the priest-kings, for they were the
sole descendants of former kings and the only ones
qualified to offer sacrifice to them. They performed
divination to receive oracles from their deceased royal
ancestors. They were also sacred kings, since they
were the only ones who could mediate between their people and the supreme God Ti (帝) through the interces-
sion of their royal ancestors. Thus, in the Shang oracle inscriptions, they claimed themselves as "I am the
Only One" (Yu I Jen 余乙人). In order to augment their
autocracy with divine sanction, they performed quite
extensive divination and even ordered their diviners to
inscribe oracle records on bones and tortoise-shells.
From these more than one-hundred-thousand pieces of
such oracle inscriptions, we begin to realize that
there were well-established sacrificial systems and
ritual calendars made by the Shang kings and an incredi-
ble numbers of animals slaughtered for royal sacrifices to the deceased royal ancestors and gods and
goddesses in the pantheon of Ti. Moreover, the arche-
ologists who have dug out the foundations of the royal
court--possibly the royal ancestral shrine as well--
and the royal tombs, had also discovered that a tremendous number of human sacrifices and companion burials
were conducted by Shang kings. More than a thousand
of these human sacrifices had their heads cut off from
their bodies and buried separately under the tomb pits
and house foundations. Some soldiers and subordinates
were apparently buried alive with their uniforms and
armor. There was even a horse-driven chariot and
horses unearthed from the pit of a royal tomb. It is
comparable to the ancient Pharaohs of Egypt and kings
of Mesopotamia, who, for the sacredness of kingship,
conducted an enormous number of sacrifices both human
and animal in order to consecrate the king and to appease the divinity.

Because of such tremendous practices of human
sacrifices conducted by the Shang kings, many Sinologists, especially the Communist Sinologists, have
designated and condemned the Shang society as a "slave-
society." Apparently these slaves were prisoners-of-

war and their descendants, and were at the lowest
status level of Shang society. Archaeologists found
that they lived in cave pits dug from the outscart
hillsides and had almost nothing of their own belong-
ings. They were entirely at the mercy of the Shang
kings, nobles, and landlords and were sold, exchanged,
and traded like merchandise. They were forced into
hard labor and treated inhumanely without welfare and
recreation. The male slaves were called Chen (臣) and
female slaves were called Chieh (妾), and they were
commonly called Chung Jen (眾人), namely, the multitude.

Soldiers in the Shang society were not much better
off than these slaves. Of course, their position was
higher than slaves and they wore uniforms and armor,
engaged in warfare, and accompanied the royal hunts,
but they were at the mercy of Shang kings and ruling
nobles as well. They were not only under the total
command of their superiors while they were alive, but
when their superiors died, they were forced to be
buried alive, still wearing their uniforms. Sometimes
even 10 percent of the whole troop was buried alive
to accompany their superiors in their journey to the
next world. Under such dictatorship and inhumane
treatment, it is no wonder that we have seen many
records in the oracle inscriptions about the rebellions and insurrections among vassals, subordinates,
and distant tribes, and innumerable oracle inquiries
made by the Shang kings about the military campaigns
to subdue rebellions. Among these records, the name
of the Ch'iang tribe (姜方) appeared most often. They
had the largest number of slaves exploited by the
Shang kings and were also the greatest number of humans victimized in the royal sacrifices. The historians also told us that it was the alliance of this
Ch'iang tribe and the Chou tribe that finally over-
threw the Shang dynasty and established the Chou dynasty in 1111 B.C.

The Book of History preserved some records about
the vices and corruption of the Shang rulers who exploited their people, levying heavy taxes, being ex-
traordinarily luxurious in their living style, with
constant enjoyment of hunting, feasting, and drinking.
Nobility surrounded themselves with women and enjoyed
sex orgies; the seductions of evil queens and their
consorts were often blamed for the fall of the dynasty.

King Wen (文王), the chief of the Chou tribe,

finally rose in rebellion against the Shang, rallying
behind him an alliance of the dissident tribes from the
Western part of Shang empire, but he became ill and
died without completing his will. His son, King Wu
(武王) succeeded him and engaged in his final battle
at the Field of Mu (牧野), forcing Shang King Hsin
(帝辛) to commit suicide by setting fire to himself in
his royal palace. Thus, was the Shang dynasty over-
thrown in 1111 B.C. In order to pacify the survivors
of Shang, King Wu appointed the son of Shang King Hsin,
Lu Fu (祿父) to head the fief of the old Shang territory and appointed two of his own brothers to watch
over him. But, unfortunately, King Wu died two years
later, and his young son, King Cheng, succeeded him,
assisted by Duke Chou (周公), the brother of King Wu.
Seeing weakness in the central authority, Lu Fu and
two brothers of King Wu rose in rebellion against the
new king, but they were soon suppressed by an army led
by Duke Chou. It took time for the new dynasty to establish itself and to pacify the new domain, but once
it had settled, the Chou dynasty made great success in
expanding its territory and strengthening its central
authority and fiefdom. Duke Chou made two significant
changes in the governmental system and social structure.

First, he established a feudal system by appoint-
ing members of the royal family as Dukes, Marquis, Earls,
Viscounts, and Barons to govern the divided fiefs. Besides the main capital Chung Chou (宗周) in the home
state, Duke Chou also built a new sub-capital at Cheng
Chou (成宗) in the east to oversee the eastern region.
He allowed feudal lords to independently govern their
fiefs with the condition that they would pay homage
and bring tribute to the central authority, and supply
the military in times of emergency. He recognized that
it was impossible and also outdated to govern such a
larger territory with a single autocratic power. Thus,
a certain form of "government by consent" was shaped in
the early Chou dynasty which distinguished it from the
rule of the Shang. In this new feudal kingdom, the
process of decision making had gradually become more
democratic. A cabinet was instituted to assist the
king for decision making at the ruling center and an
assembly of feudal lords was summoned from time to time
to consult and make decisions on significant matters of
the whole kingdom. While each fief had obtained its
relative independence, the feudal lords also realized
that they had to invite the local nobles, powerful
landlords, wealthy merchants, and even military officers and government officials for consultaion and

decision making on matters of the local fief. At the
time of a national or local emergency, the whole male
population was even summoned to the city gate to make
a major decision for engagement in warfare.

     Second, along with gradual democratization, Duke
Chou also made a radical change in the theocratic
monarchy of the Shang by announcing the kingly rule
under "the mandate of Heaven" which was based on morality rather than hereditary and military force. The
mandate of Heaven is not a priori of kingship, but conditioned under the terms of the moral conduct and self-
discipline of the king. In other words, the Shang King
Hsin (辛) lost his mandate because of his vicious rule
and moral corruption, but the Chou kings obtained the
mandate because of the virtues of King Wen and King Wu
and their conscientious care of the people. Thus, the
practice of divination which was monopolized by the
Shang kings stopped, and government based on the
"Principle of Propriety" (Li Chih 禮制) was instituted.
In the new system of Propriety, the moral disciplines,
administrative duties, hierarchical status of the king,
feudal lord, government officials, and the duties of
citizens were clearly specified. Of course, sacrifices
to the ancestors and supreme God and his pantheon were
still continued, but magical theocracy was replaced by
a morally responsible monarchy and feudal system. The
Book of Rites and the Book of Ceremonies have still
preserved for us the valuable records of this "Propriety System." They prescribed the Rites of Capping
(Initiation), Wedding, Funeral, Court Diplomacy, Military and Communal Fellowship, etc. These rituals were
no longer the monopoly of the king, but to be participated by all members involved in government, arranged
according to rank and order, and performed with elegance
and precision in public places. The name of God was
even gradually changed from Ti to T'ien (Heaven) in
order to dissociate from the notion of Ti as patron
deity of the Shang royal house, and to stress the
transcendental and moral character of God as Heaven.
T'ien was worshipped as a "personal" God who had strong
moral concern for the moral behavior of the ruler and
the welfare of the ruled. This was truly a great reformation brought about by Duke Chou and the early kings
of the Chou dynasty.

     However, the fate of those slaves and landless
peasants, spoken of earlier, was not radically improved. Many of them were simply handed over to the
new ruler and new taskmasters who treated them as a

part of the spoils. There is a debate among the Communist scholars in the People's Republic of China about whether the Chou society was still a "slave-society" or a "feudal society." There is no consensus yet, but there is some information indicating that while the Chou society was still carrying over the slave system of the Shang, there was a gradual change in that, while some slavery remained, some were allowed to become independent farmers allocated with land to produce revenue for the government. There was a certain degree of relaxation in harsh treatment of slaves and rigid seclusion of the slaves from their participation and involvement in social affairs. Most important of all is that the human sacrifice of slaves was stopped and soldiers were not buried alive, but effigies made to substitute for them.

However, it is an exaggeration to say that the Chou society was a free and democratic society, it was a feudalistic society with a well-defined hierarchical stratification. Under the king, the rank and order among the feudal lords, the government officials, military personnel, merchants and artisans, farmers and peasants were all clearly distinguished. Nonetheless, the rivalries and intrigue among the rank and file were conspicuous and concurrent, and the possibility of upward mobility on the ladder of success became realizable during the latter period of the Western Chou period (1050-771 B.C.).

There were two episodes which illustrate such significant change and further advance toward democratization from feudalism. The Kuo Yu (國語), a collection of discussions on the affairs of state, recorded an episode about a minister's advice to his king. King Mu (穆王) of Chou (1001-946 B.C.) wanted to engage in military campaigns against the northwestern nomadic tribe Chüan-jung (犬戎), but the minister Tsai-Kung Mu-fu (蔡公謀父) advised against it, saying, "The ancient sage kings might illustrate their virtues, but did not demonstrate their military force. If you tried to show off your powers by playing the games of military campaigns, your enemy would think that you were merely joking and not be afraid of you." He also mentioned that since the Chüan-jung tribe paid regular tribute, it was not right to break trust and make a sudden attack. The purpose of hunting albino (white) wolf and deer for sacrifice cannot justify a military campaign, for it would rather cause hostility of the tribal people and their refusal to pay their homage

and tributes. This episode illustrates that there was
already a wise and moral minister who dared to oppose
and criticize the king and to defend the welfare of the
ruled.

     The other episode was much more radical. By the
time of the reign of King Li (878-827 B.C.), the Chou
society had become much more advanced in commerce and
crafts, and the voices and power of merchants, craftsmen, and land-owner farmers were felt in the central
government, as well as local administration. Many of
these well-to-do merchants, artisans, and landlords
moved to the city, which was the center of feudal power
and authority. Seeing this, King Li rallied behind
him the alliance of merchants and craftsmen together
with the government bureaucrats and caused a great
threat to the declining force of the old feudal lords,
who were still scattered at the edge of the empire.
The contrast between the increasing rich merchant and
craftsmen class and the declining rural feudal lords
had become so critical that the feudal lords began to
ally themselves to resist the trend. They gathered together at the capital and made pleas to the king not to
one-sidedly support the newly risen power block, and
complained and criticized the breach of the old royal
trust. In spite of prodigious advice given by his
ministers, King Li not only refused to yield but also
started to interrogate the dissidents and suppress
them. Because of this, the citizens of the capital
made an open demonstration at the city gate and rose
in rebellion in 841 B.C. King Li was so surprised at
this unexpected riot that he hid himself and did not
dare show himself at the throne. Thus, the citizens
appointed the minister Kung Po Fo (共伯和) in charge
of the central administration, which was designated as
the First Year of the Republic (共和), and the new
Republic lasted for thirteen years until the death of
King Li in his exile and his son was inaugurated to
become the new king, King Hsuan (宣王). This thirteen
years of Republic marked the beginning of the decline
of the autocratic monarch of Chou and a significant
step toward humanization and the democratic right of
citizenship and of the individual.

     There was a record of a statement made by the
cabinet to King Li when he challenged his cabinet that
he was able to silence the dissident voices by interro-
gation, torture, and execution.

     O! King, you have only embanked temporarily

the rising flood by shutting the dissident
voices. But the dissidence of the people is
more than rising flood. You might be able to
embank the flood, but you may not be able to
embank the voice of the people. Like the
rising flood would sooner or later break the
bank, the destruction would be much greater
if you keep resisting against the voice of
the people."

We shall see that this statement made by courageous
ministers was to become the foundation and development
of various schools of political-religious-philosophical
thought in ancient China. Following, there will be an
elaboration on the four representative schools which
championed their views about the status of the individual. They are the Confucius-Mencius' view of the "responsible self," Mo Tzu's view of the "universal self,"
Chuang Tzu's view of the "transcendental self," and
Han Confucianists' view of the "integrated self."

The Responsible Self of Confucius
and Mencius

        The riot in 841 B.C. may earmark a step toward
democracy, but it did not create a democratic society;
instead, it created great chaos and caused the downfall of the Western Chou and the disintegration of the
Chou feudal system. Once order was challenged and disturbed, rivalry and conflicts increased; and before a
new order was created, the society had to undergo a
period of transition and chaos. After the fall of the
Chou capital, Chung Chou, in 771 B.C., which was destroyed by invasion of foreign tribes and riots and
insurrections, King P'ing had to abandon it and move
to the eastern capital Cheng Chou, which signified the
end of Western Chou and the beginning of the Eastern
Chou period. However, by then, the Chou kings were no
longer able to restore the ancient glory, but it remained only as a city-state surrounded by other city-
states transformed from the former feudal states.
Even though the Eastern Chou kings claimed their royal
lineage and legitimacy, they had to look up to the
political leadership of Ten States: Lu, Ch'i, Ch'in,
Sung, Wei, Tsin, Ts'ai, Tsao, Cheng, Yen. Among these
ten states, Duke Heng of Ch'i, Duke Wen of Ts'in, Duke
Jang of Sung, Duke Mu of Ch'in, and King Chuan of Ch'u
had become rival tyrants (Pa 霸) of the time. Political struggles and maneuvers among them created continuous warfare and conflicts through the entire period of

the Eastern Chou. Thus, it is also called the Ch'un
Ch'iu or Spring-Autumn period (春秋, 772-481 B.C.)
and the Warring States period (戰國, 403-222 B.C.).
Confucius edited from the archives of the Lu State a
chronicle of state affairs from 722 to 481 B.C. and
called it <u>Ch'un Ch'iu</u>, which means the spring and
autumn, for they are the two most transient seasons in
the year.

Initially, these ten states were governed by the
feudal lords, but gradually they were replaced by the
newly risen oligarchies which were no longer related
to the royal family of the Chou. These oligarchies were
made up of military officers, well-to-do merchants,
powerful craftsmen, and local landlords who ascended to
power by political alliance and intrigue. They built
the city-states with their independent military defense
and bureaucratic organization by hiring soldiers and
officials who pledged loyalty to them. They also built
the state-shrines to worship and offer sacrifices to
the common ancestors of their clans. Hence, a theocratic oligarchy based on common ancestor worship and
kinship marriage was innovated to substitute for the
declining theocratic monarchy of the Chou house. Religion and state were still inseparable, and sacrifice
and politics were identical with the Eastern Chou
period.

However, the traditional order, moral behavior,
and hierarchical authority crumbled along with the
downfall of the Chou feudal system. Many feudal lords
and oligarchies were assassinated and their houses
plundered, many superiors and seniors were assassinated
by their own subordinates and family members, and homi-
cide and patricide were almost a daily occurrence.
Order and authority were gone, loyalty and trust no
longer existed, and court intrigues and political maneuvers became rampant. Treatise and alliance made yes-
terday were soon broken, and safety and security were
lacking. The tactic for survival in this chaotic society was to maneuver, take chances, and to compete
continuously. Lamenting upon such a chaotic situation,
Confucius and many other wise men appeared to give
counsel for a solution, and attempted to restore the
society to its sanity.

The ancestors of Confucius were possibly the nobles of the Shang dynasty who fell to the level of
government officials serving the Chou royal court after
the fall of Shang. With the decline of central

authority, many government officials who served in the
royal court lost their jobs and became wandering intellectuals seeking employment in the state oligarchies.
Confucius' father was one such government official who
had served in the Chou royal court but died when Confucius was still young. Raised by his widow-mother,
Confucius was determined to carry on his father's
honor and tradition of being an intellectual by keeping
up his self-studies of ancient culture and history. He
found a job as an officer in charge of state sacrifices
and ceremonies in the State of Lu which still honored
the lineage and legitimacy of the Chou royal court.
After many years of meritorious works, Confucius was
appointed as Prime Minister of Lu in 501 B.C. However,
he soon discovered many court intrigues and corruption
in the royal house he respected; he resigned his position in 497 B.C. and started to gather around him a
small group of students and set to wandering around
other states trying to persuade the oligarchies to
adopt his political ideas and reforms. He completely
failed in convincing these oligarchies to adopt his
ideas, but he was successful in training his students
to become efficient government officials with integrity who carried on his political ideas and reforms.
After thirteen years of wandering, Confucius came back
to his home state, where he spend the last three years
of his life editing his writings and teaching his disciples. He died in 479 B.C. and was buried in the district of Chu-fu (曲埠), where his tomb still survives.

One of the great contributions Confucius made was
his democratization of education. Hitherto, education
was only given to the children of the rulers, but Confucius offered his education to anyone who wanted to
learn from him. He said: "In teaching there should be
no class distinctions" and "From him who has brought
his simple present of dried meat, seeking to enter my
school, I have never withheld instruction."[1]

He taught his students with the Six Disciplines,
the best learning available to the princes in the royal
house. This system was instituted reputedly by Duke
Chou, and Confucius transmitted it diligently. The Six
Disciplines were Poetry, History, Rites, Music, Political Science, and Metaphysics. He edited the Book of
Poetry (Shih Ching) which instructed not only writing
and composition but also the refinement of the senses
and elegance in expression. He also edited the Book of
History (Shu Ching) to give knowledge of the origin and
the earliest development of Chinese history and culture.

Confucius edited the Book of Rites from various sources,
practiced them, and commented on their motifs and purposes. He regarded the discipline of proper ritual and
restoration of the Principle of Propriety (Li chih 禮
制) laid out by Duke Chou as the key for restoring
orderly government and society. Along with the rites,
Confucius had personally loved music, performed on some
musical instruments, and wrote essays on the meaning
and functions of music. Unfortunately, not all his essays have survived, we have only one chapter preserved
in the Book of Rites to give us a perspective on the
fine essays he wrote about music. He believed that
proper education in music would encourage accord in
government and harmony in society, for while the music
allowed each one to perform one's individual cord on
special instruments, the orchestra would incorporate
each sound into a harmonious symphony. He also edited
the Book of Ch'un Ch'iu (春秋, Spring and Autumn Annals) from the archives of the State of Lu which recorded, chronologically, the major events of political
affairs that took place from 722 to 481 B.C. It was
not merely a chronicle, but a book of moral judgment
on good and evil, merits and demerits of the feudal
lords and oligarchies. It was not only an ineradicable
historical record of what really happened but also a
textbook of political science with moral philosophy.
It was the tool Confucius found as an historian and as
an intellectual to check and balance power politics
without which there would be political chaos. In this
sense, he was a pioneer of political sciences and
praised by his followers as an "uncrowned king." The
last discipline was instruction on metaphysics in the
Book of Changes. It was believed that Confucius had
written the last ten chapters of appendix-essays in the
Book of Changes to give his view of the state of the
individual in the universe and to guide an individual,
at any moment and place, to find harmony with the universe. Accordingly, we can see that his education was
quite comprehensive and well-balanced, and his purpose
in education was to produce "civilized man."

    Noting the compliable acceptance of his society
to the chaos and immorality, Confucius assiduously
strived to restore order and peace. In spite of considerable counsel and proposals already made by many
eminent ministers, Confucius insisted that cultural
restoration and moral reform were the only ways to re-
establish a sane and ongoing society. He emphasized
the reinstitution of the Propriety System established

by Duke Chou with moral reform beginning at the top of
the social hieracy. Owing to this, he was criticized
as being a traditionalist and conservative, if not a
fundamentalist, and he himself admitted that he was a
"transmitter" and not an "innovator." He felt a strong
sense of divine commission to preserve and revive the
Chou culture founded by King Wen. He said while on
his journey to a heckler who tried to stop him from
persuading the state oligarchies to accept the Propriety System, "Since King Wen is no longer alive, does
not his culture rest with me? If Heaven were going to
destroy this culture, a later mortal like me could not
have gained such a close association with it. Since
Heaven has not yet destroyed this culture, what can
the men of K'uang [hecklers] do to me?"[2]

However, he was not merely a transmitter, he was
also a great innovator. First, he demonstrated that
each "civilized person" has a divine commission (T'ien
Ming) to carry on the sacred cultural tradition and
revive it when it is about to decline. The mandate of
Heaven is no longer the monopoly of the king, but is to
be shared by each individual who is educated and realizes his social responsibility. This democratization
of the sacred duty was a giant step toward humanization
of the individual person and society. It could be compared to Martin Luther's proclamation that "All Men are
Priests," which was one of the cardinal principles of
the Reformation that opened up the avenue for modern
democracy in the West.

Second, he believed the civilized individual was
always to be a responsible self, aware of his/her
position in society and the world, performing his/her
duty accordingly. He called this sense of responsibility the "Rectification of Names," and emphasized that
it is to be the first step to save society from chaos.
On one occasion, the prince of Wei came to ask Confucius who would take control of his administration, and
Confucius replied, "The one thing needed is the rectification of names." On another occasion, Duke Ching of
Ch'i inquired of Confucius about the principles of
government, to which Confucius answered: "Let the ruler
be the ruler, the minister minister; let the father be
the father, and the son son." In this simple statement, he tried to emphasize that the actuality of an
individual's conduct should correspond with the quali-
fication of status, otherwise the names (or titles) of
status would become empty names. Each individual, at
a certain time and place, should be conscious of his

or her status and specific duty and he and she should
fulfill that duty to be qualified to stay at that level.
In other words, an individual should be a responsible
self in society and in the world, for every individual
is related mutually to others. Even a king or ruler is
not totally independent and isolated, so he cannot
selfishly do whatever he wants to do. He became a king
because the nation trusted him to be the king with a
certain social contract agreed upon when he took the
throne. He had to adhere to that responsibility and
diligently fulfill that obligation to maintain his
kingship. When he became neglectful of his duty and
irresponsible to his status, he would lose his mandate
to be a king. Likewise, at home he is the father to
his son, the husband to his wife, and the brother to
his brother and sister; and in each different status,
there is a different duty he has to fulfill. Every
name has its own specific definition, which designates
the quality which makes the status to which the name is
applied and to no other. The name is the essence of
the status,and essence should be actualized all the
time, otherwise the name would become empty. Confucius
identified the irresponsibility of each individual and
distortion in human relationships as the major cause of
disorder in his society. Therefore, he urged the "rectification of names," on the one hand, and the promotion of the practice of Jen (仁) or human-heartedness,
on the other.

Chinese lexicographer Hsu Hsin interpreted Jen to
be Jen (人) which means human or humanity itself. Confucius emphasized that Jen is to be human, the cardinal
principle of human relatedness. In other words, "being
human" always takes place in the context of relatedness. Martin Buber phrased it the "I and Thou" and
"Between Man and Man." Similarly, Confucius had long
ago stressed that the authentic self must be contextual, relational, and responsible. "No man is an island." The quality of Jen is interpreted as "love,
loyalty, altruism, mutuality, commiseration," etc., and
they are all virtues of interpersonal relationship.

Confucius strongly believed that the rectification
of names by injecting the quality of Jen into human
relatedness is the only way a chaotic society could be
saved and the sanity of humanity restored. It was
neither the reaffirmation of ancient theocratic autocracy and oligarchy, nor promotion of unlimited free
enterprise of the new commerce and crafts sponsored by
some ministers, but a thorough moral reformation and

rectification of human relationships by which he would
be able to eradicate the fundamental evil of his time.
Of course, he knew that it was a difficult fight and
bound to fail because the trend of the time was rapid
commercialization and a strong buildup of military
power. No one would listen to his moral exhortation.
But he was committed to it because he believed it to be
his "Heavenly mandate." This dedication to his moral
mission, supported by strong religious conviction, made
him the most revered Teacher of All Seasons (Wang-shu
Shu-piao萬世師表). Although during his lifetime, he
failed to realize his moral reform, he was quite successful in leaving his legacy to well-educated disciples, who carried on his mission after his death.
One of the most illustrious students was Mencius.

Mencius received his education from the grandson
of Confucius, Tsu Ssu (子思), and after its completion,
he sought employment in the state government, but was
unsuccessful, for many states were already engaged in
warfare and more interested in hiring military officers and engineers to make weapons. As Ssu-ma Ch'ien
described:

> The empire was then engaged in forming verti-
> cal (north-to-south) and horizontal (east-to-
> west) alliances among states, and held fight-
> ing as something worthy. Whereas Mencius in-
> tended to transmit the virtues of ancient
> sage kings and three dynasties, so those whom
> he visited were not willing to listen to him.
> Discouraged he retired and together with his
> disciple, Wan Chang, and others, put the
> teaching of the <u>Books of Poetry</u> and <u>History</u>
> in order, transmitted the doctrines of Con-
> fucius, and composed the Work <u>Mencius</u> in
> seven books.[3]

Through his work, we learn that Mencius not only
transmitted Confucius' teachings, but also innovated
some of his own. This study will cover at least three
significant teachings relating to individuality.

First, he believed that each individual is endowed
with good nature from Heaven and the potential to do
good without being instructed to do so. He observed
that each human being has a mind of commiseration which
cannot bear to see the suffering of others; a feeling
of shame when one does evil; a feeling of modesty and
of yielding; and a sense of right and wrong. For

example, even a thief would jump to rescue a child who
is about to fall into a well. So he came to the conclusion that, fundamentally and originally, human nature is good. Thereby, each individual has inherited
this equal potentiality to do good, and every individual is capable of becoming a sage like the ancient
sages, Yao (堯) and Shun (舜). Moreover, he stressed
that each individual has the liberty of choosing to do
good, since good nature has been implanted within him.
He regarded virtue as genuine when it was conducted by
free choice and spontaneous, individual decision
rather than enforced by an external force such as
government. However, he realized that such liberty had
been often negated and such innate good nature had been
oppressed by evil rulers, so that good nature could not
have its independent and autonomous growth. He pro-
claimed to King Hsüan of Ch'i State:

> When the prince regards his ministers as his
> hands and feet, his ministers shall regard
> their prince as their belly and heart. When
> he regards them as his dogs and horses, they
> shall regard him as any other man of the
> state. When he regards them as the ground
> and the grass to be tramped down, they shall
> regard him as a thief and and an enemy.[4]

Second, Mencius challenged such evil rulers and
openly rebuked them as Pa (霸), literally "tyrant,"
and distinguished them from the virtuous ruler Chün
(君). There were five such notorious Pa during the
period Ch'un-Ch'iu: Duke Huan of Ch'i, Duke Mu of
Ch'in, Duke Hsiang of Sung, Duke Wen of Chin, and King
Chuang of Ch'u. The basic distinction between these
Pa and Chün was that while the Chün governed the state
with the principle of propriety and took the welfare of
the people as their primary concern, the Pa were more
interested in appropriating to themselves political and
economical powers and used military force to gain the
allegiance of the people. The Chün took great care of
their people because they governed with the principle
of Jen and could not tolerate seeing the suffering of
their people. Mencius predicated:

> He who uses force, but pretends it to be a
> virtue is a tyrant. . . . He who uses
> virtue and practices love is a virtuous
> ruler. . . . When a tyrant oppresses the
> people by force, they may obey outwardly
> to him because they have insufficient

strength, but they do not submit to him in
their hearts. When a virtuous ruler governs
his people with virtue, the people are
pleased and submit to him willingly from
their hearts. This was the way how seventy
disciples of Confucius paid their respect to
Confucius.[5]

When he was asked about which element was most
important in a state, Mencius replied, "The people are
the most important element in a state; then the spirits
of the earth and grain (she-chi 社稷) are the next,
and the rulers are the least."[6] Thus, Mencius as an
intellectual regarded himself a champion of such democratic causes, who had to voice his criticism of the
vicious rulers and tyrannic government. Oppression of
the people is not only a violation of the social trust,
but also the abrogation of human right and moral principle.

Third, Mencius proposed to the rulers to institute a public educational system to provide an education for any individual who wanted one. Hitherto education was only given to the children of the rulers,
nobles, and elites. Confucius tried to change it by
establishing a school that offered an education to anyone, regardless of social status, since he felt that
education should not be limited only to the privileged
class. Mencius went a step further, he wanted the institution of schools to be a necessary government
function at proper places which would be available to
any and all children.

> Build hsiang(庠), Hsü(序), hsüeh(學), and hsiao
> (校) in order to promote education. The
> hsiang is to nurture, the hsiao is to in-
> struct, and the hsü is for physical exer-
> cise. . . [the hsüeh is for learning]. . . .
> They all serve to clarify the basic human
> relationships. When these human relation-
> ships are exemplified by the superiors,
> there will be kindly feelings fostered among
> the common people.[7]

It was only through education that the poor and
lowly people had a possibility of ascending the ladder
of success in ancient China, and it really was a great
contribution made by Confucius and Mencius to open
such opportunity. However, they strongly felt that
the primary purpose of education was to admonish the

responsible self and the ultimate realization of human-
heartedness, not simply to gain power and fame.

<u>The Universal Self of Mo Tzu</u> (墨子, C. 479-C. 381 B.C.)

About a century after Confucius, Mo Tzu came out
to champion the cause of oppressed people and advocate
his idea of the nonclass, nondiscriminatory society and
the universal self who treats everybody as equal. There
have been many interpretations regarding the social
background of Mo Tzu. One of them is that he was a native of Lu State and studied in the Confucian school,
gaining employment by the State of Sung, which was promoting the practice of universal love and pacifism.
Mo Tzu was, then, becoming critical of Confucian
ritualism, fatalism, and the doctrine of discriminative
love. Because of Confucian adoption of the Propriety
System established by Duke Chou, it had emphasized
many elaborate rites and ceremonies, which Mo Tzu criticized as a waste of time and money and ineffective in
the correction of the cause of evil in society. He
also opposed the Confucian beliefs in the mandate of
Heaven which produced the belief in fatalism and the
mood of resignation which caused the downgrading of
morale and individual incentive. Although he agreed
to the teaching of human heartedness (Jen) itself, yet
because Confucianists put that principle into a rigid
framework of the so-called Five Human Relationships
(Wu Lun, 五倫), authentic love became graded and discriminatory. The five human relationships were: the
ruler-and-the-subject, father-and-son, husband-and-
wife, brother-and-brother, and friend-and-friend, differentiated by senior and junior. As each relationship is in different context, the virtue should differ
accordingly. For example, between the ruler and the
subject, loyalty and submission are to be the virtues.
Likewise, filial piety between the father-son, propriety between the husband-wife, wisdom between the
brother-brother, and faithfulness between friend-friend
relationships. As can be seen, the stress of duty and
virtue is much more on the inferior and junior side,
and mutuality and reciprocity are not emphasized.
Furthermore, since Confucianists had strongly advocated
ancestral worship, eventually filial piety between the
father-son relationship became the criterion of all
other virtues. Accordingly, the subjects were encouraged to look up to their ruler as a filial son
would to his father; and, likewise, a wife should respect her husband; a younger brother would pay homage

to his older brother; and a junior friend should be
submissive to his senior friend. The whole scheme of
social ethics had thus become oriented by familial
ethics. Inevitably, foreigners, strangers, travelers,
and nonrelated members in society would not have any
status or integral position in this structure unless he
became a friend to some member in the family. Especially, while upper-class family members would enjoy
higher esteem and benefits of their close ties with
the high echelon of society, the lower class and the
poor would definitely suffer humiliation and be pre-
vented from climbing the higher ladder of success.
Resultantly, Mo Tzu criticized that while the principle
of Jen was desirable, the Five Human Relationship System was discriminatory and differential and he wanted
to promote nondiscriminative universal love (Chien ai
兼愛).

   Another interpretation of the social background of
Mo Tzu indicated that the name "Mo" (墨) which means
"black" or "black mark" might not be the family name
of Mo Tzu, but the brand name for a group of criminal
slaves who were branded with "black marks." In ancient
China, "mo" was a form of punishment, and a person
bearing such a mark, like the mark of Cain in the West,
would be permanently discriminated against as an out-
cast or outlaw. This interpretation does not necessarily imply that Mo Tzu himself was such a criminal
slave, but he was a leader of a group of criminal
slaves who championed for fair treatment and criminal
justice, if not ultimate liberation from slavery.
Hence, he strongly advocated that if love is to be
genuine, it should be nongraded and all inclusive. Instead of using the term Jen, Mo Tzu now used the term
Chien ai (兼愛), which literally means "all inclusive
love." The word "love" is the most common word used in
expressing human cares, concerns, passion, sympathy,
and fraternity. It is a universal sentiment applicable
to any person at any place and time, and is not to be
confined to any particular scheme or framework of a
social system.

   Mo Tzu utilized three arguments to promote the
cause of this universal love. First, he advocated
that universal love is the norm sanctioned by Heaven
because "Heaven Himself is universal love." Long before Jesus taught the universal love of his Father God,
Mo Tzu had already stated that Heaven loves all the
people and His will is to promote social justice.

How do we know that Heaven loves the people?
Because he enlightens them all. How do we
know that he enlightens them all? Because
he takes all of them into account. How do we
know that he takes all of them into account?
Because he accepts all of their sacrifices.
. . . For all the civilized people offered
sacrifices to the supreme God. (Shang Ti)
and the spirits.[8]

The will of Heaven abominates the large state
attacking the small states, the rich householders molesting the poor householders, the
strong oppressing the weak, the clever ones
deceiving the simple ones, and the honoured
condemning the humble. Moreover, Heaven
wishes the people who have powers working to
help each other, the people who are intelligent teaching to guide each other, and the
rich sharing their wealth to benefit each
other. . . .
     Therefore, when the will of Heaven is
understood and widely obeyed in the world,
justice and government will be orderly, the
multitude ill be harmonious, the country will
be wealthy, the supplies will be sufficient,
and the people will be warmly clothed and
sufficiently fed, peaceful and without
worry.[9]

     Second, benefits of the practice of universal love
are historically proven by the rule of ancient sages
who obeyed the will of Heaven, and the calamity caused
by those rulers who disobeyed the will of Heaven. Mo
Tzu argued:

The son of Heaven is the most honourable and
richest in the world. . . . Those who obey
the will of Heaven, love universally, and
benefit others will be inevitably rewarded
[by Heaven]. Those who oppose the will of
Heaven are partial and unfriendly and harming
others. They will inevitably incur the punishment [of Heaven]. . . .
     The ancient Sage-kings of the Three Dy-
nasties, Yü, T'ang, Wen, and Wu, were those
who obeyed the will of Heaven and obtained
reward. And the wicked kings of the Three
Dynasties, Chieh, Chou, Yü, and Li, were
those who opposed the will of Heaven and

incurred punishment.[10]

Third, the practice of universal love is the most
profitable to the majority of the people. This util-
itarianistic argument for the cause of universal love
is one of the characteristics of Mohist philosophy.
Mo Tzu did not simply ciritcize Confucian doctrine,
but presented his point of view quite emphatically.

> Partiality should be replaced by universality.
> But how. . . .? I say that when everyone re-
> gards the states of others as he regards his
> own, who would attack the states of others?
> . . . Now when states and capitals do not
> attack and occupy each other, . . . is it a
> calamity or benefit to the world? It is
> definitely a benefit. What then is the ori-
> gin of this benefit? We must say that it
> arises from love and not hate . . . univer-
> sality and not partiality.[11]

Even though Confucianists counterargued that Mo
Tzu's idea of universal was not realistic and his argument based on utility and profitability was not morally
justified, we can see that Mo Tsu's principle of universal love was more democratic and his argument more
modern and convincing. Especially his advocacy for
the equal right and fair justice for the slaves and
criminals at the bottom level of society, which appears
more admirable than the Confucian ideas which were supportive of kings and feudal lords who were at the top
of social hierarchy. He demanded that each individual,
regardless of status, should treat one another impar-
tially and respectively. Mo Tzu's social ethic is different from the Confucian one, for it emphasized the
principle of mutuality and reciprocity. The virtue
between a father-son relationship should not only be
filial piety of son to father but should also be a
responsible parenthood of father to son. Likewise, the
ruler should not demand loyalty and obedience from his
subjects and ignore his duties to, and attentive care
of, his people. Moreover, there should not be any discrimination based upon the difference in family relationship, tribal kinship, guild of profession, and
status in hierarchy. Each individual, in whatever
place and time, should be treated as equal and bene-
fited with impartial love. As Mo Tzu said, "Others
should be regarded as the self," his ideal of authentic
selfhood is to be all-embracing and universal.

The Transcendental Self of Chuang Tsu
(莊子, 369?-286? B.C.)

Chuang Tzu's idea of the individual represented
a group of recluses who were very disappointed with
the chaotic situation in society and chose to separate
themselves from society and refused to be involved with
any political and social affairs. There was a recluse
called Yang Chu (楊朱) whose principle was "Each one
for himself," and he "would not even pluck a single
hair to benefit the world even though it might very
well do so"! His philosophy of life was "completion
of one's life" (ch'uan sheng 全生), preservation of what
is genuine, and not allowing outside things to entangle
one's person![12] Another recluse Tzu Hua Tzu (子華子)
was saying:

> Completeness of living is the best. Life
> which is incomplete is second to it. Death
> comes last. But life constrained is the
> worst. Therefore what is called the exalta-
> tion of life means completeness of living.
> What is called completeness of living is a
> life in which six desires all reach a proper
> harmony. Life which is incomplete is one in
> which a person fails to value what he should
> value. The more incomplete it is, the less
> he values it. . . .What is called constrained
> life, is one in which none of the six de-
> sires reaches a proper harmony in any degree,
> and all get what they dislike. Such are
> submission and shame.[13]

Succeeding such sentiment of distrust in society
and search for self-preservation and completeness of
life, Chuang Tzu made a more articulate argument for
the recluses' aspiration for transcendental selfhood.
Of course, we have the teaching of Lao Tzu prior to
Chuang Tzu, in which Taoist metaphysic was fully elaborated, but Chuang Tzu had much more to say about the
status of the individual and the meaning of authentic
selfhood than Lao Tzu.

First, he advocated the universal equality of self
like Mo Tzu, but he went further to emphasize that the
value of each individual is intrinsic and should not be
judged by any other external criteria. In the first
chapter of his work, Chuang Tzu told an interesting
parable to demonstrate the equality of all things.

> When the p'eng [giant bird] is flying to the
> southern ocean, it flaps along the water for
> three thousand miles. Then it ascends on a
> whirlwind to a height of ninety thousand
> miles, for a flight of six months' duration.
> But the cicada and dove laugh at the p'eng
> bird, saying "When we make our effort to fly
> up, we fly up to the trees. Sometimes, not
> able to reach, we fall to the ground midway.
> What is the use of climbing up ninety thou-
> sand miles in order to start for the south?[14]

This parable is to illustrate that each one has a
given nature and life accorded to them and enjoys one's
own happiness. The p'eng bird, representing those who
are on high and great, should not look down at the
small birds hopping below. Meanwhile, the small birds
like doves and insects like the cicada, representing
those who are small and below, do not need to be jealous of what they are not. Regardless of largeness or
smallness, each one has one's intrinsic value and
equality of enjoyment. Another parable runs as follows:

> May I ask you some questions: If a man sleeps
> in a damp place, his loins may have pain and
> his body become numb. But is it so with an
> eel? If a man lives up in a tree, he may be
> frightened and tremble. But is it so with a
> monkey? Of these three, who knows the right
> way of habitation? Men love to eat meat;
> deers feed on grass. Centipedes love to eat
> snakes; owls and crows delight in mice. Of
> these four, who knows the right taste?
> Monkey mates with monkey; the buck with the
> doe; male fish with female fish. Mao Ch'iang
> and Li Chi were considered by men as the most
> beautiful women; but at the sight of them
> fish will dive deep into the water, birds
> will soar high in the sky, and deer will rush
> away. Of these four, who knows the right
> standard of beauty?[15]

This parable illustrates that each individual
living being has its own way of life and standard of
judgment and that to use one's own standard to judge
other's ways and values is unjustifiable. Each individual being has its own complete freedom to live according to one's given nature and enjoy one's own happiness without being interfered with by external

criteria and judgment imposed upon them. Universal
equality and complete freedom are the essential quality of authentic selfhood.

     Second, one should be impartial, indiscriminative,
and nonjudgmental to maintain the equality and freedom
of the individual self. Chuang Tzu saw the problem of
his time as each different school trying to establish
its own criterion to make judgment on others and claiming its own to be the only truth there was. The Confucian school advocated the Propriety System established by a group of ruling elite, and it was imposed
upon the majority of people to obey unconditionally.
Thereby, the framework of Five Human Relationships was
made and Five Cardinal Virtues were set as the standard and all individuals were to follow that standard,
regardless of their particular situation or condition.
Although the school of Mohists had advanced in advocating universal equality of the self, it still con-
tended against other schools by claiming that the worship of God and spirits, theocratic monarchy, and exaltation of the sages were essential and more beneficial to society. Just as there was constant warfare
among the contending states and their lords, the scholars of the times were also contending among themselves.
Each one set up its own criterion to judge others while
defending its own to be the absolute truth. Seeing
this, Chuang Tzu tried to totally discard criteria and
strip off the parochial mentality and dogmatism which
characterized its thought. He tried to attain a transcendental dimension in which the dichotomy between
"this" and "that," "mine" and "yours," "human" and
"animal" was completely dissolved. He called this
transcendental view the standpoint of Tao.

          From the standpoint of Tao, there is nothing
          which is valuable or valueless. Whereas
          from the standpoint of the vulgar, each
          thing is divided between the valuable and
          the valueless. We see the things as either
          large or small, but, in reality, there is
          nothing in the universe is not big and there
          is nothing in the universe is not small. To
          realize that Heaven and Earth are but as a
          tare-seed, and that the tip of hair is a
          mountain: this is the truth of relativity.
          Tao is without beginning and end, where-
          as things are born and die. They do not have
          permanence. Now full, now empty, they have
          no set form. Past years cannot be recalled;

218

and time cannot be arrested. Growth and decay are the successive process of transformations.[16]

Third, both the individual and the world are
transcended and the union with Tao is realized. In
this final union with Tao, there is no more differentiation between subject and object, life and death,
and the human and the divine, but they are integrated
into one mind which Chuang Tzu described as "the fast
of the mind" (hsin chai 心齊) and "sitting in forget-
fulness" (tso wang 坐忘), which are similar to the
state of samadhi the Yogin reaches at the end of meditation. He also called the person who reached that
state of mystical union the True Man (chen jen, 真人)
or the Perfect Man (chih jen, 至人) or the Spiritual Man
(shen jen, 神人). It is best to let Chuang Tzu speak
for himself:

> Now the universe is the unity of all things.
> If we realize this unity and identify our-
> selves with it, we shall know that the mem-
> bers of our body are but parts of the uni-
> verse, and our life and death are but the
> succession of day and night, so that their
> changes cannot disturb our inner peace. Thus,
> how much less the worldly gain and loss,
> good fortunes and calamities shall trouble
> our mind.[17]

> Through the cultivation of one's nature, one
> shall return to the original state of what
> is given (te 得). Having returned to the
> original state of what is given, one shall
> identify with the Beginning. Being thus
> identified, the realization of emptiness
> shall come. With this emptiness, vastness
> will be realized. Being like this, one shall
> reach a union with the universe. . . . This
> state is called the Mysterious Primordial
> Virtue (Hsüan Te 玄德). It is the identifica-
> tion with the great flux.[18]

> The True Man of ancient time slept without
> dreaming and waked without anxiety. He ate
> without discrimination, and his breathing was
> very deep. . . . The True Man of ancient time
> knew neither to love life nor to hate death.
> In living, he felt no excitement; in dying,
> he did not resist. Unconsciously he came and

and unconsciously he went; that was all.
. . . He received with delight anything
that came to him; let go anything willingly
whatever he had.[19]

Such is the view of transcendental selfhood realized
through the mystical experience of Chuang Tzu.

The Integrated Self in the Books of Rites
(Li Chi 禮記)

There are three chapters in the Book of Rites:
Great Learning (Ta Hsüeh, 大學), the Golden Mean (Chung
Yung, 中庸), and the Evolution of Rites (Li Yung, 禮運),
which represent a new synthesis of the ideas of selfhood developed so far in ancient China. Exact authorship of these three essays is unknown, but generally
they were assumed to be students of Confucianism in the
early Han dynasty (206 B.C.-A.D.200). They tried to
integrate the Confucius-Mencius' idea of the responsible self, the Mohist idea of the universal self, and
the Taoistic idea of the transcendental self, into a
unified idea of the integrated self who aspired for
Great Unity (ta t'ung 大同). Their new synthesis is a
timely reflection of the early Han era when the Warring
States period ended and the dictatorial rule of the
Ch'in dynasty (244-207 B.C.) was taken over by the Han
emperors who desired to reconstruct a new empire which
would incorporate all the ancient cultural traditions.

The chapter Great Learning tried to describe what
an individual (like a Han emperor) who aspired to
govern the whole world should do to prepare and cultivate one's own personality. Its introductory statement
stated most succintly its viewpoint.

What does the Great Learning teach is to
exemplify virtue, to love people and to rest
in the highest good. . . .
When one knows in which situation and
position one is in, one can become calm.
After calming down, one can be tranquil.
After being tranquil, one can have peaceful
repose. Having peaceful repose, one shall
be liberated. After being liberated, the
ultimate goal can be attained. Thus to know
how to begin and how to reach the goal will
guide one nearer to the Tao.
Those ancient sages who wanted to exemplify their virtues throughout the universe,

started first by governing well their own
states. Wishing to govern well their states,
they started first by regulating well their
own families. Wishing to regulate well their
families, they started first by cultivating
their own personal characters. Wishing to
cultivate their personal character, they
started first by rectifying their own minds.
Wishing to rectify their minds, they started
first by seeking absolute sincerity in their
thoughts. Wishing for sincerity in their
thoughts, they started first by extending
their knowledge. This extension of knowledge
starts with the investigation of things.

From the son of Heaven [emperors] down
to the common people, all must consider the
cultivation of personal character to be
basic. It will not grow when the root is
neglected.[20]

The above statement indicates clearly the summary
of the Confucian idea of cultivation of virtue, the
Mohist ideal of universal love and the Taoist aspiration for transcendental tranquility. The first method
to attain this great synthesis is to do Taoistic meditation to liberate oneself, and then to practice Confucian self-cultivation to be a responsible self in
society, so that the Mohist universal love and world
peace can be realized. The final paragraph indicates
that this goal of attaining the integrated self should
be the aim of every individual including an emperor
and the common people. This is the core statement of
the Great Learning chapter, and it is also a manifesto
of Han syncreticism.

In the chapter on the Golden Mean, the principle
of the Golden Mean and the concept of timeliness are
expounded. The word "Golden Mean" in Chinese has two
characters: Chung (中) which means "centrality" and
"equilibrium"; and Yung (庸) which means "normality"
and "consistency." This indicates that the authentic
self is the one who knows one's position in the universe and keeps one's relationships with all others in
harmony. The first two paragraphs of the first chapter
explain well the meaning of Chung Yung.

What Heaven imparts in human beings is called
nature. Thus to follow one's given nature
within oneself is called the Tao. To cultivate the Tao within oneself is the goal of

221

education.

Before all the feelings of pleasure,
anger, sorrow and joy are aroused, there
existed equilibrium. It is the foundation
of the world. When these feelings are
aroused, each and all should attain their due
measure and degree, then harmony of them can
be attained. This harmony is the path of
universe. When both equilibrium and harmony
are fully realized, heaven and earth will
attain their proper order and all things
shall flourish.[21]

Centrality (chung) has an implication of being
well adjusted to one's position no matter which position one is in. One clearly knows one's position and
acts properly according to the given situation. In a
sense, one is flexible, but at the same time, is at
home.

The superior man does according to the order
of his position and does not want to go beyond it. If he is in a noble position, he
behaves according to it. If he is in a
humble position, he also behaves according
to it. He can be at ease in either position.
. . . He rectifies himself and seeks nothing
from others, hence he does not have any complaints. He does not complain against
Heaven above or blame the people below.[22]

Chung also implies "timeliness" or "timely mean"
(shih chung, 時中). Human existence is in constant
change like the four seasons, so that an individual
who is in union with the universe shall be aware of
changes and be able to adjust with it. This dynamic
concept of timeliness in the flux of the universe is
neither fixed nor codified, but is to be enacted continuously from time to time.

Confucius conformed with the natural order
of heaven and followed the principle of
earth. Like earth, he supports all things,
and like heaven, he embraces all things. He
can be compared to the four seasons in their
successions, and to the sun and moon which
pursue one another without conflicts. . . .
Only the perfect sage in this world has
quickness of apprehension, understanding, insight and wisdom, which enable him to govern

all people; magnanimity, generosity, sincerity, and tenderness, which enable him to
tolerate all people; vitality, strength,
firmness and determination, which enable
him to be steadfast and reliable; orderliness, seriousness, timeliness and correct-
ness, which enable him to command a respect;
integrity, refinement and thoroughness,
which enable him to make proper judgment.[23]

In contrast, a ritual system and moral code established and imposed upon the people to obey and observe without questioning, the Golden Mean presented
here a more existential and contextual form of moral
action which exemplifies the dynamic personality of
an integrated selfhood.

The Golden Mean also indicates the tranquility,
equilibrium, and peacefulness that an integrated self
maintains in whatever situation one is in. The dichotomy between temporality of earthly time and eternity
of the universe and finitude of mundane place and infinite space is totally overcome and reconciled. The
Golden Mean called this state of mind "Ch'eng (誠)"
or "complete sincerity." It illustrates the meaning
of Yung (庸), namely constancy, permanence, un-
changeableness, and steadfastness.

Sincerity means the full realization of the
self, and the Tao is self-oriented. Sincerity is the beginning and end of all
things. . . . Therefore absolute sincerity
is continuously creative. By being continuously creative, it is everlasting. By
being everlasting, it is constantly realizing. By being constantly realizing, it is
inexhaustible and infinite. By being inexhaustible and infinite, it is extensive and
profound. By being extensive and profound,
it contains all things.[24]

Thus, the chapter, the Evolution of Rites (Li Yün
禮運) concludes the description of the state of authentic selfhood, "Great Unity" (Ta T'ung), as follows:

Confucius said: . . . When the great Tao is
fully realized, the whole world will become
equal to all, and sincerity will be emphasized, friendship cultivated, and all those
who have virtue, talent, and ability

223

equally honored. The people will not only
love their own parents, nor care only their
own children. A sufficient provision will
be secured for the elderly, full employment
for the able-bodied, and good education for
the young. Kindness and compassion will be
shown to the widows, orphans, childless-peo-
ple, and those who are disabled by disease,
so that they will have all the necessary supports. Men will have their proper works and
women have their homes. They shall hate to
see that the wealth of natural resources un-
developed, but will not hoard the wealth for
their own use. They shall hate that they do
not exert themselves to their capacity, but
will not exert themselves just for their own
benefits. Thus selfish schemings will be
repressed and found no development. Robbers,
flichers and traitors will be disappeared,
and hence the outdoors shall be left open.
This shall be the situation in the period of
Great Unity [Ta T'ung].[25]

The author of this chapter used the saying of Confucius to describe an ideal state of totally integrated individuals and great harmony realized in a
welfare society of ancient time, but, in fact, he was
describing his own vision of an ideal paradise in which
every individual would have his/her place in the world
and would be well cared for in spite of unfortunate
circumstances. Sin and crimes would recede and disappear from society, but love and sincerity would prevail and permeate all corners of the world.

Thus, we have made a brief survey of a long search
for authentic selfhood from the beginning of the Shang
dynasty to the Han dynasty and discovered that there
are various understandings and interpretations of the
status of the individual in society and the world.
There appeared four different ideas of selfhood advocated by four different groups of religious thinkers;
namely, the responsible selfhood, advocated by Confucius and Mencius; universal selfhood by the Mohists;
transcendental selfhood championed by chuang Tzu; and
integrated selfhood synthesized by the unknown authors
of three chapters in the Book of Rites. Search for
self-identity and authentic selfhood is an audacious
task and a long journey which never ends. In each
country and culture, both in the West and the East,
we should be able to find such men and women who

struggle to discover and fight for the authenticity
of selfhood, because it is a religious quest, universal
and perennial. The four ideas of authentic selfhood
developed in ancient China may even be a reference for
your own personal search for self-identity.

Footnotes

1. Lun Yü, XV, 38; VII, 7.

2. Lun Yü, IX, 5.

3. Shih Chih, Chap. 74.

4. Mencius, IVb, 3.

5. Mencius, IIa, 3.

6. Mencius, VIIb, 4.

7. Mencius, IIIa, 3.

8. Mo/Tzu, Chap. 26.

9. Mo Tzu, Chap. 27.

10. Mo Tzu, Chap. 26.

11. Mo Tzu, Chap. 16.

12. Mencius, IIIb, 9.

13. Lü Shih Ch'un Ch'iu, II, 2.

14. Chuang Tzu, Chap. 1.

15. Chaung Tzu, Chap. 2.

16. Chaung Tzu, Chap. 17.

17. Chaung Tzu, Chap. 21.

18. Chuang Tzu, Chap. 12.

19. Chaung Tzu, Chap. 6.

20. Ta Hsüeh, I.

21. Chung Yung, I, 1-5.

22. Chung Yung, XIV.

23. Chung Yung, XXX-XXXI.

24. Chung Yung, XXIV.

25. <u>Li Chih</u>, Chap. 7.

<u>Suggested Readings</u>

Yi-pao Mei, "The Status of the Individual in Chinese Thought and Practice," <u>The Chinese Mind</u>, ed. Charles A. Moore (Honolulu: University of Hawaii Press, 1967), pp. 323-339.

Wing-tsit Chan, "The Evolution of the Confucian Concept <u>Jen</u>," <u>Philosophy East and West</u> 4 (1955):295-301.

Homer H. Dubs , "The Development of Altruism in Confucianism," <u>Philosophy East and West</u> 1 (1951):48-55.

Yi-pao Mei, <u>Motse, The Neglected Rival of Confucius</u> (London: Probsthain, 1934).

Chun-i T'ang, "The Individual and the World in Chinese Methodology," <u>The Chinese Mind</u>, ed. Charles A. Moore (Honolulu: University of Hawaii Press, 1967), pp. 264-285.

Arthur Waley, <u>Three Ways of Thought in Ancient China</u> (New York: Doubleday, 1956).

Vitaly A. Rubin, <u>Individual and State in Ancient China</u>, tr. Steven I. Levine (New York: Columbia University Press, 1976).

CHAPTER 9

IS HUMAN NATURE GOOD OR EVIL?

Is human nature good or evil? This was one of the most keenly debated questions among ancient Chinese religious thinkers. As we have surveyed in the last chapter on the Search for Authentic Selfhood, there were long struggles of many individuals who had fought against the evils of oppression, warfare, exploitation, injustice, and discrimination in order to maintain their integrity. Why are there so many evils in this world? Why are there some people fighting back against the evils, while there are some people so aggressive and vicious? Where do these evils come from? Where do those people obtain the knowledge of goodness and the courage to fight back against the evils? Do the good and evil come from extra-human origin or basically from humanness itself? If the good and evil both had human origins, was it apriori already inborn in human nature or was it aposteriori that humans learned it? These questions are not only important to ancient Chinese people but also are significant for us, because we are confronted with the same questions everyday. The question of good and evil is a fundamental question to human existence, and it is not only a moral issue but also an issue related to religion, education, metaphysics, sociology, psychology, politics, and history. But among these disciplines, religion has been taken seriously from ancient times and has given many different answers. The following will present the issues and answers produced in ancient China, for they have written extensively on the question, and their answers can be a good reference for our thinking.

The basic premise of Chinese answers to the question of where good and evil come from is not metaphysical, but a human problem, and specifically related to human nature itself. This is possibly one of the basic differences between Chinese religion and Christianity. For traditional Christianity, the origin of evil or sin is described as originating through certain extra-human or metaphysical beings such as Satan, who induced human beings to rebel against God. It implies that there are two metaphysical beings or forces, good and evil, and they are in contention with each other. Human beings are simply caught up in the struggle between them and forced to make decisions as to which they should follow: good or evil. Thus, the issue of good or evil is both a metaphysical and human problem, and

they are inseparable. But in contrast to it, ancient
Chinese religion regarded the issue to be primarily a
human question and did not postulate mainly a metaphysical origin. Good is thought to be either innate
in human nature or earned by human effort; evil is regarded as what humans do to one another in a social
context, and they are not primarily related to a creator God and his opponent Satan as such. The problem of
"Good and Evil" is fundamentally understood as a human
problem, and only human beings are responsible for it;
and this is what makes various answers made by ancient
Chinese thinkers more existential and realistic to us
than that of Christianity. Because the Chinese considered "good and evil" basically a human problem, it
followed that each and every individual could become
involved in the resultant various debates, opinions,
and answers. It can be said that almost any thinkers
of ancient China, whether they were well-known or
little-known, Confucianist or non-Confucianist, had
something to say about the issue. So it is not very
easy to present all of the individualistic viewpoints.
What will be presented is a summary of the most representative ones, which will indicate major viewpoints.

So far, many Chinese scholars have classified
them into five categories: (1) Human nature is basically Good; (2) Human nature is basically Evil; (3) Human nature is neither Good nor Evil; (4) Human nature
is both Good and Evil; (5) Some have good nature, some
have evil nature. As one can see, this classification
is all based on the issue of human nature and different interpretations of it; therefore, it is most important to know what is this human nature that Chinese
thinkers were talking about. However, as we shall soon
see, they had no common consensus among themselves as
to the definition of human nature and the constituent
elements of human nature. It is also important to pay
attention to what concept of good and evil each thinker
was talking about, because they may not have the same
criterion to differentiate between good and evil.
Finally, it will be very interesting to discern what
implications and applications one can draw from each
thinker concerning the ethics, metaphysics, education,
politics, and religions disciplines. With these remarks in mind, let us examine these five different
viewpoints of human nature.

Human Nature is Basically Good

The first one to champion this view was Mencius.

Carrying his master Confucius's saying that "Human nature is the same in the beginning, but the learning
later on makes it different," Mencius stated that "Human nature is originally Good." How did he come to
such a conclusion? Because he had observed that human
beings have four virtues which he perceived to be intrinsic to human nature. They are the feeling of commiseration, the feeling of shame and dislike, the feeling of modesty and yielding and the sense of right and
wrong.

> All human beings are supposed to have a
> mind which cannot bear to see the suffering
> of other people. . . . For example, today men
> have seen suddenly a child about to fall into
> a well, they will without exception feel a
> sense of alarm and distress. . . .
> From this case, we can perceive that the
> one who does not have the sense of commisera-
> tion is not a human being. Likewise, the one
> who does not have the sense of shame and dis-
> like of the evil is not a human being. The
> one who does not have sense of modesty and
> yielding is not a human being. The one who
> does not have the sense of right and wrong is
> not a human being.
> The sense of commiseration is the begin-
> ning (tuan 端) of human relatedness (Jen).
> The sense of shame and dislike of the evil
> is the beginning of righteousness. The sense
> of modesty and yielding is the beginning of
> propriety. The sense of right and wrong is
> the beginning of wisdom. [<u>Mencius</u>, IIa, 6]

We can see here that Mencius deduced human heartedness, righteousness, propriety, and wisdom from the
four cardinal virtues, which Confucianism had strongly
advocated as the four beginnings of virtue. In other
words, he wanted to know what the potentiality and motivation are which produce morality, and he found them
in these four feelings and senses. He said that these
are the "beginnings," which could be interpreted to
mean potentiality, capacity, motivation, and initial
indications of goodness in human nature. Since society
has a moral code requiring all citizens to observe it,
there is an assumption that they have a capacity or potentiality to do good, otherwise such requirement will
be unreasonable and the institution of moral code mean-
ingless. Once you say, "one should do good," you are
already assuming that one is capable of doing good.

And it also implies that there must be something in
human nature that motivates to do good as well as being
good itself. Mencius found that initial indication in
the feeling of commiseration. All human beings,
whether they are rich or poor, nobles or lowly, men or
women, according to Mencius, would have great alarm
and a sense of distress, and spontaneity in jumping
forward to rescue when they saw a child about to fall
into a well. He explained that such spontaneity was
not caused by ulterior motivations of seeking praise
or fear of being criticized. These feelings and senses
were authentic, pure, and genuine; therefore, Mencius
affirmed they must be innate and original in human nature. Furthermore, he wanted to emphasize that such
genuine indications in human nature were the distinctive marks of human beings that distinguish humans
from animals. There were many elements or constituents
in human nature similar to animal nature, but Mencius
insisted that only human nature can do good; therefore,
only that part of nature in humans is distinguished as
human nature per se, or par excellence. Thus, he dared
to say that if one does not have such feelings and
sensitivity, one is categorically not a human being.
Mencius was not talking about the nature of living
beings in general, but specifically about human nature;
therefore, he stated that these four feelings and sen-
sitivities are the norm of human nature.

Thus Mencius made the claim:

> The sense of commiseration belongs to all
> human beings; so does that of shame and dis-
> like; that of reverence and respect; and
> that of right and wrong. . . . These are not
> fused into us from without. We originally
> are possessed of them. [_Mencius_, VIa, 6]

Now, if according to Mencius's statement that human nature is originally good, where does evil come
from? Or why do humans do wrong? There are possibly
two explanations in the teachings of Mencius. One is
to say that human nature has only provided the beginnings or potentiality for humans to do good, but not
all humans extend those beginnings to perfection or
realize that potentiality fully. Yes, Heaven gave us
that good nature within us when we were born, but not
all of us are developing that innate goodness to completion. In other words, the evilness is due to nondevelopment or incompletion on man's part. Therefore,
Mencius differentiated two parts in human beings: one

231

part which he called "the great part" (ta t'k 大体) is
the noble one, which has the mind to reflect the genuine nature of humanity and develops one's nature according to the principle of reason and righteousness.
The other part which he called "the small part" (hsiao
t'i 小体) is the lowly one, which does not have mind to
reflect the genuine nature of humanity, but behaves not
differently from animals. Originally, human nature is
all equal and good, but due to development and nondevelopment after birth that differentiates humankind
into two groups, there are those who are good and those
who are not good. The basic distinction between them
is that the former one has the mind to reflect and remind constantly of the good nature within and to make
effort to develop it to its completion. Mencius explained:

> Since [the good nature] belongs properly
> to all human beings, how it happened that
> some are lacking in human-relatedness and
> righteousness? Because, it is like the way
> in which trees are denuded by axes and bills,
> hewn down day after day, and cannot retain
> their beauty, the goodness of human mind
> (liang hsin 良心) cannot develop [to its full
> potential].
> And yet there is a possibility for its
> [the mind's] restoration. In the calm at-
> mosphere of deep night and early morning,
> trees try to restore and grow.
> But there is a restorative influence of
> night, and in the calm atmosphere of early
> morning, it returns to its pristine nature
> of humanity, tries to grow. And yet, if it
> is to be cut down again during the day, and
> the restorative influence of night is not
> sufficient to preserve the mind's natural
> goodness, what difference can you find be-
> tween human beings and irrational animals?
> But is this the reality of humanity?
> [Mencius, VIa, 8]

Mencius' use of the metaphor of a tree being cut
every day by axes and bills seems to imply that the
nondevelopment of good human nature is due to external
forces, of which he did not elaborate. But what he
wanted to indicate was that the tree is cut in such a
way that it simply does not have a chance to restore
its original pristine nature, not to mention its full
growth. However, he also hinted that good human nature

is not entirely uprooted, and there is still "the
restorative influence of the night" and "the calm atmosphere of early morning" for possible growth. The
conscientious one would still struggle to utilize this
"influence of night" and "calm atmosphere of morning"
to restore integrity, but if one no longer struggles
and lets it die out, then one can no longer be human,
but becomes no more than an animal. Of course, we cannot stretch the metaphor too far, but it may indicate
what Mencius meant by the difference between the "great
part" and the "small part."

The other intepretation of the origin of evil
might be that there are some beginnings in human nature, which lead one into doing evil. Mencius only
stated the four beginnings which lead towards goodness,
and he did not mention the beginnings which lead toward
evilness. So far, we did not see Mencius was denying
the possibility that as there is a potentiality of
doing good, so there may be a potentiality of doing
evil. The reason he did not mention that the possibility or beginnings leading towards evilness existed
was that it should not be called "human" or "human nature." In other words, Mencius was thinking categorically "to be human" is to be moral; therefore, he did
not bother to mention it nor elaborate on it. It was,
however, developed by other religious thinkers that
either human nature has some leadings toward evilness
or human nature itself has duality: one leading toward
goodness and the other evilness.

Mencius' view had many significant implications
and applications. Metaphysically, his view confirmed
that Heaven,which gave such "good human nature" to human beings, must itself be "Good," and the universe is
fundamentally "good." Moral force is more positive,
constructive, and normative than evil force. Evil is
not taken too seriously by Mencius, for it is just a
nondevelopment, passivity, deprivation, degradation,
and incompletion of good nature. Since original goodness is not totally eradicated, education and exhortation would be good enough to restore the good nature
of human beings and to encourage its development. Such
radical treatment as redemption, atonement, forgiveness
of sin and salvation are not needed. Wisemen and
teachers would be sufficient to cope with the problem
of evil, and saviour and messiah are not needed. The
method of education would be more in the way of "en-
lightening" rather than "inspiring." To pull out what
is innate and good inside of human nature than to

233

impose upon it from outside would be the proper method
for education. Government should acknowledge and respect such innate good nature in each individual and
allow for each one to develop one's own potentiality.
Provision of better educational facility is better than
building many prisons to jail the evil ones. True
goodness is to be spontaneous and voluntary, but not
coersive and compulsory. Basically, Mencius' view of
human life is optimistic and positive and stresses
human effort rather than merely relying on human nature.

Mencius believed in the ultimate goodness of Heav-
en as the source of goodness. Heaven conferred His
sanction or decree to the sages to promote the good
cause on earth. Although it was only human conduct
and effort that produced good in society, humans can
aspire for the "moving force" (huo jan chih ch'i 浩然
之氣) to strengthen and nourish moral consciousness.
The rituals for Mencius were for the proper expression
of morality and virtue.

Good will and moral action need proper form of
expression, and various rites are for the expression
of various virtues. For example, ancestral worship is
an expression of the sense of respect, and the rite of
court diplomacy is the feeling of modesty. All the
rituals are an expression of the virtue of propriety.
The ideal religious leader in Mencius' view would be
the exemplary sage who has accomplished the virtues
and received the Heavenly sanction to be a model of
good deeds.

Human Nature is Originally Evil

Hsün Tzu, another great disciple of Confucianism,
contradicted Mencius's viewpoint and claimed that the
nature of man (hsing 性) is evil and his goodness is
only acquired training (wei 偽). In other words, human nature itself is evil, and goodness is only what
one has accomplished by one's learning and moral efforts. Wei literary means "human action" (jen wei 人
為) and implies "human accomplishment" such as culture,
education, institution, moral code. Like Jesus said,
"One cannot expect to collect grapes from thistles,"
Hsün Tzu regarded it impossible to produce any goodness
out of the basic nature in humanness. Perhaps he had
quite a different view of human nature from that of
Mencius, which is why he came to such a diametrically
opposite stand. Let us see what he described about
human nature, and how goodness fared, in his view.

234

That in human beings which does not acquire
by learning and cannot be worked for, is
what we mean by nature (性 hsing). That in
human beings which acquires by learning and
can be worked for, is called human action
[wei]. [Hsün-Tzu, XXIII]

Now human beings, by their nature, from birth
love profit, and when they continue this tendency, bitter conflicts and inordinate greeds
will increase, whereas courtesy and modesty
will disappear. From birth, human beings are
envious and hateful, and when they follow
this tendency, injuries and destructions will
increase, whereas sincerity and faithfulness
will disappear. . . .
    Therefore, to control and harness human
nature which produces these evils is essential. . . . The civilizing influence of
teachers and laws, and the guidance of propriety and righteousness are absolutely necessary. Thereupon courtesy will appear, culture develop, and orderly society realize.
[Hsün-Tzu, XIX]

    The people in the street are all capable
of becoming a sage like Yü (禹). What made
Yü as a sage was that he practiced human-
relatedness, righteousness, obedience to law,
and uprightness. So there is a possibility
for everyone to know these virtues. Then, if
everyone in the street knows these virtues and
put them into practice, it is obvious that
everyone can become a sage like Yü. [Hsün-
Tzu, XXIII]

Human nature, according to Hsün Tzu is "the un-
wrought material of the original" given at birth by
Heaven who is rather mechanistic, and lacks any moral
principle, therefore nothing good is to be associated
with it. And why did Hsün Tzu judge human nature to
be evil? Because he observed that it loves profit,
tends to strive and plunder, to envy and hate, and
possesses the desires of the ear and eye. These are
the evil tendencies in human nature which produce in-
jury, destruction, impurity, and disorder in society
and also cause the virtues of courtesy, yielding,
loyalty, faithfulness, and proper conduct to disappear
from human relationships.

We can see that Hsün Tzu had rather a negative
view of human nature. So, if humankind was left to
itself, it would not produce any goodness and culture,
but would destroy itself by its own evil nature. He
could not and did not see what Mencius saw--the beginnings or potentiality of goodness in human nature and
transformation of human nature by education and civilization. To him, human nature is like a jungle, from it
a culture could not be produced, but civilization can
carve into the jungle to build a culture. Or, human
nature is like a savage, uneducated and undisciplined,
and culture is like a mandarin adult who is civilized.
His view reflected a traditional mentality which looked
at foreigners as savages and only Chinese as civilized.

However, he did not deny that there is the possibility to do good, and that possibility could come from
two sources. One source comes from the requirements of
society. If humans are to be entirely isolated and
live independently, there is no need to do good, but
since humans have to live together and form a society,
eventually a social code and moral discipline are required, and each and every individual has to acquire
that moral obligation. Whether one likes it or not,
education becomes a compulsory condition to being a
citizen; and in education, moral education is essential in producing goodness. Therefore, the civilizing
influence of teachers and laws and the guidance of the
rules of proper conduct and standard of justice are
absolutely necessary. Through education, one acquires
the learning and knowledge of culture and training of
moral conduct, and one can even become a sage, like the
ancient, virtuous, King Yü, the founder of Hsia dynasty. Morality is basically made by man, and so is
called "acquired".

But a question might be raised as to this source
of goodness, that is "What is the ultimate origin of
this source?" Where did King Yü derive his sense of
virtue and the cause for a moral code? And even though
goodness comes from education, can you educate the one
who does not have any good nature to receive and become civilized? How is human nature to be transformed
by education and civilization unless there is some potentiality in human nature to be civilized? Apparently,
although Hsün Tzu did not try to elaborate, because he
wanted to emphasize that morality is acquired, he
hinted that there is "a possibility for knowing and
practicing human-heartedness, righteousness, obedience
to law and uprightness." He also said that "man on the

street can direct his capacities to learning, concentrating his mind on one object, thinking and studying and investigating thoroughly, adding daily to his knowledge and long retaining it," he can become a sage too. So after all, there is a possibility and capacity in spite of evil human nature. In fact, Hsün Tzu was not dissimilar from Mencius in his view of human capacity to learn, that there is a mind in humans to reflect and to know what is right and what is wrong. So, on the surface, one might think that Hsün Tzu's view is entirely different from Mencius', but as a matter of fact, both of them recognize that in human nature, there are potentiality and capacity for doing good and doing evil. The only difference is that while Mencius emphasized that only human nature leading to do good should be counted as human, Hsün Tzu stressed that education and civilization are needed to control evil nature and let the good capacity develop. They used the same word "hsin" to designate human nature, but they focus differently on the different tendencies or potentialities in human nature.

Another thing common between Mencius and Hsün Tzu was that both were quite orthodox, dogmatic, and normative in their thinking about human nature. They both carried the same orthodox tradition of Confucius' hierarchical and authoritarian ethics codified as the principles of human-heartedness, righteousness, propriety and wisdom, and tried to read those principles into human nature. The only difference is that while Mencius found these four feelings and senses correlative to the cardinal principles and judged that thereby human nature must be good, Hsün Tzu could not find such direct correlation with the cardinal principles and judged that thereby human nature must be evil. But setting aside their dogmatic judgments and normative views of human nature, both of them had to acknowledge that human nature has a larger possibility or capacity in evil human nature to learn and accomplish the good as Mencius had suggested. So that, in spite of their diametrically opposing views, there is not only something in common, but also some alternative views needed to adjust their differences. But before discussing other alternative views, let us first consider the implications and applications of Hsün Tzu's view.

Logically speaking, if Hsün Tzu said that human nature is evil, then Heaven which gave human nature to human beings should be described as evil as well, and

likewise, the universe is also evil, and the environment humans live in is rather negative and passive to
human goodness. But Hsün Tzu did not describe Heaven,
the universe, and environment as evil, but rather neutral or mechanical. He simply stated that "Heaven has
a constant regular movement and it did not exist for
the sake of Yao [a virtuous king] nor cease to exist
for the sake of Chieh [an evil king]." (Hsün Tzu,
XVII). Hsün Tzu even discouraged the people from worshipping and offering sacrifices to Heaven, because one
would not receive any inspiration from Heaven to do
good, nor any reward to human moral conduct.

Religion to Hsün Tzu was only a matter of human
affairs and social conduct. Rituals were not for the
worship of God, but merely the expression of civilized
behavior and for promotion of social harmony. Education was more important than religion and essential for
the survival of a society and culture. Since human nature cannot produce goodness, and only education can,
education should be compulsory and obligatory to all
citizens. The method of education should be authoritative, normative, and dogmatic. Teachers should have
full authority and power to enforce learning. Laws
should be rigidly codified and strictly enforced.
Proper reward and punishment should be the significant
functions of government, the clear distinction and
stratification among the members in the society according to merits and demerits should be enforced. Because of his strong emphasis on law and order, Hsün Tzu
has been regarded as the father of legalism, and we can
see that "legalism" originated with his view that "human nature is evil."

It may appear that it was because of Hsün Tzu's
negative and pessimistic view of human nature that his
authoritarian and legalistic orthodoxy developed, but
we should not forget that he still felt that evil human nature, in spite of its evilness,could be transformed and corrected. Each individual who walks the
street can become a sage if the right education and
moral discipline is properly applied. However, no matter how morality is perceived by humans, goodness is
what humans have acquired.

Human Nature is Neither Good nor Evil

Kao Tzu (告子), a contemporary of Mencius, appeared to challenge Mencius' view by stating: "Nature
is neither good nor bad." It has been designated

either good or bad depending on the criteria of good
and evil one has and how one looks at human nature.
Good and evil are all judgmental and external to nature
itself. When one no longer applies one's value judgment, but calmly takes human nature as it is, one could
honestly say that it is neither good nor bad. This is
an interesting argument developed by Kao Tzu, but, unfortunately, we no longer have the writing of Kao Tzu
to know the entire scope of his argument. We only have
some fragments of his sayings recorded in the works of
Mencius, the one he challenged, so we should expect
that his view would be limited to only what Mencius
wanted to put in his work. Besides, it was in the context of polemics; therefore, the weakness of his view
would have been more exposed. However, we should read
whatever was recorded and make our own judgment of Kao
Tzu's view. Kao Tzu noted:

> The nature is like whirling water. If you
> open a passage for it to the east, it will
> flow to the east; open a passage to the west,
> and it will flow to the west. Human nature
> does not make distinction between good and
> evil, just as the water makes no distinction
> between east and west. [Mencius VIa, 3]

> The nature may be made to be either good or
> evil. Under the rules of the virtuous kings
> like Wen and Wu, eventually the people loved
> what was good, whereas under the rules of
> evil kings like Yu and Li, the people loved
> what was cruel. [Mencius VIa, 6]

Kao Tzu's view of the neutrality of human nature
has certain validity because "good and evil" are relative, and there is no absolute criterion to make a
final judgment on human nature, good or evil. In addition, making judgment upon human nature is rather artificial; furthermore, it's destructive, like making a
cup or bowl from a willow tree. It distorts the intrinsic and pristine nature and produces rather a superficial and utilitarian view of nature. In this way,
humans no longer enjoy nature as it is, but always look
at nature from the moral point of view or attempt to
exploit it according to the needs and desires of human
society.

Mencius acknowledged that Kao Tzu had attained to
a state of undisturbed mind (pu tung hsin 不動心);
thus, Kao Tzu could come to realize that we are

239

imposing our subjective minds upon nature, and that we
should let nature alone, to be as it is. However, Mencius tried to interpret Kao Tzu's "state of undisturbed
mind" as the result of moral cultivation and the ex-
altedness of righteousness, but Kao Tzu refused to
agree with him. The state of undisturbed mind is
amoral, like a blank sheet of white paper or a flat,
clean mirror. Goodness or evilness is just an objective reflection of whatever comes into contact with it.
Human-heartedness is an internal reflection, and righteousness is an external reflection. It is interesting
to note that Kao Tzu's description of the state of undisturbed mind was quite similar to Hsün Tzu's description of Heaven which is "neutral and mechanical."

Taoists were also generally in support of Kao Tzu's
view that human nature is neither good nor evil. Among
the Taoists, Chuang Tzu was the one who most often
ridiculed the Confucianist's view (including both Mencius and Hsün Tzu), so let us present Chuang Tzu's view
to supplement Kao Tzu's.

> To act by way of non-action (wu wei 無為) is
> called the nature. . . . That is of the na-
> ture is internal, whereas that is of the
> artificial is external. To put a halter on
> a horse's head and put a string through an
> ox's nose are that which is artificial.
> [Chaung Tzu, XVII]

> The people have generally a constant nature:
> to weave and clothe themselves, till and
> feed themselves. This is the common nature
> to all people, and everyone agrees with it.
> This is believed to be given by Nature. In
> the age when the human nature was perfect,
> the people moved quietly and gazed stead-
> fastly. There were no highways running over
> the mountains and no bridges to cross over
> the waters. Things were all born and able to
> mature, and each one found home in its native
> place. . . . In this age of perfect nature,
> human beings dwelt together with birds and
> beasts, and human race was one with all
> things. Why should there be distinctions of
> superior man or inferior man? All beings are
> equally lacking in desires, for they are all
> in the state of "Unadorned Simplicity" (su
> p'u 素僕). Being in this state, they all had
> possessed their primordial nature. [Chuang

240

<u>Tzu</u>, IX]

Bring your mind into a state of quietitude,
and your spirit (ch'i 氣) into a state of
non-differentiation. Follow the spontaneity
of things and hold within you no elements of
ego. Then the entire nation will be governed
by itself. [<u>Chuang Tzu</u>, VII]

Let the people alone, and not try to govern
them for the sake of your success. Let the
people be as they are without polluting their
innate natures or stimulating their instincts
[with your power and glory]. When the people
do not pollute their natures and stir their
instincts, then is it really necessary to
have a government? [<u>Chuang Tzu</u>, XI]

From the above quotations, one can see a great
similarity between the views of Kao Tzu and those of
Chuang Tzu. Nature by itself is transcending human
criteria of good and evil. Chuang Tzu was quite cyni-
cal about the endless argument and hot debate among
Confucian scholars of what is right and what is wrong.
After all, moral codes made by humans are relative and
temporal to one another, and there is no absolute goodness or evilness. However, Chuang Tzu's emphasis on
the transcendental quality of nature and his ridiculing
human artificiality and arbitrariness did not stop his
claim that nature itself is, to him, the absolute good,
and "returning back to nature" is the goodness of humanity. The "state of Unadorned Simplicity" (su p'u)
is the highest good and the most original of human nature. He believed that human nature, in spite of all
its distortion, disintegration, artificiality, and
arbitrariness can still restore one to a pristine state.
As he said, "Bring your mind into a state of quiet, and
your energy into a state of indifference, follow the
spontaneity of things and hold within you no element of
ego," and one can return and restore one's lost state
and original nature.

Of course, to Chuang Tzu, evilness is human artificiality, arbitrariness, and distortion, which are all
deviations from the pristine nature. But the worst of
all is the human coercion of other living beings to
conform to human principle and the moral dictatorship
to force upon others submission to one's selfish interest. Chuang Tzu stated this evilness in a most
simple way.

The duck's legs are by nature short, but if
we lengthen them, the duck will feel pain.
The crane's legs are by nature long, but if
we cut them short, the crane will feel grief.
Therefore, we should not amputate what is by
nature long, nor to lengthen what is by nature short. [Chuang Tzu, VIII]

In a sense, Chuang Tzu's view was not entirely
different from Mencius' view. He agreed to Mencius'
definition that human nature is originally good, although what he meant by good might have been different
from Mencius' understanding of goodness. Both Chuang
Tzu and Mencius would like to have seen the spontaneous
development of human nature without being obstructed
and oppressed by external forces. Both of them also
stated that the ultimate goodness is the human union
with the universe and the ultimate harmony of the whole
universe. However, Chuang Tzu must have vehemently
opposed the viewpoint of Hsün Tzu. He could not agree
with Hsün Tzu's definition of human nature as evil,
because he did not see the evilness that Hsün Tzu saw
as original to human nature. The vices of selfishness,
destructiveness, greed, and desire are, to Chuang Tzu,
manmade rather than originally given by Tao. Therefore, he strongly opposed Hsün Tzu's emphasis of authoritarian education and law enforcement to transform
human nature from evilness to goodness. Instead, he
accused Hsün Tzu of creating and promoting more evils,
because such coercion is the cause of all evils. But
even though he disagreed with Hsün Tzu, Chuang Tzu had
to answer the question: Where does evil really come
from? He could simply say that evil came from external
coercion and blame the society and institutions for the
cause of all evils. But, there must be something in
human nature that leads humans into doing evils,
whether it is a tendency, disposition, or potentiality
or capacity. Of course, Chuang Tzu did not elaborate
on this because he denied that there would be evilness
in the original nature. However, it could be, and it
is only the author's speculation that from the time an
individual is born and separated from the ultimate origin (or stated metaphysically as when Te has separated
from Tao) and individuation took place, certain differentiation and distinction were brought in and the cause
of alienation and discrimination already started. As
Chuang Tzu himself said:

What each individual thing obtained [from
Tao] to become existant is called Te [virtue].

> . . . Each physical form encloses within it-
> self the spiritual substance which is pri-
> vate and special. This spiritual substance
> is what we called as its nature (hsing 心生).
> [Chuang Tzu, XII]

This primordial separation caused by individuation
might be the initial tendency leading toward evil.
Since Chuang Tzu did not specifically state it as "original evil" or "original sin," we should hold our own
questions in abeyance here.

Let us see the implications and applications of
Chuang Tzu's view. Metaphysically, he thought that the
nature was absolutely good, and that nature should be
left alone without any interference by humans. Human
goodness is to return to pristine nature and reunite
with the universe. Evilness is human artificiality,
arbitrariness, and coercion. Ethics and morality are
not needed, for they are rather obstructive to the
process of returning back to nature. Ritual and ceremony are insignificant and superficial, but meditation
and self-discipline are essential for reunion with
nature. Education is not needed, for self-enlighten-
ment is possible. Teachers and law-enforcement officers are the most abhorent professions and are to be
avoided. Government should govern without governing
and leave the people alone. Absolute freedom and total
liberation from social fetters were the most desirable
for the Taoists. Free roaming in the universe and enjoyment of ectasy was the happiest state of all.

Human Nature is Both Good and Evil

Wang Ch'ung (王充 ,A.D. 27-c. 79) mentioned in his
book Lun Heng that there was a group of Confucianists
led by Shih Shih (世碩) who proposed a new interpretation of human nature. They claimed that human nature is partly good and partly bad, and that, if the
good nature in man be cultivated and developed, his
goodness increases; whereas if his bad nature be cultivated and developed, his badness increases. But this
view was more fully developed by Tung Chung-hsu. He
adopted Mencius' view of the four good beginnings in
human nature, but he did not agree that they are by
themselves good, for they need to be cultivated and
developed to become good. He also found that Hsün Tzu's
view had certain truth that there was some evilness in
human nature and unless controlled or transformed will
lead to evil. Initially, he stated that human nature

243

itself has both characters: good and evil, but later
on, he seemed to say that the evil character in nature
is more an emotional feeling (rather than rational).

> Truly, there exist in human beings both love
> and covetousness, each of which lies within
> their bodies. Since the body is received
> from Heaven and Heaven has its dual manifes-
> tations of Yin and Yang, the body likewise
> has the dual qualities of love and covetous-
> ness. [Ch'un Ch'iu Fan Lu, XXXV]

> Goodness is like a kernal of grain; the na-
> ture is like the growing stalk of that grain.
> Although the stalk produces the kernal, we
> cannot say that the stalk is itself the ker-
> nal, so even though the nature produces good-
> ness, we cannot say that the nature itself is
> good. . . . Therefore, I say that the nature
> possess the stuff of goodness, but that it
> cannot by itself act for goodness. This is
> mere rhetoric on my part, because it repre-
> sents actual truth. [Ch'un Ch'iu Fan Lu,
> XXXVI]

> Some would argue that since the nature con-
> tains the beginnings of goodness, how can the
> nature itself not be good? But I reply that
> it is not so. For like the silk cocoon con-
> tains the silk fibers and yet itself is not
> silk; like the eggs contain the chicken and
> yet themselves are not chicken, so if we fol-
> low these analogies, what can we doubt more?
> [Ch'un Ch'iu Fan Lu, XXXV]

Tung Chung-shu's view is perhaps the most sensible
and realistic view of all, for it acknowledges the fact
that both good and evil exist, and there must be some
correlations between good and evil of human nature.
Human nature must have two characters or elements or
tendencies relating respectively to either good or evil.
Meantime, each character is only potentiality or indication and cannot fully count as morally good or evil.
It needs to be cultivated and developed to become realization, like "an egg has to be hatched to become a
chicken, and a silk cocoon has to be unraveled to make
silk." Tung's view is really a good combination of
Mencius' and Hsün Tzu's views, because both of them
recognized that good and evil must relate to human

nature. His view is also easier and simpler to grasp
in describing the cause and origin of good and evil.

However, a difficult question arose from his view:
How could two opposite qualities and values come from
the same origin? Can the same fountain produce sweet
and bitter waters simultaneously? It could be explained that the difference between good and evil is
relative and artificially made by humans, like the Taoists did. But Tung explained that the difference was,
rather, due to the metaphysical difference. Like Heav-
en has two forces: Yin and Yang, when humans were born,
"the dual qualities of covetousness and love" were
given, however, in a dormant situation. It is up to an
individual to develop those "dual qualities" into good
or evil. This correlation between the Yin-Yang forces
with the good-evil morality would easily develop into
a Zoroastrian metaphysical dualism, which believes that
there is the Good God Ahra Mazda and the Evil God
Ahriman who are in contention with each other. However, Tung did not go to far into that dualism.

Several implications can be drawn from Tung's
views. Since he tried to emphasize that both good and
evil are within human nature and both are correlated
with the Yin and Yang cosmic forces, there is an implication of moral dualism in the universe and the conflict between good and evil might be related to the
cosmic battle between the Good Yang force and the Evil
Yin force. Hitherto, Yin-Yang philosophers did not
correlate the Yin-Yang forces with the morality of
humankind, it was started by Tung and followed by
later Neo-Confucian scholars like Chang Tsai, Cheng
Hao, and Chu Hsi.

Tung's view also implies that there is an existential dichotomy in human moral conduct. In each and
every human action, one has to decide which path to
follow, and such a decision involves certain tension
and conflict within one's self. When such existential
dichotomy has deepened, it will create a moral antinomy
and spiritual quandary such as Paul experienced. Paul
wrote:

> In my inmost self I delight in the law of
> God, but I perceive that there is by my
> bodily members a different law, fighting
> against the law that my reason approves and
> making me a prisoner under the law that is
> in my members, the law of sin. Miserable

creature that I am, who is there to rescue
me out of this body doomed to death? [<u>New
English Bible</u>, Romans 7:22-24]

Instead of seeking a saviour for salvation, Tung
emphasized that hard discipline and authoritarian education should control evil nature while cultivating
and developing good nature. Ho took the side of Hsün
Tzu's emphasis on rigid law enforcement and totalitar-
ian control of government. If an individual is incapable or indecisive in choosing good over evil, the
society has to take over the moral responsibility to
control the conduct of an individual.

Moreover, when human nature can be divided into
both good and evil simultaneously, eventually more
diversification of human nature could be developed.
Thus, we see that not only Tung himself divided human
nature into "nature and feeling," but many of his followers also divided human nature into three levels.
Wang Chung asserted:

> I am quite decisive in my opinion that what
> Mencius meant by the goodness in human na-
> ture refers only to the people who are above
> the average, and what Hsün Tzu meant by the
> evilness in human nature refers only to the
> people who are below the average, and what
> Yang Hsung meant by the mixture of good and
> evil in human nature refers to the people of
> average. [<u>Wang Chung</u>, XIII]

This further division extends into a new view
which classifies humankind into two groups: the good
and the evil ones.

<u>Some People Have a Good Nature and Some
People Have an Evil Nature</u>

As you can see, this view was an extension from
the fourth view which divided human nature into a dualism of good and evil. However, this view instead of
dividing human nature, divided human beings into two
groups. Wang Chung said:

> When we speak of the natures of human beings,
> there are in fact some who are good and some
> who are bad. The good ones are definitely so
> of themselves, whereas the bad ones can also
> be transformed to become good by exerting

themselves. When the rulers or parents see
the natures of their subjects or children
are good, they should support, encourage and
lead them on to do good and not allow them to
come in contact with evil. But if their subjects or children are bad, they should shield
them from evil and place prohibitions upon
them, so that they can gradually shift to
goodness. It is through the gradual transi-
tions of goodness into evil, and the transformation of evil into goodness, that the
process of nature reaches to its final form.
[<u>Wang Chung</u>, IV]

Such distinction between the good people and evil
people will be further extended into a more rigid classification developed by Han Yü (786-824 A.D.). He says
that the evil ones are somewhat predestined and not able
to be educated.

There are three grades of human nature: the
superior, the medium and the inferior. The
superior is good, and good only. The medium
may be either superior or inferior. The inferior is evil, and evil only. . . .
    In discussion about human nature, Men-
cius said that human nature is good, but
Hsün Tzu said that human nature is evil. And
Yang Hsiung said that human nature is a mixture of good and evil. Their sayings that
human nature is good at first but subsequently
becomes evil, or bad at first and subsequently
become good, or mixed at first and now becomes either good or evil, are all concerning
the medium grade only and ignoring the superior and inferior grades. . . .
    The nature of the superior grade shall
become more intelligent through education,
whereas the nature of inferior grade shall
have fewer faults by prohibition and control.
. . . But their grades have been pronounced
by Confucius to be unchangeable. [<u>Han Yu</u>, I]

It is easier for a moralist to distinguish and
classify the people according to his moral criterion
and judgment than to make a tedious analysis into the
complex nature of human beings. However, as you can
see, such social division and stratification into the
"good guy" or the "bad guy" have implied certain discrimination and segregation, which is unfair and

unjustifiable. It will also produce a predeterminism
like Arthur Jensen's theory that certain groups of people or races are born with low I.Q.'s and impossible
of improvement. Such racial discrimination and predeterminism have created many tensions in society and
also many crimes like Hitler's (or Nazi's) massacre
of six million Jews.

This view also implied that the universe is divided into good and evil and a mixture of these, and
they are all predetermined without any rational explanation or moral justification. Biological and psychological predeterminism will take precedence over the
freedom of will and possibility of social change.
Morality, education, civilization, and administration
are only available to the "chosen ones" who are capable
of doing good. Those born to do evil are eternally
condemned. Sociologically, this view will enhance the
discrimination, segregation, and elitism. Government
will only provide opportunity for the good ones to
ascend the ladder of success, while the bad ones are
to be subdued and oppressed or exploited. Two-class
society or hierarchical systems will be produced by
this view when it is applied to specific societal conditions.

As a conclusion to our study of the various views
of human nature developed in ancient China, we can make
a chart to summarize and compare their differences and
suggest possible applications in terms of metaphysics,
ethics, education, government, and religion.

As can be seen from the chart, there are various
answers to the question: Is human nature Good or Evil?
Each different answer would have its related implications to various other fields such as metaphysics,
ethics, education, government (politics), and religion.
A simple statement representing a certain (or casual)
attitude to human life is really involved and related
to many other issues in society and the world. Of
course, the chart reflecting only the representative
views of ancient China does not cover the entire scope
of the possible answers to the question, but, at least,
it can provide for us a reference for our study and
thinking.

It helps us see the range of thinking reflected in
ancient Chinese religious thinkers on this basic moral
issue. We can also gain a reference point and comparative perspective from which to compare our own modern

VARIOUS VIEWS OF HUMAN NATURE IN ANCIENT CHINA

	A	B	C	D	E
1. Theorist:	Mencius	Hsün Tzu	Chuang Tzu (Kao Tzu)	Tung Chung-shu (Shih Shih)	Wang Chung Han Yü
2. Statement-- Human Nature is:	Good	Evil	Neither Good nor Evil	Both Good and Evil	Some are Good Some are Evil
3. View of Nature:	Human	Uncivilized	Natural	Divided	Differentiated (classified)
4. Criterion of Morality:	Normative	Dogmatic	Descriptive (amoral)	Relativistic	Selective
5. Principle of Metaphysics:	Ultimate Goodness	Mechanistic	Transcendental	Dualistic	Predeterministic
6. Method of Education:	Enlightenment	Authoritarian	Spontaneity	Doctrinal	Aristocratic
7. Function of Government:	Provisional	Legalistic	Non-Inter-ference	Authoritarian	Bureaucratic
8. Religion:					
a. Concept of God	The Source of Goodness	The Mechanical Heaven	The Inter-personal Tao	The Dual Gods: God of Goodness; God of Evil	The Hierarchy of Gods
b. Purpose of the Ritual	Expression of Propriety	Training and Discipline	Meditative and Contemplation	Distinction and Sanctification	Classification and Stratification
c. Ideal Person	The Exemplary Sage	The Disciplin-ary Teacher	Nature-Mystic	The Prophet and Judge	The Noble and Elite

thought on this issue.[1]

FOOTNOTES

1. For further studies on the goodness and evilness of human nature in Chinese thought, please refer to the following works: Wing-tsit Chan, "The Concept of Man in Chinese Thought" in The Concept of Man, ed. Radhakrishna, S., and P. T. Raju (London: George Allen and Unwin, 2d., 1966); John Wu, "Mencius' Philosophy of Human Nature and Natural Law," in Chinese Culture 1, No. 1 (1957):1-19; A. S. Cua, "The Quasi-Empirical Aspect of Hsün Tzu's Philosophy of Human Nature" in Philosophy East and West 28, No. 1 (1979):3-19.

Suggested Readings

Homer H. Dubs, "Mencius and Sun-dz on Human Nature," Philosophy East and West 6 (1956):213-222.

D. C. Lau, "Theories of Human Nature in Mencius and Shyuntzyy," Bulletin of the School of Oriental and African Studies 15 (1953):541-565.

Donald J. Munro, The Concept of Man in Early China (Stanford: Stanford University Press, 1968).

250

CHAPTER 10

THE IDEAL IMAGE OF HUMANITY

Chapter 8 described how the ancient Chinese struggled to find their authentic selfhood. It was a long search under oppression and against many hostile forces, and yet each religious leader of different schools was able to come up with reasonable claims for an authentic selfhood. Then, in chapter 9, we discussed five different answers to the question, Is Human Nature Good or Evil? Apparently all answers assumed that there exists both good and evil, and, ultimately, one must seek doing more good and avoid doing evil. In other words, ancient Chinese were quite realistic in acknowledging that the present human life is not ideal, and the goal of human life is to seek and perfect the ideal each one has envisioned for one's life. The following will elaborate on the ideal images of humanity that ancient Chinese sages envisioned accomplishing. Confucius was the first one to present the ideal image of Chün Tzu (君子) or the Noble Man as his ideal of humanity. Although Mo Tzu did not particularly present his ideal image of humanity, he himself was called by his followers as Chü Tzu (鉅子) or the Great Man, and his conduct was regarded as the exemplary model for those who followed him. Therefore, we shall elaborate on the Mohist notion of Chü Tzu as the ideal image of humanity for Mohism. For the Taoistic image of humanity, it was Chuang Tzu, rather than Lao Tzu, who described more clearly the ideal image of Chen Jen (真人) or the True Man.

Confucius' Image of the Noble Man
(Chün Tzu, 君子)

Confucius had borrowed the term Chün Tzu from the Book of Poetry which he edited and used as a textbook in teaching his disciples. In the Book of Poetry, Chün Tzu appeared altogether 90 times. Among them, 36 times were used in a domestic sense--"my lord"--as spoken by wife, mistress, girl, or retainer. They were mostly used by women in calling their men. There were 36 uses in public, in an administrative and political sense. They were addressed to the feudal lords and aristocrats indicating their rank and honor. There were three instances applied to women, and two instances contrasting with small men (hsiao jen 小人). Lastly, there were 14 instances in which Chün Tzu had distinctive moral overtones, signifying the moral character and duties of feudal lords and aristocrats.[1]

However, when Confucius borrowed the term Chün Tzu from the Book of Poetry, he had stressed much more the moral character and conduct of Chün Tzu even though he did not radically negate the hereditary nature of feudal lordship that Chün Tzu always implied. In other words, he did not apply the term to everyone with the idea that all are capable of becoming a Chün Tzu as long as one has reached the moral standard Chün Tzu would require. Instead, Confucius acknowledged that those feudal lords were the rulers, and what he fervently hoped was that the feudal lords would not take for granted their hereditary lordship and govern their states according to their desires, but take their position and duties seriously and cultivate their moral character worthy of being a ruler. In the Analects of Confucius, the word Chün Tzu appeared 65 times; and in all but three instances, it was clearly used in a moral sense, signifying a "noble man" or an "ideal man."[2]

Chün Tzu originally indicated aristocratic birth, but Confucius had changed its meaning (or rather idealized it) to become an exemplary model of personality. It is quite parallel to the semantic change from the medieval "noble" to the modern "noble man." From numerous sayings of Confucius in the Analects, this study revealed the following characteristics in the quality of humanity that the word Chün Tzu implied.

First, Chün Tzu is the Person of Principle (Tao). The following passages quoted from the Analects of Confucius makes it very clear that Chün Tzu is a person who dedicates himself to the cause of Tao, regardless of his circumstances.

> Chün Tzu does not seek satisfaction in eating nor comfort in lodging. Instead, he is diligent in his works and careful in his speech. He associates with the people of principle [Tao] that he may be rectified. Such a person may be said to be a person who loves learning. [I:14]

> Chün Tzu seeks the Tao and not mere living. Regardless of whether there is starvation in farming or riches in the pursuit of studies, Chün Tzu worries about the Tao and not about poverty. [XV:31]

> Chü Po-yü is indeed a Chün Tzu: When the

state seeks to follow the Tao, he served it.
When the state discards the Tao, he rolls his
principle up and keeps it in his breast.
[XV:6]

Wealth and honor are what everybody desires.
But if they are to be obtained in violation
of the principles [Tao], one should not do it.
Poverty and humble place are what everybody
dislikes. But if they are to be avoided by
the violation of the principles [Tao], one
should not avoid it. If a Chün Tzu departs
from humanity, how can he fulfill that name?
A Chün Tzu should never act contrary to humanity even for a lapse of a single meal. In
moments of haste, he acts according to it.
In times of danger and confusion, he still
acts according to it. [IV:5]

If a person listens to the Tao in the morning, one will die content in the evening.
[IV:8]

If Chün Tzu is not steadfast, he will not be
respected, and his learning will not be on a
firm foundation. Hold loyalty and faithfulness to be the first principles. Have no
friends who are not compatible as you in holding the principles. But when you have made
mistakes, do not be afraid to correct them.
[I:8]

A Chün Tzu dedicates himself to the fundamentals [the root]. When the root is firmly
established, the Tao will grow. Filial piety
and fraternal cares are the root of humanity
[Jen]. [I:2]

It is really a surprise to read in the above passages that Confucius himself so often used the word
Tao to describe the quality of Chün Tzu. We often
think that only the Taoists like Lao Tzu and Chuang Tzu
used the word Tao to indicate their fundamental principle. As a matter of fact, the word Tao was a cardinal
principle of common faith at the time of Confucius and
not the monopoly of the Taoists. The Tao was the common denominator of truth and the fundamental criterion
of moral conduct to all different schools of religion
and philosophy. Thus, Confucius emphasized that the
Chün Tzu should be dedicated personally to the cause of

Tao, no matter what one's personal fortune and destiny
would be. "Chün Tzu seeks the Tao and not a mere
living." Even if one is in poverty and danger, one
should not deviate from the Tao. Chün Tzu associates
with those who are determined to follow the Tao and
serve the state which seeks to promote the Tao. Tao
was, to Confucius, the ultimate reality he is concerned
with. He used many religious terms such as "to seek,"
"worries about," "listen to," "acts according to," "be
steadfast with," "dedicates oneself to" in addressing
the Tao. To Confucius, the Tao is not merely a metaphysical idea to be speculated upon nor a mysterious
being to be meditated with, but the fundamental cause
of humanity to be enacted in life. He was not interested in the question, "What is Tao?" but more concerned with the question, "How to act out Tao?" Some
scholars felt Confucius was an agnostic because he did
not believe in the actual existence of God nor life
after death. So, he must be a nonreligious humanist.
But by looking at the way he described his dedication
to the cause of Tao, and his description of the ideal
image of humanness as ultimate concern with the Tao,
one cannot but think of him as a religious man. Although his religion or religious commitment did not
coincide with that of other religions or our Western
understanding of religious commitment, he definitely
had his own religion, and his religious ideal could be
described as the realization of Tao in human life. Because of such religious belief, he portrayed his ideal
human being--Chün Tzu--as the Man of Tao or the Man of
Principle. However, instead of trying to speculate or
argue about what Tao was, he was more concerned about
how to act out the Tao in human life, so he also postulated that Chün Tzu should be a Man of Virtue or Jen.

Second, Chün Tzu is the person of virtue. In contrast to the notion of Tao, which is One, the notion
of virtue is multifarious due to complex human situations and relationships. Several passages from the
Analects to illustrate various virtues Confucius mentioned as the moral quality of Chün Tzu will be quoted
below.

In the Analects, Book IV, verse 5, quoted above,
it clearly indicates that Chün Tzu would not deviate
from Tao in spite of poverty and danger, and immediately following that sentence, Confucius said, "A Chün
Tzu should never act contrary to humanity [Jen] even
for a lapse of a single meal. In moments of haste, he
acts according to it. In times of danger and confusion,

254

he still acts according to it." One can see from this passage that Confucius regarded acting according to the virtue of Jen or humanity is in itself following the Tao. In other words, the conduct of Jen is the Tao of life in reality and in a concrete sense. Jen is the cardinal principle of morality in the teachings of Confucius. Confucius said, "Set your mind on the Tao. Have a firm grasp on virtue. Rely on humanity. Find recreation in the arts [VII:6]." He also said to his disciple Ts'an, "Ts'an, there is one thread that runs through my teachings." And that thread was interpreted to be Jen, which consists of Chung (忠) and Shu (恕). Chung means loyalty to the Way of Heaven and conscientiousness to one's own personality. Shu means the altruistic way of human relationships and the extension of care and consideration to others. In other words, Jen is the moral principle existing in the context of human relationships and the union between the way of humanity and the ways of Heaven and Earth.

In other passages, Confucius also described the other virtues of Chün Tzu.

> The Master [Confucius] said with regard to Tzu Ch'an that he had four of the characteristics of the Way of Chün Tzu. "In his private conduct, he was courteous; in serving his superiors, he was respectful; in providing the needs for the people, he was graceful; in exacting services from the people, he was just." [V:15]

> Confucius said, "The Chün Tzu regards righteousness (I 義) as the substance of all things. He practices it according to the guide of propriety (Li 禮). He brings it forth in modesty. And he carries it to its conclusion with faithfulness. This man is indeed a Chün Tzu." [XV:17]

> Confucius said, "The way of Chün Tzu is threefold, but I have not been able to attain it. The man of wisdom who has no perplexities; the man of humanity [Jen] has no anxiety. The man of courage has no fear." Tzu-kung, his disciple said, "You are talking about yourself." [XIV:30]

> Tsu-lu asked, "Does Chün Tzu esteem courage? Confucius answered, "Chün Tzu considers

righteousness as the most important. When
Chün Tzu has courage but no righteousness, he
becomes turbulent. When the inferior man has
courage but no righteousness, he becomes a
thief. [XVII:23]

Chün Tzu is dignified, but does not quarrel.
He is sociable, but not a partisan. [XV:21]

Confucius said, "Chün Tzu is conciliatory
even though he does not agree with others.
The inferior man is not conciliatory even
though he agrees with others." [XIII:23]

Tzu-kung asked about Chün Tzu. Confucius
answered, "He acts before he speaks and then
speaks according to his action." [II:13]

Confucius said, "Chün Tzu is ashamed that his
words exceed his deeds." [XIV:29]

The virtues such as righteousness, courage, wisdom, conciliation, and broadmindedness are mentioned
by Confucius as the moral quality of Chün Tzu. The way
of humanity is one, but moral conduct in human life are
various. In each different situation and different
context of human relationships, a specific, special
virtue is called for. In the context of father-son relationship, parental care and concern are required of a
father, and filial piety and respect are required for
a son. In the context of ruler-subject relationship,
the ruler is to be responsible and credible, and the
subject is to be loyal and supportive. Love of husband
is to be expressed for his courtesy and consideration,
and love of wife for her chastity and understanding.
It is impossible to itemize all the virtues, but Chün
Tzu should be the person of many virtues and have the
wisdom of applying the moral principle properly according to each given circumstance. This is what Confucius tried to emphasize when he was asked how to save
society from chaos and conflicts. "Tsu-lu reported,
'The prince of Wei is awaiting you, Sir, to take control of his administration. What will you undertake
first?' The Master answered: 'The one thing needed is
the rectification of names [XIII:3].'" "When Duke
Ching of Ch'i inquired of Confucius the principles of
government, Confucius answered saying, 'Let the ruler
be ruler: the minister minister; let the father be
father, and the son son.' 'Excellent!' said the
Duke [XII:1]." The rectification of names means that

the quality of <u>status quo</u> should be fulfilled by the corresponding virtues. If a ruler does not fulfill his duties as the ruler, he disqualifies himself. Since one individual can be at the same time a ruler, a father, a husband, a brother, and friend, one has to know each different human relationship he is in and fulfill his duties accordingly. Thus, a Chün Tzu should have a good sense of moral judgment of knowing the human relationships and the social situations at the given time and space and have the wisdom to conduct himself properly. This requires that Chün Tzu should also be a person of culture and propriety.

Third, Chün Tzu is a person of culture (Wen 文).

> Confucius said, "When nature exceeds culture, one becomes rude. When culture exceeds nature, one becomes pedantic. It is only when one's nature and culture are properly blended that one becomes a Chün Tzu. [VI:16]

> Tzu-lu asked about the qualities of a true Chün Tzu. The Master said, "The Chün Tzu is the one who cultivates himself with seriousness." Tsu-lu said, "Is that all?" The Master said, "He cultivates himself so as to give the common people security and peace." Tsu-lu again said, "Is that all?" The Master said, "He cultivates himself in order to give security and peace to his people. To cultivate himself in order to give security and peace to his people, even [the ancient sage-kings] Yao and Shun found it difficult to do. [XIV:45]

> Confucius said, "A Chün Tzu has three disciplines to observe. When he is young and his 'blood and breath' [physical forces] are not settled down, he should be on guard against lust. When he matures and his physical powers are full of vigor, he should be on guard against strife. When he is old, and his physical forces are decaying, he should be on guard against avarice." [XVI:7]

> Confucius said, "There are nine things a Chün Tzu should be careful about. In seeing he is careful to see clearly. In hearing he is careful to hear distinctly. In his appearance, he is careful to be kindly. In his

manner, he is careful to be respectful. In
his speech, he is careful to be sincere. In
his works, he is careful to be superior.
When in doubt, he is careful to ask for information. When he is angry, he is careful
of thinking about the consequences. And when
he sees a chance of gain, he is careful of
thinking whether it is righteous." [XIV:10]

Confucius wanted to settle among the Nine
Wild Tribes of the East. Someone said,
"They are rude. How can you put up with
them?" Confucius said, "If a Chün Tzu [who
is civilized] lives there, what rudeness
would there be?" [IX:13]

Chi Tzu-cheng said, "A Chün Tzu is noble because of his inborn nature. Culture cannot
make a Chün Tzu." Tzu-kung, a Confucian disciple said, "I am sorry to hear what you said
about Chün Tzu. For the saying goes that
when a Chün Tzu has spoken, a team of four
horses cannot take away his words." Culture
is just as important as inborn nature; and
inborn nature, no less important than culture. Remove the hairs from the skin of a
tiger or panther, and what is left looks
just like the hairless hide of a dog or a
sheep. [XII:8]

Except the last passage, all of the above passages are
what Confucius said about the cultural qualities of
Chün Tzu. A Chün Tzu is not hereditary nor born by nature, but acquired by education of the Six Disciplines
and strenuous effort of moral cultivation. The Six
Disciplines Confucius used for educating his disciples
are the studies of poetry for refinement of thought and
expression; the studies of history for identification
of tradition and refinement of moral judgment; the
studies of propriety and music for the proper manner
and social integration; the studies of Ch'un Ch'iu for
the sciences of government and politics, and the
studies of the Book of Changes for the knowledge of
cosmology and one's destiny. It is only those who are
civilized that would be qualified to govern, because
the primary purpose of the state is to promote civilization.

Fourth, Chün Tzu is in contrast to the small man

(Hsiao Jen). There are many passages in the <u>Analects</u>
in which Confucius contrasted Chün Tzu with the small
man (Hsiao Jen). Derk Bodde and Wing-tsit Chan preferred to translate Chün Tzu as the "superior man" and
Hsiao Jen as the "inferior man." Arthur Waley translated Chün Tzu as "gentleman" and Hsiao Jen as the
"commoners." The basic difference between Chün Tzu and
Hsiao Jen in the sayings of Confucius is not class nor
rank in society, but moral qualities and the level of
nobility. Perhaps we can better judge which is a better translation after we have read what Confucius said
about Chün Tzu and Hsiao Jen.

> Confucius said, "Chün Tzu is broadminded but
> not partisan. Hsiao Jen is partisan but not
> broadminded." [II:14]

> Chün Tzu thinks of virtue; Hsiao Jen thinks
> of possession. Chün Tzu thinks of legal
> sanction; Hsiao Jen thinks of personal
> favors. [IV:11]

> Chün Tzu attempts to illustrate what is righ-
> teous; Hsiao Jen attempts to illustrate what
> is profitable. [IV:16]

> Chün Tzu is calm and at ease; Hsiao Jen is
> full of distress and ill at ease. [VII:36]

> Chün Tzu is conciliatory even though he does
> not agree with others. The inferior man is
> not conciliatory even though he agrees with
> others. [XIII:23]

> Chün Tzu is dignified but not arrogant; Hsiao
> Jen is arrogant but not dignified. [XIII:26]

> There might be some Chün Tzu who are not hu-
> manitarian [Jen]; but there could not be a
> Hsiao Jen who is humanitarian [Jen]. [XIV:7]

> While Chün Tzu can influence those who are
> above him; Hsiao Jen can only influence those
> who are below him. [XIV:24]

> Chün Tzu seeks demands upon himself; Hsiao
> Jen seeks demands upon others. [XV:20]

Fifth, Chün Tzu is the person who knows one's

destiny (Chih Ming 知命). Chün Tzu is the person who
has great ideals to improve one's personality and to
promote culture in society, but he also knows that the
ideals may or may not be realized as he wishes. He
would do his best,and he would not deviate from the
principle of Tao, even if he is to face poverty and
dangers; yet he realizes that his goals may not be accomplished. He is not quarrelsome, but rather concili-
iatory in dealing with others, and yet he knows that
there will be much opposition. Confucius had such ex-
periences in his own life. In spite of his great dedication in serving his state and trying to restore his
society to orderliness and sanity, he saw many vices in
high offices and increasing crimes in society and the
victories of violence and the defeat of justice. He
resigned from his government position and roamed for
thirteen years among the states to pursuade the rulers
to listen to his ideals. In the end, he still failed.
And yet he did not blame others and complain to the
Heaven, instead he kept on with his faith in the mandate of Heaven. Thus, he could say that Chün Tzu, the
ideal image of humanity, is the one who knows destiny.

> Confucius siad, "The Chün Tzu stands in awe
> of three things. He stands in awe of the
> mandate of Heaven [T'ien Ming]; he stands in
> awe of great men [or the sage-rulers]; he
> stands in awe of the teachings of the sages."
> [XVI:8]

> Confucius said, "He who does not know the
> mandate of Heaven cannot be regarded as a
> Chün Tzu." [XX:3]

> Ssu-ma Niu was sad and said, "All people have
> brothers but I have none." Tsu-hisa said,
> "I have heard [from Confucius] this saying:
> 'Life and death are the decree of Heaven
> [Ming]; wealth and honor depend on Heaven.
> If a Chün Tzu is reverential without fail,
> and is respectful in dealing with others and
> follows the rules of propriety, then all
> within the four seas [the world] shall be his
> brothers.' Why should a Chün Tzu be sad
> about having no brothers?" [XII:5]

> Confucius said, "Alas! No one knows me!"
> His disciple Tzu-kung said, "Why is there no
> one that knows you?" Confucius said, "I do
> not complain against Heaven. I do not blame

men. I study things on the lower level but
my understanding penetrates the higher level.
It is Heaven that knows me." [XIV:37]

The lower level that Confucius studied refers to
mundane matters and the higher level refers to matters
of Heaven, such as the mandate of Heaven and the principles of the universe. Thus, in all of the above passages, Confucius stressed that Chün Tzu should be the
one who really knows the destiny of one's life and the
mandate of Heaven. It is not a resignation of one's
ill fortune to the fate of Heaven, nor a blind faith
in the promise of good fortune believed to be given to
him. It is rather a courageous commitment to, and
trust in, the will of Heaven who commissioned him to
carry on the culture at the times of chaos and disorder.
During his thirteen years of roaming among the states,
Confucius was once confronted by the danger of assas-
sination by the people of K'uang who mistook him for
Yang Hu, their enemy. At that moment of crisis, Confucius said, "Since the death of King Wen [the founder
of Chou dynasty], is not the course of culture in my
keeping? If it had been the will of Heaven to destroy
this culture, it would not have been given to a mortal
[like me]. But if it is the will of Heaven that this
culture should not perish, what can the people of
K'uang do to me? [IX:5]." This is the best example to
illustrate what Confucius meant by "knowing the mandate
of Heaven." Confucius knew that his destiny was to
carry on the culture established by King Wen who was
the first to acknowedge the mandate of Heaven. Because
of such a sense of calling, Confucius was not afraid of
the imminent danger and death threatened by the people
of K'uang. He was already at age 56, and he had just
resigned from his position as prime-minister from the
State Lu because his policies were rejected by his
king, and yet he was not disappointed nor depressed.
Thus, he emphasized that Chün Tzu should not be only a
person who dedicates himself to follow the Tao, cultivates his virtues, and is well civilized, but also
should be a person with a deep sense of Heavenly commission and knowledge of one's destiny. To Confucius,
"knowing the mandate of Heaven" was the foundation of
his moral conduct and civil qualities. It was the
source of his moral courage and the untimate goal of
his life. Thus, Chün Tzu is not only a man of virtue
and nobility, but a deeply committed religious man.

<u>The Mohist Image of the Great Man</u>
(<u>Chü Tzu</u>, 鉅子)

According to Fung Yi-lan, the Mohists had a well-knit organization under the leadership of Chü Tzu.[3] Chü Tzu (鉅子) literally means a great man or magnate. Chuang Tzu said the Mohists regarded Chü Tzu a sage, and each group wished him to be its leader, hoping to be his successor.[4] Mo Tzu was apparently the first Chü Tzu, and after his death, the post of Chü Tzu was succeeded at least by three generations. Thus, it is adequate to say that Chü Tzu was the ideal image of humanity in Mohism. The following will depict several characteristics of the personality of Mo Tzu (the first and most respected Chü Tzu of the Mohists) to illustrate what the Mohists meant by Chü Tzu.

<u>Chü Tzu as a Champion for the</u>
<u>Cause of Common People</u>

Formerly the name Mo Tzu was understood to be "Master Mo" and Mo as his family or clan name. But recently, Chiang Ch'uan has suggested that Mo is rather the name of the religious organization founded by Mo Tzu. For in ancient China, <u>Mo</u> (墨) meant "black ink," and it was used for branding prisoners of war and criminals and marking them as criminals or slaves.[5] As we have already noted, both the Shang and Chou societies owned a large number of slaves who were harshly treated by their masters. Coming at the time of the collapse of the Chou feudal system and the rise of the middle-class, land-owning farmers and merchants, Mo Tzu rallied behind him a group of humble people branded as the Mo Family and voiced for fair and equal treatment. Although the name Mo was an insult, Mo Tzu and his disciples gladly took it as the name of their organization in order to challenge the regime and other societies.

Mo Tzu was originally a native of the State Lu, and possibly studied for a while in the Confucian school. Later, he became an official in the State of Sung, where he was influenced by the simplicity and frugality of the common people and their ideals of universal love and pacifism. He organized the Mo Family and championed their cause. Eventually, he became critical of Confucian teachings, even though he still shared some of their ideas. Because of his identification with, and advocacy of, the cause of the common laborers, he disliked the aristocratic nature of Chün Tzu that Confucius portrayed as his ideal image of humanity. Confucius regarded himself as the transmitter

262

of Chou culture and feudalism, attempting to uphold the
Confucian advocacy of feudalism, aristocracy, familyism,
excessive ritualism, and fatalism. In opposition to
the hereditary rule of feudalism, Mo Tzu advocated the
equal employment of worthy people to be government officials regardless of their aristocratic or humble origin. In the chapter Equal Elevation of the Worthy
(Shang Hsien 尚賢), Mo Tzu remarked:

> The rulers and officials all desire their
> states to be prosperous, their population in-
> creased, and their society orderly. But,
> instead of achieving wealth, they obtain pov-
> erty, instead of increase in population, the
> loss of man power, and instead of order, the
> disorder in society. Why does this happen?
> . . . It is because the rulers and officials
> do not elevate the worthy and employ the
> capable in their administration. If a govern-
> ment has many worthy men, then its adminis-
> tration will be weighy and substantial.
> Therefore one of the urgent tasks to the high
> officials is to increase the number of worthy
> men. [Mo Tzu, VIII]

Confucius was the one to emphasize the rule of the
virtuous, but he was not radical enough to challenge
the hereditary nature of officialdom and family ties in
the Chou employment system. Mo Tzu was the first to
challenge it and advocated the equal employment of the
righteous and worthy. Ascension in the ladder of success should be based solely on the merit of individuals,
and not on kinship and intimacy with the ruler. Only
equal opportunity in government employment ensures that
a state can conduct a righteous rule and enrich the
wealth, peace, and prosperity of the state. Instead of
tracing the righteous rule to the Chou feudal system
that Confucius admired and imitated, Mo Tzu traced back
further to the rule of the sage kings, Yao, Shun and
Yu T'ang and Wen, to demonstrate that their yielding of
the thrones to the virtuous ones instead of their kin
had created the golden age of ancient China. Mo Tzu
related:

> According to ancient tradition, Yao had pro-
> moted Shun at the sunny side of Fu Lake and
> entrusted the government to him, and the
> world enjoyed its peace. Yu had promoted Yi
> at the land of Yin and entrusted the govern-
> ment to him, and the nine provinces were well

ordered. T'ang promoted Yi Yin from his low
position as a cook to become a prime minister,
and his plan of enriching the state was successful. [<u>Mo Tzu</u>, VIII]

Chü Tzu is the Man of Universal Love (Chien Ai 兼愛)

Along with his advocacy of the equal elevation of
the worthy in order to uplift the status of common
laborers, Mo Tzu also championed the cause of universal
love. He found that Confucian notion of Jen or human
relatedness based on the Five Human Relationships was
centered in the family-relationship and the grade of
rank and file. The relationships between the ruler and
subject, husband and wife, brother and brother, and
friend and friend tended to be dominated by the father-
son relationship, and the patriarchal authority and
filial piety of family ethics tended to control the
moral principle of Jen. Thus, Jen was conditioned by
ethnocentrism and could not fully extend to become a
universalistic and open principle of humanity. Mo Tzu
tried to overcome this ethnocentrism and the hierarchical gradation of Confucian Jen and to promote universal
love or Chien Ai, which means literally "all-embracing
love."

Universal love has no racial, linguistic, and
national boundaries, but respects equally of each individual's human right. The following are the sayings of
Mo Tzu concerning universal love:

> The principle of universality was the way of
> the sage kings, the means of bringing secur-
> ity to the society, and the methods of feed-
> ing and clothing of the people. Therefore
> the superior man should learn it carefully
> and strive to put it into practice. If he
> does, then as a ruler he shall be generous,
> as a subject loyal, as a father kind, as a
> son filial, as an older brother compassion-
> ate, and as a younger bother respectful.
> [<u>Mo Tzu</u>, XIV]

Long before Jesus taught that God is the Father of
all humankind and "love thy enemy," Mo Tzu was already advocating universal love in China.

<u>Chü Tzu is a Man of Active Pacifism</u>

Along with his teaching of universal love, Mo Tzu

strongly opposed warfare and militarism. There is a
special chapter in his work entitled "Against Warfare,"
in which he renounced rampant warfare and the increasing fanaticism of military aggression.

> When a state delights in aggressive warfares,
> it must raise an army of several hundred high
> officers, several thousand regular officers,
> and a hundred thousand soldiers, before it
> can set out. The time required for the ex-
> pedition will be several years at the longest;
> several months at the least. During that
> time the leaders cannot attend to government
> affairs, the officials cannot manage their
> department affairs, the farmers cannot sow
> and reap, and the women cannot spin and
> weave. The state has to loose its man power,
> and the people their jobs. Moreover, taming
> horses, building chariots, hanging tents,
> supplying food and weapons are to be con-
> sidered. In the course of war, a countless
> number of soldiers will desert, or become
> lost along the way, or will die. . . . And
> when it is lucky for the state to win, it
> only wins a ruined state [which will add more
> debts to itself]. [<u>Mo Tzu</u>, XVII]

Mo Tzu also argued that even if a state won the
victory and conquered the other state, there was no
benefit. It only annexed a state destroyed and im-
poverished by warfare and added heavy burden and defi-
cit upon itself. But no matter what it is, warfare is
not acting in accordance with the Tao. However, Mo Tzu
was not only a moralist or theorist of pacifism, he was
also a courageous activist of pacifism. In Chapter 50
of the work of Mo Tzu, there described a story of Mo
Tzu's heroic act in defending a small state which was
about to be attacked by a larger state.

> When Mo Tzu heard that Kung Shu Pan, a mili-
> tary engineer, had built the cloud-ladders
> for the state of Ch'u to attack the state of
> Sung, he went to see the king of Ch'u to per-
> suade him to desist. In front of the King,
> Mo Tzu and Kung demonstrated their military
> games. Mo Tzu untied his belt to lay out a
> city and used a small stick as his weapon,
> while Kung set up his nine miniature machines
> of attack. Mo Tzu was able to repulse Kung's
> attacks for nine times and never exhausted

his defenses. Then Kung said: "I know how to
defeat you, but I will not say it." In re-
plying to it, Mo Tzu said: "I know what you
have in your mind, but I too will not say
it." The King became curious and asked Mo
Tzu what was meant, Mo Tzu continued: "Kung
is thinking of assassinating me. But I have
already trained three hundred disciples like
Ch'in and Ku-li with my strategies of defense, and they are all well prepared waiting
on the city wall of Sung for the invasion
from Ch'u. So even though I might be assassinated, you cannot conquer them." After
hearing what Mo Tzu said, the King exclaimed:
"Very well! Let us do not attack Sung."
[<u>Mo Tzu</u>, L]

This story indicates that Mo Tzu was a great champion and leader of pacifism and he had a group of dedicated followers who dared to follow the same courageous and sacrificial venture as Mo Tzu. Mo Tzu was
not entirely a nonviolent pacifist, for he apparently
organized an army of self-defense and engaged in violent resistance; but, nonetheless, he was one of the
great pacifists, for he dared to defend the defenseless
to oppose aggressors and oppressors.

<u>Chü Tzu was a Man of Great Leadership</u>

As we have already noticed, Mo Tzu was a great or-
ganizer and a charismatic leader. As the passage we
have just quoted illustrates, he had three hundred dedicated disciples ready to follow him in the defense
of the State of Sung. Apparently Mo Tzu had educated
his disciples like Confucius did, but he also taught
them engineering skills and military strategy for self-
defense. From the fact that his school had "knights-
errant" (義俠 Yi Hsia) that went to various places to
fight against corrupt officials and gangsters in defense of the weak and oppressed, we can assume that he
must have taught them the martial arts. Several of his
disciples were hired by various states to serve in the
government and received high honors and salaries. And
yet, Mo Tzu seemed to have total control of his organization and movement of his disciples. Following is an
instance to witness such control.

Mo Tzu recommended Kao Shih Tzu to serve in
the state of Wei. The ruler of Wei gave Kao
a large salary and ranked him among the

266

ministers. Kao offered three times his counsel to the court, but none of them was carried out. So he left for the State of Ch'i,
where he met Mo Tzu, and said to him: "On
your recommendation, the Lord of Wei gave me
high salary and honorable position, but he
never carried out the counsel I offered him
for three times. So I left him. Do you
think the Lord of Wei would think that I am
foolish?" Mo Tzu replied: "If you left him
to be in accordance with the Tao, what harm
is it to be considered as foolish?" Kao then
said: "How dare I would leave him unless it
were not in accordance with the Tao?". . . .
Hearing it, Mo Tzu was pleased. [Mo Tzu,
XLVI]

Mo Tzu sent Sheng Cho to serve the Lord
Hsiang Tzu Niu. When the Lord Hsiang had
invaded three times the State of Lu, Sheng
Cho had three times accompanied him. Hearing
it, Mo Tzu sent Kao Sun Tzu to recall him.
[Mo Tzu, XLIX]

These stories indicate that Mo Tzu had a tight
control of the employment and activities of his disciples. If the state did not carry the Mohist doctrine, he recalled his disciples, even if it offered
a high salary. If his disciple did not practice pacifism but went along with warfare, he immediately recalled him. His organization seemed to be a well-knit
commune system to which all the members contributed
their individual earnings. Moreover his disciples
rendered absolute homage to Mo Tzu. Huai-nan Tzu, a
Taoist, mentioned that "there were 180 men who followed Mo Tzu; all dared to jump into fire or tread on
knife-blades [to carry out his mission]. To them, even
death could not prevent them from following him [Huai
Nan Tzu, XX]." Mo Tzu's disciples called Mo Tzu, Chü
Tzu (鉅子), which means a Great Leader, or rather a
Charismatic Leader.

Chü Tzu as a Sage

The great Taoist Chuang Tzu, in describing the
leadership of Mo Tzu, said that the Mohists all regarded the Chü Tzu a sage, which would appear to be substantial evidence that Chü Tzu was a religious leader
and a man of strong faith and total dedication. The
Record of the Former Han Dynasty (Ch'ien Han Shu)

indicated that "the Mohist teachings began with the
guardian of the temples."6 Whether Mo Tzu was a temple
keeper or not, Mo Tzu had strongly advocated absolute
homage to the will of Heaven and promoted the worship
of the Heaven and the Spirits. He was very critical of
Confucius and his followers for they only believed in
the mandate of Heaven, but did not really worship Heav-
en and the Spirits like the ancient sage kings did.
Confucius said, "Offer sacrifice to God as if God
exists; offer sacrifice to the Spirits as if the
Spirits exist." Hu Shih commented that the religion of
Confucius is an as-if religion (pseudo religion). Following passages in the Work of Mo Tzu illustrate Mo
Tzu's criticism on the inconsistency of Confucianism.

> Kung-meng Tzu [a Confucian] said: "There are
> no spirits." Again he said: "The superior
> man [Chün Tzu] should learn the rituals of
> sacrifice." Mo Tzu said: "To hold that there
> are no spirits, and yet to learn the sacrifi-
> cial ceremonies, is like learning the cere-
> monies of hospitality when there are no
> guests, or throwing fish nets when there are
> no fish."7

But the most harsh criticism Mo Tzu made against Confucian teaching is aimed at its fatalism.

> In addition, the Confucians believe in the
> predetermination of fate and propagate their
> doctrine. They claimed that long life or
> early death, wealth and poverty, safety or
> danger, order and disorder are all decreed by
> the will of Heaven and cannot be altered.
> . . . Man's wisdom and power can not change
> anything. If the officials believe such
> ideas, they will be loose in their duties;
> and if the common people believe them, they
> will ignore their tasks. If the officials
> do not govern properly, and the common people
> do not do their works, eventually disorder
> and poverty will result, and the foundation
> of society will be destroyed. And yet the
> Confucians believed in such ideas and even
> considered it as the doctrine of Tao. In
> fact, they are destroying the people of the
> world. [Mo Tzu, XXXV]

In fact, both Confucius and Mo Tzu believed in the
will of Heaven, but Mo Tzu argued that Confucians made

the will of Heaven into a decree and fate and taught
that it is fixed and cannot be modified. But Mo Tzu
understood that the will of Heaven is moral, and good
fortune or bad depends upon the moral response of human
beings to the moral will of Heaven. The following is
what Mo Tzu said about the will of Heaven.

> I know that Heaven is superior and wiser than
> the son of Heaven [king] because when the son
> of Heaven does something good, Heaven gives
> him reward and when the son of Heaven does
> something evil, Heaven punishes him. . . .
> The will of Heaven abominates the large
> state attacking the small states, the rich
> householders molesting the poor householders,
> the strong oppressing the weak, the clever
> ones deceiving the simple ones, and the hon-
> oured condemning the humble. Moreover, Heav-
> en wishes the people who have powers working
> to help each other, the people who are intel-
> ligent teaching to guide each other, and the
> rich sharing their wealth to benefit each
> other. . . .
> Therefore, when the will of Heaven is
> understood and widely obeyed in the world,
> justice and government will be orderly, the
> multitude ill be harmonious, the country will
> be wealthy, the supplies will be sufficient,
> and the people will be warmly clothed and
> sufficiently fed, peaceful and without worry.
> [<u>Mo Tzu</u>, XXVII]

Mo Tzu understood the will of Heaven to be universal love and righteousness, but not predetermined and
unchangeable. When a king repented his wrong doings,
Heaven is willing to take away the punishment. Heaven
is the origin of universal love and righteousness, and
he is constantly inspiring and exhorting his people to
promote morality and discouraging them from harming one
another. The way to maintain an orderly government, a
harmonious population, a rich state, and a prosperous
society is to obey the will of Heaven and practice the
worship of Heaven. It was simple logic for Mo Tzu to
say that the welfare of the state depended upon the
moral conduct of its citizens, and the moral impera-
tives to do good depended upon devotion and obedience
to the will of Heaven. Thus, we can conclude by saying
that the ideal image of humanity portrayed as Chü Tzu
in Mohism is ultimately a person with religious dedication. Chü Tzu was not only a great leader of a

religious organization, a champion of pacifism and a
practioner of love, but most of all he himself was a
"sage."

The Taoist Image of the True Man
(Chen Jen, 真人)

In contrast to Confucianists and Mohists who had
engaged in the worldly affairs of sociopolitics, there
was a group of ascetics who were called the Taoists
seeking to transcend worldly affairs and to attain
union with the Tao. Lao Tzu was the most eminent among
these Taoists; and from the writings named after him,
we can read about the metaphysics and mysticism the
Taoists had advocated. But it is in the writings of
Chuang Tzu, another great Taoist, that we can see more
clearly the ideal image of human beings portrayed by
the Taoists. They called his ideal person various
names: Shen Jen (神人) or the God Man; Sheng Jen
(聖人) or the Holy Man; Chih Jen (至人) or the Perfect
Man; Chen Jan (真人) or the True Man. It might be due
to several different groups of ascetics, each coming up
with a different name to describe the ideal image in
Taoism, that there were such different names which appeared in the record of Chuang Tzu. As we shall see in
the following passages about the descriptions of the
Taoist image of humanity, there are some difference in
their attributes, but, generally, there are more common
characteristics in the personality of the ideal human
being they all sought to identify. I shall quote the
passages separately according to each different name in
the order of the God Man, the Holy Man, the Perfect Man,
and the True Man.

The God Man (Shen Jen)

> There is a God Man living on a distant moun-
> tain called Ku-she, and his skin is like
> snow, and he is gentle and shy like a young
> girl. He does not eat the five grains, but
> sucks the wind, drinks the morning dew, as-
> cends to the clouds and fogs, rides a flying
> dragon, and wanders over the four seas. By
> concentrating his spirit, he can produce en-
> ergy to heal the sick and to make the people
> prosperous. [Chuang Tzu, Chap. 1]

The Holy Man (Sheng Jen)

> The Holy Man leans upon the sun and moon, em-
> braces the universe under his arms, unites

himself with all things, leaves the chaos as
it is, and respects the lowly as the exalted.
In contrast to the ordinary people who strive
and struggle, the Holy Man appears to be
stupid and blockish. He participates in all
ages and achieves simplicity in oneness.
[Chaung Tzu, Ch. 2]

The Perfect Man (Chih Jen)

The Perfect Man is like a god. When the
great forest blaze, they cannot consume him;
when the great streams freeze, they cannot
chill him; when the great lightenings strike
the hills and roaring storms shake the ocean,
they cannot scare him. A man like this can
ride the clouds and fogs, and straddle the
sun and moon, and wander over the four seas.
Since life and death could not effect him, how
much less the rules of profit and loss!
[Chaung Tzu, Ch. 2]

The True Man (Chen Jen)

What do I mean by a True Man? The True Man
of ancient times did not resist against his
desire, did not boast his richness, and did
not arrange his plans. He could commit an
error but not regret it, and could enjoy his
success and not brag about it. He could
climb up to a high place and not be frightened,
could enter into the deep and not get wet, and
could jump into the fire and not get burned.
His knowledge could ascend all the way up to
the Tao.
The True Man of ancient times slept
without dreaming and woke without worries;
he ate without spicy and he breathed from
deep inside. While the common people breathe
with their throats, the True Man breathes
with his heels. [Chuang Tzu, Ch. 6]

From the above passages, we can see that although
the names of the ideal person are various, the descriptions of the character and personality are more or less
the same. There are at least four characteristics of
the Taoist Ideal Personality that we can describe as
follows:

The True Man Has No Worries
and Anxiety

Perhaps we can use the name "the True Man" to gen-
eralize all the ideal images of Taoism. The first characteristic common to all descriptions is that the True
Man has no worries and anxiety about worldly affairs.
The affairs such as where to live, what to eat and wear,
what occupation and position to occupy, are not of their
primary concern. They are not concerned about matters
such as profit or loss, fame or obscurity, success or
failure, riches or poverty. Beside these, the True Man
also tries to transcend the knowledge of the world, for
it is relative and circumstantial. To an ordinary man
and Confucian and Mohist politicians, the relativity of
"this" or "that" is very important and the difference
between them is serious, but to the Taoist, such hair-
splitting arguments and hot debates are simply a waste
of time and energy. From a relative knowledge, the absolute truth cannot be obtained. Following are the sayings of Chuang Tzu about the relativity of knowledge
and futility of argument.

> Suppose you and I have engaged in an argu-
> ment, and you have beaten me instead of I
> beating you, but does this necessarily mean
> that you are right and I am wrong? If I have
> beaten you instead of you beating me, does
> this necessarily mean that I am right and you
> are wrong? Is it necessarily that one of us
> be right and the other wrong? Or, is it ne-
> cessarily that both of us be right or wrong?
> If we can not decide by ourselves and we want
> to invite someone to decide for us, can he do
> it? Because if he agrees with you, how can
> he be fair? And if he agrees with me, how
> can he judge? Should we get someone who
> agrees with both of us? But if he already
> agrees with both of us, how can he decide?
> Obviously, neither you nor I nor anyone else
> can solve for one another the argument.
> Should we wait on still another person?
> [Chaung Tzu, Chap. 2]

Likewise, in terms of moral principle, the Confucianists claimed it to be "Jen" or human heartedness,
and the Mohists criticized that it was "graded or discriminatory, so they emphasized it to be "Chien Ai" or
universal love. So, the Confucianists counter-attacked,
criticizing Chien Ai as immoral for it treated one's

own father equally with strangers. The Taoists tried
to avoid this moral relativism and to seek a transcen-
dent life without involvement with worldly ethics. In
fact, they looked down on Confucian moralism as a sign
of degradation from the original state of Tao. In
order to avoid the involvement with worldly affairs
and moral relativism, the Taoists tended to withdraw
from government offices and urban living and seek
seclusion and isolation in the mountain regions. They
loved to live modestly and enjoyed nature. "Return
back to Nature" and "Harmony with Heaven and Earth" became the motto of their life. They were critical of
worldly philosophy and current politics, and they loved
to use satires and parables to ridicule them. But they
loved to compose poems and prose to fantasize their ro-
manticism and ideals.

The True Man has Overcome
the Fear of Death

Since the True Man has no concern for wordly affairs and moral relativism, he has also overcome the
boundaries of life and death. To an ordinary man, life
is joyful and valuable, while death is sad and unde-
sirable; but the True Man should overcome such discrimination. Life is like spring, and death is like
winter; they are but the passaging of seasonal change
that we all have to accept equally. We cannot say that
we only love the spring and refuse to accept the winter.
Once we are born and enjoy the sweetness of life, we
should also be ready to accept death as it comes. The
Taoists regard the True Man to be a person who accepts
whatever life gives and whatever death takes away.
"He came briskly, he went briskly, and that was all."
Following are the sayings of Chuang Tzu with regard to
life and death.

> I receive my life when the time has come; I
> shall lose it when the order of things moves
> on. If we are content with this life-time
> and abide in this order, then neither sorrow
> nor joy can disturb us. In ancient proverb,
> this is called the "liberation from the bond-
> age." However, there are many who cannot
> liberate themselves from their bonds. But
> no matter what, nobody can ever win against
> Heaven . . . because that is the way it has
> always been. Why should I have to resist?
> [Chaung Tzu, Chap. 6]

273

Here is the best illustration of a Taoist's attitude toward death.

> Hearing Chuang Tzu's wife died, Hui Tzu went to see Chaung Tzu to convey his condolence, but he was surprised to find Chuang Tzu sitting on the ground, singing, and beating on a tab. He said, "She has lived with you, raised your children, and now she is aged and dead. It might be alright if you do not weep and cry, but singing and beating a tab--aren't you going too far?"
>
> "No!" Chuang Tzu replied, "When she just died, I grieved like everybody else. But as I reflect the matter over, I realize that in the beginning she had no life; and not only no life, she had no form; and not only no form, she had no vital force. In the primordial chaos of being and non-being, there occurred a transformation, and the vital force was evolved. The vital force was transformed to become a form, and a form was transformed to become a life, and now the birth of life is transformed to become the death. This process of transformation is like the rotation of four seasons: spring, summer, autumn, and winter. Now she returns back to sleep in the grand mansion [of the universe'. Therefore, for me to go around weeping and wailing would show that I am ignorant of the human destiny. So I desist. [Chaung Tzu, Chap. 9]

The True Man is Invincible and Immortal

Since the True Man is capable of transcending beyond the boundary of life and death, the Taoists believed that he has also reached to the stage of invincibility and immortality. He is no longer of this world and mortal. He no longer lives by bread or grain, but by the cosmic air and spiritual breath. His body has gone through metamorphosis and transformed into an "immortal body." Hunger and thirst, heat and cold, water and fire, and life and death no longer have any effect upon him. Although his appearance may be as withered wood or a dried fish, in reality he becomes invincible because of his transcendence from the relativity of the world. "The Perfect Man can walk under water without choking, can tread on fire without being

burned, and can travel above the ten thousand things
without being frightened." His body becoming refined,
he can ride the cloud and fly into the sky and travel
freely. His eyesight is no longer limited and his
vision becomes clear, he can see all things past-pres-
ent-future simultaneously from the standpoint of the
Tao. Being a spiritual being, the form and formless
are all penetrating to him. As an ideal human being
standing between Heaven and Earth, he becomes the perfect mediator between the divine beings, the natural
forces and human beings. "So the Holy Man harmonizes
with both right and wrong and rests in Heaven the
Equalizer (T'ien Chun 天鈞)."

     It is clear that such an invincible and immortal
True Man is no longer an historical person, but a
fantasized or romanticized character of Taoist imagination. But the Taoists did not merely make up such an
imaginary character, they were quite seriously thinking
that it was possible for a Taoist to reach that stage
through spiritual cultivation and transmutation of the
body. Since there will be a more detailed description
of the method of spiritual discipline of Taoism in
chapter 12, it will not be enlarged upon at this time.
In fact, it was not the Taoists alone that envisioned
such immortal life in ancient China, the <u>Book of the
Ch'u Tz'u</u> (楚辭) or the <u>Songs of the South</u> and the
<u>Mythology of Mountain and Seas</u> (Shan Hai Ching 山海經)
also contained many records of the immortals and mythic
or spiritual beings who lived beyond the realm of human
beings. Toshihiko Izutsu felt it was possible that the
Taoists were decendents of the ancient shamans and inherited the shamanistic vision of the immortals for
their portrayal of the True Man.[8]

     In Chapter 1 of the <u>Ch'u Tz'u</u> entitled Li Sao
(離騷) meaning "Leaving the Noise [of this world],"
there is described Ch'ü Yüan, a noble poet who served
in the government and being ousted and put in exile by
court intrigues and royal slanders, now is seeking to
leave this worldly misery and folly and make a journey
into the supernatural world. This is what Ch'ü Yüan
sings:

          I have looked back into the past and forward
             to later ages,
          Examining the outcome of men's different
             designs.
          Where is the unrighteous man who could be
             trusted?

> Where is the wicked man whose service could
>   be used?
> Though I stand at the pit's mouth and death
>   yawns before me,
> I still feel no regret at the course I have
>   chosen.
> Straightening the handle, regardless of the
>   socket's shape:
> For that crime the good men of old were
>   hacked in pieces.
> Many a heavy sign I heaved in my despair,
> Grieving that I was born in such an unlucky
>   time.
> I plucked soft lotus petals to wipe my
>   welling tears
> That fell down in rivers and wet my coat
>   front.
> I knelt on my outspread skirts and poured my
>   plaint out,
> And the righteousness within me was clearly
>   manifest.
> I yoked a team of jade dragons to a phoenic-
>   figure car
> And waited for the wind to come, to soar up
>   on my journey.
>
> I watered my dragon steeds at the Pool of
>   Heaven,
> And tied the reins up to the Fu-sang Tree
>   [where the sun rises].
> I broke a sprig of the Jo-tree to strike the
>   sun with:
> I wanted to roam a little for enjoyment.
> I sent Wang Shu [the charioteer of the moon]
>   ahead to ride before me;
> The Wind God sent behind as my outrider;
> The Bird of Heaven gave notice of my coming;
> And the Thunder God told me when all was not
>   ready.[9]

Then, in the chapter called Chiu Ko (Nine Songs), there
was described the journey of shamans to the heavenly
courts of gods and goddesses and the frolicing and ro-
mances with divine beings. In the chapter called Yuan
Yu (The Far-Off Journey), another poet also sang a
melancholy and yet fascinating journey into the supernatural world.

> Grieved at the parlous state of this world's
>   ways,

I wanted to float up and away from them.
But my powers were too weak to give me sup-
    port:
What could I ride on to bear me upwards?
Fallen on a time of foulness and impurity,
Alone with my misery, I had no one to confide
    in.
In the night time I lay, wide-eyed, without
    sleeping;
My unquiet soul was active until the day
    light.
I thought of the vastness of the universe,
And wept for the long affliction of man's
    life.
Those that had gone before I should never
    see;
And those yet to come I could never know of.
Restless I placed, with my mind on distant
    things;
Despairing, frustrated, consumed with con-
    stant yearning.
My thoughts were wild and wandered dis-
    tractedly;
My heart was melancholy with mounting sadness.
My spirit darted forth and did not return to
    me;
And my body, left tenantless, grew withered
    and lifeless.
Then I looked into myself to strengthen my
    resolution,
And sought to learn from where the primal
    spirits issues.
In emptiness and silence I found serenity;
In tranquil Inaction I gained true satis-
    faction.
I heard how Ch'ih Sung had washed the world's
    dust off:
I would model myself on the pattern he had
    left me.
I honored the wonderous powers of the Pure
    Ones;
I admired of the past ages who had become
    Immortals.
They departed in the flux of change and
    vanished from men's sight,
Leaving a famous name that long endures after
    them.
I marvelled how Fu Yüeh lived on in a star;
I admired Han Chung for attaining Unity.
Their bodies grew dim and faded in the

distance;
They left the crowd of men and withdrew them-
selves.
With the ether's transformations they rose
upwards,
With godlike swiftness miraculously moving.
The world became hazy, viewed from the great
distance;
The spirit essence dazzled as it flashed back
and forth.
Leaving the dust behind, shedding their im-
purities,--
Never to return again to their old homes.
Escaping unafraid from all life's troubles:
No one in the world knows where they went to.
I was afraid at the passing of the seasons,
As the bright sun in splendour rode on his
western journey.
The fine front descended and fell upon the
earth;
And I feared the fragrant flowers would fade
permanently.
I wanted to roam about in leisurely enjoy-
ment:
I had gone through the length of years with
nothing yet achieved.
With whom can I enjoy this fragrance that is
left me?
Long I stand against the wind unburdening my
heart.
But Kao Yang [a divine king] lived far from
me in a distant time:
How can I. . . .?[10]

From the above elegies we can see the similarity between the aspiration of the Taoists and that of the ancient shamans. Both of them were disappointed in this
world's affairs and sought to escape from them. Both
of them sought to journey into the supernatural world
and enjoy immortality. Both of them believed that it
was possible for human beings to attain the status of
immortality through shamanistic ecstacy or Taoist
transformation. In a later development of Taoism,
many methods were devised to assist the Taoists attain
such stages. The book <u>Pao-p'u Tzu</u> (抱朴子) written
around A.D. 320 collected much valuable information
about ancient alchemy and medicine and spiritual disciplines for attaining longevity of life.[11] The mythological lore of those ancient sages and immortals also
multiplied to inspire the Taoists to search after the

pattern of their lives. Among them, the most popular
ones are called the Eight Immortals.[12]

The True Man is the Person Who
Attained the Tao

     What really made a True Man? What made a True
Man capable of being without worries and anxiety, overcoming the fear of death and becoming invincible and
immortal? Was it because of his divine origin that he
was an incarnation of a God? So far, Chuang Tzu did
not make such claim. Or was it because the True Man
performed certain magic and was capable of manipulating
divine beings? Again, we do not have such an indication of magical performances by the True Man in Chuang
Tzu. While the shamans had certain training and skills
to attain ecstacy and mystical union with their patron
deities and guiding spirits, the Taoists seemed not to
emphasize the significance of such assistance. The
main emphasis Chuang Tzu mentioned for a True Man to
be able to reach that high stage of life was "to attain
the Tao" (Te Tao 得道). Chuang Tzu said, "His knowledge was able to climb all the way up to the Tao like
this." It was not an ordinary knowledge, but the true
knowledge of the union of Heaven, Earth, and Human.
Chuang Tzu had illustrated fourteen such persons who
had attained the Tao to become the True Man.

          The Tao has its reality and symbols but
     is without actions and forms. . . . Itself
     is its own source and its own root. Before
     heaven and earth existed, it was already
     there a long time ago. It endows spiritual-
     ity to all gods and spiritual beings, and it
     gave birth to heaven and earth. . . .
          Hsi-wei received Tao and was able to
     lift up heaven and earth. Fu-hsi received
     Tao and entered into the womb of vital force.
     The Big Dipper received Tao and has never
     changed its course since ancient times.
     K'an-p'i received Tao and lived on the moun-
     tain of immortality. P'ing-i received Tao
     and was able to wander in the great ocean.
     Chien-wu received Tao and climbed to the
     great mountain. The Yellow Emperor received
     Tao and was able to ascend to the cloudy heav-
     en. Chuan-hsü received Tao and was able to
     dwell in the Palace of Mystery. Yü-ch'iang
     received Tao and was able to stand at the
     pinnacle of North. The Queen Mother of the

279

> West received Tao and able to sit on Shao-
> kuang [to grant immortality]--for nobody
> knows her beginning nor her end. P'eng-tsu
> received Tao and was able to have long life
> from the age of Shun to the age of the Five
> dynasties. Fü-yüeh received Tao and was able
> to become the minister to Wu-ting and ascend
> to become the Eastern Governor straddling the
> Stars of Winnowing Basket and the Tail.
> [<u>Chaung Tzu</u>, Chap. 6]

The above fourteen figures are all well-known gods, goddesses, and cultural heroes in ancient Chinese myth- ologies, and Chuang Tzu pointed out that what made all of them powerful and virtuous was nothing but their attainment of the ultimate Tao. Likewise, one can be- come a True Man by attaining the Tao, and that is the only clue. To attain the Tao means to know the Tao, to accept the Tao, to live according to the Tao, and to be one with the Tao. There are innumerable passages in the writings of Lao Tzu, Chuang Tzu, and other Tao- ists describing tirelessly the receiving of the Tao, returning back to the Tao and living in accordance with the Tao. The True Man, the Taoist ideal image of hu- man beings is no other than the Person who attained the Tao, the Man of Tao.

Thus, in the above, we have discussed three types of ideal images of humanity portrayed by the Confucian- ists, Mohists, and Taoists in ancient China. Chün Tzu represents the ideal person who has accomplished the virtues of Confucianism. Chü Tzu exemplified the per- sonality which has realized the teachings of Mohism. Chen Jen symbolized the state of humanity which at- tained to the highest ideal of Taoism. Each image of humanity has its distinctive quality and characteris- tics, and yet they are common in acknowledging that present humanity is not ideal and still has need to grow to its maturity. Of course, each imagery is oriented toward the accomplishment of its own philos- ophy and religious aspiration, but there is one thing in common in the acknowledgment that ideal humanity cannot exclude religious devotion and commitment. Chün Tzu is the person who knows the mandate of Heaven and is dedicated to the cause of Tao. Chü Tzu is the per- son who dares to self-sacrifice in order to promote the cause of universal love. Chen Jen is the person who overcomes the fear of death and lives in union with the Tao. However, more important than their personal reli- gious commitment, they all work for the same common

goal, that is to unite Heaven, Earth, and Man. They
are the ones who know the way of Heaven, the way of
the Earth, and the way of Humanity, and strive to attain the ultimate harmony of three ways into the Tao.

FOOTNOTES

1. W. Scott Morton, "The Confucian Concept of
Man: The Original Formulation," in Philosophy East and
West (Honolulu: The University of Hawaii Press, 1971),
vol. XXI, no. 1, p. 70.

2. Morton, "The Confucian Concept of Man," p. 70.

3. See Fung Yu-lan, A History of Chinese Philosophy (Princeton: Princeton University Press, 1952),
vol. I, pp. 81-84.

4. Fung, A History of Chinese Philosophy, p. 87.

5. Chiang Ch'üan, "Lun Mo Tzu fei Hsing Mo" in
Tu Tzu Chih Yen (Shang-ahi, 1917), p. 79.

6. Fung, A History of Chinese Philosophy, p. 77.

7. Fung, Yu-lan, A Short History of Chinese
Philosophy (New York: Macmillan, 1948), p. 57.

8. Toshihiko Izutsu, The Key Philosophical Concepts of Sufism and Taoism (Tokyo, 1967), Chapter II,
pp. 15-24.

9. David Hawkes, tr., Ch'u Tz'u: The Songs of the
South (London: Oxford University Press, 1959), pp. 27-
28.

10. Hawkes, Ch'u Tz'u, pp. 81-82.

11. Alchemy, Medicine, Religion in the China of
A.D. 32: The Nei P'ien of Ko Hung (Pao-p'u Tzu),
tr. James R. Ware (Cambridge: The MIT Press, 1966).

12. T. C. Lai, The Eight Immortals (Hong Kong:
Swindon Book Co., 1972).

Suggested Readings

W. Scott Morton, The Chün Tzu, Ideal Man in the

Analects of Confucius Compared to the Greek and Christian Concepts (University of Edinburgh Thesis, 1964),
162 pp.

Toshihiko Izutsu, "The Absolute and the Perfect Man in
Taoism," Eranos-Jahrbuch 1967 (Zürich: Rhein-Verlag,
1968), pp. 379-441.

Anna K. Seidel, "The Image of Perfect Ruler in Early
Taoist Messianism: Lao Tzu and Li Hung," History of
Religions 9 (1969-1970):216-247.

CHAPTER 11

THE STRUCTURE AND MEANING OF RITUAL

Why is ritual necessary? Isn't religion a personal and private matter? Why, then, do we have regular gatherings and formal, lengthy ceremonies? Besides,
many rituals were formed centuries ago to suit the interest of earlier peoples and are no longer meaningful
to us who live in the twentieth century. Most of us
at one time or another have attended some religious
ceremonies, ofttimes conducted by clergymen in a manner
not unlike a one-man show, within which we feel little
sense of participation. Again, many of the rituals
have become such a routine that we find little excitement, and if we keep attending, feel more a part of the
outdated past than the relevant present. These are
the questions and complaints often raised by modern
students attending religion classes.

And yet, in spite of many such complaints and cri-
ticisms, we still find that rituals are a necessary
part of our lives. At specific times, i.e., graduation, wedding, inauguration, public celebration,
funeral, whether it is sacred or secular, we all feel
it is essential to conduct certain rituals to meet the
occasion. And if we do not perform and participate in
these rituals, we often feel we have missed something
valuable and/or significant.

For example, do you remember the last time you
participated in a graduation ceremony? You were all
dressed up and rushed to the commencement exercises,
excited to see so many people gathering, cheering, and
congratulating. During the ceremony, how attentively
you had listened for your name to be called to receive
a diploma, and what a great thrill you felt when everyone applauded you. You were very much at the center of
attention, feeling significant and valuable because
the school and community had approved of you. At
least the ceremony was meaningful to you, for it was
"your" graduation ceremonial, and it signified an important point in your life. The ritual, which you
might have once deemed unnecessary, now became meaningful and valuable because "you" participated in it, and
it marked a transition in "your" life. With the passing of time, many of us like to think back to that
graduation experience (reliving the excitement), and
many even look forward to class or alumni reunions in
order to further rekindle the memory of the event.

From that standpoint, most of us would agree that the
observance of a ritual serves the purpose of making an
occasion more meaningful and more valuable. It plays
a very important operative role in that it has the
power to make specific times more distinctive, particular places more central, memorable actions more illustrious, and noteworthy people more respected.

If you can understand and appreciate the significance of your graduation, then you should be able to
understand the values of the rituals relating to weddings, inaugurations, public celebrations, memorials
and funerals, plus many other religious services. Of
course, each ritual is different from the other. Some
are more religious, and some are more secular, but
once we have fully participated, we begin to realize
the meaning of it, and the ritual process begins to
make more sense.

There have been many theories about the origin,
structure, function, and meaning of ritual. Some
theories stress psychological analysis and are concerned with its origin and function; whereas others emphasize its sociological cause and function. Priest,
minister, fakir, and shaman are still practicing many
ancient rituals, and many theologians are trying to
innovate new forms. Historians and anthropologists
have collected innumerable records of rituals practiced
throughout the world. However, it should be noted that
this is hardly a new, modern enterprise. Many scholars
of ancient China, and other countries, left records of
their collection and systematizing of rituals, along
with their interpretations as to theory and meaning.
For our purposes, let us take a specific Chinese ritual
and examine it from the standpoint of earlier Chinese
scholars, so that we can gain a comparative perspective
on ritual treatment in the East. The following will
introduce one of the ancient Chinese rituals called
"the Capping" and the theory of rituals expounded by an
eminent Confucian scholar, Hsün Tzu (荀子 313-238 B.C.).

The ritual of Capping is an initiation ceremony
practiced among the families of elite and educated in
China and recorded in the <u>Book of Rites</u> (Li Chi禮記),
presumed to be edited by the Elder Tai (大載) and the
Young Tai (小載) in the first century B.C.

The Ceremony of Capping

The ceremony of Capping is an initiation rite for

284

boys to attain manhood and become part of the adult
society. After the proper schooling and upon reaching the age of twenty, a male was to be capped. The
<u>Book of Rites</u> described the schooling of boys as fol-
lows:

> When they are six years old, they are taught
> the numbers and the names of the cardinal
> points. When they are seven, they do not
> sit nor eat together with girls. When they
> are eight, they learn the etiquette of en-
> trance and exit; eating and drinking. . . .
> When they are nine, they are taught how to
> number the days.
> When they are ten, they go out with their
> master and stay with him overnight to learn
> the different classes of characters and cal-
> culation. In morning and evening, they learn
> the behaviour of a youth and the form of po-
> lite conversation.
> When they are thirteen, they learn music,
> recite poetry, and practice the dance of the
> Ko [the civic dance]. When they become full-
> grown lad, they learn the dance of the
> Hsiang [the military dance].
> When they are twenty, they are capped, and
> learn the different classes of ceremonies.
> They also learn the advanced dance of the
> Ta Hsia [the combination of the civil and
> military dances], and attend to the final
> fraternal duties. [<u>Li Chi</u>, X][1]

As we can discern, there are some similarities
between ancient Chinese education and our own. Education started at the age of six which is the same as our
kindergarten age, and was completed at age twenty which
is equivalent to our completion of junior college. The
contents of education varied, broadly covering the basic
skills of etiquette. According to the Confucian tradition, Confucius prescribed the Six Disciplines (六藝
liu i) as the basic requirement for the education of
government officials. These Six Disciplines were the
studies of the <u>Book of Poetry</u>, the <u>Book of History</u>,
the <u>Book of Rites</u>, the <u>Book of Music</u>, the <u>Annals of
Spring and Autumn</u>, and the <u>Book of Changes</u>. The <u>Book
of Poetry</u> was for reading, writing, and fostering of
poetic ethos. The <u>Book of History</u>, which recorded the
mythological origins and the history of ancient dynasties, taught the student to know his roots and identity.
The <u>Book of Rites</u>, which recorded all the necessary

rites, ceremonies, and etiquette, trained the students
with proper behavior and official duties. The Book of
Music, the original of which was lost, has only several
fragments left in the Book of Rites. It gave an account of the meaning and function of music in the
court and office, which was to enhance the spirit of
harmony in society. The Annals of Spring and Autumn,
believed to be compiled and edited by Confucius himself from the archives of the State of Lu, contained
the political and moral judgment of Confucius on the
rule and character of kings from 722 B.C. to 481 B.C.
It was used to teach the students moral philosophy and
political science. The Book of Changes contained the
commentaries of the sixty-four hexagrams and ten essays on the theory of cosmological change. It taught
the student to understand the position and function of
human beings in the universe.

Fung Yu-lan, one of the eminent philosophers of
modern China, has mentioned that Confucius closely re-
sembled the Greek Sophists and Socrates.

> Both alike broke earlier conventions by being
> the first to teach students on a large scale.
> . . . Another respect in which Confucius re-
> sembles the Sophists, is that though these
> were all men of wide learning and talents,
> and hence capable of giving instruction in
> all fields of study, yet their primary aim
> was to enable their students to lead lives
> of government activity. . . . Confucius in
> many ways resembles Socrates. . . . Socrates
> regarded himself as a person who had been
> given a divine mission, and considered it
> his duty to bring enlightenment to the
> Greeks. So also with Confucius, who once
> exclaimed: "Heaven begat the virtue that is
> in me" [Lun-yu, VII, 22]. And again: "Since
> Heaven is not yet ready to destroy this
> cause of truth, what can the men of K'uang
> do to me?" [Lun-yu, IX, 5]. . . . Again
> Socrates, according to Aristotle, sought
> through inductive reasoning to frame univer-
> sal definitions, from which standards might
> be made for human conduct. Confucius, like-
> wise, expounded the doctrine of the Rectifi-
> cation of Names (cheng ming), believing that
> once the meaning of names were made fixed,
> they would serve as the standards of conduct.
> Socrates laid emphasis upon man's ethical

nature, and Confucius also looked upon a man's complete virtue (jen 仁) as of even greater importance than his capacity for government service.[2]

While we note the similarities, we can also detect some differences between the ancient Chinese educational system and ours. For example, while Confucian education strongly emphasized moral education and the learning of etiquette and general behavioral patterns, our educational system does not stress them at present. While Confucian education was primarily for a career in government service, our education does not focus on that narrow area. Religious education through the practice of rituals and music was compulsory in the Confucian system, but, for the most part, in our system, it is voluntary. While teaching was regarded as a divine mission to ancient teachers, it is no longer felt to be so for modern teachers and professors.

Let us now observe the procedures of the ceremony of Capping as described in the <u>Book of Ceremonies</u>.[3]

1. <u>Divining for the day</u>. Divining with stalks is carried on in the doorway of the ancestral temple to determine proper and sacred times to perform the Rite of Capping.

The father of the boy, as master of ceremonies, dressed up in his dark cap, black silk girdle, and white knee pads, takes his place on the east side of the doorway to conduct the divination facing to the west.

The divining stalks, the mat, and the recording materials, are all laid out in the western gatehouse.

The diviner takes up the stalks and goes to the master of ceremonies to obtain approval for divining with the stalks. After his approval, he conducts the divination and shows the result to the master of ceremonies.

If the result is favorable, the divination ceremony will come to an end, but if the result is unfavorable, they will reconduct the divination on the next day, until they obtain a favorable result.

2. <u>Invitation of the guests</u>. The master of

ceremonies will decide the name list of guests to attend the Rite of Capping, and the invitations are to
be sent out. Then he will visit again personally to
extend invitations to his guests.

3. <u>Divining for the principal guest</u>. From these
guests, the principal guest is to be chosen through
the divination which is to be conducted three days before the fixed date for the ceremony.

4. <u>The bidding of the principal guest</u>. Once again
the master of ceremonies visits personally the principal guest and bids for the honor of his guest to be
the principal guest of the ceremonies. Meantime,
other assistants at the Capping are also invited in a
similar manner.

5. <u>Announcement of the time</u>. On the eve of the
day the exact time of conducting the Capping is divined outside the door of the ancestral temple. Then
the master of ceremonies makes an announcement at the
east side of the door to the relatives, guests, and
assistants of the ceremonies.

6. <u>Dressing up of the novice</u>. The novice rises
early in the morning, cleanses himself, and dresses
in the crimson skirt, the black silk coat, and the red
leather knee-cap.

7. <u>Taking places</u>. The master of ceremonies, in
dark square clothes and russet knee-caps, stands at
the foot of the eastern steps facing westward. The
relatives, in black suits, stand behind him to the
east of the water-jar, facing westward. The usher, in
black square clothes, stands with his back to the east
gatehouse. The novice, in colored clothes, and with
his hair tied together, stands in the chamber with his
face southward.

8. <u>Receiving the guests</u>. The guests, dressed like
the master of ceremonies, and followed by his attendants in black square clothes, stand outside the outer
gate. The usher announces their coming to the master
of ceremonies, and he goes to meet them by the left of
the door. Turning his face west, he bows twice; the
guests bow in return. When they arrive at the door of
of the temple, he salutes three times.

9. <u>The first Capping</u>. The attendants all wash
their hands at the westside of the used-water jar, and

then go up and stand within the chamber, facing west,
and grade from the south. The assistant to the master of ceremonies spreads a mat near the end of the
east inner wall, a little to the north, and stands
facing west. Then, the novice proceeds from the chamber and stands with his face to the south. The assistant lays out the coif-cloth, hatpin, and comb on the
southern end of the mat. The novice goes forward to
the mat and sits down; after which the assistant combs
his hair and puts the coif-cloth on him. The guests
go down the western steps to wash their hands and then
go to sit down in front of the mat. The principal
guest then takes the back of the capband in his right
hand, and the front of it in his left, going forward
in steady fashion, pronouncing a blessing, sits down
as before, and puts the cap on the novice. He then
gets up and returns to his place, after which the assistant finishes the fixing on of the cap. When the
capped youth rises, the guests salute him, and he goes
to the chamber, puts on the black square clothes and
the russet knee-caps, and proceeding again from the
chamber, stands with his face to the south.

Then the master of ceremonies announces: "In this
auspicious month, and on this lucky day, we endue you
with the headgear for the first time. Put away your
childish thoughts from now on, and see that you keep
guard upon the virtues of your manhood. Then shall
your years all be fair, and your good fortune grow
from more to more."

10. <u>The second Capping</u>. The guests salute the
novice, who then advances to the mat and sits down.
His hair is combed and the hairpin adjusted by the assistant. Then the principal guest proceeds to put the
skin cap on the novice after he pronounces the following blessing: "In this lucky month, at this auspicious
hour, we add to you new garments. Guard reverently
your demeanour, preserve the integrity of your virtue.
Then will your years be without end, and good luck attend you for ever and ever." After this the assistant
finishes the tying of the pin-cord. Then, the novice
stands up, and all the guests salute him, he goes to
the chamber and puts on the white surcingle and knee-
caps, and, assuming a grave air, proceeds from the
chamber again and stands with his face to the south.

11. <u>The third Capping</u>. The principal guest goes
down all three of the western steps, and receiving the
russet cap, puts it on the novice. For this occasion,

he puts on the crimson skirt and the red knee-caps.
The remainder of the procedures is the same as before.
Then the skin cap, the cloth cap, the comb, and the
mat are removed and taken into the chamber to signify
the end of the Capping ceremony.

12. <u>The pledging of the novice</u>. In the room, a
mat is spread to the west of the door. As the novice
enters, all the guests salute him, and he goes to the
west side of the mat and stands with his face to the
south. The principal guest at the east of the door
receives drink and presents it to the novice. The
novice bows and accepts the goblet. The assistant
then brings in relishes, dried meat, and hash to the
novice. The novice goes to the mat and sits down.
With his left hand he grasps the goblet, while his
right hand dips a piece of the dried meat into the
hash, he makes an offering of the relishes. Then he
pours three libations of the drink, using a spoon provided, and gets up. Going to the end of the mat, he
seats himself and tastes the drink. Then he steps off
the mat, sits down, puts down the goblet and bows to
all the guests. The guests bow in return, whereupon
the novice puts down the goblet to the east of the
relishes. In return, the master of ceremonies and all
the guests also offer a drink of pledging to the
novice.

13. <u>Visiting the mother</u>. The novice then leaves
his mat, and facing north, sits down, takes the dried
meat, descends the west steps, and goes to the eastern
outer wall, where facing north, he presents himself
before his mother. The mother bows on receiving the
meat, the son bowing as he invites her to accept it,
the mother bowing once more.

14. <u>Giving a new name</u>. The guests then go down
the west steps, and take their place in line with the
western inner wall, facing east. The master of ceremonies goes down the eastern steps and returns to his
former place. The novice stands to the east of the
western steps with his face to the south, and the
guests call him by his "New Name" which his parents
designated, and the novice responds suitably.

15. <u>Reception</u>. When the guests are leaving the
ceremonial hall, the master of ceremonies accompanies
them and offers drinks to them. Then they all go out
to the robin-tent for the reception.

16. <u>Visiting relatives and officials</u>. The novice
goes to visit and greet his relatives, both female and
male. He bows to them twice, and they return his bows.
Then the novice also goes to the assistant of ceremonies to express his gratitude by bowing to him. He
then changes his clothes, puts on the black cap, black
square-clothes, and russett knee-cap, lays a present
of a pheasant before the palace, and asks permission
to visit the Ruler. Following, he takes presents and
visits the ministers and retired officials.

By this time, you are no doubt aware that the
ceremony of Capping is fairly elaborate and solemn.
It demands careful preparation and involves a large
number of people in family and society. Its procedure
is orderly, punctual, correct, and harmonious. Although the feeling on the part of the novice was not
expressed, the significance of Capping to him is obvious. He is at the center of attention, he receives
new clothing, new cap, new name, and the blessings and
acknowledgment of family and society. He becomes a new
man through the Rite of Capping and enters into a new
realm of life. In a sense, the Capping is similar to
a Christian confirmation, graduation, or university
convocation, through which young people are acknowledged into adulthood and maturity.

In addition to the above mentioned Rite of Capping,
the <u>Book of Rites</u> and <u>Book of Ceremonies</u> also described
the ceremonies of wedding, diplomatic exchange, district symposium, archery contest, state visits, and
funeral and mourning. These ceremonies are essentially
what the historian of religion call the "Rites of Passage." The purpose of the Rites of Passage are primarily to give orientation for one to pass through various phases of human life. There are certain significant times in human life that one cannot simply pass
by routinely, but must be punctuated with certain actions appropriate to that occasion. Whether or not
the occasion is a happy or sorrowful, enjoyable or
critical, festive or commemorative one, it is to be
distinguished from other ordinary times by performing
certain rituals to consecrate it. On these occasions,
ancient Chinese were very careful in their preparation
and performance of the rituals. And as these rituals
became fixed, they tended to become the custom and tradition and even controlled etiquette in society. Thus,
to the Chinese, the rituals (Li 示豊) started primary as
religious rites gradually extented to determine also
the mores of society and even to symbolize culture

(文化 wen-hua) itself.

     The ritual in Chinese characters 禮 has two radi-
cals: 示 which means "something divine or spiritual"
and 豊 which illustrates sacrificial offerings placed
on the altar. Therefore, in its original meaning,
ritual is essentially a religious practice. However,
as the ritual is conducted in public, such as a royal
court and government office, it begins to function not
only for religious purposes but also for social, educational, and political purposes. And as the rituals
are most often conducted by a family or a community,
they have also become an important function to integrate the society. Then, the rituals themselves are
regarded as the fundamental vehicles for educating the
young to be assimiliated into adult society. Inevitably, the royal court and government have to conduct the rituals to legitimate their authority and to
enhance harmony among the rank and file. Especially
in an authoritarian and hierarchical society, the rituals would become an essential means to impose the
domain of ruler and superior upon the ruled and juniors.
As Confucius and his followers had advocated in the
ordering of the Chou feudal system, they found great
value in utilizing rituals to solidify their position
and power in the politics of their times.

<u>A Theory of Ritual</u>

<u>The Source or Origin of Ritual</u>

     Hsün Tzu, a Confucian scholar during the Warring
States period, realized that the restoration of ancient
rituals practiced in the beginning of the Chou dynasty
was the way to rectify the chaotic situation of his
time, he composed two chapters in his work to elaborate
a theory on the meaning and function of ritual. In the
following, we shall note his doctrinal statements.

          The code of ritual has three sources: Heaven
          and Earth gave birth to it; our ancestors
          made it to fit the society; the rulers and
          teachers codified it. . . . If one of these
          is lacking, people could not have peace.
          Thus, the purpose of the code of ritual is
          to serve Heaven and Earth, to honor our an-
          cestors, and to magnify the rulers and
          teachers. [<u>Hsün Tzu</u>, XIX]

          By the rituals, Heaven and Earth can unite,

> the sun and moon can shine forth, the four
> seasons can proceed orderly, the stars can
> move in the courses, rivers can flow, all
> things can prosper, love and hatred are tem-
> pered, and joy and anger can keep their pro-
> per place. It causes the lower orders to be
> obedient, and the upper orders to be illus-
> trious; through a myriad changes, it pre-
> vents all things from going astray. . . .
> Is not the ritual the greatest of all prin-
> ciples? [Hsün Tzu, XIX]

According to Hsün Tzu, ritual has both cosmic and
social origin. It has its sacred origin in that it
was issued from Heaven and Earth. Then it was transmitted by ancestors and formed by ruler and teachers.
The ritual is patterned after the principle and structure of Heaven, Earth, and Man. Thus, the ritual is
itself a cosmological principle intended to unite and
harmonize all parts in the universe. It tries to unite
Heaven and Earth, and makes a harmony in human society.
Observance of ritual is not to be merely a custom or
tradition, but to attain the spirit of cosmic integration. Ritual provides the orientation for one to participate in the cosmic movement and to identify one's
position and significance in the universe. Ritual enables one to understand the fundamental questions of
religion: where do you come from, why you are here,
and where you are going. Ritual establishes an integral relationship between the microcosm and the macrocosm, in other words, "you and the universe." For this
reason, in the Capping, divination is conducted to discern the will of Heaven and facing in a proper direction on Earth is carefully oriented.

Proper grading according to the rank and file of
family and society is systematically arranged. The
Capping is therefore an initiation of a young man into
a cosmic order, integrated with the universe.

Psychological Function of Ritual

With this basic belief that ritual is a cosmological principle, Hsün Tzu proceeded to apply it for practical purposes to human society.

First, he tried to explain why we need ritual,
even though it is a cosmological principle. What are
the causes for our ancestors, rulers, and teachers to
initiate and institute rituals? Hsün Tzu explained:

How did the rules of proper conducts in ritual come into being? They came because human beings have their desires to express.
When human desire is not satisfied, human
beings try to find its satisfaction. But in
seeking their satisfaction, without proper
control, they definitely would create con-
tentions and conflicts, disorder and chaos,
and destruction and poverty. The ancient
sage kings hated this confusion, so they
established the rules of ritual and righteousness in order to set limits to this confusion,
to educate and nourish human desires, and to
provide the proper channels to fulfill their
satisfaction of desires. [Hsün Tzu, XIX]

Hsün Tzu stoically maintained his view of human
nature as basically evil, believing human beings were
primarily selfish, violent, and greedy from the time
of their birth. Without education and discipline,
human beings would become like wild animals. Because
of this rather negative view of human nature, Hsün Tzu
emphasized more authoritarian, doctrinal, and compul-
sive methods of education. Likewise, he regarded the
codes of rituals and righteousness as the codes most
needed to control excessive and extreme desires and
to guide persons to proper conduct in maintaining harmony in society.

However, we cannot ignore the fact that Hsün Tzu
also saw a positive aspect ritual: ritual was to enhance and promote the proper emotional outlet which is
very much needed in human life. He stated:

Pleasure, agreeableness, sorrow, and pa-
tience demonstrated in the rituals are the
expression of human emotion produced by the
happy and tragic occasions. Singing, jest-
ing, weeping, and wailing are the expressions of such emotions shown in the sounds.
Meat, grain, wine, fish, pork, and various
vegetables prepared in the banquet are the
expressions of such emotions shown in food
and drink. Caps, crowns, garments, and
sandals dressed up for the rituals are the
expressions of such emotions in clothing.
Shrines, temples, furnitures, mats, and
decorations for the rituals are the expressions of such emotions shown in dwelling.
These emotions are certainly the integral

> parts of human life. . . . The rituals allow
> these emotions to express fully and try to
> glorify and beautify them, so that their
> original motivation and consequent behavior
> can be harmonized. Thus, the ritual can
> become the pattern for all generations.
> [Hsün Tzu, XIX]

In another passage, Hsün Tzu also explained that ritual is the catharsis of emotion.

> Ritual is the catharsis of the emotions
> produced by memories, appreciation, medita-
> tion, and longings. It is the proper ex-
> pression of loyalty, faithfulness, love, and
> veneration. It is the most proper perfor-
> mance of human behaviors and the most beau-
> tiful action of human conducts. The sages
> had fully understood the meaning of ritual;
> the scholars had diligently performed it,
> the officials had regularly observed it;
> and the common people had annually practiced
> it as an established custom. [Hsün Tzu,
> XIX]

In the above two passages, Hsün Tzu explained the psychological aspect of ritual. The cosmological principle of ritual should become internalized to relate with the emotional needs of human beings. This emphasis of humanizing the transcendental principle and the traditional belief of gods and spirits into a corrective and integrative expression of human emotions was one of the contributions and characteristics of Confucianism. Hsün Tsu voiced that while the common people still regarded rituals as the way to serve the spirits, for the intellectuals, ritual was to be the way of human practice. Hsün Tzu did not talk too much about the ritual as worship of gods and goddesses and sacrifices, appeasing various spiritual beings. Instead, ritual is a refined and cultured expression of the gentleman and civility. Human beings carry within them a very complex and sometimes confusing variety of emotion and feeling, but the noble man (Chün Tzu),as Hsün Tzu said, should be able to control and integrate them, expressing them with elegance and sublimity through various forms of ritual. Thus, ritual is to be the highest accomplishment of human virtue and character. A proper performance of ritual with dignity and beauty is, to Hsün Tzu, the sign of a great personality who has totally integrated the cosmological principle with his psychological problems.

The ideals of ritual accomplishment are further explained by Hsün Tzu in the following quote.

> Ritual is embellished when the problems of human emotions are simplified and beautified. . . . Ritual accomplishes its golden mean when its emotions are well harmonized internally and externally; when the inner emotion and external action are well balanced. [Hsün Tzu, XIX]

Sociological Functions of Ritual

While Hsün Tzu has elaborated on the psychological need of ritual, his emphasis was more on the sociological function of ritual for establishing the order in society. He became more and more convinced, particularly during the Warring States period, that the re-establishment of order through the proper performance and strict discipline of ritual was the best way to save his society from disintegration. First, he pointed out the educational function of ritual.

> The purpose of rituals is to educate and to nourish. Meat, grain, and the blending of the five spices in dishes are to educate and nourish the taste. The pepper, the orchid, fragrance and incense are to educate and nourish the scent. Sculpture, ornament, cut gems, and elegant compositions are to educate and nourish the sight. Shrines, temples, altars, and mats are to educate and nourish the habitation. [Hsün Tzu, XIX]

Rituals provide the proper necessities and facilities of human life to cultivate noble taste and behavior. In ritual, the proper etiquette and behaviorial patterns are well demonstrated to give specific guidance for students to follow the principles of society. The educational function of ritual was particularly significant to Hsün Tzu, because, as was stated earlier, he viewed the original nature of humankind as being radically evil; he further felt that the only means with which to inculcate society with virtue, morality, and culture was by way of ritual.

In another passage, Hsün Tzu also denotes a

study pattern:

> What should one study? How should one be-
> gin? Art begins by reciting the classics,
> and ends in learning the rituals. Its pur-
> pose begins with making the scholar and ends
> in making the sage. [Hsün Tzu, I]

What Hsün Tzu meant by the classics were the Book of
Poetry, the Book of History, the Book of Ritual, the
Book of Music, and the Book of Spring and Autumn.

> The sage is the instrument of the Tao. The
> way of all rulers is united in it. The way
> of poetry, history, ritual, music all fol-
> lows it. The Book of Poetry teaches that
> the Tao is the final goal. The Book of His-
> tory teaches that the Tao is the process of
> all happenings. The Book of Ritual teaches
> that the Tao is the principle of all con-
> ducts. . . . He who follows the Tao will be
> preserved; he who rebels against the Tao
> will perish. [Hsün Tzu, VIII]

Among these classics, Hsün Tzu particularly esteemed the Book of Ritual as the most important of all.

> Without the rules of ritual, how could I
> correct myself? Without a teacher, how
> could I know whether or not my particular
> action is in accordance with the rules of
> ritual? [Hsün Tzu, II]

For Hsün Tzu, then, the goal of human life is to
become a scholar (士 Shu) and attain the state of noble
man (Chün Tzu) and finally to accomplish sagehood
(Sheng Jen). "He who loves to follow the Way and
carries it out is a 'scholar.' He who has a firm purpose and treads the Way is a 'noble man.' He who is
inexhaustively wise and illustrious in virtue is a
sage." [Hsün Tzu, II]

Second, in addition to the educational function
of ritual, Hsün Tzu also emphasized the ritual function
of classifying rank and file in society. For in the
performance of ritual, orderliness and distinction of
hierarchical stratification are fully demonstrated.

> What do I mean by distinction? I meant the
> distinctions in the society. There are the

> classes of the nobles and the commoners;
> there are the differences of seniors and
> juniors; there are the goupings of the rich
> and the poor; there are the positions of
> heavy and light responsibilities. [Hsün Tzu,
> XIX]

Hsün Tzu observed that the reality of society is
the inequality among human beings, even though he believed that inequality is not innate. Men's capacities
and capabilities are equal in that all have the opportunity to reach out and attain one's utmost development. However, since efforts and accomplishments widely
differ, wisdom and/or stupidity become apparent, whereby humankind are commissioned for different stations
in the hierarchy of society. Moreover, instead of
pointing to the hereditary factors of social stratification during his time, Hsün Tzu tried to emphasize
that social distinction is also due to moral and intellectual qualifications.

> The ruler is ruler because of his virtue and
> character are great, his wisdom and power of
> thought are exemplary. The feudal lords
> obey their ruler in their administration of
> military and public services and in their
> cares of the people. The government offi-
> cials obey their feudal lords in their ful-
> fillment of duties and works. The clerks
> carefully keep the archives and records.
> The common people show their respect of the
> elders and filial piety to their parents,
> and they work hard in their fields and busi-
> nesses to gain food, clothing, and health.
> However, the evil doers only gain uneasiness,
> shame, punishment, and death because of
> their wickedness and immorality. [Hsün Tzu,
> IV]

For this, it becomes more important to uphold
such distinction of wisdom and virtue by the proper
observance of the rules and conduct of rituals. Furthermore, Hsün Tzu had already become aware that regardless of class distinction, every human being has
the desire to be as honorable as the emperor and as
wealthy as the nobles. However, the problem is that
not all desires can be satisfied to their upmost. Even
though everybody wanted to be emperor, there can only
be one emperor. Therefore, the great social problem
is how to deal with this inextinguishable and

insatiable desire so as to avoid social upheaval.
Moreover, in a society, there are always some people
who are not guided by the ideal method of following
the Tao, and who follow, instead, their instinctive
desires; so there must be certain methods of social
control of these people. Hsün Tzu felt that such control could only be achieved by dividing the people into classes of inferior and superior, so that each class
would only expect the conditions of life and the particular satisfactions that naturally came to it. In this
way, their expectational scope would be narrowed and
desires would be controllable. In Hsün Tzu's opinion,
the most effective way of imposing such control was
through the discipline of ritual.

> When is it that man is truly man? Because
> he makes distinctions. When he is hungry,
> he desires to eat; when he is cold, he de-
> sires to be warm; when he is tired, he de-
> sires to rest; he likes what is helpful and
> dislikes what is injurious. Hence, the path
> of human life cannot be without its dis-
> tinctions; no distinction is greater than
> social divisions; no social division is
> greater than the rule of ritual. [Hsün Tzu,
> V]

Thusly Hsün Tzu regarded the great significance
of ritual, for it has the educational function of integrating youth into the society and cultivating the
moral virtues needed to maintain a society. It has
another function of classifying the rank and file in
society and maintaining its status quo. As we noted
in the ceremony of Capping, each member who participated in the ritual was assigned to a certain specific
position and role, so that rank and file, seniority
and authority can be clearly demonstrated. Hsün Tzu
therefore felt that ritual could control and supress
undue ambitions and desires and maintain peace and
harmony in a society. This helps us delineate the
high regard that Hsün Tzu also had for the political
function of ritual in a society.

The Political Function of Ritual

Since ritual has a social function of maintaining
the status quo and avoiding disturbances and conflicts,
Hsün Tzu also regarded ritual as the cardinal principle of government.

> The rules of ritual are the greatest thing
> in government and in making social distinc-
> tions; they are the foundation of strength
> and security; they are the Way of being ma-
> jestic; they are the focus of honor. Kings
> and dukes gained the empire by following them.
> By not following them, they lost their terri-
> tory. Hence, the strong armor and trained
> armies were insufficient to gain virtue; high
> city walls and deep moats were insufficient
> to make those rules feared. If they followed
> this principle [Tao], they were successful;
> if they did not follow this principle [Tao],
> then they failed.
>
> The soldiers of ancient times had only
> spears, shields, bows, and arrows; yet enemy
> states came to submit themselves without at-
> tempting a battle. They did not build inner
> or outer city walls; they did not dig moats.
> They did not establish outposts; they did not
> make much of strategems. Yet states were
> peaceful, unafraid of outside enemies, and
> secure.
>
> There was no other reason but that they
> knew the right way of action [Tao] and were
> fair to the people, and sincerely loved
> them; the subject accorded with his ruler
> like a shadow to its object or an echo to
> its source. If anyone did not obey the law,
> then only did they visit him with punishment.
> Hence, they only needed one man and the whole
> country obeyed. It is said: the majesty and
> fearfulness of the ruler should be great, but
> it should not be tried out; punishment should
> be established, but not used--this expresses
> what I meant by the ritual. [<u>Hsün Tzu</u>, XIX]

One of the most significant functions of government is to educate its people to the observance of law
and order of a particular society. But the government
officials, who are to educate the people, are to be
educated first, according to the rules of ritual. In
this respect, ritual is regarded as not only the
method of governing but also the principle of politics.
To Hsün Tzu, there was no separation between religion
and state, ritual and politics, or sacrifice and government. Such identification between religion and state
has been one of the distinctive traditions of China,
which also influenced many neighboring countries such
as Korea, Japan, and Tibet.

<u>Ritual as a Moral Principle</u>

As a summary to the above analysis of the meaning and functions of ritual, Hsün Tzu was convinced that it should also be one of the cardinal principles of morality. For ritual is the cosmological principle uniting Heaven, Earth, and Man, upon which the harmony and order of society stand, and through which an individual cultivates his or her morality and culture to attain sagehood. It is the fundamental discipline to be instituted by government and to be promoted by the scholar-officials of government, which was understood to be the primary duties of Confucianists. Hsün Tzu amplified his posture:

> Of the things that are in heaven, there are none brighter than the sun and moon . . . of the things that are human, there are none brighter than the rules of ritual and righteousness. . . . The destiny of men is from Heaven; the destiny of a country is from observing the rules of ritual. . . . The principles of ritual have remained unchanged through the time of all kings. They are sufficient to permeate the Way of life [Tao]. One king fell and another rose; that which conformed to these principles permeate them all. When these principles permeate the government, there can be no misgovernment and disorder. He who does not know how to make them permeate his actions does not know how to alter his actions to suit changing conditions. When they permeate the whole of a person's conduct, he can never fail. Ill-government and calamity are born of their lack; good government comes from exhausting their trivial details. . . . The one who governs the people tests their virtue. . . . That which he tests it by are the rule of ritual. [<u>Hsün Tzu</u>, XVII]

To Hsün Tzu, the principles of ritual were identical with moral principle itself. Human beings need this moral principle of ritual because human nature is basically evil and needs ritual to set up a standard for human beings to be able to know what is right and what is wrong, and to cultivate personality to reach its conceivable perfection. For human beings by nature do not have an innate motivation to do good nor innate knowledge of what is right or wrong. Ritual as

the rule of ethics accumulated by the ancient sages
and established by the government could give proper
guidance, stimulation, and discipline for human beings
to learn and to cultivate their character and to accomplish their acme of perfection to become sages.
Thus, even though ritual is an external standard of
conduct and, at times, ceremonious, it was well-suited
to Hsün Tzu's pessimistic view of human nature and his
emphasis on authoritarian ethical doctrine. For he
was convinced that without ritual, there would be no
morality and culture. This was especially true during
the Warring States period, at which time he saw rampant chaos and ever-deteriorating human conduct. This
resulted in his becoming even more emphatic in stress-
ing the necessity of imposing the rules of ritual as
the urgent duty of government and scholar officials.

> The principle of ritual is truly deep. . . .
> Its principle is truly great. Its principle
> is truly high. . . . When the superior man
> has investigated ritual, he cannot be
> cheated as to what is false. . . . The rules
> of ritual are the utmost of human morality.
> . . . The student who resolutely studies
> ritual becomes a sage; without specially
> studying it, he becomes a directionless
> person. [<u>Hsün Tzu</u>, XIX]

From the above quotes, we are amply aware that
Hsün Tzu emphatically presented his theory of the
ritual: it originated from a pattern in the universe
and was adapted to the psychological needs of human
beings. It had served various functions such as educational, political, and social in order to integrate
society. Ritual was so significant and valuable that
Hsün Tzu simply had to identify it as the cardinal
principle of morality.

The Meaning and Function of Music

One final aspect of Hsün Tze's interpretation of
ritual is the meaning and function of music in the
performance of rituals. Education in music was regarded as one of the six major arts of Confucian disciplines, and there was believed to be a classic on
music edited by Confucius himself, but, unfortunately,
it is no longer in existence. However, we do have a
chapter in Hsün Tzu's writings on music, which is now
believed by many scholars to possibly be a part of
that ancient Confucian classic. Even though it is a

short chapter, it does contain the most beautiful treatise on the meaning and function of music.

Music played an important role in ancient Chinese culture. The <u>Book of Poetry</u>, probably the first literary composition, collected three hundred and five songs primarily sung either in the ceremonies or festivals. Chinese language is monosyllabic and is easy to compose into rhymes and poems. Thus, poetic style and proverbial form are regarded as the epitome of Chinese composition in ancient times. The first lesson Confucius taught his students was the composition of poetry, which became a tradition in Chinese education until the end of the Manchu dynasty, at which time the educational system was influenced by Westernization. But even today the standard of Chinese scholarship is measured by the level of elegance and nobility of poetic expression among the conservative Chinese scholars. It should be noted that the definition of music to the ancient Chinese was far more extensive than that which we adhere to in the twentieth century. It meant the arts which include both instrumental and vocal music plus rhythmical chanting and pantomimic dance. Of the musical instruments, Hsün Tzu listed quite a few: drums, bells, stone chimes, reed organs of thirty-six and thirteen reeds, flagolets flutes, lutes, and various percussion instruments. Vocally, Chinese songs were rich in homonyms composed as poetry, and it is necessary to know Chinese poetry to understand Chinese vocal music. However, almost every educated Chinese would memorize the <u>Book of Poetry</u>, or any significant songs sung in the rituals, so that they did not need to see the words to comprehend the songs. In ancient Chinese music, rhythm was considered to be more important than melody. Dancing consisted of pantomiming by a group of performers who acted out the meaning of the music. For example, they marched north to illustrate the attack of a king and his army upon their enemy and marched south to indicate their victorious return. They moved their arms violently and stamped their feet to demonstrate the beginning of battle, and kneeled at the end to represent a happy end and the beginning of peaceful dynasty. In military dance, they used poleaxes and shields, and wore armor; and in the dance of peace, they used feathers and yak-tails, and wore official robes. Modern Peking Opera still carries this ancient tradition of pantomimic dance.

The music was, of course, an integral part of all

religious ceremonies, especially in ancestral worship,
the court ceremonies, and the district gathering of
nobles.

Confucius was apparently one of the ancient music
lovers. It was said that he was so impressed by the
performance of the Shao-Shun's music when he first
heard it that for three months he was unconscious of
the kind of meat he was eating. It is also recorded
that he himself performed on the stone chimes and liked
to sing a good song. However, not all ancient Chinese
liked the music Confucius loved. There was an occasion when one duke complained to one of Confucius'
disciples that when ancient music was performed, he
could hardly keep awake. This duke was a zealous Confucianist, so apparently by the time of Confucius, the
ancient music was no longer enjoyed by everybody, and
newer forms of music were introduced to accommodate
the spirit of the times. More melodic than monotonous
performances were by both male and female characters
rather than mere male performance; also, an addition
of dwarf characters or monkey characters took place in
pantomime. Confucius was very much offended by this
newer form of music, so much so, he even proposed a
ban on it by law. This was because he thought music
had a profound influence upon the manners and customs
of the people, and the newer music tended to be licentious and relaxed the moral tone of the community. We
can depict here a kind of puritanic ethos and moralistic interpretation of music in Confucius.

Succeeding this Confucian view of music, Hsün Tzu,
however, developed and elaborated more fully his own
theory of music.

First, he found the beginning of music in human
emotions.

> Now music is the expression of joy. Men's
> feelings make this inevitable. For man must
> need to be joyous; when joyous, his feelings
> must need to be expressed in sound, and
> acted out in movements. . . .
> In a man's conduct, his sounds, move-
> ments and pauses are expressive of all the
> changes in his mood. Hence, man cannot be
> without joy, it must have a physical em-
> bodiment. When this embodiment does not
> conform to the right principle [Tao], there
> will be disorder. The early kings hated

this disorder, and so they established the
music of Ya (雅) and Sung (頌) to guide
it. They caused its music to be joyful and
not to degenerate, and its beauty to be distinct and not limited. They caused in its
direct and indirect appeals, its complexes
and simplicity, its frugality and richness,
its rests and notes, to stir up the goodness
in men's minds and to prevent evil feelings
from gaining any foothold. This is the manner in which the early kings established
music. [Hsün Tzu, XX]

Second, one of the major functions of music was
to harmonize and unite the people. Hsün Tzu said:

For when music is performed in the ancestral
temple, for prince and minister, the ruler
and ruled hear it together, and they become
harmonious and reverent. When it is performed in the inner apartment of a house,
father and son, older and younger brothers
hear it together and become harmonious and
affectionate. When it is performed before
the elders of village and clan, old and
young hear it together and become harmonious
and obedient. For music discriminates and
unites in order to establish harmony. It
compares and distinguishes in order to beau-
tify its measures; it is performed in harmony in order to create beauty, so that it
leads everything in accordance with Tao and
control all changes.
     When I hear the music of the Ya (雅,
Court Music) and Sung (頌, Hymns), my sense
of destiny is broadened. When I see the
dancers grasping their shields and poleaxes, practicing the lowering and raising of
their heads, bending and straightening of
their bodies, my course of conduct and behavior becomes dignified. From the way they
move in groups and adapt themselves to the
music, the rank and order are exemplified,
and their advancing and retreating are made
harmonious
     In the performance of music, when the
dancers step forward, it is of attacking and
dealing with death; when they step back, it
is of courtesy and humility. Hence, music
is the greatest unifier in the world, the

bond of inner harmony, the inevitable con-
sequence of human emotion. [Hsün Tzu, XX]

Thus, music, together with ritual, work to promote
the harmony and order of society. <u>Li Chi</u> stated most
succintly:

> Music makes for common union. Ritual makes
> for difference and distinction. From common
> union comes mutual affection; from differ-
> ence, mutual respect. Where music prevails,
> we find a weak coalescence; where ritual
> prevails, a tendency to separation. It is
> the business of the two to harmonize peo-
> ple's feelings and give elegance to their
> outward manifestations. . . .
> Music comes from within; ritual acts
> from without. Coming from within, music
> produces the serenity of the mind. Acting
> from without, ritual produces the finished
> elegance of manner. Great music must be
> easy. Great ritual must be simple. Let
> music achieve its full results, and there
> will be no resentments. Let ritual achieve
> its full results, and there will be no con-
> tentions. The reason why bowings and cour-
> tesies could set the world in order is that
> there are music and ritual. [<u>Li Chi</u>, Yueh
> Chi]

Third and finally, like ritual, music has also
its ultimate purpose in attaining a cosmic harmony.

> Hence, in the fine and distinct notes [of
> music], we have an image of heaven; in the
> ample and grand, an image of earth; in their
> beginning and ending, an image of the four
> seasons; in the wheelings and revolutions of
> the pantomimes, an image of the wind and
> rain. The five notes, like the five colors,
> from a complete and elegant whole, without
> any confusion. . . . The small and the great
> complete one another. The end leads on to
> the beginning, and the beginning to the end.
> The key notes and those harmonizing with
> them, the sharp and the bass, succeed one
> another in their regular order. [<u>Li Chi</u>,
> Yueh Chi]

Music echoes the harmony between Heaven

and Earth; rites reflect the orderly distinctions in the operation of Heaven and
Earth. From that harmony all things come
into existence; to those orderly distinctions all things contribute their indivi-
dualities. Music originated from Heaven,
and rites immitated the forms of Earth. . . .
       Harmony is the final goal sought in
music. Thereby music follows Heaven in order
to manifest the spirit-like expansive influence of heavenly atmosphere. Orderly
distinction is the final goal of rites.
Thereby rites follow Earth in order to ex-
hibit the spirit-like retractive influence
of earthly formation. [<u>Li Chi</u>, Yueh Chi]

     Thus this chapter has examined the germane em-
bodiments of the theory of ritual and the consciousness of music as expounded by the Confucian scholars
of ancient China. Reading of this chapter may enhance
your better appreciation of ritual when you "participate" in a ritual next time.

FOOTNOTES

1. Cf. _Li Khi_ (_Book of Rites_), tr. Jemes Legge
(London: Oxford University Press, 1885). Reprinted
in _The Sacred Books of the East_, Vols. XXVII-XXVIII.

2. Fung Yu-lan, _A History of Chinese Philosophy_,
tr. Derk Bodde (Princeton: Princeton University Press,
1952) vol. I, pp. 52-54, passim.

3. Cf. _The I Li_ or _Book of Etiquette and Cere-
monial_, tr John Stelle (London: Probsthain & Co.,
1917).

Suggested Readings

Noah E. Fehl, _Li: Rites and Propriety in Literature
and Life_ (Hong Kong: The Chinese University of Hong
Kong, 1971).

Kathleen Higgins, "Music in Confucian and Neo-Confucian Philosophy," _International Philosophical Quarterly_
20 (1980):433-451.

D. L. Phelps, "The Place of Music in the Platonic and
Confucian Systems of Moral Education," _Journal of the
North China Branch of the Royal Asiatic Society_ 59
(1928):128-145.

Marcel Granet, _Festivals and Songs of Ancient China_,
tr. E. D. Edwards (New York, 1932).

Derk Bodde, _Festivals in Classical China_ (Princeton:
Princeton University Press, 1975).

Henri Maspero, _China in Antiquity_, tr. Frank A. Kierman, Jr. (Amherst, MA: The University of Massachusetts
Press, 1978), Book II.

Emily M. Ahern, _Chinese Ritual and Politics_ (Cambridge:
Cambridge University Press, 1981).

Mircea Eliade, _Rites and Symbols of Initiation_ (New
York: Harper Torchbooks, 1958).

CHAPTER 12

THE WAYS OF SELF-DISCIPLINE

Chapter 10 adduced the philosophy of the ideal
image of humanity as portrayed by the Confucianists,
Mohists, and Taoists. However, the question of accomplishing that ideal goal and reaching the stage of
perfection remains to be answered. What method or discipline would or could lead one to attain the ideal
personality? Realizing that setting up a high ideal
without giving proper instruction and training is ir-
relevant and impractical, ancient Chinese religious
masters developed various disciplines to cultivate
moral and spiritual character for their disciples, as
well as for themselves. This section will address the
available substratum on four types of self-discipline
developed in ancient China. The first is the way of
shamanistic ecstasy developed by the shamans in
the Shang dynasty. The second is the process of moral
and spiritual cultivation developed by the Confucianists and recorded in the <u>Book of Great Learning</u> (<u>Tah
Hsieh</u>,大學). The third is the education of knights-
errants developed by the Mohists. The fourth is the
way of immortality developed by the Taoists, especially expounded in the Book of <u>Pao-p'u Tze</u> (抱朴子).

In contrast to the preceding chapter, which discussed the structure and meaning of public rituals,
this chapter will focus more on the personal disciplines or self-development methods through which an
individual cultivated privately. Of course, a person
did not isolate himself from others entirely,for one
needed the instruction of a master and the assistance
of the group. However, the ultimate goal was still
self-realization of the ideal image of humanity which
each individual had set up for himself. Through various methods of training, one experienced, personally,
the reality of authentic selfhood and one's integral
relationship with the universe. This self-realization was called "wu" (小吾) by Chinese and "Satori" by
Japanese, and the word wu indicates that the mind
(小,心) becomes conscious of oneself (吾), that is,
self-awareness or self-awakening. As Socrates' phrase
"Know thyself" is the beginning of philosophy, the
ancient Chinese masters also regarded wu, self-realization, as the first step toward enlightenment.[1] However, it is not an easy process to describe what goes
through one's own mind during the training and in the

enlightenment experience unless one confesses personal experience. Besides, it is quite possible that even using the same methods or disciplines, two persons may differ in experience and realization. Therefore, what is presented here is only a general guideline or introductory manual of various disciplines developed in ancient China along with the few personal confessions that were available. It is also to be noted that not all the disciplines were well systematized and formulated as a manual in the beginning. Except for the case of the Confucian disciplines recorded in the <u>Book of Great Learning</u>, the other disciplines were rather fragmentary in nature and in need of artificial and even arbitrary rearrangement. The purpose of this chapter, therefore, is not to reproduce the manual of discipline, as such, but to point out the basic tennets of the training and to make some remarks on its significance as fostered by the ancient masters.

<u>The Shamanistic Way of Ecstasy</u>

In the Shang oracle inscriptions, there appeared a word 巫, indicating the existence of shamans or wu (巫). The oracle inscript of wu seems to portray a dignified figure standing in front and raising two arms to display long sleeves which were decorated with many ornaments. Paleographer Chen Meng-chia suggested that ancient Chinese shamans were also government officials who served in the royal court and performed various duties, including rituals and dances.[2] There were both male and female shamans, and they seemed to have their own groupings, traditions, and possibly their own special roles. Chen Meng-chia discovered that wu originally referred to the female shamans who worked as spirit mediums for transmitting revelations and oracles from divine beings. But by the time of the Shang dynasty, the number of female shamans decreased, and their role diminished to merely a dancing performance in the rain-begging rituals. Dancing was also called wu (舞) in Chinese, and in these dances, the performers wore a robe with long ornamented sleeves, so that the dancers were also identified as female shamans. It might be that in the prehistoric stage of agricultural life, the female shamans occupied a more important role of invoking the rain gods to send down rain to meet agricultural needs. By the time of the Shang dynasty, the official duties multiplied in the royal court so that male shamans had increased in number and power. As a matter of fact, Shang kings themselves were shamans or chief-shamans, who were

310

regarded as the head of shaman groupings. The Shang
oracle inscriptions have indicated that the Shang kings
themselves had, on several occasions, performed divinations interpreting the cracks on tortoise shells to determine the future. Ito Michiharu also discovered that
some of the shamans were identified not only as diviners but also as tribal chiefs, military leaders,
district officials, and priests. So he suggested that
in the theocratic state of Shang, the shamans were both
religious leaders and government officials, and the
king was both the head and high-priest of the state.
He further assumed that since the Shang dynasty was established by the formation of a tribal confederation
centered in the Shang royal house, the Shang kings often
summoned the assembly of the local tribal chiefs and
priests to conduct the royal ceremonies in their court,
enhancing central authority. This explained why there
were different groupings of shamans participating in
the government of the Shang royal house and their different roles due to their different offices.[3]

Chen Meng-chia has summarized that there were at
least five offices that the Shang shamans occupied in
the central administration: (1) the Priesthood (祝史);
(2) Divination (予卜); (3) Healing (医); (4) Dream Interpretation (卜夢); (5) Dancing (舞). In the office
of the priesthood, the shamans conducted the rituals,
sacrifices, ceremonies, blessings, and cursings. As a
diviner, a shaman prepared the tortoise shell or animal bone for divinations, conducted the divination,
and recorded the oracle inquiries and their consequences.
The shamans were also known to be the divine healers
because they performed exorcism, sorcery, and faith
healing by using medicine, magic, and incantation.
They were also the dream interpreters who could predict coming fortunes and events by reading the signs
in dreams. Shamans were also the dancers and singers
who could evoke the spirits of divine beings by their
incantations and entertain them with their dancing,
using various gestures and postures to induce the
spirits to grant their wishes.[4]

To perform these duties, shaman underwent specific
procedures (listed below). It was not noted whether
these procedures were in such procession at each performance, but they are a good indication of the significant disciplines essential to shamanism.

<u>Purification Rites</u>

There are extensive records in the Shang oracle
inscriptions and the Chou classics that stressed the
significance of purification prior to all the shamanistic practices. First of all, shamans and shamanesses
were to purify their bodies by three methods:
(1) water-bathing; (2) fire-purgation; (3) and the annointment of perfume. Bathing in a river or pond to
cleanse oneself before entering into the holy ground to
engage in the sacred rites not only symbolized the
purification of past sinful deeds but also signified
the rebirth into a new mode of life. Like Christian
baptism, bathing in a river was the initiatory rite
for shamans and shamanesses, symbolizing abandonment of
their profane lives and admission into the sacred. Instead of water bathing, fire was also used by the shamans to purge, for it was believed to be able to consume the unclean and burn out the sinful. It was not
clear how the Shang shamans practiced fire purgation;
but from the modern practice, we can assume that the
shamans were either purified by torch fires circling
around their bodies or by walking through charcoals of
fire with bare feet. The annointment of perfume was
done either by bathing in a hot tub of water boiled
with the fragrant grasses (hsing tsau 香草) or by putting perfumed oils on the body. The annointment of
perfume was conducted more often by the shamanesses for
their dancing and entertainment for their patron deities.[5]

In addition to the purification of the body, the
shamans also conducted quite extensive purification
rites of their clothing, vestments, tools, ritual vessels, and the rooms where they conducted the rituals.
They used water to cleanse them, fire to purge them,
blood to annoint them, or a libation of wine to pour
upon them. For example, a modern shaman takes up a
torch in his hand, enters into the room and waves the
torch around the door posts, the walls, the tables,
the chairs, and all the corners of the room while he
is chanting and making gestures of chasing the evil
away. Dogs, cattle, and sheep were offered as sacrifices, and their blood was smeared on the things or
the bodies they wanted to consecrate. The wine was
used very often, not only for the purpose of intoxi-
cating the shamans to induce them into a trance but
also for the libation of the sacrificial offerings and
holy places. With all these elaborate purification
rites, we can understand how seriously the shamans took

312

the observance of purity and holiness. In order to
make contact with the holy, one had to completely
cleanse one's uncleanliness, both physically and spiritually. It was imperative that both the body and the
environment be purified so that the shaman could be
initiated into the world of the sacred. The profane
was transformed by destroying its old mode of life in
order to be reborn into the life of holiness. Purification of the novice shamans included various stages
of initiation ordeals. It was believed that not only
would the initiation give the shamans the right to officiate at rituals but it would contribute to the
ritual's effectiveness. It was with great pain and
agony that shamans went through their initiation journey and purging ordeals, but it seems that they were
not alone. The Chinese word for purification, Fu (示友),
has a radical of 示 , which means "holiness" or "divine," and a radical of 友 which means a "friend."
Now, who would this friend be? Chen Meng-chia believed
that it was a dog, because the word "friend" (Yu 友)
came from the word Chuan (犬) which means "a dog."6
Dogs have been the companion of human beings from prehistoric time. And from the recent archaeological discovery of the burial of many dogs in the Shang tombs
and the oracle inscriptions recording innumerable dog
sacrifices conducted in the Shang rituals, we can assume that the Shang shamans were accompanied by dogs
in their initiation journeys. For dogs were sensitive
to enemies on the road and gave the alarm at imminent
danger; moreover, they were good guides on a hazardous
journey. Dogs were also faithful friends who would
defend their masters from being attacked by enemies
and/or devils. Therefore, ancient Chinese must have
believed that dogs would be good guides and companions
to go through the journey of death by sacrificing or
burying the dogs to accompany them in their tombs.
The Shang oracle inscriptions mentioned particularly
that dogs were crucified and offered as sacrifices to
the gods of four corners and winds for the purpose of
calming storms. The blood of a dog and exposure of a
crucified dog were believed to be capable of calming
the anger of the storm gods. Very similar to the
paschal lamb of the Hebrew passover, crucifying dogs
which atoned the sin of human beings was believed to
be effective in appeasing the wrath of gods and to pass
over the imminent danger of death. To the modern
world, it may sound inhumane to kill a dog or bury a
dog as was the custom in ancient China, but we have to
remember that the dogs were not killed at random, but
only at the most crucial time and in the midst of

purification rites. We can also empathize with the
shaman's distress at having to kill one's beloved dog
and best friend. This reminds us once again of just
how serious the shamans were in their purification of
sin and evil and of their desire to be born again into
a new mode of life.

The Knowledge possessed by God and Goddesses

Both male and female shamans were primarily the
media of divine oracle and their primary role was to
communicate with the divine beings. Thus, the knowledge possessed by the gods and goddesses was essential
to the practice of shamanism. Whether or not the duty
of the Shang shamans was an hereditary one is not clear;
however, at the time of initiation, they were given the
secret names of their patron deities, and they would be
sworn to become the sons or daughters of their particular deities. It was not only the name of a god or
goddess, but the knowledge of the attribute, position,
and especially the power and functions of god or goddess that was very important. For example, at the time
of a storm, when the shamans were requested to perform
the sacrifice to calm the winds, they had to know from
which corner the wind came and the god of that corner,
why the god caused the storm, what sacrificial offerings could appease his anger, what incantations and
sacred words would soothe his spirit before they were
able to conduct the proper rite to calm the wind.

From the Shang oracle inscriptions, we are able
to know the names of these gods and their special domains in the pantheon of the Supreme God Ti. As we
have already discussed in the third chapter, these
gods and goddesses were the agents of the God Ti, whom
the shamans seemed to know well and were able to communicate with for special needs. Of course, for every
communication, every shaman had to contact their own
patron deity first before proceeding to communicate
with other deities, accomplished only by the mediatorship of the patron deity. However, all the efforts and
maneuvers of the shamans might fail, and the mediatorship of the patron deity could come to no avail, especially at a time of drought and famine. Then, ultimately, the king himself as the arch-shaman and high
priest had to make the most solemn sacrifice to evoke
his deceased ancestral kings and all the patron deities
to appease the Supreme God Ti. This was an ultimate
sacrifice and the last appeal the shamans could

possibly make. In this sacrifice, it was not only the
crucifixion of dogs and other animals but also the torture and exposure and even cruifixion of the shamans
that were conducted to make their desperate appeal to
God Ti. The Shang oracle inscription called this sacrifice Ch'ih (赤) which means Red, Burning, or Naked.
It included the burnt offering of animals, the naked
exposure of the shamans under the sun, the affliction
of the shamans by fire, and the burnt offering of shamans.[7] Of course, it should be noted that these ordeals were not part of the shamans' daily routine. For
the most part, the Ch'ih Sacrifice was only conducted
during the most crucial crises, e.g., wars, famines,
etc. During times of peace and contentment, the shamans could enjoy their privileged places with their
patron deities and other deities as well. We can see
this romantic side of the mystical journey in the following shamanistic ecstasy.

The Shamanistic Ecstasy

     As the entertainers of gods and goddesses, the
shamans had to learn how to sing. The singing was
primarily an incantation to evoke the deity and to invite the deity to descend. Depending on each different
deity and each different circumstance, the incantation
could be long or short, sharp or heavy, joyous or sad,
crying or wailing, monotonous chanting or melodic song,
and magical spell or urgent prayer. Along with the incantation of singing, the shamans also learned how to
perform various forms of gestures, postures, and
dances. Again, depending upon each different deity and
different circumstance, the dancing and gestures would
vary.

     While the primary purpose of singing and dancing
was to evoke and entertain the deities, they also became the means by which to induce the spirits of the
shamans into their ecstatic journeys. Their spirits
soared into the sky, riding the clouds and winds, roaming with the stars, and playing with gods and goddesses. Such joyfulness and ecstasy of having mystical union with divine beings were fortunately recorded
in the Ch'u Tz'u. Here are two songs just to illustrate the inner joy of shamans in their ecstatic journey.

                 Meeting with the Great One,
                 Lord of the Eastern World

On a lucky day with an auspicious name,
Reverently we come to delight the Lord on
   High.
We grasp the long sword's haft of jade,
And our girdle pendants clash and chime.
Jade weights fasten the God's jeweled mat.
Now take up the rich and fragrant flower-
   offerings.
The meats cooked in melilotus, served on
   orchid mats,
And libation of cinnamon wine and pepper
   sauces!
Flourish the drumsticks and beat all the
   drums!

. . . .

The singing begins softly to a slow, solemn
   measure;
Then, as pipes and zithers join in, the
   singing grows shriller.
Now the priestesses come, splendid in their
   gorgeous apparel,
The five sounds mingle in a rich harmony;
And the god is merry and takes his pleasure.[8]

                 Meeting with the Great Master of Fate

Open wide the door of heaven!
On a black cloud I ride in splendour,
Bidding the whirlwind drive before me,
Causing the rainstorm to lay the dust.
In sweeping circles my lord is descending:
"Let me follow you over the K'ung-sang
   Mountain".
See the teeming people of the Nine lands!
"What is the span of man's life to me?"

Flying aloft, he soars serenely,
Riding the pure vapour, guiding yin and yang.
Speedily, lord, I will go with you,
Conducting High God on his way to Chiu Kang.

My cloud-coat hangs in billowing folds;
My jade girdle-pendants dangle low:
A yin and a yang, a yin and a yang:
None of the common folk know what I am doing.

I have plucked the glistening flower of the
   Holy Hemp
To give to one who lives far away.
Old age has already crept upon me:
I am no longer near him, fast growing with
   a stranger.

He drives his dragon chariot with thunder of
   wheels;
High up he rides, careening heavenwards.
But I stand where I am, twisting a spray of
   cassia:
The longing for him pains my heart.

It pains my heart, but what can I do?
I only wish the present could always stay
   the same.
But all man's life is fated,
Its meetings and partings not his to
   arrange.[9]

There are other similar elegant elegies recorded in
Ch'u Tz'u, but, unfortunately, much too extensive to
include in this study. However, from the above brief
survey of the role and discipline of the shamans, we
can see how seriously they took their position as
mediator between man and gods and the difficult training and ordeals they had to face in order to communicate with the divine beings. Faced with a crisis,
they were even ready for self-sacrifice to rescue the
people from famines. Moreover, they were great artists
who could sing, dance, and even compose beautiful poetry. Their contribution to the birth of Chinese culture should be always acclaimed and accredited. But,
most of all, they were first-rank mystics who knew
gods, spirits, and the universe, seeking the eternal
harmony of all things.

The Moral and Spiritual Cultivation
of Confucianists

   While Confucius taught his disciples with the Six
Disciplines (poetry, history, ritual, music, political
science, and cosmology), in order to train them as
public officials, his followers realized that the moral
and spiritual cultivation of individual personality
should be the beginning and foundation of all learning.
Thus, we have in the Book of Great Learning (Tah Hsieh),
purportedly edited either by Tseng Tzu, a disciple of
Confucius, or Tzu Ssu the grandson of Confucius,

317

instruction in eight steps toward self cultivation of
moral character and completion of the ideal world
peace. Originally, the <u>Book of Great Learning</u> was only
preserved as a chapter in the <u>Book of Rites</u>, but after
Chu Hsi (1130-1200 A.D.), a great Neo-Confucianist of
the Sung dynasty, re-edited it and gave it a full commentary, it became one of the four classics of Confucianism. The following is the main text of the <u>Book
of Great Learning</u>:

> The Way of learning to be great consists in
> mainifesting clean character, loving people,
> and abiding (chih) in the highest good.
> Only after knowing what to abide in can
> one be calm. Only after having been calm
> can one be tranquil. Only after having
> achieved tranquility can one have peaceful
> repose. Only after having peaceful repose
> can one begin to deliberate. Only after
> deliberation can the end be attained. Things
> have their roots and branches. Affairs have
> their beginnings and their ends. To know
> what is first and what is last will lead one
> near the Way.
> The ancients who wished to manifest
> their clean character to the world would
> first bring order to their states. Those who
> wished to bring order to their states would
> first regulate their families. Those who
> wished to regulate their families would first
> cultivate their personal lives. Those who
> wished to cultivate their personal lives
> would first rectify their minds. Those who
> wished to rectify their minds would first
> make their will sincere. Those who wished
> to make their wills sincere would first ex-
> tend their knowledge. The extension of knowl-
> edge consists in the investigation of things.
> When things are investigated, knowledge is
> extended; when knowledge is extended, the
> will becomes sincere; when the will is sin-
> cere, the mind is rectified; when the mind is
> rectified, the personal life is cultivated;
> when the personal life is cultivated, the
> family will be regulated; when the family is
> regulated, the state will be in order; and
> when the state is in order, there will be
> peace throughout the world. From the Son of
> Heaven down to the common people; all must
> regard cultivation of the personal life as

the root or foundation. There is never a
case when the root is in disorder and yet
branches are in order. There has never been
a case when what is treated with great importance becomes a matter of slight importance
or what is treated with slight importance
becomes a matter of great importance.[10]

The extention of knowledge consisted mainly of
classification of subjects, comprehensive knowledge of
the six disciplines, and firm understanding of the
principles. But since the knowledge is unlimited and
demands endless pursuit, an extension of such infinite
knowledge will become futile and fruitless. The wise
one should know "where to rest." The Great Learning
said to rest in the highest goodness, but what is the
highest goodness? It is interpreted to mean "to rest
in human-heartedness (jen) as a ruler, in reverence as
a minister; in filial piety as a son; in kindness as
a father; in good faith when dealing with the people."
In other words, the true knowledge is to know oneself,
to know one's position in society, and to fulfill the
duties assigned to one's position.

The Investigation of Things
(Ko-wu 格物)

Chu Hsi interpreted Ko-wu as follows:

> The meaning of the expression "The perfection
> of knowledge depends on the investigation to
> things (Ko-wu)" is this: If we wish to ex-
> tend our knowledge to the utmost, we must in-
> vestigate the principles of all things we
> come into contact with, for the intelligent
> mind of man is certainly formed to know, and
> there is not a single thing in which its
> principles do not inhere. It is only because
> all principles are not investigated that man's
> knowledge is incomplete. For this reason, the
> first step in the education of the adult is to
> instruct the learner, in regard to all things
> in the world, to proceed from what knowledge
> he has of their principles, and investigate
> further until he reaches the limit. After
> exerting himself in this way for a long time,
> he will one day achieve a wide and far-reach-
> ing penetration. Then the qualities of all
> things, whether internal or external, the re-
> fined or the coarse, will all be apprehended,

and the mind, in its total substance and great
functioning, will be perfectly intelligent.
This is called the investigation of things.
This is called the perfection of knowledge.[12]

Chu Hsi, the leader of the Rationalist school of
Neo-Confucianism, emphasized that the rational principle
of being is inherent in things themselves and both in-
ductive and deductive investigation of things will lead
one to a clear understanding of the principle (li 理)
of all things. But Wang Yang-ming (A.D. 1427-1529), the
leader of the Idealist school of Neo-Confucianism, rejected Chu Hsi's interpretation and emphasized that the
principle (li 理) is already inherent in the mind, and
investigation is to mean to "correct" what is wrong in
the mind, so that one can have accurate knowledge of
the principle of things. In other words, he thought
that sincerity of the will should come before the investigation of things; because without sincerity of the
will, no true knowledge is possible. The debate between
these two schools still continues to this day.

Sincerity of the Will (I Cheng 意誠)

In the <u>Great Learning</u>, the meaning of sincerity of
will was explained as follows:

> What is meant by "making the will sincere" is
> allowing no self-deception as when we hate a
> bad smell or love a beautiful color. This is
> called satisfying oneself. Therefore, the
> superior man will always be watchful over
> himself when alone. When the inferior man is
> alone and leisurely, there is no limit to
> which he does not go in his evil deeds. Only
> when he sees a superior man does he then try
> to disguise himself, concealing the evil and
> showing off the good in him. But what is the
> use? For other people see him as if they see
> his very heart. This is what is meant by
> saying that what is true in a man's heart
> will be shown in his outward appearance.
> Therefore the superior man will always be
> watchful over himself when alone. Tseng Tzu
> said, "What ten eyes are beholding and what
> ten hands are pointing to--isn't it frighten-
> ing?" Wealth makes a house shining and vir-
> tue makes a person shining. When one's mind
> is broad and his heart generous, his body
> becomes big and is at ease. Therefore the

superior man always makes his will sincere.[13]

Apparently sincerity of the will means non-selfishness and non-subjectivism. In the introductory statement of the main text, the <u>Great Learning</u> already said that by knowing what to abide in, one can attain calmness. With calmness, one also attains tranquility, peaceful repose, and careful deliberation, until, finally, one strives to know the beginning and the end, which is the Way (Tao). Wang Yang-ming regarded this introspection and meditation so significant that he adopted the Zen method to train himself and his disciples to attain sincerity of the will.

<u>Rectification of the Mind</u>
<u>(Cheng Hsin 正心)</u>

In the <u>Great Learning</u>, the rectification of the mind was explained as follows:

> What is meant by saying that cultivation of the personal life depends on the rectification of the mind is that when one is affected by wrath to any extent, his mind will not be correct. When one is affected by fear to any extent, his mind will not be correct. When he is affected by fondness to any extent, his mind will not be correct. When he is affected by worries and anxieties, his mind will not be correct. When the mind is not present, we look but do not see, listen but do not hear, and eat but do not know the taste of the food. This is what is meant by saying that the cultivation of the personal life depends on the rectification of the mind.[14]

The mind freed from fear and fondness, worries and anxiety, and fully concentrated and awakened, is the source of integral personality and the beginning step towards the cultivation of personal life. It is apparent that the rationalist interpretation of Chu Hsi and idealist explanation of Wang Yang-ming are really complementary to one another. Chu Hsi tried to emphasize that only an objective and clear understanding of the principle in things can help to rectify the mind and make the will sincere. Wang Yang-ming then stressed that unless one has a pure and rectified mind, one cannot attain a clear and objective understanding of the principle of things. Chu Hsi claimed

321

that extension of knowledge and investigation of things
can set the mind free from anxieties and worries. Wang
Yang-ming insisted that only the rectification of the
mind and sincerity of the will can produce the accurate
investigation of things and extension of knowledge. In
fact, they are complementary to one another.

The Cultivation of the Personal Life
(Hsiu Shen 修身)

> What is meant by saying that the regulation
> of the family depends on the cultivation of
> the personal life is this: Men are partial
> toward those for whom they have affection and
> whom they love, partial towards those whom
> they despise and dislike, partial toward
> those whom they pity and for thom they have
> compassion, and partial toward those whom
> they do not respect. Therefore, there are
> few people in the world who know what is bad
> in those whom they love and what is good in
> those whom they dislike. Hence, it is said,
> "People do not know the faults of their sons
> and do not know [are not satisfied with] the
> bigness of their seedlings." This is what
> is meant by saying that if the personal life
> is not cultivated, one cannot regulate his
> family.[15]

There is every indication that it was adoption of
the Mohist teaching of all-embracing love which was to
overcome partiality and promote universality. However,
universality can only be established on the respect of
individuality. The value of each person should be acknowledged and weighed justly without being interfered
with by personal relatedness or favoritism. For this,
the Confucianists promoted a state examination system
to select the wise and the worthy to become government
officials. Beyond this, it was the cultivation of personal character and constant self-discipline that enabled an individual to become a respectful person in
the family and in society.

Regulation of the Family
(Ch'i Chia 齊家)

The Great Learning made the following comments on
the regulation of family:

> What is meant by saying that in order to

govern the state it is necessary first to
regulate the family is this: There is no one
who cannot teach his own family and yet can
teach others. Therefore the superior man
[ruler] without going beyond his family, can
bring education into completion in the whole
state. Filial piety is that with which one
serves his ruler. Brotherly respect is that
with which one serves his elders, and deep
love is that with which one treats the multitude. The "Announcement of K'ang" says, "Act
as if you were watching over an infant." If
a mother sincerely and earnestly looks for
what the infant wants, she may not hit the
mark but she will not be far from it. A
young woman has never had to learn about
nursing a baby before she marries. When the
individual families have become humane, then
the whole country will be aroused toward humanity. When the individual families have
become compliant, then the whole country will
be aroused toward compliance. When one man
is greedy or avaricious, the whole country
will be plunged into disorder. Such is the
subtle, incipient activating force of things.
This is what is meant by saying that a single
word may spoil an affair and a single man may
put the country in order. [Sage emperors]
Yao and Shun led the world with humanity and
the people followed them. [Wicked kings]
Chieh and Chou led the world with violence
and the people followed them. The people
did not follow their orders which were contrary to what they themselves liked. Therefore the superior man must have the good
qualities in himself before he may require
them in other people. He must not have the
bad qualities in himself before he may require others not to have them. There has
never been a man who does not cherish altruism [shu] in himself and yet can teach other
people. Therefore the order of the state
depends on the regulation of the family.[16]

Inasmuch as the family was the basic unit of the
society, it was quite clear that anyone wanting to
prove themselves qualified to govern the state should
first be representative of a well-regulated family.
As we have already noted, family ethics is the foundation of Confucian morality, and the <u>Great Learning</u>

emphasized that filial piety, brotherly respect, and
fraternal love are the basic virtues of those who desire to be the rulers and officials. The Confucianists believed strongly that the family is the training
station for the cultivation of the morality and spir-
tuality, for one's personality, and for social ethics.
A filial son will learn from his father's care of him
how to take care of the people when he becomes an official. A filial daughter learns from her mother's
nursing of the baby how to take care of her own baby
when the time comes. So the <u>Great Learning</u> said,
"When the individual families have become humane, then
the whole country will be aroused toward humanity."

<u>The Order of the State</u>
(<u>Ch'ih Kuo</u> 治國)

The <u>Great Learning</u> explained the order of the
state as follows:

> What is meant by saying that peace of the
> world depends on the order of the state is
> this: When the ruler treats the elders with
> respect, then the people will be aroused to-
> ward filial piety. When the ruler treats
> the aged with respect, then the people will
> be aroused toward brotherly respect. When
> the ruler treats compassionately the young
> and the helpless, then the common people
> will not follow the opposite course. There-
> fore the ruler has a principle with which,
> as with a measuring square, he may regulate
> his conduct. . . . Take warning from the Yin
> dynasty. It is not easy to keep the mandate
> of Heaven. This shows that by having the
> support of the people, they have their coun-
> tries, and by losing the support of the peo-
> ple, they lose their countries. Therefore
> the ruler will first be watchful over his
> own virtue. If he has virtue, he will have
> the people with him. If he has the people
> with him, he will have the territory. If he
> has the territory, he will have wealth. And
> if he has wealth, he will have its use. Vir-
> tue is the root, while wealth is the branch.
> . . . In the Oath of "Ch'in" it is said,
> "Let me have but one minister, sincere and
> single-minded, not pretending to other abili-
> ties, but broad and upright of mind, generous
> and tolerant toward others. When he sees
> that another person has a certain kind of

ability, he is as happy as though he himself
had it, and when he sees another man who is
elegant and wise, he loves him in his heart
as much as if he said so in so many words,
thus showing that he can really tolerate
others. Such a person can preserve my sons
and grandsons and black-haired people [the
common people]. He may well be a great benefit to the country.[17]

The emphasis here is in the virtue and personality
of the ruler and government officials. "Virtue is the
root" of wealth and prosperity of the state. There are
two criteria of virtue, one is the mandate of Heaven
and the other is the support of the people. But, in
fact, they are all in one, for the mandate of Heaven
depends on the consent and support of the people, and
the consent of the people depends upon the virtue of
the ruler and officials. So basically, it is still
virtue that counts. Mencius differentiated two kinds
of rulers: one is called the Virtuous Ruler (Jen Chün
仁=君) and the other is the Tyrant called the Pa Wang
(霸王). He said, "He who, using force, makes a pretense
at virtue, is a Pa. He who, using virtue, practices
human-heartedness is a virtuous King." Mencius thought
that it was legitimate for the people to revolt against
the Pa and to cause a change of heavenly mandate.

Peace of the World
(P'ing T'ien Hsia 平天下)

This is the ultimate goal of the moral and spiritual disciplines. Unfortunately the Great Learning
did not elaborate on this. Perhaps it assumed that
once the seven steps had been taken, peace would inevitably come to the world. If a person cultivated
moral and spiritual values and was proven capable of
regulating the family, putting the state in order, he/
she should be able to bring peace to the world. However, we have to wait for the later development of
Confucianism to see how to work out world peace con-
cretely (see chapter 14).

So the above eight steps expounded in the Great
Learning represent Confucian self-discipline, not only
to perfect one's own personality but also to promote
world peace. The following will discuss Mohist education.

The Mohist Education of Knights-
Errants (I Hsieh 義俠)

Mo Tzu was the founder of Mohism and Mohist organization. He recruited his disciples, training them to practice all-embracing love, social justice, and the defense of the oppressed. He had his religious philosophy and political ideology, but he respected individual personality and emphasized personal development. Therefore, although he had a rigid organizational rule and collective disciplines, he allowed the individual to choose and develop his own talent and vocation. General guidelines of Mo Tzu's educational philosophy and some concrete examples of the disciplines and training he gave to his disciples will be described below.

Religious Education

Mo Tzu believe in Heaven who is the moral example and standard of all humankind and whose will everyone should obey. He criticized Confucianists for being hypocritical, because while they assumed the existence of Heaven, they did not practice worship and obedience. Adhering to this reasoning, Mo Tzu emphasized that faith in the moral will of Heaven and total dedication to the cause of Heaven should be the beginning of personal education and social reform.

> To accomplish anything whatsoever, one must have standards. None has yet accomplished anything without them. The gentlemen fulfilling their duties as generals and councelors have their standards.
> . . . What, then, should be taken as the proper standard in government? Nothing better than following Heaven. Heaven is all inclusive and impartial in his activities, abundant and unceasing in his blessings, and lasting and untiring in his guidance. And, so, when the sage kings had accepted Heaven as their standard, they measured every action and enterprise by Heaven. What Heaven desired they would carry out, and what Heaven abominated they refrained from.
> Now, what is it that Heaven desires, and what is it that he abominates? Certainly Heaven desires to have men benefit and love one another and abominates to have them hate and harm one another. . . . How do we know . . . .? Because he loves and benefits

humankind universally.[18]

Heaven created the universe, set up the sun, moon,
and stars to regulate the seasons and grow vegetation
to feed humankind and living things. Heaven also appointed rulers and officials to govern and setup laws
and rules to maintain peace and prosperity in society.
Heaven is almighty, all-knowing, and omnipresent. He
is the highest authority who governs the moral and political conduct of humankind, and he has many spiritual
beings (Kuei 鬼) as his agents to carry out his rewards and punishments. Moral principles such as universal love and social justice originated from Heaven,
because Heaven represented the exemplary model of love
and righteousness. All the ancient sage kings worshipped and obeyed the will of Heaven to carry out his
moral principles, so that the people enjoyed peace and
prosperity in ancient times. Noting that society was
in great chaos and the states were in constant warfare,
Mo Tzu felt that the only means by which to save this
situation was to restore faith in Heaven and revive the
moral principles Heaven had appointed. Therefore, Mo
Tzu circumspected:

> Therefore, the will of Heaven is like the
> compasses to the wheelwright and the square
> to the carpenter. . . . If the rulers and
> gentlemen of the world really desire to
> follow the Way and benefit the people, they
> have only to obey the will of Heaven, the
> origin of universal love and righteousness.
> One cannot be too cautious not to obey the
> will of Heaven.[19]

Thus, he subscribed to religious education as the
first step to revitalize personal commitment and moral
courage to engage in social reform and to promote universal love and social justice. The propagation of the
worship of Heaven and the teaching of the will of Heav-
en would, he felt, have moral effects on the reduction
of crimes in society and warfare among the states.
However, Mo Tzu opposed the fatalism taught by Confucianists in their religious education. Although Heav-
en is almighty and his will pervasive, Mo Tzu claimed
that Heaven was not mechanistic and the will of Heaven
not predeterministic. Instead, Heaven himself was the
perfect example to inspire an individual to follow,
and his will was the way to encourage the individual
to practice morality in spite of evil circumstances.
Heaven allows personal choice and freedom, and endows

the rewards to encourage good conduct, as well as punishments to deter the propagation of evil. Mo Tzu rejected the idea that one's own destiny was predetermined by fate, but emphasized it was shaped by one's
self and one's personal conduct.

Moral Education

Since universal love and social justice were considered the will of Heaven and the standard of society,
Mo Tzu trained his disciples to practice vigorously
these two moral principles. Since he believed that the
cause of social evil was in individual selfishness,
family centered ethnicism, inequal hierarchy and feudalism, and aggression and warfare of large states,
Mo Tzu took the following concrete measure to promote
his ideals of universal love and social justice. First,
he trained his disciples to control their selfish desires and dedicate themselves to the cause of public
welfare. In order to control selfish desires, he
himself exemplified in a simple and thrifty life. He
advocated content with basic subsistence without waste
and luxuries. Willingness to share personal gains and
private profits with others and to contribute them to
public welfare was also part of his code. Second, he
encouraged his disciples to respect individual personality and to treat others equally regardless of
creed, racial, or economical status. One should love
the parents of others as one's own, and treat foreigners and strangers with equality. Individual talent and
merit was to be equally elevated and credited without
bias and discrimination. Third, collective consciousness and voluntary contribution were to be encouraged.
Mo Tzu trained his disciples according to their individual talents and abilities, and he earnestly sought
them jobs that would enable them to promote their
ideals. He expected that they would contribute their
earnings and profits to the Mohist organization to be
shared by all; in so doing, it would not only benefit
others but would also attain moral benefactions for
them. Fourth, the spirit of self-sacrifice was to be
fostered. In an evil society, it is never easy to
promote universal love and social justice without
self-sacrifice. When a large state engaged an invasion of a small state, Mo Tzu did not only make a
venture to the large state to argue against such invasion, he also trained his disciples to go to the
small state and defend it. For any moral cause, the
spirit of self-sacrifice was needed. Huai-nan Tzu mentioned that Mo Tzu had one hundred and eighty disciples

who would have dared to jump into fire, to confront
swords, and to die without hesitation. Fifth, be in-
dustrious and positive. Mo Tzu had been criticized for
his harsh training and rigid discipline, for he did
not only encourage a thrifty life but also hard work.
Ch'in Hua-li, a disciple of Mo Tzu had served Mo Tzu
for three years. His hands and feet had become flat-
ened and his face black because of hard labor, yet he
dared not ask what he desired. The Book of Lu-shi
Ch'un ch'iu mentioned that Mohist scholars dressed in
rags and served by creeping, regarding self-torture a
privilege. These were rather extreme, but thrift and
diligence were definitely enforced by Mo Tzu in his
discipline. But more important was the positive attitude and the spirit of creativity that Mo Tzu emphasized. Because the people tended to become resigned and passive when they were confronted with the
overwhelming evil and massive task of social problems,
and delighted in taking refugee in fatalism to console
themselves, Mo Tzu urged his disciples to be courageous, creative, and positive. Be courageous, because
Heaven is on the side of the righteous. Be creative,
because there is no fate, and the future is to be
created now. Be positive, because passivity cannot
construct and reform society. When Mo Tzu went to the
State of Ch'i, a passerby asked him why he worked so
hard for social justice while the whole world no longer
cared for it. In reply to him, Mo Tzu said, "There is
a farmer who has ten sons, and only one son works while
the other nine do not. Does not this make that one
son's work more urgent? Thus, why do you want to dis-
courage me to work for social justice while the world
no longer cares?" This is the spirit of positivism
and creativity he exalted and encouraged his disciples
to foster.

<u>Pragmatic Education</u>

        Since most of the disciples of Mo Tzu came from
the poor and low classes, they could not benefit from
official education, which was only allowable to the
children of the nobles and officials. Since they had
to work and earn their educations and continued to
support themselves after their educations, they were
more concerned about practicality and usefulness. Education was not merely to gain information, accumulate
knowledge and be mindful of theories, but to put knowledge into practice and work constructively in daily
life and in society. He lamented that the nobles of
his time merely proposed the ideals of achieving

justice, and yet would not cultivate their own personalities. They handled their personalities with even
less care than the merchants would handle a bale of
cloth. This is like desiring the completion of a wall
and becoming resentful of working to build it. Therefore, Mo Tzu exhorted his disciples to remove the six
selfish desires: pleasure, anger, joy, sorrow, like,
and dislike, and to replace them with universal love
and righteousness. "When silent, one should be delib-
erating; when talking, one should instruct; when acting, one should achieve something." Beside this self
discipline, Mo Tzu also taught the methods of acquiring
accurate knowledge. First, determine whether the
knowledge has originated from meritous deeds of the
ancient sage kings or not. Second, whether the knowledge has common consensus with the opinions and needs
of the common people or not. Third, whether the knowledge is profitable to the majority of the people when
it is to be put into practice. Mo Tzu trained his
disciples to make critical judgments, careful analysis,
and accurate verification. He also used these three
methods in his own argument and in teaching his disciples to argue for their ideals and objectives.[20]

Mo Tzu was unfairly criticized by Confucianists,
especially Mencius, of advocating profitability more
than righteousness, because in his arguments, he often
made his point by appealing to profitability. For
example, in his opposition to warfare, he argued that
warfare was most unprofitable. For the engagement of
warfare, the state had to draft young people at an inopportune time, exhaust economical resources, destroy
a well-established state, and, finally, with a lucky
victory, to win an already destroyed and poverty-
stricken state to add more burdens upon itself. Of
course, Mo Tzu argued also that warfare was against
the will of Heaven, the moral principle of universal
love, and contradictory to the deeds of ancient sage
kings and the opinion of the people, but the people
would not listen to these arguments. So Mo Tzu developed an argument based on profitability and utility
in the hopes they would listen, because people were more
concerned with profit and usefulness.

Military Education

Even though Mo Tzu was a pacifist strongly opposed
to the rampant warfare of his time, he was also an activist who dared to go to aggressors to disuade them
from attacking and oppressing others. However, he

also realized that mere argument and negotiation might
not work to stop such aggression. So he himself, as
an engineer and military strategist, had to plan the
defensive strategies and build the defensive mechanism
and weapons to resist aggressions. Eleven chapters in
the work of Mo Tzu were entirely dedicated to elaborating defense plans and mechanisms. How to prepare the
city gates, towers, ladders, water storage, ditches,
holes, and how to coordinate the common defense by
invoking help from Heaven and spiritual beings, as-
signing mutual assistance and aids, and taking commands under talented leadership were fully described.
For this self-defense, Mo Tzu must also have developed
a method of personal military education, including
physical exercises, martial arts, defense strategies,
diplomatic negotiations and arguments, and leadership
training. Unfortunately, we do not have a detailed
record of this training. However, from the records of
personal conduct of Mo Tzu and his disciples, we can
assume that they must have had a fairly advanced self-
defense training. Some historians even suggested that
the knights-errants (I Hsieh) might be offsprings of
Mohists. The knights-errants, who acquired martial
arts for self-defense, often roamed around the country
fighting against corrupted officials, local mobsters,
evil merchants, and landlords who oppressed the innocent and weak. They took the law into their own hands
and punished evil with their sense of righteousness and
love for the oppressed. Chinese popular folk literature is full of the heroic stories of these knights-
errants, and Chinese common people admired them as
folk-heroes and heroines.[21]

In military education, Mo Tzu emphasized several
significant steps. First, one should be personally
strong in one's conviction that warfare was evil and
that warfare could be overcome. Pacifism should be a
strength, not a passivity and evasion. Second, diplomatic argument and negotiation should take place before any confrontation. Accumulation of all sources
of information about evilness and non-profitableness
of warfare and the documentation of the benefit of
pacifism should be always ready and available.

Diplomatic skill and persuasiveness of argument
were to be constantly practiced. Discouraging the enemy and oppressors of the futility of their engagement in warfare and making the enemy soldiers tired of
fighting for the evil cause were considered to be constant goals. Third, he postulated careful study of

war plans of the enemy and developing defense strategies. When the state of Ch'u hired Kung Sun-pang to
build nine war machines to attack the small State of
Lu, Mo Tzu went to the royal court of Ch'u to demonstrate his defense mechanism in front of the King of
Ch'u to convince him of the futility of Kung's war
plans, thereby stopping the warfare. Fourth was the
common defense system. In order to confront the emergency of an enemy's invasion, the total cooperation of
citizens and a well-organized coordination of strategies were essential. Thusly, mutual assistance and
joint obligation among all the members of a city were
organized and trained. In order to resist war, it was
not only the father and older brothers who had to engage in defense, but the mothers, younger brothers,
and even sisters who were involved. So it follows that
there were women soldiers existing in Mo Tzu's military
defense. Apparently, Mo Tzu knew that nobody could win
against people committed to self defense, and the success of such organization itself was a great victory
for fighting against warfare. In order to exhort the
people to rally for the common defense and coordinate
them for a successful campaign to stop aggression, a
great leadership with a strong conviction in pacifism
and skills of diplomacy and defense strategies was
essential, and Mo Tzu was training his disciples for
exactly that reason.

The preceding is a brief sketch of Mohist educational philosophy and methods that we can summarize
from the works of Mohists. Apparently, in its origin,
it was a collective discipline in a well-knit religious organization, but it had gradually become a self-
discipline of a knights-errant type of individual
when the organization was disbanded. We can therefore
establish that the self-discipline of Mohism was
really for the cultivation of the I Hsieh, the Knight
of Righteousness.

The Taoist Way of Immortality

In contrast to Confucian discipline which aimed
at serving the state and promoting world peace, the
Taoist discipline worked toward attaining immortality
of life. In chapter 10, we discussed the Taoist ideal
image of man as the True Man, the man who is capable
of transcending the life and death of this world and
lives as an Immortal (Hsien 仙).[22] In order to attain
the state of immortality, there developed various
methods such as breath control, alchemy, hygiene, and

332

and medicine in later Taoism. There were groups of the so-called Fang Shih (方士) or masters of prescription, who specialized in medicine, hygiene, alchemy, geomancy, neocromancy, etc. They were quite active around the second century B.C., and some of their great masters were even invited by the emperors to become their personal advisors in search of immortality. The Book of Lieh Tzu (列子) described an Island of "Peng-lai where the plants of immortality grew in the Eastern sea, and there were several attempts to make voyages to obtain the Grass of Ling-chih (靈芝草), or the immortal mushroom. A great number of writings also occurred with regard to the methods and formulas to obtain immortality, but many of them were lost. Fortunately, we have a symposium of such discipline and formulas preserved by Ko Hung (葛洪, A.D. 280-340) in his Pao-p'u Tzu (抱朴子). It is an encyclopedic work collecting all the methods and formulas practiced by various groups of Taoists, but it is not a systematic treatise and even contains some conflicting ideas and instructions. The following will introduce its various methods without attempting to reconcile the conflicts which existed among them.

Moral Conduct

The Taoists believed that in human bodies there existed innumerable ghosts and gods in each vital organ to control the health and fate of life, depending upon the moral conduct of each individual. Every fifty-seventh day of the sixty-day cycle, these ghosts and gods mounted to heaven and personally reported human conduct to the God of Fate, so that the length of life was determined thereby. Thus, moral conduct was the primary condition for immortality. Ko-Hung believed:

> The requirements for attaining the longevity
> of life are calmness, freedom from anxiety,
> and obliviousness of physical frames. . . .
> The other requirements are very much depen-
> ding upon extending love even to the lowliest
> things and harming nothing which breathes.
> [Pao-p'u Tzu, II]
>
> Those who are thinking of obtaining the
> longevity of life should accumulate the
> merits of moral conducts by extending deep
> sympathy with all living things, knowing the
> pains of others through one's own suffering,
> caring even for the creeping creatures,

rejoicing the good fortunes of others, and
sharing the sorrows of the people, rushing to
help those who are needy, harming nothing by
your hands, speaking no evils to cause the
miseries, regarding other's success and failures as one's own, no arrogance and no boast-
ing, no envy and no deception. Those who accumulated these merits shall receive the
blessing from the Heaven. Therefore, their
undertakings will be successful, and they
shall become the immortals. [Pao-p'u Tzu, VI]

Selection of the Right Teacher

Ko Hung also mentioned several times the significance of selecting the right teacher to teach, guide,
and train in order to attain the way of immortality.

Generally speaking, it is more important to
find a right teacher than your own hard
studies. [Pao-p'u Tzu, VI]

If one does not search for the way to attain
the immortality and meet an enlightened
teacher, there is no way of knowing the most
subtle thing in the world. [Pao-p'u Tzu, VI]

The Spiritual Anatomy and Pathology

Ko Hung lamented that the people were more concerned with worldly affairs and not with the spiritual
consitutents within themselves.

Throughout our lives, we have the heaven
above our heads, and yet we never truly understand what the heaven is. All the times, we
step upon the earth, and yet we never really
understand what the earth is. We all have
our own bodies, and yet we never fully understand how our minds operate. . . . It is even
worse in the case of the knowledge of immortality and the mysteries of Tao and Te. It
is really sad to see that the people only
rely on their superficial perception of sense
organs to make judgment on the existence of
the transcendental. [Pao-p'u Tzu, II]

The apprentice should first learn by contemplative
introspection the inner structure of spiritual life and
the function and movement of the spiritual beings and
forces within. According to the Jade Classic of the

Yellow Chamber (黃庭王經) and the <u>True Classic of the
Great Mystery</u> (大洞真經), every body contains 36,000
gods--the same number of gods to reside in various
levels of heaven to administer the physical universe.
The body is really a microcosm of the universe: its
eyes are the sun and moon, and its joints correspond
to the days of the year. The Three-in-One (San I,三乙)
gods preside over a Field of Cinnabar in the human
body, and they are all controlled by the Highest God,
T'ai I (太乙), who resides in the highest compartments
of the Field of Cinnabar. Under the God T'ai I, the
God of Destiny who keeps the Book of Life and the Book
of Death is the one who determines death and immortality. Besides the 36,000 gods, the Three Worms also
reside in the Field of Cinnabar and cause disease, old
age, and death. The masters of the Interior-gods
school of hygiene, therefore, taught their disciples
to observe a strict diet, not to feed the Three Worms,
and to practice breath control and embryonic respira-
tion (t'ai hsi 胎息.) to foster the 36,000 gods, so as
to avoid disease and cultivate immortal life. The masters were also able to train to develop interior vision
through meditation to see the inner gods and their
movement. Breath and saliva are the best nourishment
to feed these gods, and if the apprentices could acquire them properly and eat them continuously, they
could, in the end, transmutate their bodies to become
light and refined, and ride the wind and cloud. Another method was to unite the cosmic air with the
semen accumulated in the lower part of the Field of
Cinnabar to produce a mysterious embryo which would
develop into a new and pure body inside the old one.
So when the old body died, this pure body would be
released from the corpse to become an Immortal.[23]

The Elixir of Immortality

Besides the breath control developed by the hygiene
school, Ko Hung detailed the medicine or the elixir of
immortality developed by the alchemist school. In
Chapter 4 of <u>Pao-p'u Tzu</u>, Ko mentioned nine kinds of
the divine elixir; Flowers of Cinnabar, Divine Amulet,
Divine Cinnabar, Reverted Cinnabar, Gustatory Cinnabar,
Refined Cinnabar, Tender Cinnabar, Fixed Cinnabar, and
Cold Cinnabar. The processes of producing these cinnabars and their usages are various and complex; therefore, it is not the intention of this study to elaborate on them, but merely appertain briefly Ko Hung's
belief in why the cinnabar could induce the immortality of life.

335

Ordinarily, when the herbs are roasted, they
will turn immediately into ashes,but the cinnabars will produce the mercury, and after a
number of successive transformations, it re-
verts to cinnabars. Because it has such superior quality to the herbs, it can produce
the longevity of life in people. [Pao-p'u
Tzu, IV]

However, according to modern chemistry, cinnabar
(HgS) plus heating (O_2) will produce SO_2 and Hg (which
is mercury), but by heating 2 Hg with fire (O_2), it
will produce 2HgO, and not cinnabar (HgS). However,
2HgO and HgS appeared to be similar to the Taoists,
which caused the misunderstanding that the cinnabar
has reverted to itself. So alchemy to produce the
elixir of immortality is rather based on an intuitive
belief and faulty observation. Besides, the cinnabar
mercury elixir it produced may have been very toxic
or poisonous. Ko Hung apparently had only accumulated
the information of alchemy, but did not try to take
the elixir himself. There were some incidents of
poisonous death caused by taking the cinnabar-mercury.
However, the Taoist attempts to produce the elixir
of immortality has never stopped. Through many generations, the belief in the elixir of immortality persists, and search for, and experiment of, new elixires
still continues.[24]

The Way to Keep Unity

Chapter 18 of Pao-p'u Tzu expounded that the way
to keep the union with Tao is the ultimate way to attain immortality.

I heard my teacher say, "If one knows the
Unity, one knows all things." The Unity is
the origin of Tao. Lao Tzu said, "In attaining the Unity, the heaven became pure.
In attaining the Unity, the earth became
tranquil. In attaining the Unity, the people shall live [forever]." Following the
Unity is fortunate; opposing the Unity is
unfortunate. Keeping the Unity, one shall
obtain the immortal life; losing the Unity,
the life shall perish. [Pao-p'u Tzu, XIX]

Ko Hung, in Chapter 10 of Pao-p'u Tzu (Clarifying the
Basic), claimed that only the teachings of Taoism made
men's inner gods concentrate upon Unity and enjoy a
constant harmony with Tao. Taoism, according to Ko

Hung, included all the good found in Confucianism and
Mohism, embraced the essentials of the logicians and
legalists, moved with the seasons, and adapted to all
creation. The active principle of Taoists was to be
able to accomplish their interest through self-cultivation. Their inactive principle was to be adept at
fostering non-belligerence among men. Their constant
goal was skill in the use of heart and mind as they
observed people. Their repose consisted in their
ability to be free from worry as they took their repose in Tao.

In the above, we have surveyed four methods of
self-discipline developed in ancient China by four
different religious schools. Each school had its own
different orientation and goal, but they all commonly
stressed the significance of the personal cultivation
of one's own morality and spirituality and fostered
the belief that without strenuous effort and continuous
practice of self discipline, religion would only become an empty ideal and abstract theory. Of course,
not all the adherents of religion were able to accomplish their training and attain the ideal goals, but
the method of discipline was laid out and the masters
were available, the only thing left was the self-determination on the part of the disciple. Ko Hung
expressed it most succintly:

> The most decisive secret for obtaining the
> longevity of live is one's own will power,
> and not in one's riches or high position.
> . . . Why? Because the method of attaining
> the immortal life requires calmness and re-
> pose, freedom from desire and passion, deep
> introspection, and even sitting with no-
> mind like a weathered-tree. [<u>Pao-p'u Tzu</u>,
> II]

However, no matter what method of discipline one
would pursue, one was well aware that the common goal
among all these four disciplines was to attain harmony
between the self and the universe. Realization of the
Unity in the microcosmic self and the macrocosmic universe and keeping up its harmony and peace were the
ultimate goals of self-discipline.

<u>Footnotes</u>

1. It is significant to note that self-awakening and self-realization have been regarded as the first step and essential element in major religious and philosophical traditions. Cf., D. T. Suzuki, "Enlightenment" in <u>The Review of Religion</u> (New York: Columbia University Press, 1954), Vol. XVIII, Nos. 3-4, pp. 133-144.

2. Chen, Meng-chia, "Shang Tai teh Shen-hwa i Wu-shih (The Myths and Shamanism of the Shang Dynasty)" in <u>Yen-ching Hsieh-Pao</u>, Vol. XX, 1936, pp. 487-576.

3. Ito, Michiharu, <u>Chugoku Kodai Ocho no Kei-sei</u> (The Formation of Ancient Chinese Monarchies) (Tokyo, 1975), chaps. 1 & 2.

4. Chen, Meng-chia, op. cit., pp. 534-535.

5. Ibid., pp. 552-555.

6. Ibid., pp. 554-555.

7. Ibid., pp. 563-566.

8. David Hawkes, tr., <u>Ch'u Tz'u: The Songs of the South</u> (London: Oxford University Press, 1959), pp. 36-37.

9. Ibid., pp. 39-40.

10. Chen, Wing-tsit, <u>A Source Book in Chinese Philosophy</u> (Princeton, N.J.: Princeton University Press, 1963), pp. 86-87.

11. Fung Yu-lan, <u>A History of Chinese Philosophy</u> (Princeton, N.J.: Princeton University Press, 1963), Vol. I., p. 363.

12. Cheng, Wing-tsit, op. cit., p. 89.

13. Ibid., pp. 89-90.

14. Ibid., p. 90.

15. Ibid., p. 90.

16. Ibid., p. 91.

17. Ibid., pp. 92-93.

18. Yi-pao Mei, tr., <u>The Ethical and Political Works of Motse</u> (London: Probsthain, 1929), pp. 15-16 passim.

19. Ibid., p. 150.

20. Cf. Feng, Ch'eng-jung, <u>Mo Tzu Sheng-p'ing chi Ch'i Chiao-yu Shieh-shu chic Yen-chiu</u> (A Study on the Life of Mo Tzu and His Education) (Taipei, 1976), pp. 183-197.

21. In the popular folk literature is a story which exemplifies many folk heroes and heroines, <u>Shui-hu Chuan</u> or <u>the Water Margin</u>. Pearl S. Buck, however, has translated it as <u>All Men are Brothers</u>, (The John Day Company, 1968) 2 vols. Also cf., James F. Cahill, "Traditional Heroes in Chinese Popular Fiction" in <u>The Confucian Persuasion</u>, ed., Arthur F. Wright (Stanford, CA: Stanford University Press, 1960), pp. 141-176.

22. The Chinese word Hsien (仙) consists of the two elements: Man (人) and Mountain (山), which might indicate that they were originally meant to be hermits residing in the mountains. Holmes Welch argued that Lao Tzu, Chuang Tzu, and Lieh Tzu did not develop the idea of Immortals nor the techniques to attain the longevity of life (長生), for they all regarded death as a natural process and did not try to avoid death like the later Fang Shih tried to do. The True Man who transcended life and death described in Chuang Tzu and the Island of P'eng-lai in Lieh Tzu were all allegorical expressions and should not be taken literally and searched for the techniques to attain immortality of life such as alchemy, hygiene, breath control and alchemy. See Holmes Welch, <u>Taoism: the Parting of the Way</u> (Boston, MA: Beacon Press, 1957), pp. 92-95.

23. Holmes Welch, <u>Taoism: the Parting of the Way</u>, pp. 105-109.

24. Cf. Thomas Boehmer, "Taoist Alchemy: A Sympathetic Approach Through Symbols" in <u>Buddhist and Taoist Studies</u> I., ed. Michael Saso and David W. Chappel (Honolulu: The University Press of Hawaii, 1977), pp. 55-78.

Suggested Readings

Holmes Welch, <u>Taoism: The Parting of the Way</u> (Boston, MA: Beacon Press, 1957).

Henri Maspero, <u>Taoism and Chinese Religion</u>, tr. Frank Al Kierman, Jr. (Amherst, MA: The University of Massachusetts, 1981), Books 8 & 9.

Karl L. Reichelt, <u>Meditation and Piety in the Far East</u> (London: Lutterworth, 1953).

Wang Yang-ming, <u>Instructions for Practical Living and Other Neo-Confucian Writings by Wang Yang-ming</u>, tr. Wing-tsit Chan (New York: Columbia University Press, 1963).

Chu Hsi, <u>Reflections on Things at Hand</u>, tr. Wing-tsit Chan (New York: Columbia University Press, 1967).

Mircea Eliade, <u>Shamanism: Archaic Techniques of Ecstacy</u> (New York: Pantheon Books, 1964).

CHAPTER 13

THE WAYS OF COSMIC INTEGRATION

In order to unite with Tao and make harmony with
the universe, ancient Chinese religious masters developed many ways of communicating with Heaven and
Earth and integrating human society. The Shang kings
had already established a well-organized system of ancestral worship in the royal court to maintain continuity between the deceased and the living. They also offered sacrifices to the gods of the Four Corners and
all gods and goddesses in the Pantheon of Ti to enhance
harmony with their environment. The Chou kings carried
on a similar sacrificial tradition. The <u>Book of Rites</u>
recorded a ritual system instituted by the Chou dynasty.
It describes in great detail the ceremonies of initiations, weddings, gatherings, district drinking events,
district archery contests, banquets, state visits, reception of ministers, royal audiences, sacrifices, and
mournings. Confucius taught his disciples the performance of these ceremonies and the significance of propriety in social conduct. He advocated the practice
of ancestral worship in order to promote the virtue of
filial piety and to preserve continuity with the golden
past. Mo Tzu, a rival of Confucius, also emphasized
the practice of common worship of Heaven and the spirits
to promote the virtue of universal love. The shamans
had already developed very delicate and elaborate media
to communicate with gods, goddesses, and spirits. In
addition to the mysticism developed by Lao Tzu and
Chuang Tzu, the later Taoist religions had also organized well-knit religious communities with elegant rituals and doctrinal systems. Buddhism, which was introduced into China from India around the first century
A.D. not only brought with it its original Sangha system but also adopted some traditional Chinese religious
practices. Because of their extensiveness and diversity, it is impossible to list all of the religious systems developed in ancient China in this study. But they
all appeared to have one thing in common, that of integrating the human community with the universe.

In order to illustrate this point more fully,
three religious systems (which have been observed by
the Chinese people the longest and most commonly) have
been selected. The first is ancestral worship, which
started historically from the Shang dynasty, and went
through their whole history and is still practiced today among the Chinese people. The second is the Monthly

Ordinances observed in the state cult. The third is
the Rite for Universal Salvation practiced by the common people.

Ancestral Worship

From the Shang oracle inscriptions, we are able to
discern the delicate sacrificial system for ancestral
worship practiced in the Shang royal court. A geneal-
ogy of Shang kings and queens was well distinguished,
and the sixty-day cycle of sacrifices to all the deceased ancestors was well established. Divinations
were constantly performed, petitioning the deceased
ancestors to give their permission, protection, blessing, and forgiveness of sins. Elaborate sacrifices
were offered to ancestors for their mediation in order
to reach the Supreme God Ti. The homes in which the
ancestors previously lived were automatically converted
into ancestral shrines, and their possessions were preserved within them. The royal court was at the same
time the communal ancestral temple for worshipping all
the royal ancestors. In ancestral worship, all the
members of the royal family and government officials
attended a ceremony officiated by priest-shamans headed
by the living king himself as filial son (hsiao Tzu 孝
子).

It is important to note that the eldest grandson
was chosen to represent the deceased ancestor by dress-
ing up in the clothing of the ancestor, and the prayers
and sacrifices during the ceremony were all addressed
to the grandson. It was called Shih (尸) or the imper-
sonation of the dead, and it implied certain belief in
the reincarnation of the deceased ancestors in their
grandchildren. The oracle inscription Shih (宦) which
means "room" seems to indicate a special room in which
two containers with boiled water of fragrant grasses
were set up for the worship of ancestors. The other
oracle inscription Chung (宀) also indicates the house
in which an altar was set up for ancestral worship. It
was possible that a certain emblem or spirit tablet was
erected upon the altar to symbolize the presence of ancestors. The word ancestor in the oracle inscription
appeared as 且 which seems to indicate the phallic
stone erected to symbolize the fecundity of ancestors.
At the time of ancestral worship, all the members of
the clan gathered together to conduct the sacrifice to
the ancestors by inviting the spirits of ancestors to
come to join in with their descendants, renewing their
vows to support one another during the communal banquet

and sharing the sacrificial meals. Thus, the ancestral
shrine became the center of clan society (she 社). It
was not only the royal family which had its ancestral
temple to conduct ancestral worship, but the local landlords also had their own ancestral shrines and worship
to form their own clan societies.[1]

The <u>Book of Rites</u> contains an elaborate code of
mortuary rites and sacrifices to the ancestors. Chapter 10 prescribes the proper conduct of a filial son to
serve his parents while they are still alive. Chapter
19 describes in great detail the mourning rites, and
Chapter 11 gives instructions on the mourning dress indicating different relationships with the dead. There
are also four chapters (11, 23, 24, 25) that prescribe
the rules for worship and sacrifices.[2] Instead of describing these rituals and sacrifices in detail, we
will focus upon the basic beliefs of ancestral worship,
its social function, moral value, and religious significance.

Basic Beliefs of Ancestral Worship

The basic concept which gave rise to ancestral
worship was the people's belief in life after death.
Ancient Chinese believed that at the time of birth, a
spirit (hun 魂) from Heaven and the soul (p'o 魄) from
earth came to dwell in the human body; while at the
time of death, as the body decayed, the soul returned
back to the Yellow Spring (Huang Ch'üang 黄泉) of the
earth, and the spirit returned to Heaven. The returned
spirit and soul were to be recalled by their descendants through ritual invocation (tsau hun 招魂) conducted on the rooftop to come home to dwell in the
spirit tablet erected for the deceased. While phallic
stones or wooden statues were used in ancient time to
symbolize the presence of ancestors, the modern practice uses a wooden tablet inscribed with the name,
dates of birth and death, and the personal history and
merits of the deceased. The spirits that have returned
are called Kuei (鬼), literally meaning "returning."
Those spirits and souls which were not properly taken
care of became haunting ghosts, causing diseases and
harm to animals and human beings. Chinese conducted
various ceremonies to console these homeless spirits
and provided proper dwelling places for them. Later,
we will describe in detail various ancestral ceremonies,
but for the present, we will mainly focus upon the central belief in the immortality of the soul as the basis
of ancestral worship. Chinese felt that the spirits

and souls should have a proper place in which to dwell
peacefully, and the cult of ancestral worship, established in the home, was accorded to be the most proper
resting place to give their ancestors.

Chinese people also believed in the spiritual
power of their deceased ancestors. The ancestors were
not only alive but also powerful in effecting the fortunes of the living. The ancestors could endow blessings, as well as punishments, depending on the filial
piety of their descendants. As former parents, they
were believed to be still kind and caring and intimate
to their descendants. However, they were also feared
because they had now transcended their physical limits
and obtained a spiritual power which was more effective
in controlling the destiny and fortunes of their descendants. There are many stories informing us of how
an unfilial son would change his attitude toward his
parents after their death because of the fear of their
retribution. However, it is more important to note
that the deceased parents were now regarded as the
mediators between divine and spiritual beings and the
living human beings. As we have already noted, for the
Shang kings to reach to the higher spirits and gods
and finally to the Supreme God, they had to invoke and
rely first upon their immediate deceased parents as
their mediators. Many oracle inscriptions indicated
that the ancestors (especially the ancestral kings)
were in company with Ti, the Supreme God (Pin Ti 賓帝).
We can assume that the mediatorship of ancestors was
the fundamental cause for the development of ancestral
worship in ancient China. Because, in spite of the
existence of many media and methods available for the
living to communicate with divine and spiritual beings,
none of them were considered quite as intimate or reliable as the immediate ancestors. And since the ancestors had now become spiritual beings after their
death, they were believed to be able to intercede more
effectively for their descendants than before.

<u>Social Function of Ancestral Worship</u>

At the time of the death of a parent, not only
elaborate mortuary rites and burial were to be prepared, but also the notice of sad news was sent out
immediately to summon all the relatives and the friends
of the deceased. Sociologically speaking, the funeral
ceremony was a great occasion for family reunion and
even a social gathering to support the survivors in
their immediate loss and to rekindle the family and
kinship tie. Assembly of the relatives at the funeral

344

ceremony was to consolidate the family that had just
sustained a great loss with psychological and economical support and to also reassert and reinforce the
social and economical status of the bereaved family to
the public.

The erection of the cult of ancestral worship in
the home and its continuation plays very significantly
in the maintaining of historical continuity. The ongoing tradition of daily morning ritual of ancestor
worship by rekindling the light, invocation of the
names of the deceased, offering of prayers with burning incense, and reporting of the significant events
in the family allows the bereaved family members to
express their grief and lamentation, as well as to
maintain their rapport with the deceased. Confucius
regarded ancestral worship as the best means to educate the young concerning their roots. Through ancestral worship, the aged are honored, the past commem-
orated, the genealogical link maintained, and the past
and present united. The young have no identity crisis
for they know where they came from, and they are assured that they will be taken care of if they do their
duties in maintaining ancestral worship. The old who
worked hard to maintain the family need not worry and
sorrow for they are assured care even after death.
Ancient Chinese did not develop an elaborate system of
eschatology such as heaven and hell nor doctrines
such as karma and samsara (reincarnation), but they
kept up their belief in the immortality of life through
the endless chains of ancestral worship. They believed
that the grandparents would be reborn in their grandchildren, and their blood line would be carried on in
their descendants; so they all worked hard to lift up
the status of the family and looked forward to the future success of their children. It is no wonder that
ancestral worship has never ceased throughout the entire history of China. It is really the basic foundation of Chinese religion.

Besides the historical continuity that ancestral
worship has maintained, it has also served a significant function with regard to social or communal integration. Traditional Chinese society is a kinship
oriented society centered in communal ancestral worship. It is not only that each family has its own
family cult for ancestral worship, but a town, village,
and even a city has a communal ancestral shrine that
venerates the common ancestors of the town, village,
and city. In its earlier stages, when all members in

in a society were the descendants of the same patriarchs, they only worshipped their patriarchs; but as the clans intermarried, eventually they extended their worship to other clan patriarchs in the same communal ancestral shrine. As the communal ancestral shrine grew, it even became a nationwide clan or kinship association of the same surname and related family names. As we have noticed, the Shang society was centered in the Shang royal ancestral temple and the Chou dynasty organized its feudal system centered in the Chou royal lineage, where the ancestral worship had always been the center of these two ancient Chinese dynasties. Even today, homes and markets are built centering upon the ancestral shine, and the shrine becomes the meeting place of the community.

Communal ancestral worship annually renews kinship and enhances the communal fellowship. As the hierarchy of patriarchs was sanctified and the authority of elders augmented in the ancestral worship, the respect of the elderly and altruism of infants was also cultivated among members of the clan. Of course, modern industrialization and communist revolution have radically changed the traditional Chinese social system today, but we cannot deny that ancestral worship has performed a great function for social integration in the past history of China. We can still observe that the tradition of ancestral worship has been preserved in many sectors of modern Chinese society, especially among the overseas Chinese.[3]

Moral Value of Ancestral Worship

Confucius said, "The duty of a young man is to be filial to his parents at home, to be fraternal in community, to be cautious and faithful, to be kind to everyone, and to be intimate with love. If, when all that is done, he has still energy to spare, then let him study the civil arts" (Analects, I:6). His disciple Yu Tzu also said, "Those who have filial piety and altruism in family life seldom show indignation and offense against the superiors in public life. There have not been those who dislike to offend against superiors to stir a violent rebellion in society. The noble person is concerned about fundamentals. For only when the fundamental is well established that the Way (Tao) can grow. What is fundamental? Filial piety and altruism are fundamental" (Analects, I:2). Another disciple Tseng Tzu also concurred with Confucius by saying, "Only when proper respect towards the deceased has been

346

shown at the End and continued ever after they have
been departed that the moral force of a people can
reach to its highest point" (<u>Analects</u>, I:9). All the
above sayings by Confucianists stressed the moral value
of ancestral worship. Since the family is the basic
unit of society and the starting place to give moral
education for the young, the practice of ancestral
worship is regarded to be the first step of moral education, and filial piety to be the fundamental of
social ethics. Ancestral worship is to foster filial
piety, respect of the elderly, the value of tradition,
the sense of duty and care of the people. Thus, filial
piety is understood to be the source of moral force.

All the virtues such as human-heartedness (Jen),
righteousness, propriety, wisdom and faithfulness advocated by Confucianists are believed to spring spon-
taneously from filial piety. If one can respect one's
own parent, then one can extend this respect to other
persons and learn parental care in loving and caring
for other people. By honoring parents and glorifying
the merits of ancestors, the sense of refinement and
fairness will be fostered. Proper manners and etiquette
shown to the parents will eventually produce modesty
and propriety in society. Acknowledgment through
obedience to the wisdom of parents will eventually accumulate greater wisdom in life. Faith and trust in
parents will foster the spirit of loyalty and the
sense of trustworthiness. Mohists agreed that the
filial piety and fraternity fostered in the family
could be the prime motive for the development of universal love.

Moreover, Confucianists were also convinced that
filial piety could cultivate the respect of ancient
cultural tradition and great accomplishment of the
past. It would enhance more the sense of appreciation
and gratitude towards the sacrifices and merits that
the ancestors had made. Commemoration of the hard
work and great contributions made by the older generation also encouraged the younger generation to preserve
the golden past and to carry on with a new sense of responsibility. By identifying with the root, a new
sense of vision and mission would be produced to guide
the destiny of new generations. The people without a
past has no future. Of course, a blind acceptance of
the past may produce a stubborn conservatism and hin-
der future creativity and innovation, concomitantly a
homeless mind and rootless society will create an ego-
istic and alienated world.

347

<u>Religious Significance of</u>
<u>Ancestral Worship</u>

   Ancestral worship in China is primarily a religious practice even though it has its sociological function and moral value. Christian missionaries who went
to China and observed the prevailing practice of ancestral worship among the Chinese populace debated
among themselves whether it should be taken as a religious cult or merely as a manner of respect. If the
ancestors were regarded as certain divine beings and
ancestral worship contained some "superstitious" beliefs,
Christian missionaries would not allow Chinese converts
to maintain their ancestral worship in Christian families. But if it was only a moral practice of showing
the respect and gratitude to, and commemorating of, the
merits of ancestors, then it was to be allowed. However, the truth is that the demarcation line between
religious cult and moral behavior is very thin in the
practice of ancestral worship, and it is futile trying
to differentiate them sharply in order to satisfy the
religious standard Christian missionaries set up for
themselves. In the Chinese mind, religion and morality
are one, and the cult and piety are inseparable. Instead of trying to tear apart such a perenial and in-
valuable tradition that the Chinese people have per-
sisted in longer than the history of Christianity itself, it is more meaningful to discern its religious
significance.

   First, Chinese thinkers claimed that ancestral
worship, which developed primarily from filial piety,
had a cosmological orientation. <u>Hsiao Ching</u> (Book of
Filial Piety) recorded a maxim of Confucius.

> Filial piety is the first principle of heav-
> en, the ultimate standard of earth, the norm
> of conduct for the people. The people ought
> to follow the pattern of heaven and earth,
> which leads them by the brightness of the
> heavens and the benefits of the earth to
> harmonize all under heaven.[4]

In other words, family was not only understood as the
basic unit of human society, but also a microcosm of
the macrocosmic universe, and ancestral worship conducted at home would promote the filial piety which
eventually would enhance an ecological harmony of the
universe. No wonder in traditional China, Feng Shui
geomancy (風水) was conducted to determine the location

and direction of building a home, so that the family life thereon would be in accordance with the movement of the universe. Even the city planning and building of capitals had a similar cosmological orientation.[5]

Second, ancestral worship is regarded as the most distinctive expression of humanity. Tseng Tzu asked Confucius, "Is there anything in the virtues of the sages that can surpass filial piety?" The Master replied:

> Human beings excel all other beings in heaven and earth, and of all human actions, none is greater than the filial piety. In the practice of filial piety, none is greater than paying the due respect to one's father, and in paying respect to father, none is greater than venerating him as a mediator of God T'ien. The Duke of Chou had done exactly this. Anciently, the Duke of Chou had offered the sacrifices in suburbs to the Gods of the Four Corners and the Soils in order to mediate with the God T'ien. He also offered the sacrifices to his ancestor King Wen at the Hall of Light in order to mediate with the God T'ien. Therefore, all those within the four seas have followed him accordingly and offered the sacrifices to their ancestors. Thus, how can there be anything in the virtues of the sages that can surpass the filial piety?[6]

Third, ancestral worship is a sacred rite of cosmic and social integration. Again, Confucius stated succinctly:

> Anciently the illustrious kings had served the Heaven intelligently because they were filial in serving their fathers. They had served the Earth discreetly because they were filial in serving their mothers. The elderly and the young were harmonious to one another, and therefore the world above and below is all peaceful. Hence, because the Heaven was well served and the Earth honored, the divine beings have manifested themselves brilliantly. Even the king as the Son of Heaven had to have some one to pay respect to, that is his father, and he had to have some one to defer to, that is, his elder

brothers. Thus, he offered sacrifice at the
ancestral shrine in order to keep his parents
in remembrance. He also cultivated his personality and acted cautiously, lest he should
disgrace his elders. He paid the due respects to all the spiritual being at the communal ancestral temple, so that they would
be benevolent. When the filial piety and
fraternal love reached perfection, all the
divine and spiritual beings could be communi-
cated effectively. His virtue would be il-
luminated over the four seas, and there would
be no place that it could not penetrate.
Hence, the Book of Poetry said,

> From the west to the east,
> From the south to the north,
> No one would think of disobedience.[7]

As a summary to our study of the significance of
ancestral worship, we can say it was not simply an expression of human emotion that refused to let the deceased parents and ancestors disappear into oblivion
but a strong belief in the permanence of human life
and human relationships. The parent-child and ances-
tor-descendent relationships are not temporal, but
eternal and unchangeable. Moreover, the cult of ancestral worship was not only set up to commemorate
the deceased ancestors, but also a means to trace back
to the root and search for the ultimate reality by the
mediation of the ancestors. Ancestral worship is also
regarded as a center for the integration of family and
society. By commemorating the loving care and merit
of the ancestors, the spirit of fraternal love and the
bond of social commitment are renewed and strengthened.
The new and young generation identifies its root and
discovers its future destiny to carry on and uplift
the older generation it succeeds. Ancestral worship
is the Chinese religion par excellence and a perenial
institution that has prevailed through all the changes
in Chinese history, and there is every indication that
it will exist as long as Chinese people exist.

Monthly Ordinances (Yueh Ling 月令)

In the fourth chapter of the Book of Rites, there
was recorded Monthly Ordinances which described the
monthly ritual and sacrifices to be conducted by the
king and his officials in the royal court. Whether
the Monthly Ordinances were literally observed by the

ancient kings of Shang and Chou dynasties or not has
not been ascertained, but it must retain determinate
elements of pre-Han ritual practices and indicates an
effort to systematize them into a coherent system of
royal sacrifices around the end of the Chou dynasty.[8]
The following will describe the pattern in the twelve
months ritual cycles of Monthly Ordinances and point
out its leitmotifs and purposes.

Before the Monthly Ordinances were instituted, the
rituals and sacrifices were practiced at random and
more diversely according to the needs of special occasions of particular localities. With the rise of dynasties and centralization of power and authority, the
rituals were also gradually systematized and rigidly
regulated. We have already seen this in the ancestral
sacrificial system of the latter Shang dynasty. In
order to worship all the deceased royal family members,
each ancestor was given a posthumous title according
to the Ten Celestial Signs (T'ien Kan 天干) and worshipped during the ten-day week of T'ien Kan calender.
There has been much speculation as to the basis for the
sign being given to each ancestor, but one basic motivation was to organize all the individual practices of
ancestral worship into a coherent system to fit with
the celestial cycle of cosmic movement. We see a similar intention of systematizing the random rituals in
the establishment of the Monthly Ordinances.

The ritual cycle of Monthly Ordinances was oriented
by the four seasons: spring, autumn, and winter, and
each season is divided into three months. At the beginning of each monthly ordinance, the location of the sun
and the movement of constellations was identified, and
the distinctive natural phenomena of the month were
pointed out. The Book of Rites described it as follows:

> In the first month of spring, the sun and
> moon conjunct at Shih [or a Markab Pegasi],
> and the constellation of Shan [embracing
> Betelguese, Bellatrix, Rigel, γ, δ, ε, ζ, η,
> of Orion] culminates at dusk, and the con-
> stellation of Shih [embracing ε, μ, of
> Scorpio] at dawn. The Celestial stem is
> Chia Yi (甲乙), and its divine ruler is T'ai
> Hao (太皞, the God of Fire). The distinc-
> tive natural phenomena are that the east
> winds blow and resolve the cold. Creatures
> that have been torpid during the winter be-
> gin to move. The fish rise up to the ice.

Otters sacrifice fish and the wild geese
make their appearance." [Li Chi, IV]

In order to harmonize with the planetary movement
and climatic changes in nature, the Monthly Ordinances
prescribed that the son of Heaven should occupy the
office on the north-eastern corner of the royal court,
ride in the carriage with the phoenix (bells) drawn by
the azure-dragon (horses) and carrying the green flag,
and wear the green robe with pieces of green jade on
his cap and at his girdle pendant. He should eat
wheat and mutton. The utensils and vessels he uses
should be slightly carved to resemble the shooting
forth of plants.

Now as a high priest, the king has to prepare and
conduct the proper seasonal ritual and sacrifice. In
the first month of spring, the inauguration of spring
should take place. Three days before the ceremony,
the grand recorder should inform the son of Heaven,
saying, "On such and such a day is the inauguration of
the spring. The energies of the season are fully seen
in wood." On this, the son of Heaven devotes himself
to self-purification, and on that day he leads in person the three dukes, nine ministers, feudal princes,
and the prime minister to meet the spring in the eastern suburb; and on their return, he rewards them all
in the court. After this ceremony of reception of the
spring, the son of Heaven also conducted the ceremony
of ploughing to inaugurate farming. The Monthly
Ordinances described it as follows:

In this month the son of Heaven on the first
Hsin day (辛) prays to God for a good year;
and afterwards, the day of the first conjunction of the sun and moon having been
chosen, with the handle and share of the
plough in the carriage . . . to plough the
field of God. The son of Heaven turns up
three furrows, each of the ducal ministers
five, and the other ministers and feudal
princes nine. [Li Chi, IV]

In addition to the ceremony of ploughing, the son
of Heaven also issues a moral exhortation and various
orders to his officials.

He also orders the grand recorder to guard
the statues and maintain the laws, and especially to observe the motions in the

heavens of the sun and moon and of the zodiac
stars in which the conjunctions of these
planets take place, so that there should be
no error as to where they rest and what they
pass over; that there should be no failure
in the record of all things, according to
the regular practice of early times. [Li
Chi, IV]

The king gives orders to set forward the
business of husbandry. The inspectors of the
fields are ordered to reside in the lands
having an eastward exposure, and see that all
repairs of the boundaries and divisions of
the lands are done properly, and make all the
marks and signs of the paths and ditches
clearly visible. They must skillfully survey
the mounds and rising grounds, the slopes and
defiles, the plains and marshes, determining
what the different lands are suitable for,
and where the different grains will grow best.
They must thus not only instruct and lead on
the people, but also themselves engage in the
tasks. The business of the fields are thus
ordered, the guideline of husbandry is set,
and all the tasks of husbandry are carried
out without error. [Li Chi, IV]

In this month, the king also orders the chief
director of music to enter the music college
to instruct and practice music and dances.
The canons of sacrifices are also examined
and set forth, orders are given to offer
sacrifices to the spirits of the hills and
forests, the streams and lakes. Special care
is taken not to use any female animal as
sacrifice [so that the life unborn will not
be injured]. [Li Chi, IV]

    After the moral exhortation and special orders of
the month are issued, the son of Heaven also puts up
strict prohibitions of the month to be observed by his
subjects.

Prohibitions are issued against cutting down
trees. Nests should not be thrown down. Un-
formed insects should not be killed. Creatures in the womb, infant creatures, birds
just taking to the wing, fawns and eggs are
all not to be killed or destroyed.

353

Congregation of multitude and assembly of
the people are not allowed, and building of
fortifications and walls are not permitted
[because such operations would interfere
with the labors of husbandry]. Skeletons
would be covered up, and bones with the
flesh attached to them should be properly
buried. In this month no war games or
war-like campaigns should be undertaken;
the undertaking of such operation is sure to
be followed by calamities from Heaven. This
means that warfare or war games should not
be initiated in the general season of spring.
[Li Chi, IV]

Finally, the son of Heqven re-emphasizes the significance of observing the ways of heaven, earth, and
men, and also reminds his people of grave consequences
of violating the ways with ritual errors.

No change in the ways of heaven is allowed;
nor extinction of the principles of earth;
nor any confounding of the bounds of men.
If in the first month of spring the ritual
proceedings proper to summer were carried
out, the rain would fall unseasonably, plants
and trees would decay prematurely, and the
states would be seized by constant fear and
chaos. If the ritual proceedings proper to
autumn were carried out, there would be
great pestilence among the people and bois-
terous winds would work their violence; rain
would descend in torrents and weeds, fescue,
darnel, and thistles would grow wild. If
the ritual proceedings of winter were carried
out, snow and frost would destroy the living
things, the flood of water would cause great
damage, and the first sown seeds would not
root in the ground. [Li Chi, IV]

From the above delineation of the first month's
ordinances, we can discern a pattern by which ancient
Chinese kings and officials tried to conduct the proper human acts to maintain harmony with their environment. As the Chinese word for King (王) symbolized
him to be the mediator of three realms of the universe,
heaven, earth, and men, he is fully responsible to
conduct rituals to enhance cosmic harmony. He is the
son of Heaven who received the mandate of Heaven to be

the king, but at the same time, he is also the high
priest who performs the rituals to mediate between
heaven, earth, and mankind. The pattern of his ritual
action is at once religious, moral, and ecological.
We can list its major acts as follows:

1. Observation of the planetary movement and natural
     phenomena.

2. Observance of the royal habitation, behavior, diet,
     and utensils.

3. Observance of purification and ritual preparations.

4. Performance of proper ceremonies assigned to the
     month.

5. Issuance of moral exhortation and seasonal ordi-
     nances.

6. Prohibitions set up to conserve the ecology.

7. Warnings against ritual errors and violations.

The same ritual pattern is repeated again and again in
every month to ensure the ecological harmony and peaceful living which ancient Chinese people believed to be
the foundation of happiness.

The ritual pattern innovated by the Monthly Ordinances was carried into the state cult of the Han dynasty (206 B.C. - A.D. 222). The Treatises on Ritual
(Li-yi Chih 禮儀記) in the Fan Yeh's Later Han History
(Hou Han shu 後漢書) have preserved for us a detailed
record of the ritual calendar practiced during the Han
dynasty.[9]

The Cult for Universal Salvation
(P'u Tu 普渡)

While the Monthly Ordinances and the Han Treatises
on ritual represented the state cult which integrated
the Yin-Yang cosmology and Confucian moral disciplines,
the cult for universal salvation represented a popular
cult which synthesized the Taoist belief in the immortal life and the Buddhist ideal of universal salvation.

Both Lao Tzu and Chuang Tzu, two great pioneers
of Taoism, taught that the universe is created by Tao,
and the Way of Tao is cyclical for it has its beginning, growth, ending, and reversal (Fan 反). Human
life also has its cycle of birth, growth, death, and
rebirth by following the Way of Tao. In order to realize the ideal of obtaining such immortal life through

the process of regeneration, the Taoists had developed
the rites of cosmic cycle, celebrating the beginning
of the Cosmos on the fifteenth day of the first lunar
month, the zenith of cosmic process on the fifteenth
day of the seventh lunar month, and the ending or renewal of cosmic cycle on the fifteenth day of the
twelfth lunar month. They are called Shang-Chung-Hsia
Yüan, respectively. T'ien-Shih Tao, a religious
organization founded by Chang Ling in the middle of the
second century A.D., further developed the belief in
Three Ruling Dieties (San Kuan 三官): the Heavenly
Ruler, the Earthly Ruler, and the Water Ruler and practiced the expiatory rites toward these gods for forgiveness of sins and healing of sickness. The Three
Days of Assembly (San-Hui Jih), which they observed annually for offerings and expiations of Three Ruling
Deities, were gradually developed into the Three Celebrations of Cosmic Cycles by the fourth century.

Meanwhile, Mahayana Buddhism was introduced into
the south-western part of China from India by the silk
route around the first century A.D. and began to spread
into the central part of China. In order to penetrate
into the main religious movement of China, Mahayana
Buddhism assimilated various traditional Chinese beliefs and practices. One such assimilation was the
synthesis between the Buddhist ceremony of Ullambana
with the Taoist Chung-yüan Chieh, the second celebration of the cosmic cycle. The Ullambana ceremony may
have originated in ancient India as an Avalambana offering of merit toward the salvation of all sinful
ones, both alive and dead. The merits accumulated by
the saints and monks, it was believed, could be transmitted to sinful ones to redeem them from punishment.
Since Mahayana Buddhism advocated the Boddhisattva
ideal which emphasized that salvation for others was
more important than liberation for oneself, the Buddhists had regularly performed the Avalambana Festival
as one of their significant rites in the ritual calendar. It was quite possible that Chinese transcribed
the word Avalambana as Yü Lan P'en (盂蘭盆) which means
in Chinese "to turn the basin upside down." Because
in the Chinese practice of Yü Lan P'en ceremony, they
suspended the basins that contained the sacrificial
food in the air and turned them upside down in order
to feed the hungry ghosts who were believed to be tortured in hell. There is a Buddhist scripture called
Yü Lan P'en Ching, possibly composed in the fourth century, which recorded a Buddhist legend of how Moggal-
lana, a Buddhist monk, descended into deepest hell to

rescue his mother from her miseries there. After Mog-
gallana had done this, the great compassionate Buddha
then suggested the institution of the Ullambana Festival in order to unite all the merits accumulated by
faithful Buddhists to offset the demerits committed by
those unfortunate denizens in purgatory and to save
them, even temporarily, from the tortures of hell. The
main purpose for writing such a scripture was to make
an apology to those Chinese folks who rejected Buddhism as a religion of non-filiality and refused to let
their young men become celibate monks. They accomplished their goal by emphasizing that celibacy and
monkhood could accumulate merit enough to redeem the
sins of ancestors and to rescue them from the sufferings of hell. The Yü Lan Ching apparently made a great
impact on Chinese of that period, because it implanted
the beliefs in the doctrines of moral causation, heav-
en and hell, the miseries of purgatory, the way of salvation by the transmission of merit, and the significance of charity and meritorious works. Chinese Buddhists must have had foreknowledge of the Taoists' practices of the Three Celebrations of the Cosmic Cycle,
particularly of the Middle Cosmic Cycle Festival
(Chung-Yüan Chieh), in that all faithful Taoists were
summoned to appear in front of the Court of the Earthly
Ruler to confess and expiate their sins; in this way,
the Buddhists assimilated their Ullambana Festival with
Chung-Yüan Chieh. Apparently, early Chinese also wel-
comed this additional cult and integrated it with their
traditional celebration of the cosmic cycle, and thus
it has been generally called P'u Tu (普渡), which literally means "universal salvation." The following is a
brief summary concerning the practices of the festival
for universal salvation.[10]

Usually starting from the first day of the seventh
lunar month, the people prepared for the coming of
P'u Tu Festival by purification of their homes, environment, and themselves. In order to make their rites
effective, each member of the community was to be
hospitable to strangers and travelers who passed by
and to be generous to the unfortunate and outcasts in
the community. Enemies were to be forgiven, debts
pardoned, and quarrels reconciled. Since the main purpose of P'u Tu was to release and feed the hungry
ghosts, the spirit of universal love and communal care
was enhanced in advance among members of the living
community. Three days before the beginning of the
rite, all the members were to observe pennance by fast-
ing and abstinence and attending to the litanies of

repentance conducted by Buddhist monks or Taoist
priests. Slaying of any animal was forbidden during
these three days.

     After the Buddhist monks and Taoist priests, who
were invited to conduct the P'u Tu ritual, completed
their own purification and divination to determine the
site and time of the rite, a P'u Tu altar was built.
The construction of the P'u Tu altar was modeled after
the mandala of the highest heavens in which the altar
should face the direction of the north where the Three
Rulers of the Cosmos resided. On the P'u Tu altar,
offerings of tea, wine, vegetable dishes, buns, fruits,
and flowers, always in threes, were laid out. A special altar was also built in the southern side of the
ritual site which faced the north, and all the idols
and statues of lesser deities, including the Jade Emperor, were to be erected together on the same altar.
This was to demonstrate that the Three Rulers were superior to the lesser deities, who were merely the agents of the Three Rulers. It also signified that only
the Three Rulers could forgive the sins of the living
and the dead and release the dead from the tortures of
hell. Then another special altar was to be set up for
the hungry ghosts to come and participate in the P'u
Tu ritual. Because they were unclean, they could not
mingle directly with the living on the purified altar,
and yet they needed to be integrated into the rite, so
a long table was set up connecting to the altar of the
lesser deities and the Jade Emperor, while the sacrificial offerings were laid out on the table. An incense
pot was placed between the table and altar to signify
the transition and link between the underworld and
this world.

     The priests who officiated at the ritual purified
themselves by observing pennance and abstinence. The
priests all wore red robes, which were called Ho-ch'ang
or longevity robes. On the red robe of the high priest
was embroidered the eight triagrams symbolizing the
total cosmos or eight golden cranes. On the sleeves,
collar, and lower borders of the robe was embroidered
the eight treasures, which symbolize the eight im-
mortals--a fan, lotus, sword, flower basket, flute,
gourd, wooden clappers and a bamboo container. After
everything was prepared, the announcement of the P'u
Tu ritual was sent to all members of the community,
to all travelers and strangers who passed by and to
hungry ghosts. All members of the community then
brought their offerings to the altar and the priests

were seated surrounding the altar, then the formal P'u
Tu ritual began in the following manner.

Part I. K'ai T'an (開壇) or
Opening the Altar

Fa Ku: the drum of the Law. The beginning of the
P'u Tu ritual is signaled by the beating of the drum
of the Law or the Taoist's drum. Three long rolls of
the drum are sounded announcing the three stages of
the cosmos-heaven, earth, and the underworld that the
ceremony is about to begin. As the drums echo throughout the cosmos, summoning the spirits, the living, and
the deceased, the temple custodians begin to light in-
sense and candles at various altars. The gongs and
cymbals then join with the drum beat in a cadence of
purification of the sacred rite.

Priase to the Three Rulers. The high priest offers incense with chanting of a hymn in praise of the
Three Rulers accompanied by music played on drums, cymbals, gongs, and double-reeded flute. After the chant,
the chief cantor reads a lengthy petition addressed to
the Heavenly Ruler, expressing the purpose of the ritual and the prayers of the entire community, with a
list of the names of all community members who have
contributed to the sacrifice. Then, the high priest
chants hymns in praise of the Three Treasures. In
Buddhism, the Three Treasures are the Buddha, the
Dharma (teachings), and the Sangha (community), but in
Taoism, they are the Eternal Tao, the Taoist Canon, and
the Heavenly Master Chang Tao-ling (張道稜), the
founder of T'ien-shu Tao. While the three praises are
being sung, the high priest performs a meditation in
which he envisions in his mind the appearance of the
Three Rulers. In the state of union with the Tao, the
Three Rulers are now believed to be present in the
body of the high priest, the altar becomes the center
of a microcosm, and the high priest is ready to officiate the P'u Tu ritual.

A Procession to the P'u Tu altar. Leaving the
main altar, the Taoist priests make a procession to the
front of the paper image of Ta-shih-chih (Mahasthama),
the Boddhisattva who rescued his mother from hell, be-
seeching his aid in releasing the souls from hell. the
high priest chants the mantra of Ta-shih-chih and draws
secret talismans in the air, invoking the spirit of
Ta-shih-chih to descend upon the effigy. This rite is
called k'ai-kuang, or "opening the eyes" of the statue.

After the incantation, the priests proceed to the P'u
Tu altar, and the high priest and the chief cantor perform the purification by sprinkling holy water in the
ten directions. Then, the chief cantor holds three
sticks of unlit incense in his right hand and invites
the high priest to ascend the throne of the P'u Tu
altar by chanting:

>Praise the most superior and mysterious 36
>divisions [of ministers, sages, and the
>generals of the heavens].
>From the center of Dragon-tiger mountain,
>descend here.
>Guide the souls to birth in ultimate happi-
>ness.
>Come forward, master, and take the precious
>throne.

The high priest responds:

>Make it known that my origins are not sullied,
>The six roots [eyes, ears, nose, tongue, body,
>mind] will not interfere, for I am of pure
>mind.
>The compassionate sovereigns of the three
>stages, [past, present, future] whom I am
>one with!
>Be present in your multitudes as I ascend the
>throne.
>Come and save all souls and hungry ghosts!

The chief cantor responds:

>Three thousand holy ones come to the feast,
>To realize the salvation of all living beings.
>Strike the drum of the Tao three times,
>Ascend the precious throne.
>All souls and hungry ghosts, come to save
>them!

Then, while the musicians are playing the exorcism
melody called Ta-k'ai-men, or "Open wide the gate,"
the high priest and the assistant cantor enter the
area of the altar shielding their faces with their
sleeves, symbolizing the wiping away of the six roots
of desire and evil influences, and then progress to
the throne.

Consecrating the ritual site with mudras. When
the high priest has ascended the throne, the chief

cantor burns the incense and paper money in the temple
furnace. This is the signal for Ta-shih-chih to allow
the multitude of hungry ghosts waiting outside the
temple to enter. As they are entering, the musician
plays the song of exorcism, and the high priest performs a series of exorcistic mudras to form a protec-
tive circle around the altar.

<u>Part II. Ch'ing Shen (進神) or
"Inviting the Gods"</u>

<u>Incense offering to gods</u>. The high priest begins
to chant the invitation mantra to all gods and goddesses of the three realms while lifting up the lit
incense sticks to all the directions. After completing
the invitation, he reads the community petition, ex-
plaining the purpose of the P'u Tu ritual and the benefits the people seek from the gods.

<u>Welcoming the Five Sovereigns of the Five Direc-
tions</u>. The high priest puts on a five-pointed crown
and beseeches the Five Sovereigns to assist him in releasing the souls from purgatory and protecting the
living. The five-pointed crown resembles the crown
of Ti-tsan (地藏, Ksitigarbha), a Boddhisattva who
rescued souls from hell. It also symbolizes the Five
Buddhas of the Five Buddhist Worlds: (1) Aksobhya,
the Immutable and Sovereign of the Eastern World,
(2) Ratnasambhava, the Blissful and Glorious of the
Southern World, (3) Mahavairochana, the Eternal and
Pure of the Central World, (4) Amitabha, the Infinite
Life of the Western World, (5) Sakyamuni, the Incar-
nated One of the Northern World. However, Taoism assimilated these Five Buddhas with the Taoist Five
Sovereigns, namely: (1) The Green Sovereign of the
East, (2) The Red Sovereign of the South, (3) the Yellow Sovereign of the Central Earth, (4) the White
Sovereign of the West, (5) the Black Sovereign of the
North. Chinese Folk Religion has further assimilated
these Five Sovereigns as (1) Heavenly Worthy who Pro-
tects the Soul, (2) Emperor of Longevity who Prolongs
Life, (3) Jade Emperor who Rules the World, (4) Heavenly Emperor who Governs all Spirits, (5) Emperor of
the Purple Heaven who Grants Life.

By wearing the five-pointed crown, the high priest
now is representing at once the Boddhisattva Ti-tsang
and the Five Sovereigns; he is now able to descend
into the Ten Halls of hell to release the imprisoned
souls.

361

Meditation on the pearl. While other priests are
chanting the mantra inviting the Ten Kings of hell,
the high priest prays to the Heavenly Worthy to endow
the yang force on the pearl which is embroidered on
the top of the five-pointed crown, so that he can il-
luminate hell when he is descending there. The Taoists
believe that there are Ten Halls in hell, each Hall
has its king supervising punishments. When a soul of
the deceased descends into hell, he/she has to appear
first in front of the king of the First Hall, who has
both the register of the merits and demerits and the
mirror that illuminates the interior to weigh and
balance the deeds of the deceased. The king of the
First Hall then determines whether the deceased (based
on merits and demerits) is to be released from the hell
or to go through the appropriate tortures punishable
by the other nine kings of the Nine Halls. The geography of hell in the underworld is arranged according
to the magic square or mandala of the Lo-shu, an ancient Chinese book of geomancy.

     When the soul is released from hell, which could
be immediately or after torture, he/she was to be reborn according to merits or karma into six realms of
the universe through a path in the six paths of rebirth, namely: the paths of gods, human beings, immortal spirits, animals, hungry ghosts, and demons.
By concentrating his mind on the Pearl of Illumination,
the high priest envisions himself as the scion of the
Ten Halls of hell, the six paths of rebirth, and the
Eight Taoist Immortals who had overcome death and
obtained eternal life.

Part III. Releasing the Souls
from Torment

     A circular platform shaped in an octagonal form
which has a mandala of hell carved on top is placed
on the altar in front of the high priest. Then, the
high priest chants the mantra "P'o Ti-yu Chou" (破地
獄咒) to break open the gates of hell. The mentra is
chanted nine times in loud strident tones. Afterwards,
he holds the Ju-i (如意) scepter made of jade in his
left hand between the middle finger and the thumb and
pinches in his right hand a few grains of uncooked
rice, circling the Ju-i scepter twice over the mandala
of hell, while placing the grains of rice in one of
the eight directions and the center of the octagonal
box. This process is repeated nine times until all
nine gates of hell have been broken. It is believed

that as the grains of rice are laid in place and a
mantra is chanted, the tortures will be stopped, the
gates opened, and the souls therein released. Finally, holy water is sprinkled over the entire octagonal box, and the rite to set the souls free comes
to an end.

In the process of being released from hell, all
the souls go through a purgation of the magical square
of mandala to atone for their sins. The souls are
also instructed to follow the Taoists in a dance
called the Steps of Yü, because Yü, the emperor of Hsia
dynasty, used the magic square and its ritual dance to
stop floods in ancient China and restore order to nature. The Taoist priests now use their left-hand palms
to perform the secret nine-step mudra to guide souls
through the Nine Halls of hell to come to the tenth
court of judgment, whereby they are permitted to come
forth and attend the P'u Tu festival on earth.

Part IV. Preaching the Sermon of Merit

After offering incense to sanctify the temple, altar, and the new congregation of the hungry ghosts,
the high priest reads a lengthy series of sermons on
merit called Yü-chia Yen-k'ou (瑜伽焰口). The hungry
ghosts are admonished that they, too, can be converted
to become upright spirits by doing meritorious deeds
for the living community.

Part V. Feeding the Hungry Ghosts

After the sermon of merit, a huge basin piled up
with the sweet red buns in a circular pyramid shape,
the symbol of long life, will be placed on the altar.
Upon the pyramid, a left-hand shaped bun, with the
thumb and last finger bent inward and three other fingers standing straight up, is placed. The hand represents the six paths of rebirth in the incarnation of
a soul. Then the priests invoke the god Hui-hai Ch'i-
szu, or "The Merciful Worthy who returns souls to
their bones and raises the dead," to assist these hungry ghosts in their reincarnations. The priests also
chant the mantra of "healing medicine to relieve the
sufferings and cure the bruises and wounds of the tortured." After blessing the food offerings and the
buns, the priests toss the red buns onto the floor
where the hungry ghosts are supposed to be, to feed
them. They also sprinkle the elixir of sweet dew into

a paper cone to the hungry ghosts to quench their
thirst. Each time the buns are tossed out, the
priests chant a mantra and perform a lotus mudra.
Three incantations on the elixir of sweet dew are believed to be changed into the multitude of quenching
liquid like water, rain, and oceans. The community
members also partake of the red buns on the altar, but
they are not supposed to pick up the ones tossed onto
the floor. Besides the food and drink, the community
members also offer clothing, paper-money, and other
necessities for the hungry ghosts. So it is a grand
communal banquet in which all the living and the dead
are participating.

Part VI. Sending Off the Gods
and Ghosts

     Sending off Ta-shih-chih (大勢至). As the P'u Tu
ritual comes to its end, the list of the names of those
who contributed to the ritual is presented to the Heavenly Worthies so that they will be blessed. Then, the
Five Sovereigns of the Five Directions are sent off by
chanting and removal of the five-pointed crown from the
head of the high priest. Finally, the effigy of Ta-
shih-chih is burned, accompanied by paper money and
other offerings that the community members desired to
send to their deceased ancestors. It is believed that
Ta-shih-chih will lead off the souls to their individual destinies afterward. The musicians play a song
of exorcism called Ta K'ai Men, or "Opening the Gates,"
in sending off the gods and ghosts.

     Throwing of incense sticks. While the offerings
are burnt outside, the high priest opens the curtains
and commands all souls to leave the world of the living,
and go on to their own destinations. A prayer of
thanks to all the deities in the three realms of heaven,
earth, and water is chanted, and all the priests stand
up to bid farewell to the deities of each realm by
throwing the incense sticks in front of the altar. Finally, the priests chant the canons of Kung Te (功德)
or "Merit of the Universal Salvation" and the Yüan-Shih
(元始) mantra, or "the Cosmic Origin," begging continual blessings of the primordial breath. The
priests bow three times to the altar of P'u Tu and
then walk back to the altar of the Three Rulers and
prostrate themselves in front of it. Music is once
again played, and the priests all give three low bows
thanking the master, Lao Tzu, for aiding in the services. This concludes the P'u Tu ritual.

The above has presented three of the most distinctive rites of the Chinese religion to demonstrate the efforts of the Chinese to integrate the way of humanity with the ways of Heaven and Earth. Ancestral worship, the longest tradition and practice of Chinese religion, aims to perpetuate the continuity and interrelatedness of the human community. The Monthly Ordinances, the most archaic almanac of the state cult, represents the sacred duties of Chinese administration in harmonizing human community with cosmic movement. The rite for universal salvation, a syncretic rite of Taoism and Buddhism, and the most popular cult of the common folks, illustrates the common concerns for the bereaved souls and a grand celebration of the divine and human; the living and the deceased, and an effort for universal salvation. Thus, they symbolize perfectly the Chinese way of cosmic integration.

Footnotes

1. For the practices of ancestral worship in the Shang dynasty, see Kwang-chih Chang, _Shang Civilization_ (New Haven, CT.: Yale University Press, 1980), pp. 165-188. Kiyoshi Shirakawa, _Chuko-ku Kodai no Bunka_ (The Culture of Ancient China) (Tokyo, 1979), pp. 78-90. Kiyoshi Akatsuka, _Chuko-ku Kodai no Shukyo to Bunka_ (Religion and Culture of Ancient China) (Tokyo, 1977).

2. _Li Chi_ (the _Book of Rites_), trans. James Legge, _Li Khi_ (London: Oxford University Press, 1885) as vols. XXVII and XXVIII of "The Sacred Books of the East."

3. For sociological studies of Chinese ancestral worship, see C. K. Yang, _Religion in Chinese Society_ (Berkeley, CA: University of California Press, 1967). Emily M. Ahern, _The Cult of the Dead in a Chinese Village_ (Stanford, CA: Stanford University Press, 1973). Arthur P. Wolf, ed., _Religion and Ritual in Chinese Society_ (Stanford, CA: Stanford University Press, 1974). William H. Newell, ed., _Ancestors_ (Berlin, Germany: Mouton Publishers, 1976), section 3.

4. _Hsiao Ching_, Chap. VII.

5. Cf. Paul Wheatley, _The Pivot of the Four Quarters_ (Edinburgh: Edinburgh University Press, 1971).

6.   Hsiao Ching, Chap. IX.

7.   Hsiao Ching, Chap. XVI.

8.   The complete text of the Monthly Ordinances (Yueh Ling) is translated in Li Chi.

9.   Derk Bodde made an extensive study of the Han festivals in his Festivals in Classical China (Princeton: Princeton University Press, 1975)

10.   I have consulted extensively Duane Pang's article: "The P'u Tu Ritual: A Celebration of the Chinese Community of Honolulu" in Buddhist and Taoist Studies I, ed. Michael Sas and David W. Chappell (Honolulu, Hawaii: The University Press of Hawaii, 1977), pp. 75-122, passim.

Suggested Readings

J. J. M. de Groot, The Religious System of China (Leiden, Neatherlands: E. J. Brill, 1892-1910), repr. (Taipei: 1964), 6 vols. 1-3: Disposal of the Dead; 4-6: The Soul and Ancestral Worship.

Francis Hsu, Under the Ancestors' Shadow (New York: Columbia University Press, 1938).

Michael Saso, Taoism and the Rite of Cosmic Renewal (Pullman, Washington: Washington State University Press, 1972); David Jordan, Gods, Ghosts and Ancestors (Berkeley: University of California Press, 1972).

CHAPTER 14

THE WAYS OF RELIGIOUS SYNCRETISM

Throughout the history of China, people have had
to cope with the problem of religious pluralism. From
the very beginning of the establishment of the Shang
dynasty, the Shang kings had to imbibe the techniques
of pacifying various tribes and to assimilate various
cultures, customs, and religions into a coherent theocracy in order to give legitimate power and authority
to their regimes. The Chou kings who revolted against
the Shang and established the Chou dynasty had to make
the same efforts when consolidating the Shang culture
and religion to form a new hierarchical feudalism in
order to maintain their sovereignty. This was especially true during the latter part of the Chou dynasty when the central authority of the Chou collapsed
and the orthodox tradition diversified, wherein the
Chinese people became conscious of the great explosion
of religious pluralism. There was no longer a single
dominant religion; instead, there evolved a multiplication of Confucianism, Taoism, Mohism, Ying-Yang and
the Five Elements school, Shamanism, and many forms of
folk religions. Chinese historians called it the
period of the "One Hundred Schools," and similar to
the "One Hundred Flowers" blooming, they were accepted
as more beautiful than simply having one blooming
flower. Thus, religious pluralism has become the way
of life for Chinese people.

As if such diversification was not enough,
shortly after this basic religious development, the
Chinese experienced a virtual invasion of faiths:
Buddhism from India; Manichaeism and Zoroastrianism
from Persia; and Judaism and Christianity from the
Middle East. Most of these foreign religions came in
with the immigration of foreign peoples and traders,
accompanied with their own cultures and customs. From
the beginning of the Han dynasty, China has become the
melting pot and cosmopolitan world of East Asia.
Meanwhile, many neighboring tribes who were hitherto
called barbarians by the Han Chinese were influenced
by Chinese culture and gradually assimilated or ac-
culturated into its mainstream. In turn, they also
brought multifarious ethos of their tribal cultures
and religions into the melting pot of Chinese culture.
Wolfram Eberhard has pointed out many influences of
the local cultures on the central Han culture and the
fact that Chinese culture is basically a composite or

conglomeration of diverse local cultures.[1] Even
though his theory is not unanimously accepted by Sinologists, the pluralistic nature of Chinese culture
cannot be denied.

After the collapse of the Han dynasty, the
Chinese people witnessed many non-Han Chinese dynasties established whereby many foreigners became kings.
The Northern dynasties (421-589), the Mongol (Yüan)
dynasty (1260-1367), and the Manchu (Ch'ing) dynasty
(1644-1911) were typical examples of such domination
by non-Han Chinese kings. However, one interesting
common phenomenon among these foreign regimes was
that they all accepted Han-Chinese culture and adopted
Confucian bureaucracy within their own administrations.
They even made efforts to ameliorate the tensions and
conflicts occurring among the different religions and
even tried to determine a more applicable way to co-
exist together. The problem of religious pluralism
still persists at the present time. The one-party
controlled regimes of both the Republic of China in
Taiwan and the People's Republic of China in the mainland tend to exert their authoritarian control on
the matter of religion, and yet they have to make
many compromises and adaptations in their religious
policies.

Religious pluralism has only recently become an
important issue in the West, especially in America,
but it is one that the Chinese people have endured for
a long time. However, it is obvious that the Chinese
attitude toward varied religions and their method of
handling the problem of pluralism has not been uni-
form. There have been many ugly episodes of hostile
attitudes and harsh persecutions that have occurred
between the different religions. All the evils of
nationalism, racism, discrimination, and provincial-
ism can be easily spotted throughout the history of
China. At the same time, one can also detect en-
lightening moments of religious tolerance, inter-
religious cooperation, and even religious syncretism.
In a sense, almost all Chinese religions in China are,
in one way or another, syncretic religions. But then,
in every nation, there has always been "the choice
and master spirts of the age" (Shakespeare), those
who would champion a universalistic worldwide fraternal community, envisioning a utopia of "All Men are
Brothers." In this chapter and within the confines
of this study, we will delineate the pattern in the
Chinese attitude towards the different religions and

to discern the ways of Chinese religious pluralism.
Research in this area has disclosed at least three
general reactions to "other" religious ideas discernable: exclusiveness, syncretism, and universalism.
Let us examine these three reactions and their consequences.

<u>Exclusiveness and Religious Persecution</u>

<u>Ancient Imperial Persecutions</u>

Throughout the history of China, there have been
many occurrences of religious persecution which have
demonstrated an exclusive attitude toward "other"
religions. From the archaeological diggings of the
Shang royal tombs, we have discovered the remains of
seven to eight hundred human beings: some of whom gave
evidence of having been buried alive, while others
had been beheaded before the burial. In the oracle
inscriptions, there are many indications of human
sacrifices of slaves who were captured from foreign
tribes during the military campaigns of the Shang.
In order to establish a theocratic empire, many innocent human beings were victimized. The first Ch'in
emperor, who was successful in overcoming all other
six rival states and establishing a new empire, issued
an edict to burn the Confucian classics and to execute
the Confucianists in 213 B.C. Then, when the Confucianist gained power in the Han dynasty, they tried
to suppress the rise of many Taoist religious groups
such as T'ai-p'ing Tao and T'ien-shu Tao in A.D. 188,
191, 204, and between 205-211.

<u>Persecutions of Buddhism</u>

The most notorious persecutions were the so-
called "Three Wus and One Tsung": specifically, the
imperial persecutions of Buddhism in 446 A.D. under
Emperor T'ai-wu (ruled 424-452 A.D.), in 574 A.D.
under the Emperor Wu, in 845 A.D. under the Emperor
Wu-tsung, and in 955 A.D. under Emperor Shih-tsung.
Three of them were comparatively limited in the extent and scope of their persecutions, but the one in
845 A.D. under Emperor Wu-tsung was harsh and had a
lasting effect. According to the <u>T'ang-shu</u> [History
of the T'ang dynasty], more than 4,600 large temples
and monasteries and 40,000 smaller ones were de-
molished, and about 260,500 monks and nuns were forced
to return to secular life. Some 150,000 slaves were
taken, and tens of millions of acres of land was confiscated. Fortunately, Buddhism did not die out, but

Manichaeism, Zoroastrianism, and Nestorian Christianity, which were taken to be affiliated with Buddhism, suffered severe blows and ceased to exist. It was undeniably an infamous event in the religious history of China.

However, Wing-tsit Chan pointed out that the persecution had a short duration and was not intended to destroy the religion itself. His reasoning indicated:

> The issues were basically political and economic, for too many able-bodied men had joined the monasteries and thus became unavailable for agricultural production and army or labor conscription, and too much land belonged to the Buddhist church and had thus become tax exempt. In these ways Buddhism not only deserted society but actually presented a threat to national defense and national economy. Significantly, confiscated images of bronze were made into currency, those of iron made into agricultural instruments, and those of gold and silver turned over to the Treasury, while images of wood, clay, or stone were left untouched. The despotic measures are, of course, not to be excused, but the nature of action, however undemocratic, was not antireligious in the real meaning of the term.[2]

Persecution of Christianity

The expulsion of Catholic missionaries and destruction of some three hundred churches ordered by Emperor Shih-Tsung of the Manchu dynasty in 1724, was another obvious case of imperial religious persecution. The Catholic mission began by the Portuguese Jesuit missionaries in 1583, and followed by Spanish missionaries from the orders of Dominicans, Franciscans, and Augustinians. While they were successful in their mission of converting Chinese to Christianity, the rivalry and quarrels occurring between the Portuguese and Spanis trader over trading privileges and profits in China had drawn the missionaries into a lively debate concerning whether or not Chinese Christians should be allowed to observe the ancestral worship. While the Jesuits were more conciliatory and accommodating, allowing Chinese converts to retain their traditional ancestral worship and some Confucian rites, the Dominicans and Franciscans objected strongly to them and

reported the Jesuits' permissiveness to the Pope in
1704. The Pope and the Congregation of Rites took the
side of the Dominicans and Franciscans and issued the
now famous decree which stated: "One name and one only
God for Chinese, T'ien-chu or the Heavenly Lord. . . .
Ritual acts in honor of Confucius had also to stop.
. . . Veneration of ancestors and even of their tablets
were prohibited by the decree." The papal delegate was
sent to Peking, but his behavior was calculated to offend the Chinese emperor and to embitter the quarrel,
rather than effect conciliation. Thus, in 1706, Emperor Kang-hsi issued an edict expelling all missionaries from China who refused to abide with the rule
that allowed Chinese Christians to observe the Rites.
In the end, the Jesuit missionaries chose to follow
the Papal decree, and they were expelled as well in
1773, which ended the second phase of colorful Christian missions in China. Whether or not Chinese ancestral worship is an idol worship is very delicate
and is still an unsolved issue among Christians. However, some modern Chinese Catholics have restored the
ancestral worship in their families, but the Protestants generally prohibit it. Although on the surface
this religious persecution was caused by the issue of
the Rites, the main cause was political. The arrogance of the Roman papacy and the "saving face" of the
Chinese emperor, along with their mutual exclusiveness,
brought about an unfortunate event in the history of
China. The scandalous rivalry and quarrels between
the Portuguese and Spaniard missionaries, which destroyed the second phase of Christian missions in
China, had a lasting effect on later Christian missions and is, indeed, an important lesson to learn.

<u>Persecution of Religious Societies</u>

     From the beginning of the eighteenth century,
there have appeared many religious groups such as the
White Lotus Society, the Tsai-li Society, the Eight
Trigram Society, the Triad Society, the Elders Society,
etc. Many of these societies were organized by leaders
who promoted a syncretism of Buddhism, Taoism, and to
a certain extent, Confucianism and Christianity. However, their popularity among the common populace
caused great alarm and anxiety to government officials,
and in the end brought about imperial persecutions.
According to J. J. M. De Groot, such religious persecutions were caused by the exclusiveness of the Confucian bureaucrats, who occupied the official positions in the Manchu dynasty. In his book, <u>Sectarian-
ism and Religious Persecution in China</u>, he quoted

many decree statements issued by the Imperial Office
concerning the heresy and immorality of these religious societies and the orders and measurements of the
punishment upon them. Following are some of these decrees:

Emperor Shih-Tsung issued an imperial order to
the Provincial Governor of Chiang Hsi on 17 August
1724, stating:

> We considered that the weeding out of
> the tares is the means of giving rest to the
> loyal, and the expulsion of heresy is the
> way to promote orthodoxy; that from old the
> rulers of the empire brought men's minds to
> peace and concord, regulated manners and
> customs and rendered them uniform, and that
> not one has ever neglected to make the re-
> pression of sedition the first and chief ob-
> ject of his care.
> Now it has come to my knowledge that
> there are many heretical sects in Chiang Hsi,
> which confer names and titles on their
> adepts, misled the people, and meet at night.
> Because their numbers are so numerous and
> their existence is so seldom revealed, they
> must of necessity increase and spread
> rapidly, unless they are exterminated root
> and branch. If the Prefects do not perse-
> cute them, these officers themselves feed
> the spirit of resistance which possesses
> these sects; therefore the purifying of the
> manners and customs resolves itself in this,
> that the Viceroy shall instruct all his sub-
> ordinate officers to make secret and zealous
> investigations concerning the sects and
> punish the leaders. Such "conversion to
> orthodoxy by the expulsion of heresy" I will
> requit with favours, initiative taken in
> such matters shall be rewarded; slow and in-
> different officials I will severely punish.
> But the persecution must be carried out with-
> out alarm or noise, so as not to provoke
> panics and excitement among the people; only
> the leaders must be severely punished, and
> the misguided followers shall not be searched
> out too thoroughly.[3]

In 1727, the emperor issued another decree to all
governors of all provinces to enforce the persecution

of the leaders of religious societies. Then, in 1748,
there were rebellions led by the White Lotus Society
followed by many insurrections of other religious
societies. The Imperial Office became more alert and
oppressive, engaging in larger scale operations of
persecution. In 1880, Emperor Jen-tsung issued the
following decree.

> Reverently we have found in the Authen-
> tic Register of Decrees of the sixth year of
> Chien Lung period, that then an Imperial
> edict was received, to the effect that, for
> the ruling of regions where as yet no re-
> bellion against the government has arisen,
> and for the protection of a realm where the
> government is not yet in danger, it is ne-
> cessary to make the manners and customs and
> the human mind the first and chief objects
> of care.
> For where the human mind is orthodox,
> there the manners and customs are pure, and
> as a consequence the Imperial Government
> possesses integrity and wisdom, in conse-
> quence of which a long existence is ensured
> to the dynasty. This sage edict, so glori-
> ous and brilliant, truly is a political
> standard rule for myriads of generations.
> . . .
> Now the improving and perfecting of
> people's manners and customs surely de-
> mand that before all things they are to be
> prevented from being misled by heresies and
> thus made to move together in the paths of
> orthodoxy; only when this has been done can
> their improvement by doctrine take effect.
> The doctrine of Confucius is the most
> worthy, the most august for ten thousand
> generations. Beside this, other exists,
> like those coming forth from Buddhism and
> Taoism, which, though not orthodox, have
> since the Han and T'ang dynasties up to our
> time not completely scoured away with sand.
> But by their special dress and ceremonial
> attire, and because they live under abbots,
> these votaries are a separate class of
> people, so that if there are among them
> disturbers of the peace or enemies of the
> government, these can forthwith and easily
> be prosecuted or found out. But as to the
> members of the so-called White Lotus

religion of these later ages, they do not
distingush themselves from ordinary people
by separate dwellings, nor by a particular
dress, and so there is no means to sift from
each other the local heterogeneous elements
among these religionists and non-religion-
ists living in the same house.

Hence, when mandarins [officials] have
to do with a heretical religion, they as a
rule make their searches and arrests quite
at random; besides over and again they avail
themselves of such occasions to extort money,
without asking whether they have to do with
members of the religion or with non-members
--it is only bribes they seek. And, what is
worst of all--while ignorant country people
who cannot even read a single letter are
thus arbitrarily and at random arrested on
the charge of heretical rebellion, the real
sectaries and makers of proselytes are allowed to go free, and remained untried.[4]

One can see from the decree that it was a religious oppression by Confucian orthodoxy on the heterodoxy of religious societies in the name of "law and
order." Meantime, it acknowledged the difficulty of
such religious oppression and the corruption within
the administration that claimed to be keepers of law
and order. The intrinsic nature of religious societies was not fully investigated and understood by the
authorities, but branded right away as "heretic and
immoral." In return, the religious societies had to
fight back by engaging in insurrections and rebellions.
The desire and need of religion among the common people cannot be subjugated and nagated by unsympathetic
authorities. Unfortunately, orthodoxy's oppression
of heterodoxy and the scandal of religious exclusiveness continue to darken the history of China even to
modern times.

Communist Oppression

Since the Chinese defeat in the Opium War (1840-
1842), Chinese young intellectuals have blamed the
cause of such humiliation to the backwardness of
traditional culture and religions, and championed for
the cause of modernization by accepting the Western
sciences, industries, and democracy. In the process,
Western secularism, humanism, atheism, and materialism
were also absorbed by Chinese intellectuals, and they

have voiced strong anti-religious slogans, working toward the eradication of religion from Chinese society.
With the success of establishing the Republic in 1912,
nationalism and ethnocentric ethos prevailed and attacks on foreign religions began. With the Communist
takeover in 1949, the widescale policy of religious
persecution was formulated and put into practice.

The regimes of both the Republic of China and
People's Republic of China are dominated by one party
and do not tolerate the existence of competing parties,
and thereby both of them exert strong exclusive and
even dictatorial policies against other religions and
ideologies. The Kuomingtang party of the Republic of
China follows the pattern of Confucian bureaucracy and
orthodoxy, and by promoting the so-called New Life
Movement tried to eradicate the traditional faiths and
to have full control of religious organizations. The
Communist party of the People's Republic has advocated
Marxist-Leninist materialism and atheism and has been
more radical in its religious oppressions.

In the Constitution of the Chinese Soviet Republic issued in 1931, it stated that while the Soviet
Government would guarantee religious freedom to the
workers, peasants, and toiling population, it would
also advocate the right to engage in anti-religious
propaganda and would not allow those religious institutions of the imperialists that do not comply with
Soviet law to exist.[5] In other words, religious freedom includes the freedom to attack religion, and all
religions are only allowed to exist by abiding within
the Soviet law. C. K. Yang is right in interpreting
that Communism has become a "New Faith" in China and,
therefore, cannot tolerate the existence of other
faiths. Donald E. MacInnis has made a comprehensive
survey of the religious policy statements and practices of the Communist regime and pointed out its
full-scale programs for religious persecution and reform. Richard C. Bush Jr. has reported in great detail the Communist oppressions of various religious
groups in China. Following are some such examples.[6]

First, the folk religion and various religious
societies have suffered the harshest persecution, regarded as both superstitious and conspiratorial, they
are easier to subjugate due to their lack of international connections and external supports. Many of
the leaders of societies and their followers were ex-
ecuted and imprisoned and their religious properties

confiscated. However, the secret society of I Kuan
Tao (The Way of Pervading Oneness) still survivies
today, even under continuous harsh treatment by the
government.

Second, in the late 1940s, all Christian missionaries were expelled from China, being accused of working as agents of Western imperialism and capitalism,
and the foreign contacts with the native Christian
churches were completely cut off by 1951. The church
schools and hospitals run by foreign mission boards
were confiscated, and seminaries, orphanages, and
publishing houses were consolidated. Even though
Chinese Christians were allowed to survive, they had
to organize patriotic associations to support government policy and to renounce past evils of foreign missions and the scandals of Christianity. Priests and
ministers were forced to be self-supportive, and the
church activities were severely restricted. Christian
intellectuals were re-educated to make compromises of
Christian doctrines with the Communist ideology. Some
Protestant conservatives who resisted were imprisoned
and tortured. Very often, they were accused of being
either political dissenters or unrepentant "running
dogs" for Western imperialism, and not properly counted
as cases of religious oppression.

Third, Buddhist temples and monasteries were confiscated and converted to become either military bar-
racks or local schools, and monks and nuns were dispersed from their monasteries and forced to join com-
munes to engage in labor. The Chinese Buddhist Association was organized to support patriotic causes and
"reform" traditional Buddhism. Religious persecution
of Tibetan Buddhists and the expulsion of Dalai Lama
in 1951 from Tibet are rather well-known. However, in
order to maintain better diplomatic relationships with
Japan and Southeast Asian Buddhist countries, such as
Thailand, Cambodia, Burma, Buddhist leaders are utilized by the government as goodwill delegates to attend
the international Buddhist conferences and, in return,
are expected to initiate some Buddhist conferences in
China, inviting foreign Buddhist leaders to attend.
Again, Buddhists are to be re-educated and to make
Buddhist teachings compromising with the Communist
ideology.

Fourth, both Confucianism and Taoism, two major
native religious traditions of China, have not es-
caped the Communist subjugation and oppressions.

Confucius was harshly criticized as the defender of
monarchical feudalism and the Confucian bureaucrats,
the oppressors of the peasants and workers, resultantly, the Confucian temples were consolidated and
Confucian studies banned. Fung Yu-lan, an eminent
Confucian scholar, who remained in mainland China, was
under harsh criticism and had to make an open confes-
sion of the errors in his Neo-Confucianism. This
anti-Confucian ethos culminated in the so-called Cultural Revolution conducted by the "Gang of Four" and
the Red Guards in 1966. The birthplace of Confucius
at Chü-fu was raided, the portraits of Confucius were
mocked in public parades, many universities were dis-
rupted, and many professors and intellectuals were
forced to engage in farming and manual labor.

The suffering of Taoism under Communist persecution was even more severe.   Taoism was simply
equated with superstition, the Taoist temples damaged, and the Taoist priests were forced to do manual
labor and re-learn Marxism and Leninism. Since the
Taoists did not have international contacts, the
government did not find any value in utilizing Taoists to engage in international diplomacy, therefore,
the Taoist organization and activities were severely
curtailed.

Fifth, Islam fared better than other religious
groups under the Communist regime, mainly because of
the new government's strong support from the Moslem
ethnic communities and their strong will to fight
back against religious oppression. Remembering the
past failures in subjugating the Moslem ethnic communities by past regimes, the Communist authorities
did more careful planning and slow enforcement,
trying to assimilate Islam with the Communist ideology
rather than to eradicate it. Self-autonomy of Moslem communities was allowed, under condition that they
would be led by Communist trained officials and support the policy of the central Communist authority.
The re-education program of Moslems to study Chinese
language, culture, and Communist ideology was encouraged. The first translation of the Qu'ran was
officially published in 1952 and the Chinese Islamic
Association was organized in Peking in 1953. Many
goodwill missions of Chinese Moslems were sponsored
by the government to the Moslem nations in the Middle
East and Indonesia to enhance better diplomatic relations. The special treatment afforded to Chinese
Moslems by the Communist regime was by no means to

encourage the propagation of Islam, but rather to
enforce its policy of assimilation with the Communist
ideology.

In spite of its vigorous persecution of the traditional religions, the Communist regime could not
eradicate all of them. Instead, it had to revise its
practices from time to time and from one religion to
the other. After the death of Mao Tse-tung and the
reopening of diplomatic relations with the West, religious persecutions have subsided, and rigid restric-
tions on religious activities have become more relaxed. However, the Communist regime is still suspicious and not ready to open its door for the restoration of Christian foreign missions. The current Communist administration may take more pragmatic policy
than the past radical one, but its anti-religious
policy may not change as quickly as might be desired.

The above cases are examples of religious exclusiveness and religious persecutions that happened
in the history of China, and they have made dark marks
on the pages of Chinese religious history. Like many
ugly incidents of religious persecutions and violations of human rights in many other countries, China
has had her share of shame and blame and is in great
need to be enlightened and reformed. While there have
been many religious persecutions occurring throughout
Chinese history, there has also occurred an interesting religious phenomenon called "syncretism" or "syncretic religion." The following will give examples,
as well as describe, this phenomenon.

Syncretism or Syncretic Religion

Many scholars of Chinese religion have already
called attention to this syncretic nature of Chinese
religion and pointed out that it is one of the distinctive characteristics of Chinese religion.
W. E. Soothill described the religious style of the
Chinese as follows:

> While a few of the laity devote themselves,
> some solely to Buddhism, some solely to
> Taoism, the great mass of the people have
> no prejudices and make no embarrassing dis-
> tinctions; they belong to none of the three
> religions, or, more correctly, they belong
> to all three. In other words, they are
> eclectic, and use whichever from best

responds to the requirement of the occasion
for which they use religion.[7]

Wing-tsit Chan wrote in more detail about what he
preferred to call "religious pluralism" rather than
syncretism.

> . . . There has been in Chinese tradi-
> tion a strong sense of pluralism which per-
> sists even in a strongly monolithic situa-
> tion. And this pluralistic spirit has been
> the most prominent and most enduring in the
> sphere of religion. . . .
> In the realm of religion, many of them
> follow the three religions at the same time,
> visiting Buddhist or Taoist temples as the
> need arises and also perform Confucian rites
> before their ancestors. Temples dedicated
> to the Three Sages are found in all parts of
> China, and some of them even include repre-
> sentations of Islam, Christianity, and
> Judaism. In funeral and other religious
> ceremonies and in community festivals, Budd-
> hist and Taoist priests and laymen of vari-
> ous beliefs perform the rites together.
> Religious doctrines, symbols, ceremonies,
> and even deities have been so intermingled
> that scholars cannot tell if they are of
> Confucian, Buddhist, or Taoist origin. It
> is often said that the average Chinese is
> one who wears a Confucian crown, so to speak,
> a Taoist robe, and Buddhist sandals.[8]

From the viewpoint of religious orthodoxy and exclusiveness, the term "syncretism" or "syncretic religion" may appear to be perfidious, random, corrupting,
and superificial. But Judith A. Berling has defended
the syncretism against such accusations. Because
Chinese religions, in general, are not credal and exclusive, and membership in more than one religion is
possible, it is inappropriate to condemn syncretism
as betrayal and perfidious. Syncretism is different
from "Ecclecticism" which is "idio-syncratic or whim-
iscal" and a random mixture of different beliefs and
practices, for it has its own principle and structure
of reconciling various religious elements from more
than one religion. Syncretism has been often criticized as being "confused, deluded, and simpleminded"
and too eager to secure "unity at the expense of
truth." But there is a misunderstanding of "truth" as

a fixed entity in an unchangeable historical form ignoring the fact of dynamic change in religious history. Syncretism is a process of religious interaction and change. Finally, syncretism is not just a mere slogan of unity of all faiths and utopian dream of peaceful coexistence of world religions, but a concrete effort and serious enterprise at the risk of many religious persecutions, working out a harmonious view of religion to meet the spiritual need and desire of the time. In conclusion, Berling emphasized that the term syncretism should be understood as a heuristic construct of the history of religion to describe a particular religious phenomenon, and she offered the following definition: "Syncretism may be tentatively defined as the borrowing of affirmation, or integration of concepts, symbols, or practices of one religious tradition into another by process of selection and reconcilation."[9]

Of course, there have been many different forms of syncretism that appeared in the history of China, and it is important to look into each case of syncretism carefully and distinguish it from others. But at the same time, by comparison, we can discern certain patterns and structures that existed in all syncretic religions. Let us note its pattern and structure.

Conglomeration of Religious Elements

One religion adapts some religious elements from other religions. We can see that almost all Chinese religions have one way or another borrowed or adapted certain religious concepts, practices, and structures from other religions.

Tung Chung-shu, an ideologue of the Han Confucian bureaucracy and the state cult of Confucianism, borrowed a great deal of the Yin-Yang and Five Elements cosmology developed by Tso Yen to give the Confucian social ethics a metaphysical foundation and to consolidate an interpretative philosophy of history for the Confucian Bureaucracy to control dynastic changes and imperial office.[10]

The Taoist religious organization of T'ai-p'ing Tao and T'ien-shu Tao borrowed quite extensively from the newly introduced Buddhism of its confessional rites, communal disciplines and rules, and charity works and social services. They were, perhaps, the first most successful religious organizations developed in ancient China. In the end, they also imitated the Buddhist Tripitaka in canonizing their Taoist Bible called the Tao Tsang or Taoist Pitaka.[11]

The Buddhists learned very quickly in their initial phase of introducing Buddhism into China that, if it was to be accepted, they would have to assimilate and accommodate some of the religious elements that the Chinese people highly valued. They had practiced the so-called Ke-yi or "Matching ideas" with the Taoist terms. For example, tathata (thusness or ultimate reality) was equated with the Taoist term pen-wu (本無) or the original nonbeing, or pure being. The Buddhists also realized that they had to accommodate the tradition of ancestral worship and the Confucian social ethic based on the virtue of filial piety.[12]

Although the rise of Neo-Confucianism signaled the great revival of orthodox Confucianism in the Sung dynasty (960-1279), Neo-Confucianism absorbed many elements from both Taoism and Buddhism. The Buddhist meditation (samadhi) and enlightenment (buddhi) and wisdom (prajna) were synthesized with the concepts of ting, ming, and chih of Neo-Confucianism. The Taoist cosmology developed in the Ts'ang-t'ung-ch'i (參同契) and the Taoist meditation and disciplines greatly influenced the formation of Neo-Confucian metaphysics and the method of spiritual cultivation.[13]

The above examples show that all three major religions in China have borrowed from one another some religious elements to innovate a new development. Thus, syncretistic practice has strengthened and enriched one's own religion rather than weakened it. By accommodating and assimilating to the native religion, a foreign religion can itself assimilate to become an integral tradition. By tolerating a foreign religion and absorbing it, a native religion can enrich itself and innovate a new development. So far, Chinese history of religious syncretism has affirmed that the mutual borrowing and accommodation between two different religions has always been constructive and beneficial to both entities and to the advancement of religiosity.

All Religions Come From One Source

In mutual borrowing and accommodation, Chinese

people already acknowledged that each religion had
something good and valuable in it. The acknowledgment of mutual goodness in all religions eventually
led to the affirmation that all religions are harmonious in having the same origin and goal. The Unity of
all religions has thus become one of the unwritten
decrees to Chinese believers.

This new consciousness of the harmony in religions has appeared since the beginning of the Han dynasty (206 B.C.-220 A.D.). With the establishment of
Confucian bureaucracy, the Confucian officials and
intellectuals began to realize a necessity to develop
a new metaphysics they called "the Way of Heaven" to
encompass all philosophical and religious ideas and
to include all accounts of human experience and sociopolitical order. Berling described "the Way of Heav-
en" as follows:

>This belief in the unity of the Way of
>Heaven established a foundation for syncre-
>tic thought; unless religious ideas could be
>shown to be outright fantasies, they had
>some claim on truth, even if a distorted or
>partial truth. Distortion or partiality
>could be rectified; the believers were sel-
>dom called upon to choose one god or one
>truth over all others. The Way of Heaven
>included all truths of man. . . .
>Perfect moral and cosmic order had to
>embrace all reality. The broad pattern was
>no problem; as long as the Han empire re-
>mained stable, the general correspondence
>of the realms of heaven, earth and man
>seemed an obvious truism. . . .
>Han thinkers were not fussbudgets who
>created the correspondences to tidy up the
>universe and put everything in its proper
>little nook. In their eyes understanding
>the correspondences clarified the cosmic
>principles behind all processes and phenom-
>ena, and thus allowed humans to understand
>and control them. Through them the secrets
>of the universe could be controlled at the
>source. The power made available through
>understanding the cosmos was illustrated in
>the mystique of the emperor, who was the
>pivot of the triad of heaven, earth, and
>man, and thus responsible for upholding the
>entire cosmic order. . . .

The system of correspondences developed
by Han thinkers both reflected their exhil-
eration with the power of human culture and
gave them a means to solidify and extend
that power. It also gave them a means for
reconciling diverse ideas within the all-
embracing Way, which was used to advantage
by later syncretists.[14]

Wing-tsit Chan has also analyzed this Chinese
view of the harmony of religions and pointed out quite
succintly six implications:[15]

1. Each religion is understood as a branch of the ed-
    ucational system, and all founders and sages are
    but "teachers" of a particular school. Chinese
    people called religion "Chiao," or "Teaching or
    Education," and the founders of religion as "Chaio
    Tsu" (教祖) or Teaching Master. Chinese intellec-
    tuals respect Confucius and Lao Tsu as great
    teachers, but do not claim them as divine beings
    nor their teachings infallible and absolute.

2. All religions are equal. As the Taoist Ku Huan
    (392-453?) put it, "Taoism and Buddhism are equal
    in illuminating and transforming people." Differ-
    ent religions developed under a variety of condi-
    tions to meet basic needs of the times, but they
    are all "convenient means" to the same end. Sun
    Ch'o (265-420) also stated, "Confucius sought
    order and peace in society, and the Buddha sought
    enlightenment in the fundamental nature of exis-
    tence, but their goals are the same."[16]

3. All religions complement one another. While the
    distinctiveness of each religion is fully acknowl-
    edged, the uniqueness and special contribution
    claimed by each religion are understood to be
    complementary to one another. "Confucianism has
    been chiefly concerned with the social order,
    Taoism with the individual, particularly his peace
    of mind and tranquility of spirit, and Buddhism
    with previous and future lives."[17] The strength
    of Confucianism is in its sociopolitical ethics;
    Buddhism has its special methods of meditation and
    discipline; the Yin-Yang school excels in cosmol-
    ogy and metaphysics, and Taoism advances the pre-
    servation and immortality of life.

4. Mutual identification among all religions. There

is always something common and similar among different religions, and it can be mutually identified
and assimiliated. Su Ch'o said, "The enlightenment
that transforms a person into a Buddha is none
other than the awakening which Mencius said the
sage achieves for himself and helps others to
achieve."[18] The Taoist search for immortality of
life is similar to the Buddhist desire of freedom
from re-birth.

5. All religions come from one source. Emperor Wu
   (r. 502-549) said, "Traced to the source, the three
   religions are no different." K'an Tse (third century) claimed that "All these religions have their
   source in Heaven which they obey."[19] The Taoist
   concept of Wu (無) or Nothingness was identified
   with the Buddhist idea of Sunyata or the Emptiness.
   This understanding of mutual identification has developed further into the Hua-yen Buddhist logic of
   mutual penetration and non-obstruction, which shall
   be elaborated upon later.

6. All religions aim at the realization of human nature (hsing). From quite early days, Chinese intellectuals have been greatly concerned with the
   issue of human nature and the method of reaching
   its fulfillment. In chapters 8, 9, 10, and 12,
   there has already been an elaboration of this subject. Confucianists, Mencius, and Hsün Tsu and
   Tung Chung-shu all paid attention to the issue of
   good and evil in human nature. Both Lao Tzu and
   Chuang Tzu emphasized that the ultimate goal is to
   preserve the essence and purity of human nature.
   The Taoist religion worked out various methods to
   realize the Three Primordial Principles--Essence,
   Vital Force, and Spirit--within human nature. Zen
   master Hui-neng (638-713) interpreted the Buddhist
   enlightenment experience as the realization of one's
   own nature rather than taking refuge in an historical Buddha. Neo-Confucianist Ch'eng Hao (1032-
   1085) stressed that the academic and scientific
   research and investigation of all things should not
   end only in acquiring knowledge of external phenomena, but in realizing and integrating one's own
   nature and destiny. Fung Yu-lan, one of the most
   eminent Neo-Confucianists, expressed this fundamental humanistic ethos most succintly.

       People in the moral sphere fulfill human
       relations and human duties. In doing so,

they investigate human principles to the
utmost and fulfill human nature. People in
the transcendental sphere serve Heaven and
assist in the natural transformation of
things. In doing so, they investigate the
principle of the universe and fulfill the
nature of the universe. . . . To penetrate
the mysteries and know the transformation
of the universe is to complete the work of
the universe . . . and this is to serve
Heaven.[20]

The Way of Mutual Penetration

The Unity of all religions is a high ideal, but
sometimes it is difficult to realize in this world of
divisiveness. Each religion and each school within
a religion tends to claim its superiority and abso-
luteness. Dogmatism and sectarianism have been the
double disease of religion in the history of mankind.
Theological exclusiveness and mutual antagonism among
religions are still the major scandals of our day.
Religious wars or the holy wars have been the worst
warfares that human beings have ever had, and yet they
are with us today. How to put the high ideal of harmony of religion into practice among different religions has become a most urgent task, and Chinese
seemed to find a way to cope with it, even though they
couldn't completely reach the ultimate ideal. We are
referring to the way developed by the school of Hua-
yen Buddhism during the T'ang dynasty (618-907).

The T'ang dynasty has been regarded as the cosmopolitan age in Chinese history, for the great influx of the Central Asian and Middle Eastern cultures
took place, and the Koreans and Japanese came to learn
Chinese culture. China became the melting pot of
East Asia. In order to meet with the needs of the
cosmopolitanic age, the T'ang emperors not only
adopted the traditional Confucian bureaucracy and
Taoist religion but also Buddhist universalism to
accommodate their imperial policy. Interesting
enough, it was during the reign of Empress Wu Tse-
t'ien (684-704), the first and only female emperor in
China, that Hua-yen Buddhism, which had developed a
universalistic view called the Dharmadatu, was adopted
to promote the spirit of cosmopolitanism, not only in
politics but also in religion.

The Hua-yen Buddhists held that there are four

views of the universe (Dharmadhatu) possible:

(1) the phenomenal view, which sees the universe as
primarily phenomenal; (2) the view of principle, which
only conceives the principle as underlying and sus-
taining all phenomena; (3) the view of interaction and
interdependence between the phenomena and noumenon,
which comprehends that an interrelationship existed
between phenomena and noumenon; (4) the view of mutual
penetration and identification within the phenomena,
which intuits the organic relationships between phenomenon and phenomenon among all phenomena.

In order to demonstrate the subtle truth of the
Dharmadhatu, the Buddhist abbot Fa-tsang (643-712)
asked the Empress Wu to order the construction of a
ten-mirror hall which had all eight walls, ceiling,
and floor covered with reflecting mirrors. Then, as
he placed a Buddha statue in the center of the hall
and lighted a torch, he invited the empress to enter
the hall to see the instantaneous and simultaneous
interpenetration of the Buddha images in all ten-
sided mirrors. Different sides of Buddha image and
the viewers are reflected mutually without destroying
one another. The Empress Wu realized instantly the
truth of "All in One" and "One in All."

Huan-yen Buddhism utilized its logic of mutual
interpenetration and non-obstruction to successfully
reconcile the differences within the different schools
of Buddhism, and, thus, it was also adopted by the
T'ang dynasty to promote its cosmopolitanism. It
could be used for dealing with the problem of religious
pluralism as well. For it could give a better interpretation of the organic relation within all different
religions. While it upholds the principle or the
noumenal ideals of all religions, it also maintains
the organic inter-relationships among the religions
without destroying one another. While the integrity
of each religion is sustained, its organic relations
to the totality of religion is also stressed. The
similarity and differences among the religions are
thus dialectically synthesized and organically integrated.

A Higher Synthesis of All Religions

Following the process of mutual borrowing, acknowledgment of harmony in religious, and the development of an organic view of the totality of religions,

we see the rise of a higher synthesis of all religions.
Since each religion must have its good elements, the
best religion may be the religion that has assembled
all the good elements from all existing religions.
During the Sung dynasty (960-1279), various religious
societies were organized by some charismatic leaders
who incorporated various religious elements from Confucianism, Buddhism, Taoism, Yin-Yang cosmology, and
even Manichaeism to form their own religious system.
The White Lotus Society, the White Cloud Society, the
Tsai-li (Principle Abiding) Society are good examples
of such syncretism. Unfortunately, these syncretic
religious societies had suffered religious persecutions by the exclusive and orthodox authorities under
the Yüan, Ming, and Ch'ing dynasties. Because of
their strength and popularity, the central authorities had often felt great threats from them and tried
to subdue or even eradicate them. But as we have already seen, the governments were not very successful,
and these religious societies continued to spread and
grow.

At the beginning of the Twentieth Century, we
evidenced the rise of new religious societies, which
extended their syncretism not only to include the
three major traditional religions but also Christianity, Islam, and Judaism. The Society of World Religions, founded in 1915; the International Society of
Holy Religions and the Hsi-hsin (Purification of the
Heart) Society in 1917; the Tao Yuan (the Academy of
Tao) in 1921; the T'ung-Shan (Fellowship of Goodness)
Society in 1918; and the Wu-shan (Awakening for Righteousness) Society in 1915 are the contemporary religious societies in China. They have equally venerated
the founders of the world's major religions: Confucius,
Lao Tzu, the Buddha, Abraham, Jesus and Mohammed, and
they have read the major scriptures of world religions
and selected from them important texts they believe to
represent the essence of each religion to compose their
own Bible. The morality of Confucianism, the metaphysics of Taoism, the mercy of the Buddha, the method
of Yoga, the philanthropy of Christianity, the law of
Judaism, and the devotion of Islam, are the major doctrines they have adopted from world religions. In
their temples, they built several altars or halls to
venerate the major sages of world religions, but above
them, they worship a Godhead they call T'ai-shang Lao-
chün (the Supreme Primordial and Eternal Lord) who
they believed to be the transcendental ultimate reality of the universe. They are open and tolerant to

all other religions and eager to propagate their teachings and promote a fraternal world fellowship. Their claim is that all religions have evolved from the same source and that all religious communities are moving toward becoming one family. They abhor religious warfares and seek a world peace supported by world religious communities. However, they show signs of being too idealistic and appear to be rather arrogant in that they tend to behave in a superior manner toward those who still maintain the traditional religious organizations. One might even say that their fusion of the existing mass varieties of religion has created an elite religion; one that gives every indication of becoming just another isolated religion. It may be that they have advanced too fast, and that the other religions have not been able to follow them as quickly as they would have liked. Especially under the attacks of political nationalism and religious orthodoxy, as well as the pressure of current divisiveness between two Chinas. In this context, the new sects have become rather inactive or are dying out altogether.

The above has presented four patterns of religious syncretism developed in China. However, these four patterns may overlap one another, and, in fact, each syncretism or syncretic religion should be studied according to its own merit. Moreover, syncretism could be understood as either a new unification or a new diversification from the old traditions. Nonetheless, it is undeniable that religious syncretism is a pervading religious phenomenon in China.

The Voices of Universalism

Throughout the history of Chinese religions, we notice the recurrent calls for a cosmopolitan understanding of the world community and a universalistic approach to solve the problem of cultural divisiveness and religious pluralism. These calls came from the charismatic leaders and visionary prophets of all different religious traditions, and yet they seem to have one common voice and the same utopian vision of humankind. Let us hear these calls as they pertain directly to their age and times.

The Great Tao of Confucius

Chapter 7 of the <u>Book of Rites</u> quoted a statement made by Confucius after he was discussing with his disciple Yen Ten the sad state of the fallen Chou central authority:

388

I have never seen the realization of
the Great Tao and the eminent sage rulers of
the Three dynasties, but I have always envisioned them.

When the Great Tao is realized, the
spirit of openness and fareness will prevail
all under the sky. The men of talents, virtue, and ability shall be chosen equally,
and sincerity and harmony shall be cultivated.
Therefore, men did not only love their parents and not treat their children as only
children. A sufficient provision shall be
secured for the aged till their death, and
competent employment for the able-bodied,
and adequate means of upbringing for the
young. Kindness and compassion shall be
shown to widows, orphans, childless people,
and those who are disabled by disease, so
that they will have the wherewithal for support. Men will have their proper works and
women will have their homes. They shall hate
to see the wealth of natural resources underdeveloped, but also dislike to see the
hoarding of wealth for their own pleasures.
They shall regret of not exerting themselves
[of their given talents] but also hate to
exert themselves only for their own benefits. Thus, the selfish schemes shall be
repressed and found no development. Robbers, filchers, and rebellious traitors
shall not appear, and hence the out doors
shall be left open. This shall be the period
of what I called the Great Unity (ta t'ung
大同).[21]

The Confucian thought of the Great Tao or Great
Unity has become a model of Chinese utopian aspiration
and has made great impact on the later development of
universalism. We shall soon see that it has reappeared
and expanded in the universalism of K'ang Yu-wei in
modern times.

<u>All Embracing Love of Mo Tzu</u>

Even though Mo Tzu criticized many defects of
Confucianism, he advocated the similar universalistic
view of the Great Tao and promoted a worldwide fraternal community based on "All Embracing Love" (chien ai
兼愛). He also organized a cultic community to defend
the oppressed and slaves, and championed for active

pacifism. In chapter 15 of his work <u>Mo Tzu</u>, he described the main cause of world miseries and proposed
a solution with the principle of "All Embracing Love."

   The object of humanity is to promote the
benefits for the world and remove harm from
the world. This should be the goal of human
devotion. But what are the benefits and the
harms of the world?
   Take the present situations of mutual
attacks among the states, mutual usurpation
among the families, mutual injuries among
the individuals, or the lack of altruism and
loyalty between the rulers and ministers, of
parental affection and filial piety between
parents and children, and of harmony and
peace among brothers and sisters. These are
the harms in the world. In examination of
these harms, what is the cause for such
harms? . . .
   They arise out from the lack of "all
embracing love." At present, the feudal
lords know only to love their own states and
not those of others. Therefore, they do not
hesitate to mobilize their states to attack
others. The heads of families know only to
love their own families and not those of
others. Therefore, they do not hesitate to
mobilize their families to usurp others.
And individuals do not love one another, they
will injure each other. When the rulers and
ministers do not love each other, they will
not be kind and faithful. When the parents
and children do not love each other, they
will not be affectionate and filial. When
brothers and sisters do not love one another, they will not be harmonious and peaceful. When nobody in the world loves any
other, the strong will surely oppress the
weak, the many will exploit the few, and the
rich will insult the poor. The noble will
despise the humble, and the cunning will deceive the ignorant. Because of the lack of
love, all the calamities, usurpations, hos-
tilities and animosity have become rampant.
. . .
   It should be replaced by all embracing
love and mutual benevolence. What is the
way of all embracing   love and mutual

390

benevolence?

It is to regard other people's countries as one's own. Regard other people's families as one's own. Regard other people's person as one's own. Consequently, when the feudal lords love one another, there will be no warfare in the fields. When the heads of families love one another, there will be no family feuds. When the individuals love one another, there will be no mutual injuries. When the rulers and ministers love one another, there will be altruism and faithfulness. When parents and children love one another, there will be affection and filiality. When brothers and sisters love one another, there will be peace and harmony. When all the people in the world love one another, the strong will not oppress the poor, the many will not exploit the few, the rich will not insult the poor, the noble will not despise the humble, and the cunning will not deceive the ignorant. Because of all embrasive love, all the calamities, usurpations, hostility, and animosity in the world shall be ceased. . . .

But now the gentlemen of the world would say: Yes, it will be good if love becomes universal, but it is something distant and difficult to realize. This is simply because the gentlemen of the world fail to recognize its benefits and understand its reason. . . .[22]

Even though the Mohist organization was short-lived and the teachings of Mo Tzu were ignored for many centuries in China, many Christian missionaries and Communist leaders have rediscovered the great value in Mohism and readvocated the Mohist cause.

The Yin Yang Cosmology of Tsou Yen

Tsou Yen (305-240 B.C.?) was perhaps one of the most erudite scholars in ancient China. He traveled extensively, studied astronomy, history, geography, zoology, botany, agriculture, and politics, and, finally, composed the first theory of Yin and Yang and the Five Elements of cosmology. Because of his broad knowledge and grave concern concerning concurrent warfare in ancient China, he tried to remind Chinese people to know that there is a greater universe than their

"ethnocentric world," and that the political powers of
dynasties are not absolute, but have their rise and
decline. Even though we do not have his writings left
for us, we can read what the great ancient Chinese historian Ssu-ma Ch'ien wrote about Tsou Yen in his Shih
Chi.

> He first made a record of China's famous
> mountains, great rivers, deep valleys, birds
> and animals, things produced on land and
> sea, and distinctive characters of natural
> phenomena and landscapes. On the basis of
> these, he extended his survey to what is be-
> yond the seas, and to what human beings can-
> not see. He mentioned and cited the facts
> that ever happened since the separation of
> heaven and earth, and the cyclical rotation
> of the Five Elements in the universe. He
> pointed out how the reign of each element
> is quite appropriate and how the Five Ele-
> ments correspond one another!
> He reminded Chinese people that what
> scholars claimed to be the Middle Kingdom
> [China] only constituted one eighty-first of
> the whole world. The Middle Kingdom is only
> one of the nine districts in the Divine Con-
> tinent of the Red Regions. . . . Besides the
> Middle Kingdom there are continents similar
> to the Divine Continent of the Red Region
> totaling nine, which are called the Nine
> Continents. Around each of these is a small
> encircling sea. People and beasts cannot
> pass from one to another, thus making each
> a separate continent. . . . But ultimately,
> all human relations shall culminate in the
> virtues of humanity, righteousness, re-
> straint, frugality, and the practice of the
> proper relations between the ruler and min-
> ister, superior and inferior, and among the
> six family relations. . . .[23]

Tung Chung-shu, the political ideologue of the
Han Confucian bureaucracy, had adopted the theory of
mutual yielding and mutual conquest among the Five
Elements expounded by Tsou Yen in developing a Confucian philosophy of political changes to check and
balance the dictatorship of monarchic rule.

The Universal Equality of Chuang Tzu
Chuang Tzu (399 to 295 B.C.), an eminent Taoistic

mystic, tried to transcend the petty exclusive dogmatism of his time and advocated the universalistic Taoistic view that emphasized the "Free Wandering and
Equality of All Things!" In the first two chapters of
his work <u>Chuang Tzu</u>, he used the following parable to
explicate his universal aspiration.

> The Universal Harmony recorded various
> wonders of the universe, and it says: "When
> the Great Bird P'eng journeys to the south-
> ern ocean, where the waters are rolled for
> three thousand miles. He beats the whirl-
> winds to ascend ninety thousand miles first,
> and then sets off on the sixth month gale to
> fly south. . . . The cicada and sparrow laugh
> at this, saying, "When we make an effort to
> fly up, we can get as far as the branch of
> elm or sapanwood tree, but sometimes we do
> not make it and just fall down on the gound.
> So who would care to rise ninety thousand
> miles in order to fly to the south." . . .
> Little understanding cannot comprehend
> great understanding; the short-lived cannot
> comprehend the long-lived. . . .
> Great understanding is broad and un-
> hurried; little understanding is cramped and
> busy. Great words are clear and limpid;
> little words are shrill and quarrelsome. In
> sleep, human spirits go wandering; in awaken-
> ing hours, their bodies hustle. With every-
> thing they meet they become entangled. Day
> after day, they use their minds in strife,
> sometimes grandiose, sometimes sly, sometimes
> petty. Their little fears are mean and
> trembly; their great fears are stunned and
> overwhelming. They judge the things like
> shooting an arrow or crossbow pellet, for
> they pretend to be the arbiters of right and
> wrong. They cling to their position as if
> they had sworn before the gods thinking that
> they are holding on to victory. . . . Even
> though they have already drowned in what
> they are doing, you cannot make them turn
> back. They grow darker and darker as if
> they are sealed within seals--such are the
> excesses of their old age. And when their
> minds draw near to death, nothing can you do
> to restore them to the light. . . .
> The sage leans on the sun and moon,

tucks the universe under his arm, merges
himself with things, leaves the confusion and
muddle as they are, and looks on slaves as
exalted. While the ordinary men strain and
struggle, the sage is stupid and blockish.
He takes part in ten thousand ages and
achieves simplicity in oneness. For him, all
ten thousand things are what they are, and
thus they enfold one another.
  Harmonize them all with the Heavenly
Equality, leave them to their endless
changes, and so live out your years. What do
I mean by Heavenly Equality? Right is not
right; so is not so. For if right were
really right, it would differ so clearly from
not right that there would be no need for
argument. If so were really so, it would
differ so clearly from not so that there
would be no need for argument. Forget the
demarcation of time; forget the distinction
of space. Leap into the boundless and make
it your home![24]

From a worldly standpoint, we see things relative-
ly, observing differences, tending to discriminate
things from one another. But from the standpoint of
the universal Tao, such differences will be reconciled,
and discrimination cease. Merging with all things and
harmonizing with the Heavenly Equality are the secret
ways of Taoistic mysticism.

The Buddha-Nature in All Things

Mahayana Buddhism that came from India and developed in China, claimed that the Buddha-nature existed in all things, and all things are capable of
enlightenment. Such realization of the universality
of Buddha nature came to its full expression in the
Lotus Sutra or the Saddharma-Pundarika, part of which
follows:

  The Buddha appears in the world. . . .
  He saves all beings. I have realized the
  Supreme Way. The Teachings of Great Vehicles are applicable to all beings. . . . I
  desire to enable all beings to be the same
  as we are. In order to save all beings and
  enable them all to enter the Path of the
  Buddha, I have preached about Nirvana, but
  there is no real distinction between Nirvana

394

and this world. All the teachings from the
beginning are always equal and devoid of
distinction. When a follower of the Buddha
fulfills his course, he becomes a Buddha in
his next life.
     Because of my adaptability to use every
suitable means to aid human kind for salvation, I have revealed the teachings of the
Three Vehicles. Therefore, any one who had
learned from the former Buddhas, and practiced charity, or underwent disciplines and
endured forbearance and humiliation, or made
serious effort at concentration and understanding, and cultivated various kinds of
benevolence and wisdom, would reach the level
of Buddhahood. Those people who, for the
sake of the Buddha, installed the images, or
had them carved, would reach the level of
Buddhahood. Those who with a happy frame of
mind, sang the glory of the Buddha, or worshipped, or merely folded their hands, or
uttered one "Namo" [Praise be. . .], would
reach the level of the Buddhahood. . . .
There are going to be infinite numbers of the
future Buddhas. All these Tathagatas [the
ones who realized the Truthfulness] will propagate the Teachings of Salvation by all
suitable means. All these Buddhas, with an
infinite number of suitable means, will save
all living beings, and enable them to dwell
in the Pure Wisdom of the Buddha. Among
those who have heard the Teachings, None will
fail to become Buddha.[25]

From this basic belief in the universality of
Buddha nature and the potentiality of universal salvation to attain the Buddahood, Chinese Mahayana Buddhism
has promoted the understanding and realization of universal equality and mutual identification of all
things, including both the animated and non-animated.

<u>The Western Inscription of Chang Tsai</u>

     Chang Tsai (1020-1077), a pioneer of Neo-Confu-
cianism, wrote the following inscription on the western
wall of his lecture hall to inspire himself, as well
as his students, to cosmic aspiration.

     Heaven is my father and Earth is my mother.
     . . . All people are my brothers and sisters,

and all things are my companions. Respect
the aged. . . . Show deep love toward the
orphaned and the weak. . . . The sage identified his character with that of Heaven and
Earth. . . . Even those who are tired, in-
firm, crippled, or sick; those who have no
brothers or children, wives or husbands, are
all my brothers and sisters. . . . In life
I follow and serve Heaven and Earth, and in
death I will be at peace.[26]

In the first chapter of his collective work Cheng
Meng, he also explicated what he believed to be the
Great Harmony.

The Great Harmony is called the Way [Tao].
It embraces the nature which underlies all
counter processes of floating and sinking,
rising and falling, and motion and rest. It
is the origin of the process of fusion and
intermingling, of overcoming and being overcome, and of expansion and contraction. At
the commencement, these processes are incipient, subtle, obscure, easy, and simple,
but at the end they are extensive, great,
strong, and firm. It is Heaven that begins
with the knowledge of Change, and Earth
that models after simplicity. That which is
dispersed, differentiated, and capable of
assuming form becomes material force, and
that which is pure, penetrating, and not
capable of assuming form become spirit. Unless the whole universe is in the process of
fusion and intermingling like fleeting forces
moving in all directions, it may not be
called Great Harmony.[27]

The Great Unity of K'ang Yu-wei

Finally, we must examine the most elaborated universalism that ever developed in China, namely, the
Great Unity of K'ang Yu-wei (1858-1927). Growing up
as a Confucianist, K'ang also learned Taoism, Buddhism,
and especially world history and Western cultures. At
the age of twenty-seven, he composed the first draft
of what later became his magnum o'pus, Ta T'ung Shu,
or the Book of Great Unity. Some of his major statements concerning the Age of Great Peace have been
selected.

In the world of great Unity, the whole
world becomes a great unity. There is no
division into national states and no difference between races. There will be no war.
. . .

In the Age of Great Peace, there are no
emperors, kings, rulers, elders, official
titles, or ranks. All people are equal, and
do not consider position or rank as an honor
either. Only wisdom and humanity are promoted and encouraged. Wisdom is to initiate
things, accomplish undertakings, promote
utility and benefits, and advance people,
while humanity is to confer benefits extensively on all the people and bring salvation
to them, to love people and to benefit
things. There is no honor outside of wisdom
and humanity. . . .

In the Age of Great Peace, since men's
nature is already good and his ability and
intelligence is superior, they only rejoice
in matters of wisdom and humanity. New
institutions appear every day. Public benefits increase every day. The human mind gets
stronger every day. And knowledge becomes
clearer every day. People in the whole
world together reach the realm of humanity,
longevity, perfect happiness, and infinite
goodness and wisdom. . . .

In the Age of Great Peace, all people
are equal. There are no servants or slaves,
ruler or commanders, heads of religion or
popes.[28]

From the above survey, we can see that various approaches to the issue of religious pluralism existed
in Chinese history. Even in modern China, three ap-
proaches--Exclusiveness, Syncretism, and Universalism--
co-exist or vie with one another. What will become of
the future trend of Chinese religion, no one can predict, but at least we can learn from Chinese religious
history some of the possible approaches to the problem
of religious pluralism. In the future, it may be that
the division of religions will cease, or that even the
existence of religion as an entity or a criterion may
no longer be needed (as predicted by K'ang Yu-wei), because all the existing religions will have completed
their historical missions and exhausted themselves.
When that state is reached, the problem of religious

pluralism will automatically cease to be.[29]

FOOTNOTES

1. Wolfram Eberhard, The Local Cultures of South and East China (Leiden, Netherland: E. J. Brill, 1968).

2. Wing-tsit Chan, "The Historic Chinese Contribution to Religious Pluralism," in Religious Pluralism and World Community, ed. Edward J. Jurji (Leiden, Netherland: E. J. Brill, 1968), p. 118.

3. J. J. M. De Groot, Sectarianism and Religious Persecution in China (Leiden, 1901), pp. 267-268.

4. Ibid., pp. 369-371.

5. Quoted in Religious Policy and Practice in Communist China, by Donald E. MacInnis (New York: Macmillan, 1972), p. 119.

6. Richard C. Bush, Jr., Religion in Communist China (Nashville, TN: Abingdon, 1970).

7. W. E. Soothill, The Three Religions of China (London: Oxford University Press, 1923), p. 13.

8. Wing-tsit Chan, "The Historic Chinese Contribution to Religious Pluralism," pp. 114-115.

9. Judith A. Berling, The Syncretic Religion of Lin Chao-en (New York: Columbia University Press, 1980), p. 9.

10. Cf., Fung Yu-lan, A History of Chinese Philosophy (Princeton, NJ: Princeton University Press, vol. II, 1953), see chapter 2.

11. Holmes Welch, Taoism: The Parting of the Way (Boston: Beacon Press, 1957), chapter 2.

12. Cf., Kenneth K. S. Ch'en, The Chinese Transformation of Buddhism (Princeton, NJ: Princeton University Press, 1973).

13. Fung Yu-lan, A History of Chinese Philosophy, pp. 422-431.

398

14. Berling, <u>The Syncretic Religion of Lin Chao-en</u>, pp. 20-23.

15. Wing-tsit Chan, "The Historic Chinese Contribution to Religious Pluralism," pp. 12-126.

16. Ibid., p. 122.

17. Ibid.

18. Ibid., p. 123.

19. Ibid.

20. Ibid.

21. <u>Li Chi</u>, Chap. 7.

22. <u>Mo Tzu</u>, Chap. 15.

23. <u>Shih Chi</u>, Chap. 74.

24. <u>Chuang Tsu</u>, Chap. I and Chap. II.

25. <u>Taisho Daizokyo</u>, IX, 8, 9, 15.

26. Wing-tsit Chan, <u>A Sourcebook in Chinese Philosophy</u> (Princeton, NJ: Princeton University Press, 1963), p. 497.

27. Ibid., p. 500.

28. Ibid., pp. 732-734.

29. K'an Yu-wei envisioned that when the Great Unity is realized, there is no longer the existence of difference in religious, and even the necessity of having a religion. See Laurence G. Thompson, <u>Ta T'ung Shu, The One World Philosophy of K'ang Yu-wei</u> (London: Allen & Unwin, 1958). It is also interesting to note that Christian theologian Dietrich Bonhoefferalso discussed the coming age of "religion-less-ness." (See his <u>Letters and Papers from Prison</u> [New York, 1962]).

Suggested Readings

Laurence G. Thompson, tr., <u>Ta T'ung Shu: The One-World Philosophy of K'ang Yu-wei</u> (London: Allen & Unwin, 1958).

Garma C. C. Chang, The Buddhist Teaching of Totality
(University Park, PA: Pennsylvania State University
Press, 1974).

Claude Geffre and Joseph Spae, eds., China As A Challenge to the Church (New York: Seabury, 1979).

Julia Ching, Confucianism and Christianity (Tokyo:
Kodansha International, 1977).

Ross Terrill, The Future of China After Mao (New York:
Delta, 1978).

CHAPTER 15

CONCLUSION: THE CHARACTERISTICS
OF CHINESE RELIGION

We began this study with the Chinese definition of religion which is denoted as Chung, Chiao, Chia, and Tao. The word Chung (宗) indicates Chinese understanding of religion as primarily the ancestral tradition transmitted from generation to generation. Through this religious tradition, Chinese people trace their roots and reascertain their identities. Even though Chinese people have gone through many changes in their history, they still maintain this sacred tradition in order to preserve their continuity. Nakamura Hajime pointed out this characteristic of Chinese conservatism by illustrating the Chinese exaltation of antiquity. For Chinese scholarship, learning is referred to as Chi-ku (稽古), which literally means "searching out the ancient ways." The ancient classics, which have collected the wisdom of ancient sages, are regarded as Ching (經 , standard) or Tien (典 , law) or Ch'ang (常 , eternal principle). The religious classics provides for Chinese people the pattern of life and the paradigm of truth and perfection.[1] A good example can be seen in Mo Tzu's argument for the verification of truth in which he stated the truth should be based on the will of Heaven and testified by the deeds of the ancient sage kings. Enormous accumulation of historical records and respect for classical studies are well-known facts among Sinologists, witnessing Chinese exaltation of historicity.

The word Chung also implies the ritual conduct practiced in religious institutions. To Chinese people, religious experience is not only expressed in the wisdom of ancient sages but also in the ritual enactment of the primordial experience in the context of communal participation. The rites and ceremonies enable an individual to participate in the cosmic renewal, as well as to integrate oneself within the human community. The Confucian preoccupation in preserving the ancient rites and instituting the ceremonial system testified to this love of ritual among the Chinese people. In part III (chapters 11-14), we studied the theory and functions of ritual and various representative rites performed by Chinese people for initiation, moral and spiritual discipline, social

cohesion, and universal salvation. The ritual gives
individuals a personal orientation whereby to cultivate moral and spiritual character and to become integrated into society with the etiquette of mutual respect. It also assists individuals in identifying with
their past roots, their present status, and their future responsibilities, and also partake in the universal salvation and cosmic renewal. The ritual might
appear to be tedious, complex, and boring, but the
Chinese people regard it as a valuable method; one that
was exercised by ancient sages in their attempt to attain superior self-realization.

The second word Chiao (教, teachings) stresses
more on the educational and moral aspects of Chinese
religion. In order for individuals to become knowl-
edgeable with regard to the classics and rites, it is
necessary to be educated by a teacher or a master.
Because of this, teachers are highly respected and
praised, and they have also occupied highly esteemed
positions in Chinese society. In each religious school,
the founder and patriarchs are venerated, even worshipped, by their followers. Confucius is entitled as
the "the Most Illustrious Master of All Ages," Mo Tzu
is remembered as "the Great Master," and Lao Tzu (i.e.,
the ancient master) was worshipped as the "Supreme
Ancient Lord." Even to the present time, the
birthday of Confucius is chosen by the Republic of
China to be the national holiday as a sign of respect
for all teachers.

However, the significance of the word Chiao is
not limited to the paying of respect to the teachers
but also to emphasize the moral quality of the masters' teachings and instructions. Besides the transmission of historical knowledge, scientific information, and technical skills, the traditional Chinese
education has always stressed that the moral disciplines be the most essential elements in education.
The purpose of education is to cultivate the ideal
personality and moral character, not to merely produce
technological men. Part II (chapters 7-11) of this
study has described the Chinese understanding of the
human position in the universe and the struggle of
the Chinese people in their search for authentic selfhood and the ideal image of humanity.

This moral emphasis in Chinese religion has been
pointed out by many Chinese scholars. In analyzing
the modern trend of the religion of the masses,

Wing-tsit Chan described its major characteristics as
worldliness, ethical emphasis,lay-leadership, and syncretism. On ethical emphasis, he stated that each individual is instructed by all different schools in
Chinese religion, that he/she has inherent good nature
either as the Confucian Li (rationality) or the Taoist
(virtue) or the Buddhist Tathata (suchness), and that
everyone is capable of attaining his/her self-salvation
without resorting to the external helps, such as sav-
iors or redeemers.[2] However, this overemphasis of
humanism and indivudualism by modern humanist scholars
should be moderated by the traditional acknowledgment
of the divine endowment of the good nature by the ancient sages.

The word Chia (家, family) signifies the communal
expression of Chinese religious experience and the organizational aspect of Chinese religions. Historically, the ancestral worship in the family shrine is
one of the most archaic forms and perennial traditions
of Chinese religion. Joseph M. Kitagawa in his comparative studies with other religious organizations of
the Eastern religions (Hinduism, Buddhism, and Shin-
toism) characterized Chinese religious system as
"Family-ism." In his words, "Chinese Family-ism implies more than the centrality of the family cult in
the lives of Chinese people; Family-ism determines the
values and norms of behavior of the people in all
spheres of life."[3] As we saw in our study of Confucian
ethics based on the Five Human Relationships, the
filial piety is considered as the core of ethics and
the other human relationships are to be oriented by it.
Thus, Chinese people conceive the state (Kuo-chia,
i.e., nation-family) as an enlarged family. Most of
the religious organizations, such as Confucian shrine,
Taoist temple, and Buddhist monastery, are also established according to the pattern of family structure.
C. K. Yang also pointed out the religious significance
in Chinese society in that Chinese religion has pene-
trated its influences on Chinese society and culture
by the way of diffusion rather than separation. "The
beliefs and rituals of diffused religion develop their
organizational system as an integral part of the organized social pattern. In the diffused form, religion
performs a pervasive function in an organized manner
in every major aspect of Chinese social life."[4]

However, according to our studies, the word Tao
(道) is the common term used by all Chinese religious
thinkers to denote the essence of religion. While the

403

other words may demonstrate the external characteristics of Chinese religion, it is in the word Tao that
Chinese people have tried to exemplify their understanding of the most subtle nature of religious experience. In order to avoid repeating what we have
already studied in this book, the author would like
to summarize the meaning and method of Tao in the
following.

     Tao means both the essence and manifestation of
religion. As the essence of religion, it is expressed
both in negative and positive terms. Because Tao in
the sense of being the ultimate reality is beyond the
human conceptualization and the categories of knowledge, it can only be defined by such negative expressions as "Wu" (無, nothingness or non-being), "Wu-
chih" (無極, non-ultimate), "Kung" (空, emptiness).
Chinese sages wanted to preserve their sense of awe to
the numinous or mysterious nature of the ultimate
reality they had experienced by refusing the Tao to
be completely classified by the categories of human
knowledge.

     But, at the same time, the religious thinkers
have also realized the multifarious manifestations of
the ultimate reality, which they could designate by
positive expressions such as "Shang Ti" (上帝, the supreme Lord), "T'ien" (天, the Heaven), "Tao" (道, the
way or principle), Tathata or Tathagata (Ju-lai, 如來,
absolute suchness). The positive expression of the
ultimate reality is expressed both in theistic and
non-theistic terms. Therefore, it is very important
to maintain a well-balanced dialectical approach for
the understanding of the Chinese view of the ultimate
reality, because a one-sided interpretation focused
either on the negative notion or on the positive nature of it would distort the original meaning of Tao.
Likewise, a unilateral interpretation stresses either
the theistic nature of the ultimate reality or the
impersonalistic aspect of it could not lead to the
subtle understanding of Tao.

     Moreover, the word Tao not only denotes the ulti-
mate reality in Chinese religious experience but also
indicates the multifarious ways of communicating with
the ultimate reality. For the word Tao means both the
Way as principle and the ways as the means to realize
the principle. They classified these ways according
to their three dimensional world view into the way of

404

Heaven, the way of Earth, the way of Man, and the way
of Harmony.

From our study concerning the ways of Heaven and
Earth in part I (chapters 3-6), we have learned the
metaphysical or ontological aspect of Tao. In chapter
3, we discovered that the Chinese view of "god" cannot
simply be classified as animism, totemism, polytheism,
henotheism, monotheism, or pantheism. It might be
called an organic or hierarchical pantheon, which includes the worship of a Supreme God and his pantheon
of divine beings, natural forces, and deified cultural
heroes and ancestors. It resembles the hierarchy of
government officials in the Chinese traditional feudal
system. The significance of this pantheon does not
lie in the exclusive authority of the Supreme God nor
in the polymorphous manifestation of the divinity, but
in the organic interrelationship and interaction of
all things in the entire universe. The command of God,
the functions of gods and natural forces, and the
sacrificial activities of humankind are all conceived
as the integral parts of the universal organism.

Chapter 4 presented a brief history of the development of the belief in T'ien (the Heaven) which
had reenforced the significant interrelationship between God and humankind by interjecting the moral
character into the belief of the mandate of Heaven.
Therefore, the political legitimation could find its
ontological basis in the dynamic movement of the universe, and the historical changes could discern its
moral determinant in the cosmic movement. Thus, the
time has its destiny and the space its centrality as
the book of Chung Yung tried to demonstrate.

The organic movement of the universe is described
in chapter 6 to be all inclusive and intrinsic. It
contains all the views of ancient Chinese cosmological
views such as monism, dualism, and pluralism. Ultimately, however, an organistic understanding of multi-
dimensional interrelationship and interaction of the
universe is developed in the metaphysic of I (易,
Changes). The creation and permeation of Tao and the
balance between the Ying and the Yang, the mutual interactions among the Five Elements, are now all integrated in the cosmograme of the I Ching (the Book of
Changes). However, this naturalistic and mechanical
cosmology of I Ching is depicted more dramatically in
chapter 5 as the myth of P'an-ku in which the organism
of the universe was symbolized as the cosmic giant man

so that religious people could apprehend more inti-
mately their personal relationship with the universe
in terms of macrocosmic and microcosmic relationships.

The second part of this book focused on the Way
of Man and dealt with various issues of Chinese anthropology. Chapter 7 described the Chinese understanding
of human position in the universe and the distinctive
role of humankind in maintaining the ecological harmony of the universe. Chapter 8 surveyed various
searches of ancient Chinese for the realization of
selfhood. Chapter 9 dealt with the issue of good and/
or evil in human nature, and chapter 10 portrayed various ideal images envisaged by ancient sages. While
various views and options are presented, they are all
placed in the contexts of the cosmos, history, and
society, in that the Chinese people prefer to express
their beliefs in the concrete and particular forms.
Nakamura Hajime pointed out the nondevelopment of abstract thought and emphasis on the particular and fondness for complex multiplicity expressed in concrete
forms in the Chinese way of thinking.[5] Notwithstand-
ing, through this study, the author was very much impressed by the existential concern of Chinese people
and their struggles for the freedom of choice, decision making, and their collective efforts to achieve
the excellence in spite of the oppressive situations
and opposing forces they had to cope with. Under the
despotic monarchical system, the Chinese religion has
opened up various channels or ways for the people to
search for and attain their human potentials and
ideals. With the provision of multiple ways to reach
the same common goal, Chinese people learned to tolerate and compromise one another to live as a national
family. They also realized that the human search for
establishing an ideal society or Ta-t'ung Shih-chieh
(大同世界, the World of Great Unity) is a perennial
task.

The last part of this book then follows to describe Chinese efforts in developing various methods
for attaining their utopian world by various forms of
religious rites and ceremonies. Chapter 11 described
the meaning and function of the ritual in which the
notion of religious ritual (Li 禮) was extended to become the norm of human behavior and the means for social integration. Chapter 11 also described, in detail, various ways for individuals to attain their
moral cultivation and spiritual ideals. To many
Chinese religious people, religion is not merely ideas

to be conceived, but the ways to be practiced and
realized through daily rituals. However, the final
goal is not only for self-salvation or self-perfection
but also for the enrichment of the human community and
even for cosmic integration, which was demonstrated in
the rites of the Monthly Ordinance and the cult of
Universal Salvation in chapter 13. Chapter 14 presented various ways through which the Chinese people
sought to cope with the problem of religious pluralism and their ultimate search for a harmonious world
in which all humankind can live by love and in peace.

Chinese religion defined as Tao is an encompassing system in which the Tao of Heaven and Earth
provides the understanding of the origin and organic
interrelationship of all things; the Tao of Man in-
spires the meaning and responsibility of human beings
in the cosmos; the Tao of Harmony instructs the ways
and means by which the dream of ideal world can be
realized, and the Chinese people defined it as the
Harmony of Heaven, Earth, and Man (T'ine-Ti-Jen Ho-I
天地人合一).

FOOTNOTES

1. Hajime Nakamura, Ways of Thinking of Eastern
Peoples, tr. Philip P. Wiener (Honolulu: East-West
Center Press, 1964), chap. 18.

2. Wing-tsit Chan, Religious Trends in Modern
China (NY: Octagon Books, 1969), pp. 174-178.

3. Joseph M. Kitagawa, Religions of the East
(Philadelphia: Westminster Press, 1968), p. 80.

4. C. K. Yang, Religion in Chinese Society
(Berkeley: University of California Press, 1961), p. 20.

5. Hajime Nakamura, Ways of Thinking, chapters
16, 17, and 19.

SELECTED BIBLIOGRAPHY

Ahern, Emily M. Chinese Ritual and Politics. London: Cambridge University Press, 1981.

Berling, Judith. The Syncretic Religion of Lin Chao-en. NY: Columbia University Press, 1980.

Bilsky, L. J. The State Religion of Ancient China. Taipei, 1975.

Blyth, R. E. Zen in English Literature and Oriental Classics. NY: E. P. Dutton, 1960.

Bodde, Derk. Essays on Chinese Civilization. Princeton: Princeton University Press, 1981.

________. Festivals in Classical China. Princeton: Princeton University Press, 1975.

________. "Myths of Ancient China," Mythologies of the Ancient World. Edited by Samuel N. Kramer. Garden City, NY: Doubleday, 1961.

Buck, Pearl S. All Men are Brothers. NY: John Day, 1968.

Campbell, Joseph. The Masks of God: Oriental Mythology. NY: Macmillan, 1962.

Chan, Wing-tsit. A Source Book in Chinese Philosophy. Princeton: Princeton University Press, 1963.

________. "The Concept of Man in Chinese Thought." The Concept of Man. Edited by P. T. Raju. London: Allen and Unwin, 1960.

________. "The Historic Contribution to Religious Pluralism." Religious Pluralism and World Community. Edited by Edward J. Jurji. Leiden: E. J. Brill, 1968.

________. Religious Trends in Modern China. NY: Columbia University Press, 1953.

________. The Way of Lao Tzu. Indianapolis: Bobbs-Merrill, 1963.

Chang, Carson. Development of Neo-Confucian Thought.

NY: Bookman Associates, 1962. 2 vols.

Chang, C. Y. Creativity and Taoism. NY: Julian
     Press, 1963.

Chang, Garma C. C. The Buddhist Teaching of Totality.
     University Park: Pennsylvania State University
     Press, 1974.

Chang, Kwang-chih. Shang Civilization. New Haven:
     Yale University Press, 1980.

Ch'en, Kenneth K. S. Buddhism in China. Princeton:
     Princeton University Press, 1964.

________. The Chinese Transformation of Buddhism.
     Princeton: Princeton University Press, 1973.

Cheng, Te-k'un. Archaeology in China. Cambridge:
     Heffer, 1959-1963. 3 vols.

Chesneaux, Jean. Secret Societies in China in the
     Nineteenth and Twentieth Centuries. Ann Arbor:
     University of Michigan Press, 1971.

Ching, Julia. Confucianism and Christianity. Tokyo:
     Kodansha International, 1977.

Creel, Herrlee G. The Birth of China. NY: Frederick
     Ungar, 1937.

________. Confucius, the Man and the Myth. NY: John
     Day, 1949.

________. Chinese Thought from Confucius to Mao Tse-
     tung. NY: New American Library, 1960.

Chu Hsi. Reflections on Things at Hand. Translated
     by Wing-tsit Chan. NY: Columbia University
     Press, 1967.

Dubs, Homer H. The Moulder of Ancient Confucianism.
     London: Probsthain, 1927.

________, translator. The Works of Hsuntze. London:
     Probsthain, 1928.

________. "The Development of Altruism in Confucian-
     ism." Philosophy East and West 1 (1951):48-55.

__________. "Mencius and Sün-dz on Human Nature."
     Philosophy East and West 6 (1956):213-222.

Dumoulin, Heinrich. Buddhism in the Modern World.
     NY: Macmillan, 1976.

Eberhard, Wolfram. The Local Cultures of South and
     East China. Leiden: E. J. Brill, 1968.

Eliade, Mircea. Cosmos and History: The Myth of
     Eternal Return. Translated by Willard Trask.
     NY: Harper Torchbook, 1959.

__________. A History of Religious Ideas. Translated
     by Willard Trask. Chicago: University of
     Chicago Press, 1982. Vol. 2.

__________. Patterns in Comparative Religion. Trans-
     lated by Willard Trask. NY: Meridian Book,
     1958.

__________. Rites and Symbols of Initiations. NY:
     Harper Torchbook, 1958.

__________. Shamanism: Archaic Techniques of Ecstasy.
     NY: Pantheon Books, 1964.

Fang, Thomé. The Chinese View of Life. Hong Kong:
     The Union Press, 1957.

__________. Chinese Philosophy: Its Spirit and Its De-
     velopment. Taipei: Linking Publishing Co.,
     1981.

__________. "The World and the Individual in Chinese
     Metaphysics." The Chinese Mind. Edited by
     Charles A. Moore. Honolulu: University of
     Hawaii Press, 1967.

Fehl, Noah E. Li: Rites and Propriety in Literature
     and Life. Hong Kong: The Chinese University of
     Hong Kong, 1971.

Ferguson, John. "Chinese Mythologies." The Mythology
     of All Races. Edited by John A. MacCulloch.
     Boston, 1928, pp. 1-203.

Forke, Alfred. The World-Conception of the Chinese.
     London: Probsthain, 1925.

Fung, Yu-lan. A History of Chinese Philosophy.
     Translated by Derk Bodde. Princeton: Prince-
     ton University Press, 1952. 2 vols.

________. A Short History of Chinese Philosophy.
     Translated by Derk Bodde. NY: Macmillan, 1948.

________. The Spirit of Chinese Philosophy. Trans-
     lated by E. R. Hughes. London: Kegan Paul,
     1947.

Geffre, Claude and Spae, Joseph, editors. China as a
     Challenge to the Church. NY: Seabury, 1979.

Girardot, N. J. Myth and Meaning in Early Taoism.
     Berkeley: University of California Press, 1983.

________. "The Problem of Creation Mythology in the
     Study of Chinese Religion." History of Reli-
     gions 15 (1976):289-318.

Granet, Marcel. Festivals and Songs of Ancient China.
     Translated by E. D. Edwards. New York, 1932.

________. The Religions of the Chinese People.
     Translated by Maurice Freeman. NY: Harper
     Torchbooks, 1975.

Grave, Arnold. "Tao: An Aged-old Concept in its
     Modern Perspective." Philosoohy East and West
     13 (1963):235-250.

Groot, J. J. M. de. The Religion of Chinese. NY:
     Macmillan, 1910.

________. The Religious System of China. 6 vols.
     Leiden: E. J. Brill, 1892-1910. Repr. Taipei,
     1964.

________. Sectarianism and Religious Persecution in
     China. Leiden: E. J. Brill, 1901.

Hawkes, David, translator. Ch'u Tz'u: The Songs of
     the South. London: Oxford University Press,
     1959.

Haydon, Eustace, editor. Modern Trends in World Re-
     ligions. NY: Books For Libraries Press, 1968.

Higgins, Kathleen. "Music in Confucian and Neo-Confu-
     cian Philosoohy." International Philosophical
     Quarterly 20 (1980):433-451.

Ho, Ping-ti. The Cradle of the East. Chicago: Uni-
     versity of Chicago Press, 1975.

Hsü, Francis. Under the Ancestors' Shadow. NY:
     Columbia University Press, 1948.

Tzutsu, Toshihiko. "The Absolute and the Perfect Man
     in Taoism." Eranos-Jahrbuch 1967. Zürich:
     Rhein-Verlag, 1968, pp. 379-441.

__________. The Key Philosophical Concepts of Sufism and
     Taoism. Tokyo, 1967.

Jordan, David. Gods, Ghosts and Ancestors. Berkeley:
     University of California Press, 1972.

Keightley, David. N. Sources of Shang History.
     Berkeley: University of California Press, 1978.

__________. "The Religious Commitment: Shang Theology
     and the Genesis of Chinese Political Culture."
     History of Religions 17 (1978):211-225.

Kitagawa, Joseph M. The Religions of the East.
     Philadelphia: Westminster, 1968.

Lai, T. C. The Eight Immortals. Hong Kong: Swindon
     Book Co., 1972.

Lau, D. C. "Theories of Human Nature in Mencius and
     Schyuntzyy." Bulletin of the School of
     Oriental and African Studies 15 (1953):541-565.

Legge, James. The Chinese Classics. 5 vols. Hong Kong:
     Hong Kong University Press, reprinted 1970.

Long, Charles H. Alpha: The Myths of Creation. NY:
     Macmillan, 1963.

MacInnis, Donald E. Religious Policy and Practice in
     Communist China. NY: Macmillan, 1972.

MacNair, H. F. China. Berkeley: University of Cali-
     fornia Press, 1951.

Maspero, Henri. *China in Antiquity*. Translated by
     Frank A. Kierman, Jr. Amherst: University of
     Massachusetts Press, 1978.

__________. *Taoism and Chinese Religion*. Translated
     by Frank A. Kierman, Jr. Amherst: University
     of Massachusetts Press, 1981.

__________. "Mythology of Modern China." *Asiatic
     Mythology*. Edited by P. L. Couchous. London,
     1922.

Mei, Yi-pao. *The Ethical and Political Works of Motzu*.
     London: Probsthain, 1927.

__________. *Motse, The Neglected Rival of Confucius*.
     London: Probsthain, 1934.

__________. "The State of the Individual in Chinese
     Thought and Politics." *The Chinese Mind*.
     Edited by Charles A. Moore. Honolulu: Univer-
     sity of Hawaii Press, 1967, pp. 323-337.

Moore, Charles A. editor. *The Chinese Mind*. Honolulu:
     University of Hawaii Press, 1967.

Morton, W. Scott. "The Confucian Concept of Man: The
     Original Formulation." *Philosophy East and
     West* 21 (1971):69-77.

Munro, Donald J. *The Concept of Man in Early China*.
     Stanford: Stanford University Press, 1968.

Nakamura, Hajime. *Ways of Thinking of Eastern Peoples*.
     Translated by Philip P. Wiener. Honolulu:
     East-West Center Press, 1964.

Needham, Joseph. *Science and Civilization in China*.
     Vol. 2. London: Cambridge University Press,
     1956.

Otto, Rudolf. *The Idea of the Holy*. Translated by
     John Harvey. London: Oxford University Press,
     1925.

Overmeyer, Daniel L. *Folk Buddhist Religion*. Cam-
     bridge: Harvard University Press, 1976.

Phelps, D. L. "The Place of Music in the Platonic and

Confucian Systems of Moral Education." <u>Journal of the North China Branch of the Royal Asiatic Society</u> 59 (1928):128-145.

Reichelt, Karl L. <u>Meditation and Piety in the Far East</u>. London: Lutterworth, 1953.

Rubin, Vitaly A. <u>Individual and State in Ancient China</u>. Translated by Steven I. Levine. NY: Columbia Universtiy Press, 1976.

Saso, Michael and Chappel, David W., editors. <u>Buddhist and Taoist Studies I</u>. Honolulu: University Press of Hawaii, 1977.

Saso, Michael. <u>Taoism and the Rite of Cosmic Renewal</u>. Pullman: Washington State University Press, 1972.

Shryock, J. K. <u>The Origin and Development of the State Cult of Confucianism</u>. NY: The Century Co., 1932.

Smith, D. Howard. <u>Chinese Religions</u>. NY: Holt, Rinehart & Winston, 1968.

__________. <u>Confucius</u>. NY: Charles Scribner's Sons, 1973.

Soothill, W. E. <u>The Three Religions of China</u>. London: Oxford University Press, 1923.

Stelle, John, translator. <u>The I Li or Book of Etiquette and Ceremonial</u>. London: Probsthain, 1917.

Terrill, Ross. <u>The Future of China After Mao</u>. NY: Delta, 1978.

Thompson, Laurence G., translator. <u>Ta T'ung Shu, The One-world Philosophy of K'ang Yu-wei</u>. London: Allen and Unwin, 1968.

Tillich, Paul. <u>Dynamics of Faith</u>. NY: Harper Torchbooks, 1958.

Waley, Arthur, translator. <u>The Analects of Confucius</u>. NY: Vintage Press, 1938.

__________. *Three Ways of Thought in Ancient China*. Garden City, NY: Doubleday, 1956.

__________, translator. *The Book of Songs*. NY: Grove Press, 1937.

__________, translator. *The Way and Its Power*. London: Allen and Unwin, 1934.

Wang Yang-ming. *Instructions for Practical Living and Other Neo-Confucian Writings by Wang Yang-ming*. Translated by Wing-tsit Chan. NY: Columbia University Press, 1963.

Ware, James R., translator. *Alchemy, Medicine, Religion in the China of A.D. 320*. Cambridge: MIT Press, 1966.

Watson, Burton, translator. *Mo Tzu: Basic Writings*. NY: Columbia University Press, 1963.

__________., translator. *The Complete Works of Chuang Tzu*. NY: Columbia University Press, 1968.

Weber, Max. *The Religion of China*. Translated by Hans H. Gerth. NY: Macmillan, 1951.

Welch, Holmes. *Buddhism Under Mao*. Cambridge: Harvard University Press, 1953.

__________. *Taoism, The Parting of the Way*. Boston: Beacon Press, 1957.

Werner, Edward T. C. *Dictionary of Chinese Mythology*. Shanghai, 1932.

Wheatley, Paul. *The Pivot of the Four Quarters*. Edinburgh: Edinburgh University Press, 1971.

Whitehead, James, editor. *China and Christianity*. Notre Dame: University of Notre Dame Press, 1977.

Wilhelm, Helmut. *Change, Eight Lectures on the I Ching*. Translated by Cary F. Baynes. NY: Pantheon Books, 1960.

Wilhelm, Richard, translator. *I Ching*. Princeton: Princeton University Press, 1950.

Wright, Arthur F., editor. <u>The Confucian Persuasion</u>.
     Stanford: Stanford University Press, 1960.

Wu, John. "Mencius' Philosophy of Human Nature and
     Natural Law." <u>Chinese Culture</u> 1 (1957):1-19.

Yang, C. K. <u>Religion in Chinese Society</u>. Berkeley:
     University of California Press, 1961.

Yu, David C. "The Creation Myth and Its Symbolism
     in Classical Taoism." <u>Philosophy East and
     West</u> 31 (1981):479-500.

Zücher, E. <u>The Buddhist Conquest of China</u>. 2 vols.
     Leiden: E. J. Brill, 1959.

Han Yu, 247
Hsiao Ching (Book of filial piety), 348-350
Hsün Tzu, 29, 234-237, 292-302
Hua-yen Buddhism, 385-386
Human nature, 228-250
Hun-tun (chaos), 124, 142

I Ching (Book of Changes), 27, 160-166
I Li (rites and ceremonies), 27
Ideal images of humanity, 251-282
Immortality of life, 332-337
Integrated self, 220-225
Investigation of things, 319-320
Islam, 36, 37, 45

Jen (human relatedness), 180-183

K'ai-t'ien, 172-173
K'ang Yu-wei, 149, 396-398
Kao Tzu, 238-239
Kingship, 24
Knight-errants (I Hsia), 266-267, 326-332
Ko Hung, 131, 333-339
Kuan Tzu, 147-148, 153-155

Lao Tzu, 6, 30, 137
Li (rites), 283-292
Li Chi (Book of Rites), 27, 173-175, 284-292, 351-355,
     388-389
Li Yun (evolution of rites), 220, 223
Lieh Tzu, 125
Life after death, 25
Liu An, 175
Lotus Sutra, 394-395
Lu-shih Ch'un-ch'iu, 148-149, 156-157
Lun Yü, see Analects of Confucius

Manichaeism, 35
Mencius, 29, 181-184, 209-212, 227-234
Mo Tzu, 31, 212-215, 262-270, 326-332, 389-391
Mohism, 31, 326-332
Monism, 137
Monthly Ordinances (Yueh Ling), 350-355
Moon (god), 72
Mountain (god), 76
Moral cultivation, 317-325
Muslim, 36
Music (Yueh), 302-307
Mutual conquest order, 156-158

Mutual production order, 155-156
Mutual transformation, 159-160

Nature deities, 71-77
Nature of man, 173-176, 228-249
Needham, Joseph, 150-151, 158-159
New Religious Societies, 43-45
Nü Kua (the myth of), 170-173

Order (of the State), 324-325

Pacifism, 264-266
Pai Hu T'ung, 177
P'an-ku (the myth of), 122-135
Pantheon (of Ti), 77-79
Pao-p'u Tzu, 278, 333-337
Peace (of the world), 325
Peasant religion, 28
Persecution (religious), 369-378

Rain (the god of), 74-75
Rectification of the mind, 321
Rectification of names, 207-208
Religious Societies, 371-373, 387-388

Self discipline, 309-337
Selfhood, 196
Self-realization, 309-310
Shamanism, 32-33, 310-317
Shamans, 25, 310-317
Shang religion, 23-26
Shang Ti, 52, 88
Shih Ching (Book of Poetry), 26
Shu Ching (Book of History), 26
Siddhartha Gotama, 34
Sincerity of the will, 320-321
Sixty-four hexagrams, 160-166
Skepticism, 27-28, 107-108
Slave society, 197-198
Son of Heaven, 100
Ssu-ma Ch'ien, 13
Sun (the god), 71-72
Syncretism (religious), 378-388

Ta Hsüeh (the great learning), 230, 317-325
Ta T'ung (the great unity), 220, 223-225
Tao, 3-17, 279-281
Taoism, 30-31, 42, 332-333
Tao Te Ching, 5, 12, 124-127, 129, 137-146, 178-179

About the Author

Milton M. Chiu was born in Kaohsiung, Taiwan, in 1930
and received his higher education in Tainan, Taiwan
(Tainan Theological College, Th.B. 1953) and in
Chicago, Illinois (Divinity School, University of
Chicago, B.D. 1961; M.A. 1963; Ph.D. 1970). He was
an ordained minister of Formosan Presbyterian Church
and served the congregations of Tainan and Yuen-lin
(1953-1959). He taught as Associate Professor in
Tainan Theological College (1963-1967), as Assistant
Professor in Boston University (1968-1973), and as
Associate Professor in Ithaca College (1973-present).
He has read many papers in the conferences of the
American Academy of Religion and Association for Asian
Studies. He has published many articles in church
magazines and theological journals. He translated
The Religions of East by Joseph M. Kitagawa into
Chinese. His article "The Religions of Taiwan" has
recently been accepted by The Encyclopedia of Religion,
edited by Mircea Eliade, which will be published by
the Macmillan Publishers in the near future. He makes
his residence, along with his wife, Margaret, in
Newfield, New York.